Lin MacDonald
Set Decorator

Street Furniture

LINKS

STREET FURNITURE

Author: Carles Broto
Editorial coordination: Jacobo Krauel
Graphic design & production: Dimitris Kottas (www.cuboctaedro.eu)
Collaborators: Oriol Vallés & Roberto Bottura
Texts: Contributed by companies, edited by William George

©LinksBooks
Jonqueres, 10, 1-5
08003 Barcelona, Spain
Tel: +34-93-301-21-99
Fax: +34-93-301-00-21
info@linksbooks.net
www.linksbooks.net

©This is a collective work. In accordance with Intellectual Property Law "collective works" are NOT necessarily those produced by more than one author. They have been created by the initiative and coordination of one person who edits and distributes them under his/her name. A collective work constitutes a collection of contributions from different authors whose personal contributions form part of a creation, without it being possible to separately attribute rights over the work as a whole.

©All rights reserved. No part of this book may be used or reproduced in any manner whatsoever without written permission except in the case of brief quotations embodied in critical articles and reviews.

Street Furniture

LINKS

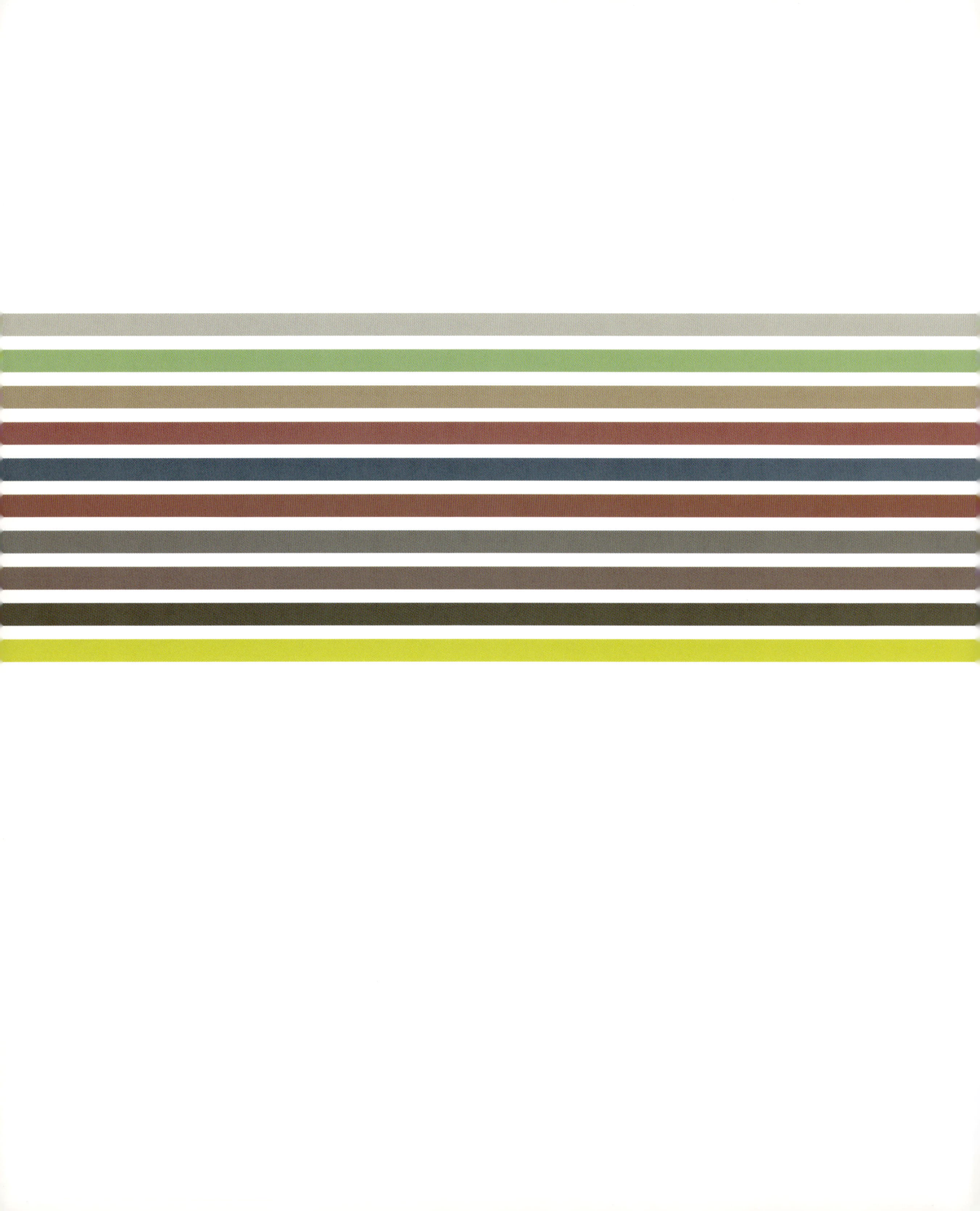

Contents

7		Introduction
8		Seats
122		Planters
140		Tree rrids
150		Bicycle racks
164		Fountains
174		Pavements
182		Wastebaskets
212		Shelters
234		Limits
258		Lights
306		Product index
310		Designer index
312		Company index

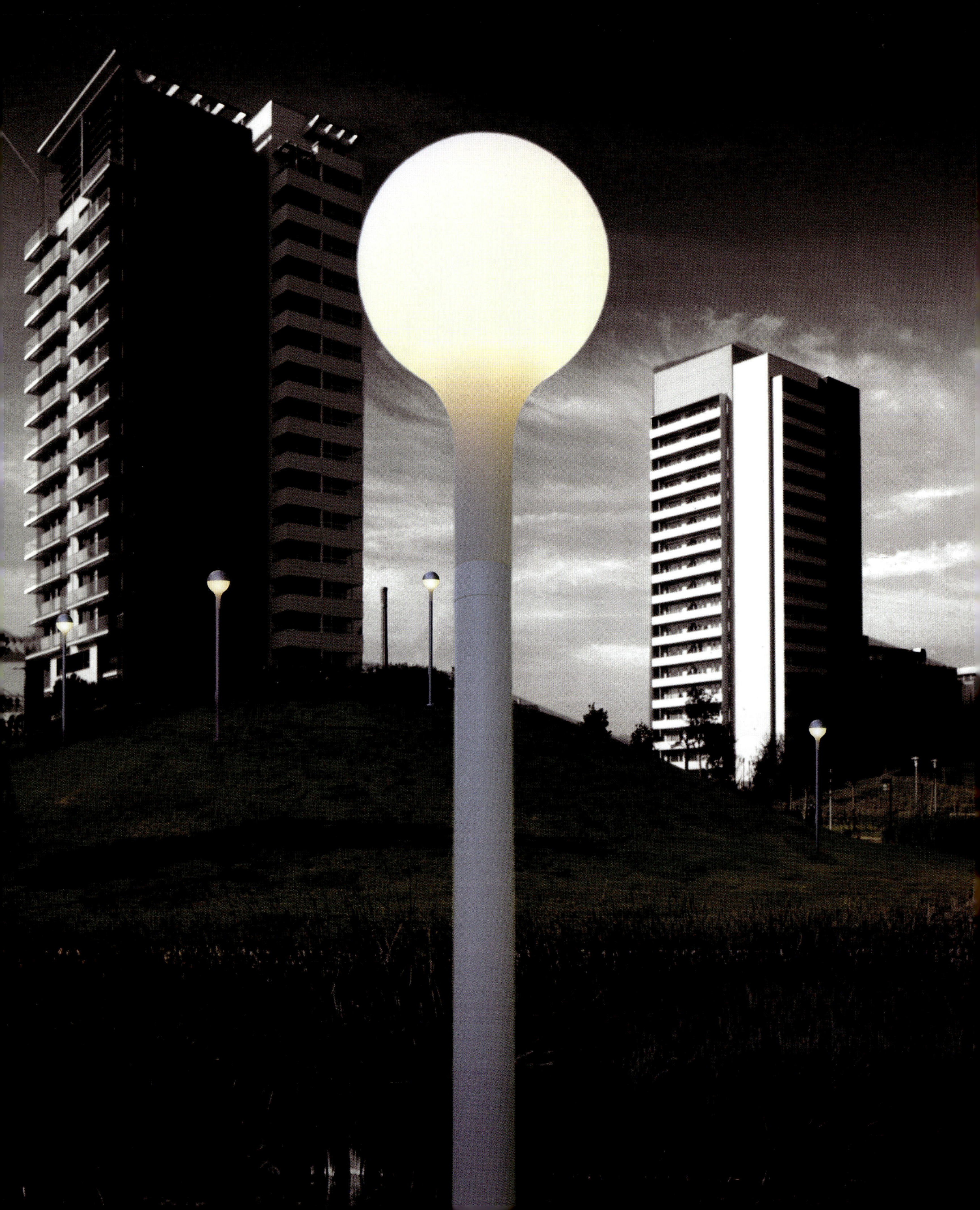

Introduction

Ever since the beginning of modern civilization, the urbanization of public space has been a prevailing subject and a subject in a constant state of mutation. Besides the structures, buildings and dwellings that serve the full range of possible requirements, cities as well as villages need streets, parks and plazas in which the inhabitants can move, rest, play, or get together. In fact, many urban design theorists consider that the life-quality of a city's inhabitants depends on the proportion of shared space available and how it is used.

There is no doubt that the urban furniture plays a leading role in making people's presence in these areas more frequent, agreeable and comfortable. A well distributed arrangement of benches, street lamps or shade will contribute to making a plaza more accessible, encouraging a more positive and lively relation between its visitors. Thus, an obvious improvement will ensue, strengthening the social links throughout the neighborhood.

Although many of us only hurry through these spaces briefly on our way to somewhere else, hardly noticing the urban furniture, these accessories are in fact a crucial component, capable of making life much more comfortable. On the other hand, for those who make public space a prolongation of their home, whether they be children, teenagers, retired people or members of any other population group, the lack of these items to which we are all accustomed would be highly traumatic. Hence, in many cities, groups of people have created associations to protest about the neglect of their neighborhoods. There are many housing estates in which local authorities have ignored these requests and the situation of neglect has become extremely chronic compared to other more fortunate districts of the same city.

Indeed, urban furniture seems to have become vital for contemporary cities. Not only can these items become a distinctive feature of a neighborhood and of a town, like London's telephone boxes, but it is their design and the degree to which they address the solution to everyday problems that proves their validity. The adaptation to different spaces, the durability or resistance to harsh atmospheric conditions or vandalism, an item's versatility or multiple use and of course its aesthetic value that are a source of inspiration to architects and designers, who have carried out their projects within the public space of the streets, squares and parks of our urban environments.

In this book we have compiled a selection of the most recent and significant contributions to this field of design. Effective and contemporary urban furniture, with designs ranging from the most classical to the most experimental and futuristic, in form as in the implementation of new materials and finishes. Each item is completely illustrated with photographs and plans, together with a full explanation of the constructive details, dimensions and weight, the installation process and the maintenance required. It is all perfectly ordered according to the functions fulfilled, and the clear and attractive layout with a file-like presentation make it ideally easy and practical to consult. We believe this book to be a good alternative to the usual collection of catalogues, providing an interesting source of inspiration for Town Halls, municipalities, town planners, architects, builders and students alike, all of whom will have access to the contact data of the makers of the outstanding items offered in this volume.

Seats

Design: Enric Batlle - Joan Roig • **Production:** Santa & Cole

This modular urban bench in rhomboid shapes is made of mass coloured concrete. The concept arose from an angle, designed to shape limits, contain and form alignments, with or without a backrest. Its geometric characteristics only permit curved alignments with large radii. Its simplicity and discretion make it fit into any urban space without prominence. The standard line is mass coloured in greyish tones, stripped finish, freestanding on the ground. Different finishes and colours can be available depending on the quantities ordered. It can also be manufactured with recyclable aggregates. It can be delivered in two combinable measures, 48 cm and 150 cm. The line is complemented by a piece of the same height and shape as the backrest, aimed to contain the ground. The designers recommend a minimum distance of 3 cm between the benches.

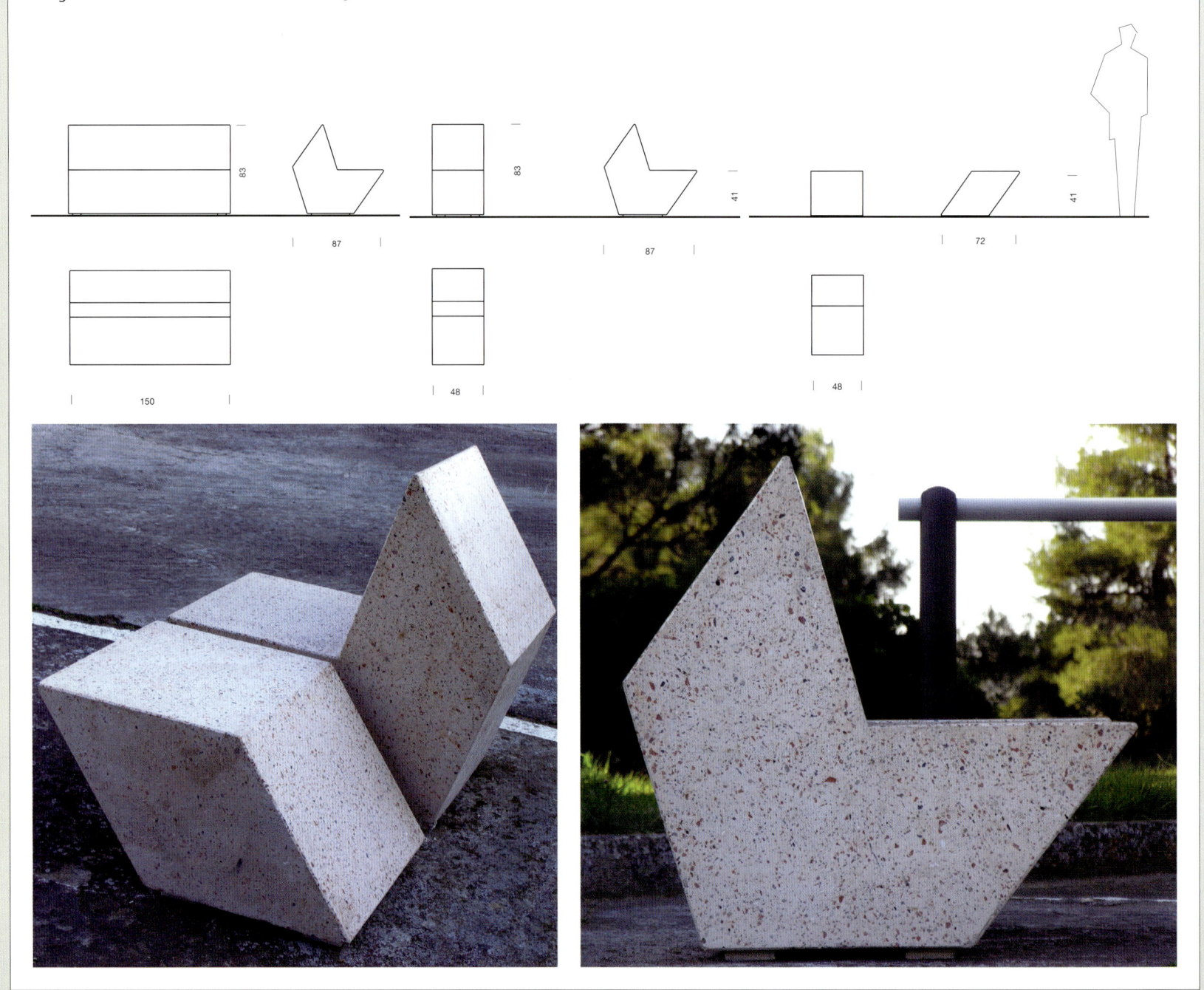

2197

Design and production: **Neri**

A fixed bench in UNI EN 1563 nodular cast iron and hot-galvanized steel, conforming to UNI EN ISO 1461 standards. The non-metal parts are of iroko wood (or equivalent). The bench consists of a hot-galvanized steel frame made of an elliptical flange, two cast iron half-shells decorated with bas-relief waves applied as covering for the flange and eight curved planks of laminated iroko wood.

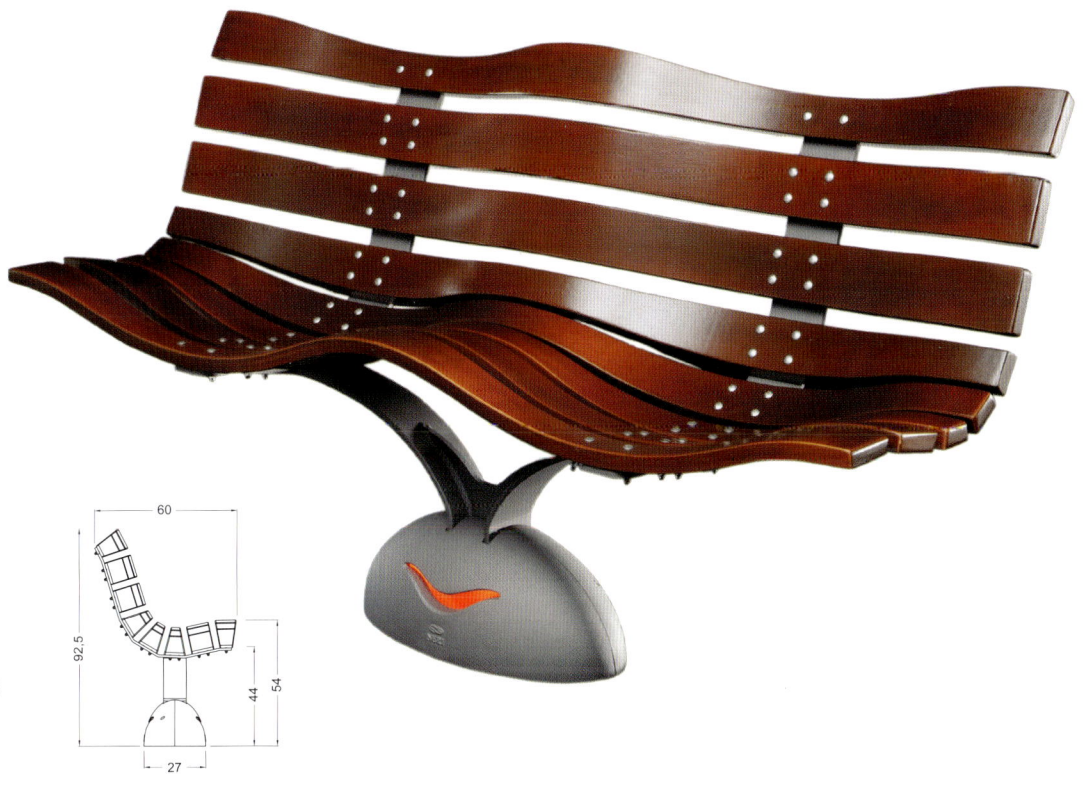

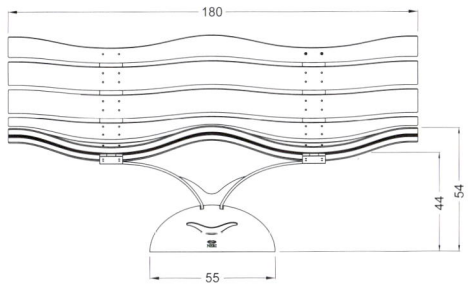

5050

Design: **Lisa Segatori** • Production: **ORA Centurelli**

Why 5050? Because 5050 is harmony and balance, anytime and anywhere. Its line is simple and clear. If you look at it, it amazes you, if you ignore it, it finds you. It joins the concept of emptiness and fullness but also the concept of fullness and emptiness, because 5050 is all and the opposite of all. It smiles to you and it winks to you, it seems to say "let's do 5050! or better fifty-fifty!". Plasma technology production and much more.
Measures: 50 x 150 x 50 cm

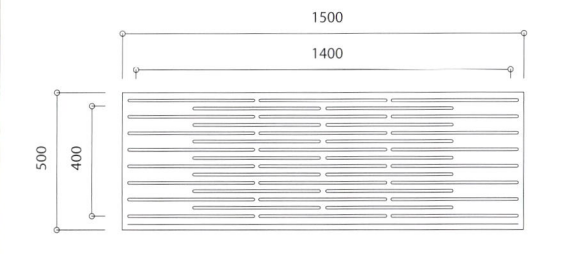

SEATS

Accesible

Design: **Diana Cabeza** • Collaborators: **L. Heine I M. Wolfson** • Production: **Estudio Cabeza**

This urban bench is ideal for resting or reading in a public open space. The different lengths of backrest and seat, along with their constructive independence, allow alternative uses such as a backrest for those sitting on the floor, or lean-to for someone standing or even a protective enclosure for a baby´s pushchair or a wheelchair for the walking-impaired. The backrest ends as a horizontal surface which can be used to lay out a picnic, as a lean-to for a standing position or as a support for reading material. Seat and backrest: solid hardwood, with penetrating sealer, natural finish.
Legs: Cast iron. Finishing: Grit blastined and painted with thermosetting polyester powder coating.

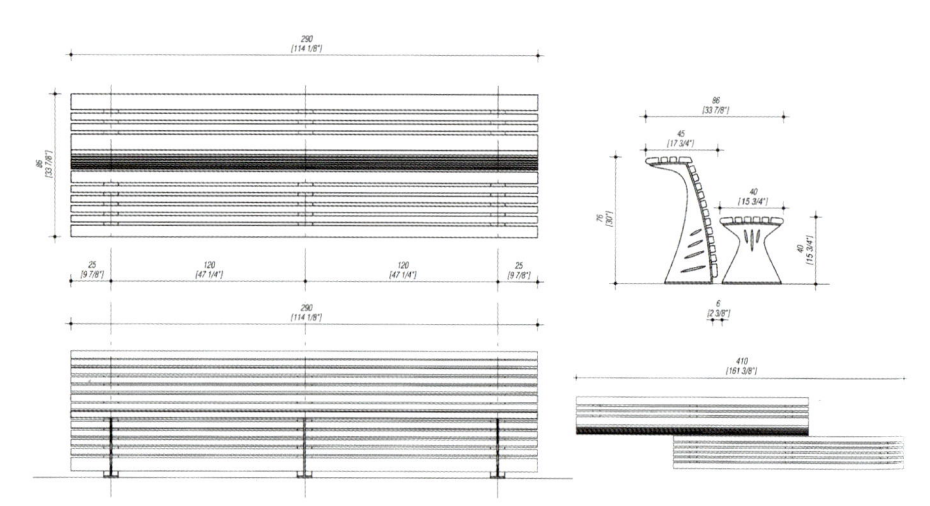

Agi

Design: **Lisa Segatori** • Production: **ORA Centurelli**

This product was born as an armchair and became a piece of outdoor seating later. Its elegance is given by the continuity of the frame and its unusual backrest. It is an item that will introduce a harmonious element of design into any kind of ambience, adapting well to natural or artificial scenery.

It is made of electrically welded tubing and tight radium hydraulic curves, with a circular section 42.4 mm (1.66 inches) diameter and a wall thickness of 2.6 mm (0.10 inches). At the base, the tube has holes for the item to be fixed to the ground with stainless steel screws. Three perforated plates welded to the frame allow the wooden seat to be attached with galvanized or stainless steel screws. The seat consists of four autoclave-treated pinewood boards 95 x 45 mm in section (3.75 x 1.76 inches), painted with waterproof varnish. The backrest is a treated and painted wooden pole, 160 mm (6.28 inches) in diameter, fixed to the frame by two perforated welded plates.

SEATS

Agrada

Design: **Quim Larrea & Associates** • Production: **ONN Outside**

Agrada proposes a new form for urban relations: designed for casual meetings, extended conversations and to give users a privileged view of the city and its inhabitants. The piece is a miniature urban stage.
The structure, in painted zinc-coated steel, is lightweight yet extraordinarily robust. The surfaces are realized in tali wood - pleasing to the touch and highly durable.
The different models in the range can be combined in an infinite number of ways.

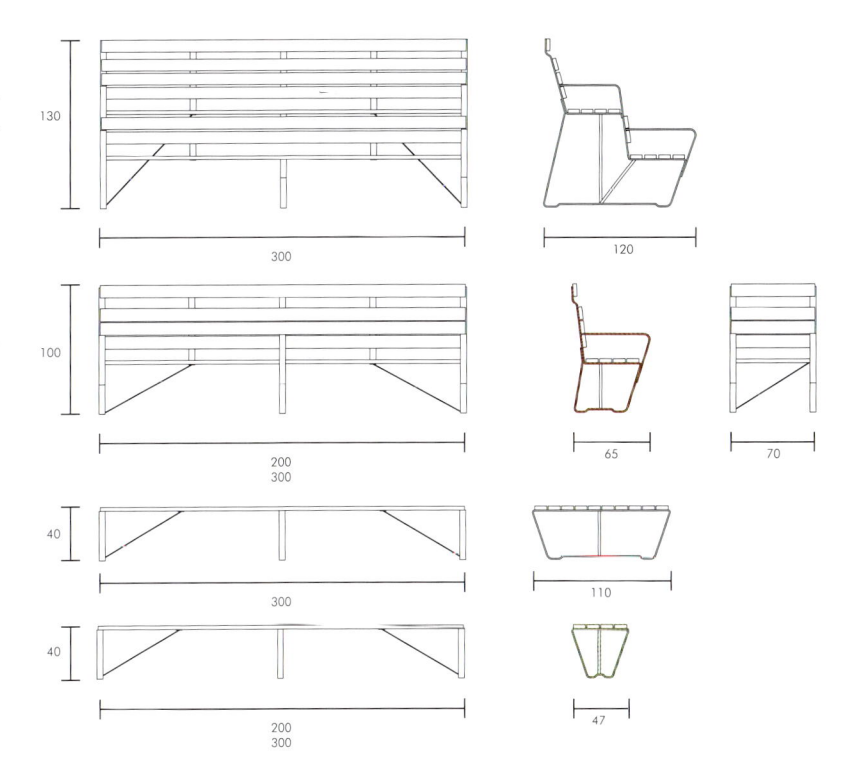

SEATS 13

AJC

Design: R + B Arquitectos • Production: Microarquitectura

Robust and simple bench seating elements.

The parallelepiped form is produced in three sizes which can be installed together to create a continuous bench or separately as a language of independent groups.

Built from 4 mm thick galvanized steel sheet reinforced internally with steel tubes, the benches are bolted to the floor.

The seat is realized in a different material, which is inserted into the top of the structure. There is a choice of seat materials available, permitting the design of the AJC bench to be customized for each application.

SEATS

Alea

Design: **Josep Suriñach** • Production: **Fundició Dúctil Benito**

Alea is an ergonomic bench. The structure is made of steel and the seat is of tropical wood, measuring 150 × 45 mm. The finish coat is with Ferrus to protect the steel from corrosion and from saline fog. The wooden parts are treated with Lignus, a fungicide, insecticide and waterproofing agent that has no effect on the natural colour of the wood. The parts are fixed with M19 screws.

Alehop

Design and production: **ONN Outside**

The Alehop perch seat redefines the whole concept of seating for urban spaces. Its perch design makes it an ideal meeting point, allowing users to converse at the same height irrespective of whether they are standing or seated. This is not possible with a standard bench. This feature means the Alehop perch bench is particularly suitable for areas such as schools or universities, leisure areas, parks, beaches... It can also be used as a handrail to define areas. In terms of ergonomics, its height and the width of its seating surface ensure the comfort of the user-type it was conceived for. It is produced in zinc plated steel, stainless steel AISI 316, or steel with an epoxy coating. The timber is Tali treated with teak oil.

SEATS

Alfil

Design: **Diana Cabeza** • Colors: **Elisabet Cabeza** • Production: **Estudio Cabeza**

The Alfil seat constitutes a versatile item for multiple indoor and outdoor scenarios. It can serve the purpose of a bench for a quick rest or stop over and can also be configured to create a dynamic interpersonal situation.
Next to a sofa or an armchair it may be used as a side table.

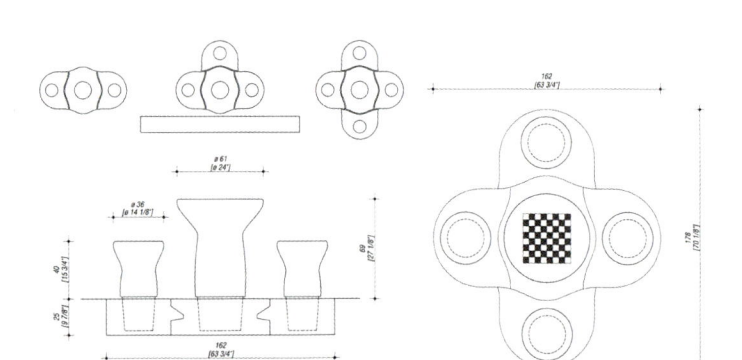

SEATS

Ambiente

Design: **Bernhard Winkler** • Production: **Euroform**

Ambiente Wood – this is the new generation of free-standing wooden benches with optimum seating comfort on ergonomically shaped seating elements. The unique design is convincing in functional terms too – because, despite its refined appearance, Ambiente is extremely stable, robust and long-lasting. This model is available in wood and expanded metal versions. The metal frame is optimally protected from corrosion by means of a process of hot-dip galvanization followed by an additional powder-coating. A litter bin has also be designed to match the "Ambiente" park bench.

Ameba

Design: **Atelier Mendini** • Production: **Ghisamestieri**

This range of Park benches consists of lateral frames in cast-iron that support alternatively twenty-nine or sixteen Iroko wooden laths. These are impregnated with protective fungicides and are available in two different lengths (1500 mm and 2000 mm); steel ties allow for fastening. The laths may be painted in the colour requested. There is a circular base-plate at the end of the cast-iron lateral components allowing the bench to be fastened to the ground with expansion bolts. The items are delivered separately, for the simple assembly operation to be carried out by the customer.

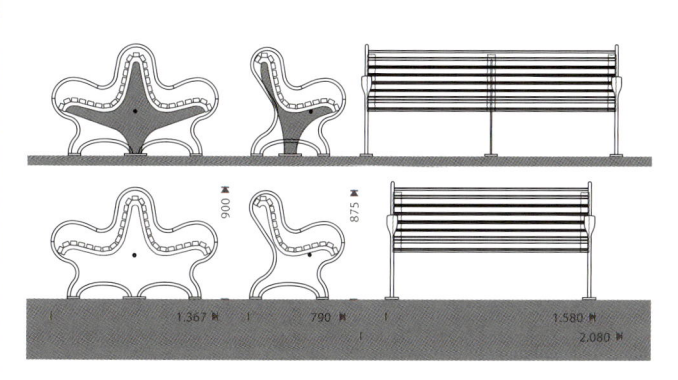

SEATS

Ara

Design: **Marta Ferraz, Paula Cabrera and T&D Cabanes** • Production: **T&D Cabanes**

Ara is a bench that combines formal equilibrium, ergonomic principles and top quality materials. The boards on the seat can be of tropical wood or of polythene in different colours. The seat rests upon a curved structure with angular steel supports. The result is a wide, comfortable and inviting piece of urban furniture. The benches can be combined together to form different configurations. Alone or in groups, standing in a row or randomly placed, they create a variety of dynamic compositions

18 SEATS

Arco

Design: **Germán Rubio** • Production: **Durban Studio**

The shape of Arco breathes geometry, which is what makes it so striking. Ergonomically designed, this bench is appropriate for various types of users. In fact it consists of two items, a chair and a bench for the elderly, Arco-senior, which has been thought of specifically for those who make the most use of public benches. It is higher so that such users can sit down and get up more easily, and the armrest is wide for better support. The Arco bench is made of cast aluminium, lacquered, or cast iron finished with an anti-corrosive paint. The seat can be of treated tropical wood, autoclave treated northern pine, or composite board made of recycled plastics.

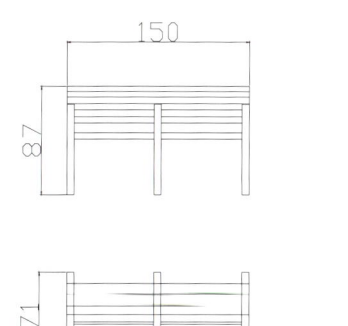

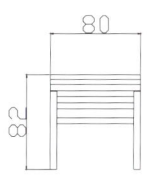

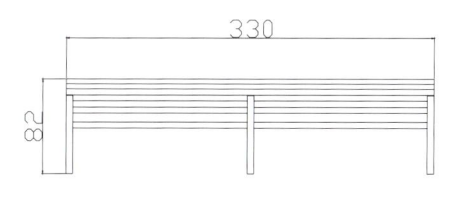

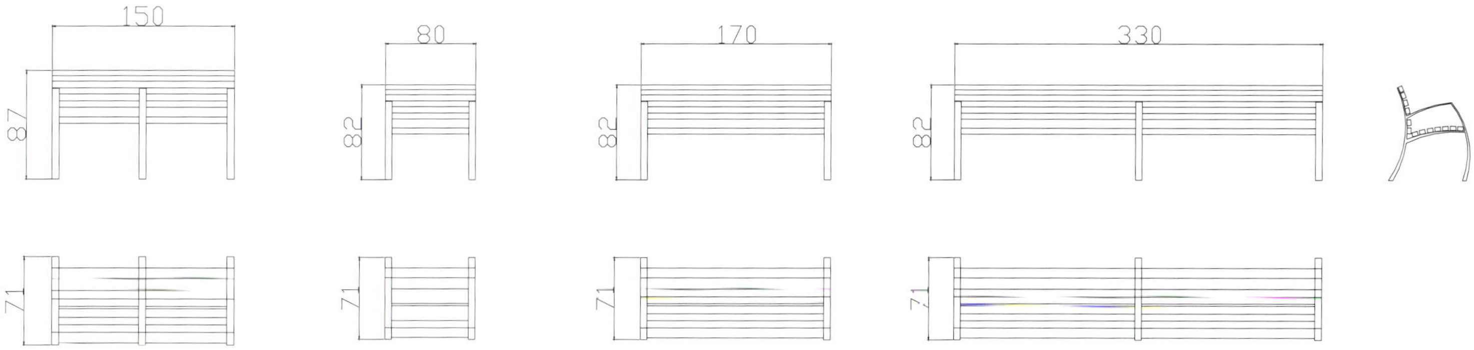

SEATS

Armonia

Design: **Bernhard Winkler** · Production: **Euroform**

A comfortable bench consisting of a 15 mm round steel frame, hot-dip galvanised and powder coated in RAL colours, while the seating surface is made of expanded metal 3 mm thick.

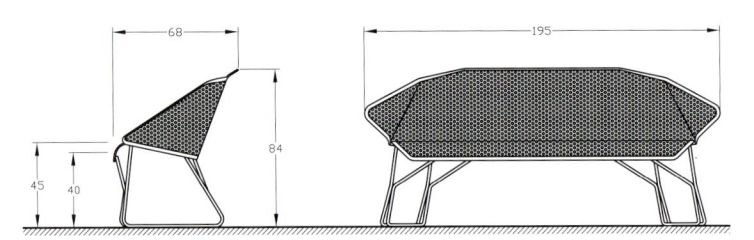

Arona

Design: **Enrico Marforio** · Production: **Ghisamestieri**

Park benches consisting of two lateral frames in cast-iron and seven Iroko wood laths (differentiated sections 50 × 33 × 1500 and 100 × 33 × 1500), impregnated with protective fungicides; steel fastening ties allow the parts to be fixed together. The laths can be supplied in other colours on demand. Semicircular feet at the end of the cast-iron lateral components allow the bench to be fastened to the ground by means of expansion bolts. The bench is delivered disassembled and the customer carries out the simple assembly operations.

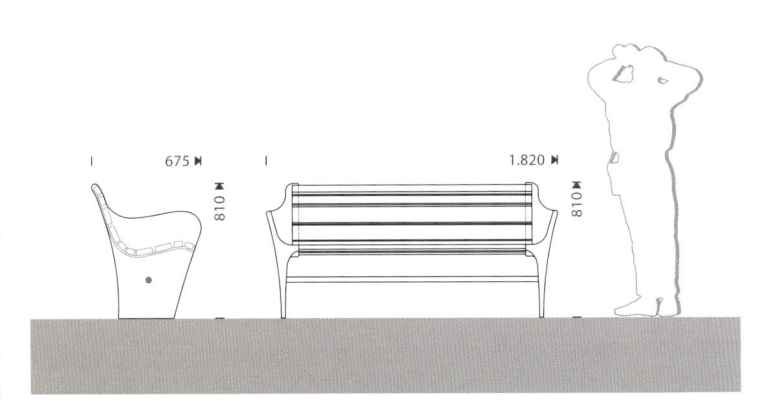

SEATS

Baf

Design: **Joan Forgas** • Production: **Alis**

The Baf bench consists of three pieces and optional armrests. The back is made of two boards of Bolondo wood, the dimensions of which may vary according to the number of armrests the bench has. The armrests consist of two boards of Bolondo or copper-treated pine measuring 540x175x50 mm, fixed to the structure with metal bolts. The seat consists of three horizontal boards of Bolondo or copper-treated pine, measuring 2000x175x50 mm. A vertically placed board conceals the edge and performs as a drip. The supporting structure is made of 6mm thick, laser-cut, galvanized steel plate, soldered and with an epoxy powder-coated finish 80 micros thick. The colour is "sable noir". The bench is fixed to the ground with special bolts and security plugs, installed previously.

Bagdad Café

Design: **Helio Piñón** • Production: **Escofet**

The Baghdad Café items, designed by architect Helio Piñón, are a risky proposition that pushes the use of one single material to the limit. A precisely folded and curved sheet of 8mm thick corten steel plate results in an ergonomic form that is clearly self-explanatory. Both items arise almost immediately from the brief encounter with certain visual references that are characteristic of the XXth century, added to the constructive possibilities of steel sheet. The associative quality of the object is obvious: its suggestive outline multiplies the possible functions it may fulfill, so being sat on may be only one of its main probable uses. Recognizing the properties of corten steel plate, the outline becomes a line and the material becomes a texture. It is constructed folding a sheet, but is perceived as the extrusion of a sign. The Baghdad Café bench and chair are delivered with an agreeable semi-gloss finish, after being sand-blasted, oxidized and stabilized with a double coat of two-component semi-gloss transparent polymer varnish. The length of the bench is 180 cm and the length of the chair is 60 cm; their weight 165 Kg and 55 Kg respectively. The items are installed directly onto the pavement, anchored with a row of concealed bolts.

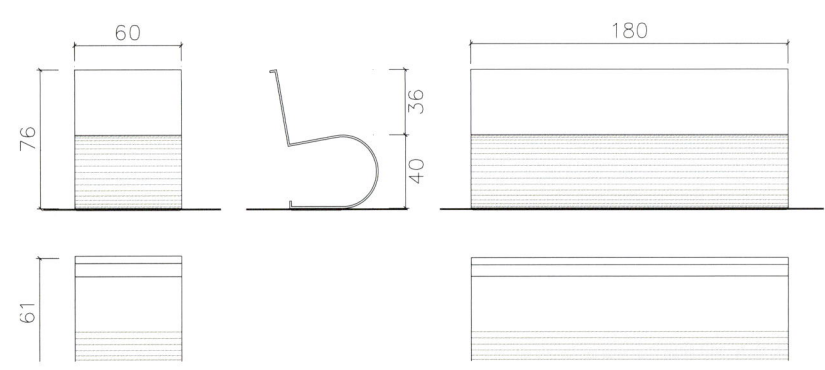

SEATS

Banca

Design: **Bernardo Gómez-Pimienta** • Production: **Alis**

There are two versions of Banca, a bench and a chair. The boards in both cases are of solid Bolondo wood or copper-treated pine, measuring 1610x90x40 mm. The back consists of four boards and the seat consists of six. The ends of the boards are held by U-shaped galvanized steel structure measuring 50x50x4 mm, with a powder-coating of epoxy 80 micros thick. The colour is "sable noir". The boards are fixed in place with countersunk bolts.

SEATS

Bancal

Design: Olga Tarrasó - Julià Espinàs • Production: Santa & Cole

This is a robust and simple bench designed for public meeting areas. It is conceived as a modular and versatile unit to provide long alignments of seating surface, with or without backrests. Its formal clarity predominates over its rhetoric value. The Bancal bench is especially designed for public use and has centuries of tradition. It is modular, solid, has a sober appearance, is designed for open spaces and is made to withstand adverse conditions. It is a linear bench for public areas and may come with or without a backrest. It consists of a steel structure and wooden boards, both common and long-lasting materials. It is designed to respond to urban plans for large benches with different needs and orientations. Its elemental but thorough design permits the backrest to be placed in two positions in the same alignment or simply omitted altogether.

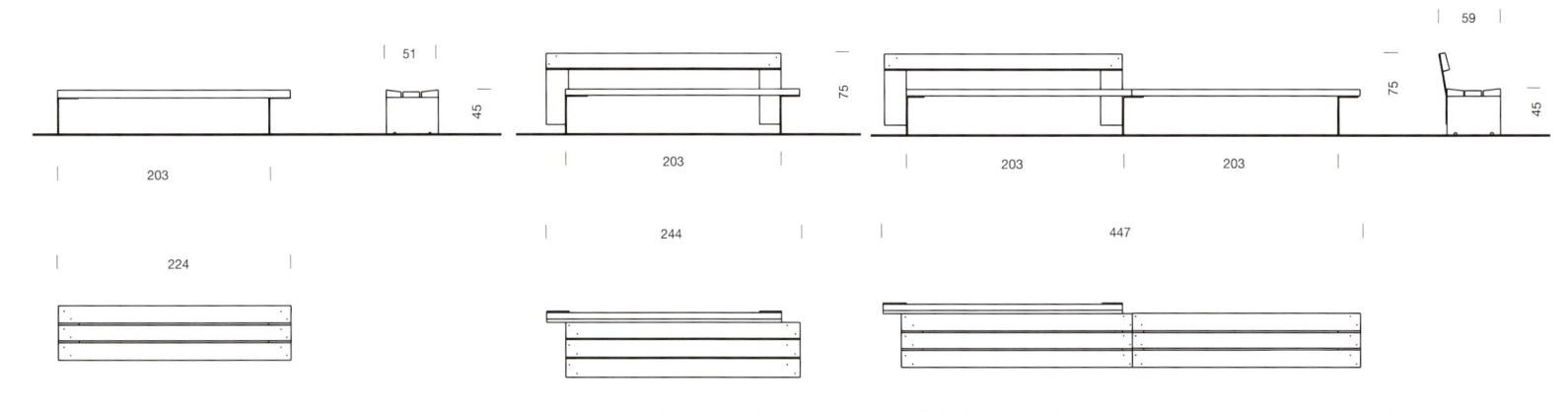

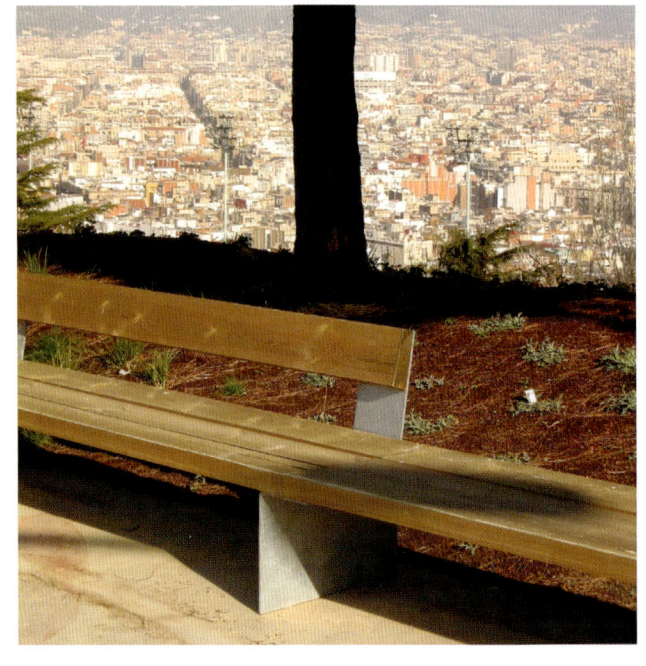

SEATS

Banda

Design: Diana Cabeza • Collaborators: L. Heine I M. Celi • Production: Estudio Cabeza

Due to its robust design, this bench is ideal for low-maintenance or marginal urban areas. The colour aggregate turns the precast concrete into a friendly item that can be used in a number of different contexts. The system of separate bench and buried base allows to first place the base, execute flooring system around base and level to achieve a perfect fitting. Final placement of bench is then accomplished with a thixotropic adhesive.

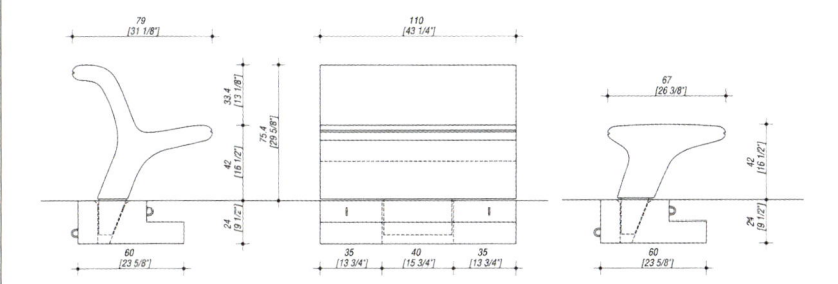

Banda Doblada

Design: Susanne Cierniak & Tran Thanh Minh Nguyen • Production: Escofet

Banda Doblada was the winning entry in the 3rd Design Competition of Urban Furniture in White Concrete, which took place in 2003 organized by the White Department of the Polytechnic University of Valencia, under the sponsorship of Cemex Spain, Ltd. The winners were the two Danish students, Susanne Cierniak y Tran Thanh Minh Nguyen.

Escofet was a member of the jury, and had accepted the commitment of producing and marketing the winning design if it was commercially viable. With the installation at the UPV Campus (Universitat Politècnica de Valencia) of the five prototypes, made of cast concrete in different colors, Escofet put the innovative seating element on the market. The bench avoids predetermining our behavior in any way, allowing users the maximum degree of freedom.

Measuring approximately 2 x 1,5 meters and weighing some 350 kilograms, the item is perfectly stable, requiring no additional anchoring system other than its own weight to attach it to the pavement, the lawn or the sand on the beach.

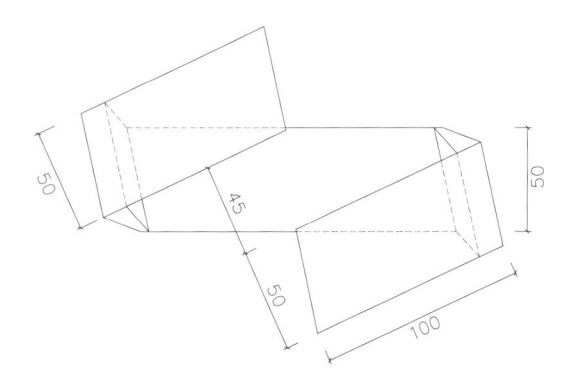

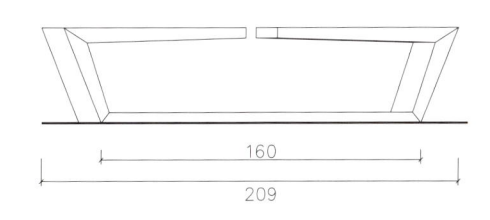

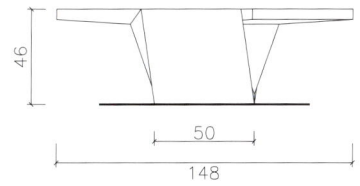

SEATS

BdLove Bench

Design: **Ross Lovegrove** • Production: **Bd**

The BD LoveBench is made of polyethylene (MDPE), of medium density, a material that can be mass pigmented in different colors. The part processing system is rotational moulding. The bench contains 5 stainless steel inserts. The item has a seating capacity for ten people. Optionally, non-slip stoppers in EPDM (rubber) can be installed, to make water drainage beneath the bench easier. It is secured using stainless steel bolts. 5 bolts supplied if required. Polyethylene PEGS close the ballasting holes (2u). A Polypropylene TRI-SURE PEG with rubber O-ring seal closes the ballast emptying hole. The bench can be ballasted with water or washed sand (max.120 Kg). The objects general measurements are 2652 × 1293 × 940 mm.

The thickness of the material varies from 9 mm near the base under 8 mm at the top of the object. The total weight of one bench (without ballast) is approximately 80Kg. The item is available in a range of standard colors: fluorescent red, beige, white, blue, green, sandstone (sand granite structured) and millstone (dark grey granite structured). It can be supplied in custom made special colors according to client requirements.

BdLove Bench

26 SEATS

Bench Seat I - Curved

Design and production: **Botton & Gardiner**

In this version of the Benchseat 1 there is an appropriate and careful combination of different woods, held by a cast aluminum frame. The original Benchseat 1, which became known as a result of its installation in the Fox studios in Sydney, Australia, was characterized by its complete simplicity. It consisted of a single well-shaped curve that fulfilled the necessary function and made it a welcome item in any park or natural area.

The wooden components of the bench have been varnished with jarrah. The bench has a maximum height of 440mm and a width of 430mm.

Big Bux

Design and production: **Miramondo**

Big Bux is a multifunctional object: The design is based on the box tree, carefully pruned into the shape of a cube. In keeping with its origins, Big Bux could and should be used as a decorative horticultural object (though it need be neither pruned nor watered). Thanks to its materials and structure, it is perfectly performant as a seat, but in conjunction with floor lighting, Big Bux becomes a lamp. Brightly illuminated from within, its leafy pattern casts exciting shadows onto the ground and neighbouring walls.

SEATS

Bilateral

Design: **Olga Tarrasó - Julià Espinàs** • Production: **Santa & Cole**

The Bilateral bench is an ergonomically shaped seat that can accommodate a number of people in a row. The optional models with or without a backrest added to its simple and versatile form allows for a number of possible compositions. The bench consists of the armrests, the support structure, and the wooden slats that provide the surface to sit on. The support structure is made of 6 mm (1/4 inch) folded steel plate, with a corrosion-proof coating and painted black.

The seating surface of the bench, with or without a backrest, is made of slats of tropical wood with an FSC certification and treated with a tannin blocking agent. The various parts of the bench are held together with screws and bolts made of steel with a rust-proof coating.

The article's modular form multiplies the possible combinations it can be installed in.

It is fixed to the pavement by means of two corrosion-proof structural steel screws.

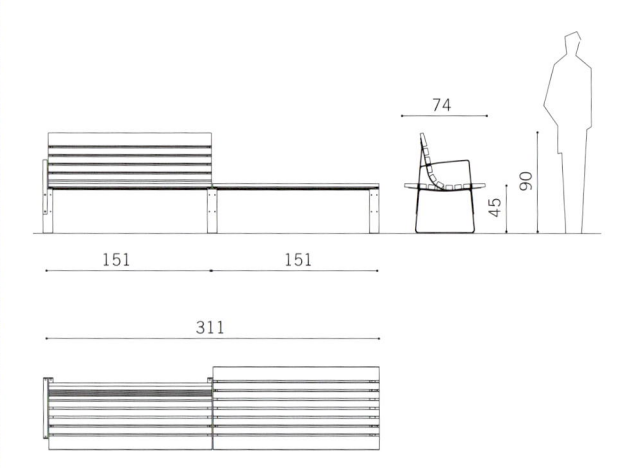

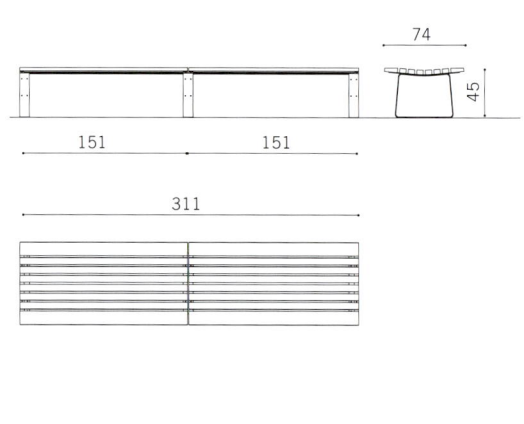

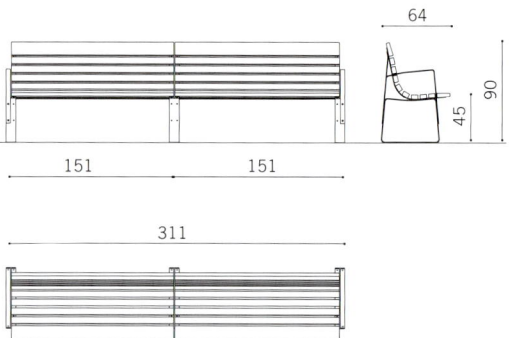

28 SEATS

Bilbao

Design: **Josep Muxart** • Production: **Escofet**

The Bilbao bench is one of a series of urban elements that come under the same name. These reinforced concrete seats have been designed to transmit a feeling of organic softness to the rigidity of the actual material. This has been achieved by using a composition of rounded forms and warped planes. The result achieved is a series of disquieting pieces that seem to be undergoing a contained state of movement. The dimensions have been kept limited to permit a more amiable interaction with the environment.

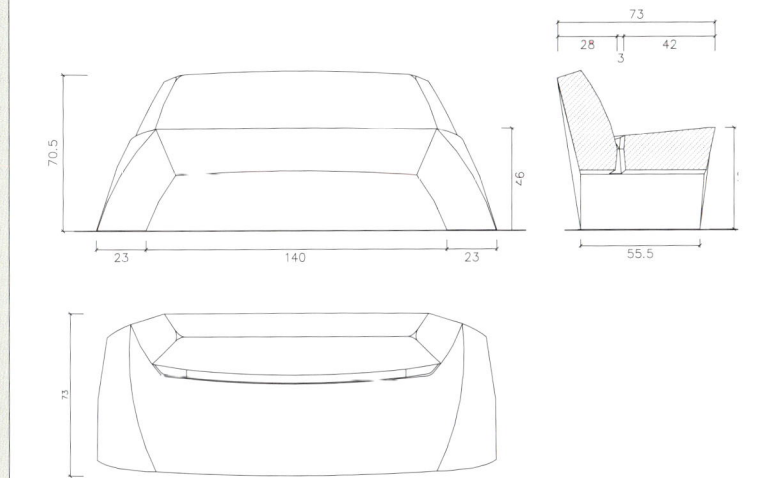

SEATS

Bloop

Design: **Ton Riera Ubía** • Production: **mago:urban**

The Bloop series, designed by Ton Riera Ubía and produced and commercialized by mago: urban, includes four different models. They share the characteristics of functional flexibility and a clearly discernible purity of line, providing a configuration that is easy to integrate in any urban environment, without forgetting the sobriety and elegance that characterise mago: urban.
The configuration of the four models is based on the idea of a bench with orthogonal lines made up of a concrete bench and four A-304 quality stainles stell supports. They differ in whether or not they have a back, located along the whole length of the bench or at one of the ends, as well as a bold pattern on the seat element of one of the models.

Blue Moon

Design: **Vicente Soto** • Production: **T&D Cabanes**

The Bluemoon bench features a conceptual design. Its ergonomic structure is a composition of purist forms, executed in an interplay of steel and tropical wood boards. The backpiece consists of one single board. It has been designed to enhance large, open air surroundings and gardens, although it performs to equal advantage next to highly technical architecture where metal prevails.

SEATS

Boa

Design: **Alberto Llorian Fueyo** • Production: **T&D Cabanes**

The "Boa" bench is one of the most important new additions to Tecnología & Diseño Cabanes' new collection of urban furniture. The uniquely sinuous curves it can adapt to, its robust structural stability, solid and secure, make this bench an extraordinary example of sculpture, made to be integrated into both urban spaces and natural environments. The possibility of creating an infinite number of configurations by placing the various modules in a correlative straight or curved position represents the system's main quality. The structure consists of steel plate, galvanized in a range of colors, adding to the system's versatility. The support members consist of a strong structure of tropical wood, resistant to average natural weather conditions.

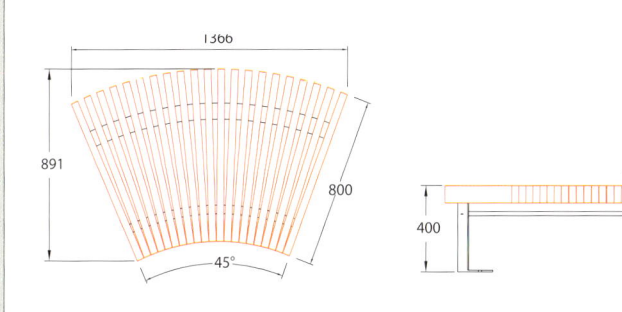

Board

Design and production: **Runge**

For those who love to socialise, Board consists of top-quality timber formed into a half-oval shape using traditional handcraft techniques.
Interchangeable, weatherproof varnished or breathing-active painted, this bench offers pure recreation whether it is used for sitting or lying on, with unlimited possibilities and variations.

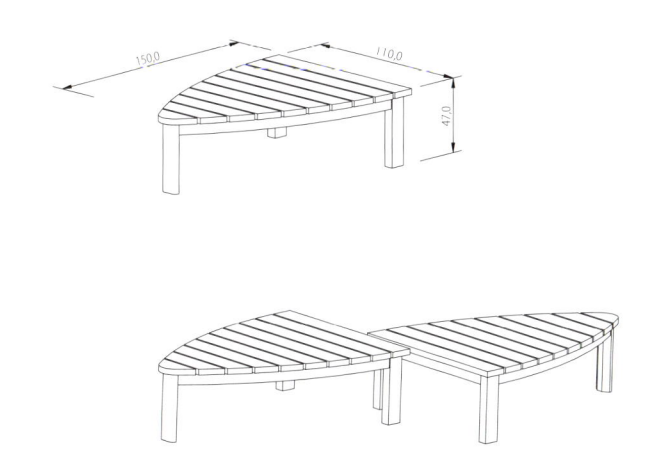

SEATS

Boomerang

Design: Andreu Arriola / Carme Fiol • Production: Escofet

Boomerang is one of a set of seats and tables made of stone. Their friendly shape invites the passers-by to rest, read or deposit what they are carrying, constituting an innovative reminder of ancestral nature and the world of fossils and seashells. These items were designed to form part of natural parks or green areas, to furnish plazas, promenades or neutral public areas in the city with an object that is rational while offering a welcoming natural counterpoint. They are outdoor sofas that can be installed in large indoor spaces such as sport pavilions, exhibition spaces, major facilities, markets and such. Boomerang introduces itself as a playful, conversational item that symbolically embodies communication and movement.

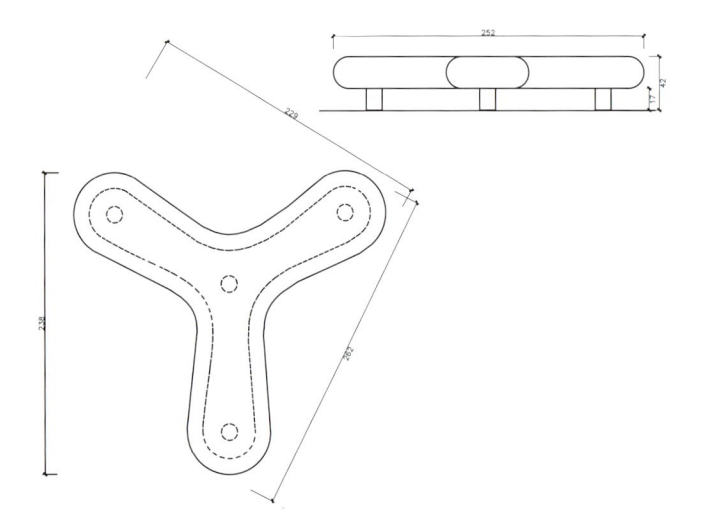

Botanic

Design: **Michelle Herbut** • Production: **Street and Park Furniture**

Michelle Herbut, who graduated as a Bachelor of Industrial Design in 2005, designed the Botanic Bench for a final year University project to suit a specific site in South Australia. Inspired by the growth and organic nature of the plants at the Botanical Gardens, she wanted to simulate the bench 'growing' out of the ground and took advantage of the resulting curve to add another possibility to the ways you can use the bench, by using it as the much sought backrest that nature so often omits. Street and Park Furniture, with whom Michelle currently works, were approached to help with production and manufacturing issues. With their specialist experience, the enterprise provides urban projects with the convenience of a single supply source of street furniture, backed by specialist experience and support. The Botanic Bench consists simply of a series of hardwood boards bolted onto the two curved end pieces made of aluminium.

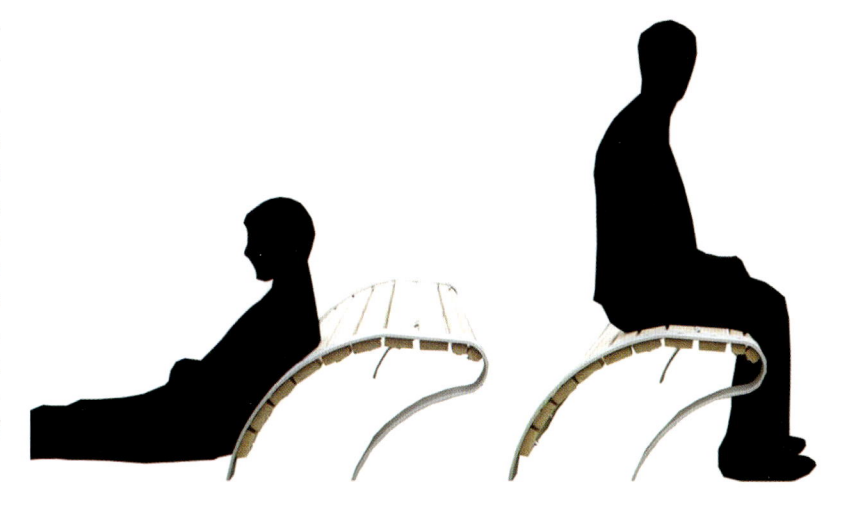

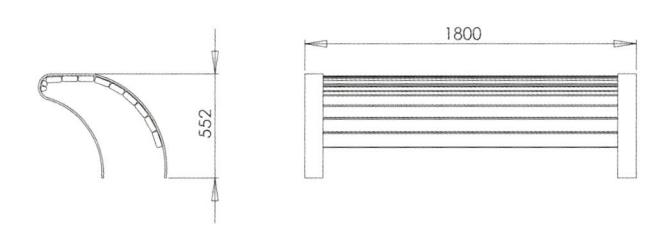

SEATS

Brunea

Design: **David Karásek & Radek Hegmon** • Production: **mmcité**

A range of benches with a sophisticated modern design to bring elegance into every outdoor and indoor environment. Despite a light visual appearance, overall sturdiness is ensured. The new versions with either straight or curved arrangements of the transversal lamellas allow for variations and original (e)motional compositions. Brunea received the "Good design 2002" award. The hot-galvanised steel frame comes painted in a standard hue. The seat and backrest are either of solid wood lamellas or of perforated metal sheet, in both cases discreetly but firmly joined to the supporting frame. All four legs can be easily fixed to the ground.

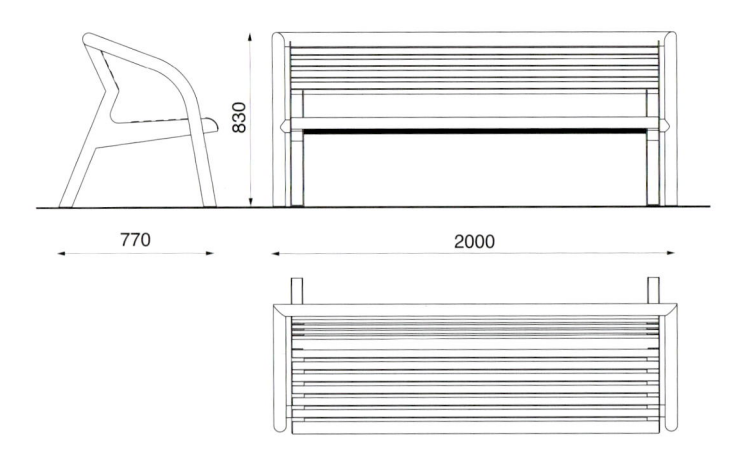

BS9

Design and production: **Bottom and Gardiner**

The Bench Seat BS9 uses a range of seat materials including hardwoods and extruded aluminium on a cast aluminium frame. This is a contemporary backless public space bench featuring a gentle wave shape, and back-to-back seating.

SEATS

Buque

Design: **Diana Cabeza** • Production: **Estudio Cabeza**

Buque owes its name to its relation with a harbour and the context of shipping. In its design old traditions are respected but its image is modernized by using a line that links modern technology to the solidity of a historical location, the language of old ships of steel sheet and wood. The structure is of steel sheet with the soldering points showing. The finish is galvanized by immersion. The seat and the back are made of solid Lapacho or Quebracho wood, planed and waterproofed.

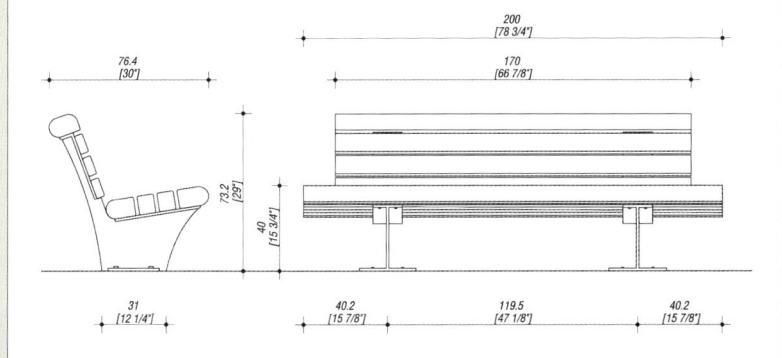

Cado

Design: **Max Wehberg** • Production: **Westeifel Werke**

The Cado seating series is based on a simple trapezoidal foot that sustains a curved sitting surface. Different configurations can be created based upon this element: with or without a backrest and with a solid or a lighter appearance.

SEATS 35

Calma

Design and production: **Runge**

Calma offers young and old a welcome place of rest and relaxation. Stable and precise feets made of cast aluminium with armrests and durable hardwood in the seat and back unite to a quite resting place with mediterranean flair. Seating made of durable hardwood niangon. 4 slats in the seat and 2 in the backrest (each 10,5 x 3,5 cm) with stabilised stainless steel bars screwd centrical unterneath the seating. The seat is cambered for the highest seating comfort. Cast aluminium bench feet with armrest and centrecal stainless steel bars coloured in DB 703 anthrazite grey. Bench for free standing, optionally with plates zu screw on the pavement or with plug-in anchors for setting in foundation.

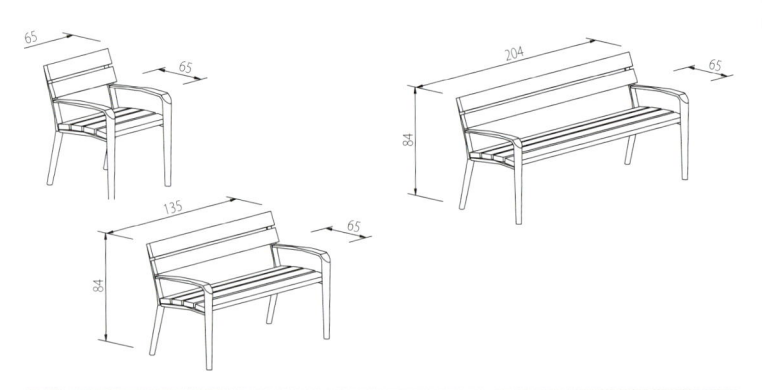

Canapino

Design and production: **Geohide**

The notably straightforward appearance of this bench for outdoor spaces enables it to be installed with equal success in a contemporary or a traditional context. Moreover, it has been especially designed to be adjustable to variable grade configurations, by the simple application of readymade steel wedges. The bench is designed to be fastened onto a stable foundation by whatever type of screws or anchorage system considered most appropriate for the specific location.

The item consists of a stainless steel structure and pipe connections. The seat and backrest are made of ash wood and are easily removable. The entire object is assembled with bolts, making it easy to disassemble for maintenance. The steel surface has a sandblasted finish (natural color for the pipes). The wooden components are treated and painted with a base coat of fungicide and two coats of slightly tinted finish varnish (other finishes can be supplied upon request).

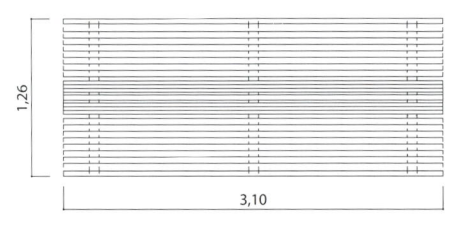

SEATS

Catalano

Design: Óscar Tusquets Blanca & Lluís Clotet • Production: Bd

One of the few pieces of Spanish design that have never been bettered and which can be expected to remain commercially viable. The secret lies in its well-known virtues. Its ergonomic shape, wisely adapted from the bench antoni Gaudí designed for Güell Park; and the deployé steel, which gives it a sense of transparency so that it blends discreetly into its setting, prevents rainwater from collecting and keeps it warm in winter and cool in summer.

"The profile of the bench that Gaudí designed for the Park Güell seemed to us to be unsurpassable, and we decided to adapt it for the Catalano. Done well, plagiarism does not necessarily have to kill the original. The quality of an imitation, as of anything else, depends on the talent of the plagiarist". On the basis of the 1 m (39.3 inches) module benches of any length can be assembled, single or back-to-back, using the type of leg desired.

Materials: Legs in galvanized, hot-dipped or electro-polished stainless steel tube. Bench in deployé steel, whith two versions: galvanized and painted in white, or hot dipped.

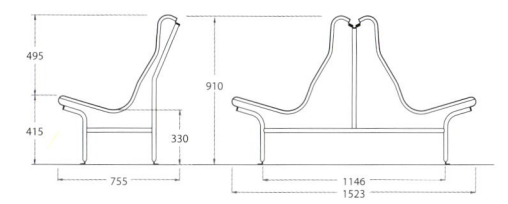

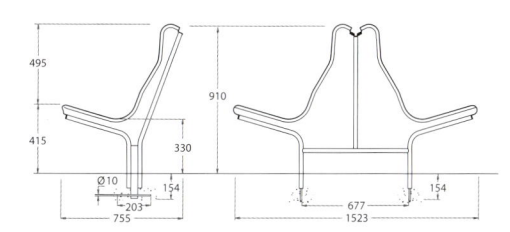

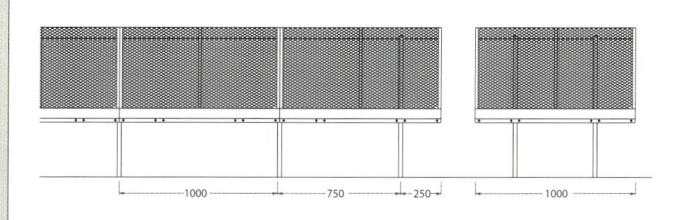

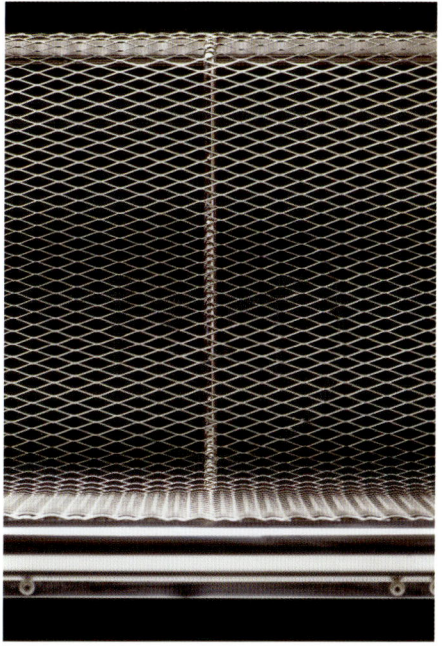

SEATS

Celesta

Design: Javier Feduchi, Alfredo Lozano y Pablo Moreno • Production: T&D Cabanes

The main characteristic of the Celesta bench is the rationality and the solidity of its form. It consists of a monolithic body of saw-cut crystal granite, and a structure of stainless carbon steel, fixed to the ground by means of a chemical adhesive.

Chill

Design: Frog Design • Production: Landscape Forms

Chill is a chaise lounge, expressed in sculptural form, appealing to those seeking new solutions to furniture in public spaces. Its form echoes the contour of the human body which it is designed to support. The ergonomically sculpted item measures 32 × 62 × 28 in. It has a weight of approximately 50 lbs. The seating surface is made of roto-molded polyethylene. All the steel parts are primed with E-coat.

SEATS

Coma

Design: **Joan Cinca** • Production: **mago:urban**

This bench, made of sandblasted reinforced concrete, weighs 250 Kg. It tries to answer a wide range of necessities with one single object that can be used in many different configurations by simply altering the direction in which it is facing. Suitable for plazas, promenades or pedestrian areas, the basic configuration of the bench is ergonomic, but used in an inverted position it can become a limit or a bollard.

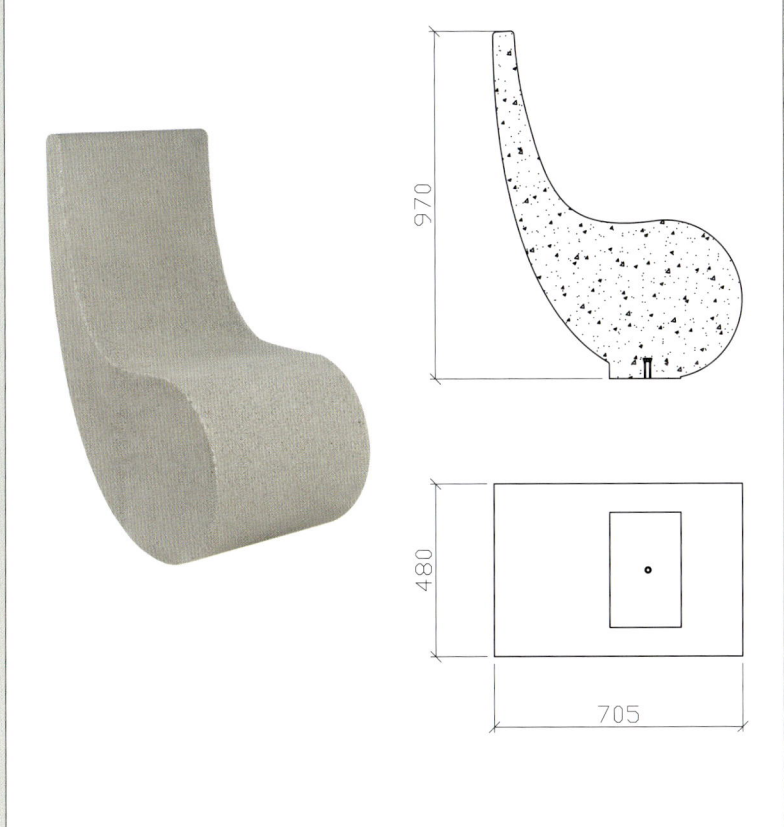

Come Back

Design: **Eveline Bijleveld** • Production: **VelopA**

The Come Back is the very first outdoor bench manufactured according to the Cradle to Cradle (C2C) sustainability principle. Developed by William McDonough and Michael Braungart, C2C is inspired by the ingenious cycles of nature. At the end of their life cycle, the product materials are separated and re-used with no loss of quality in an endless cycle.

The Come Back is manufactured fully in accordance with C2C concept, making it well and truly ready for a future in which sustainable production will play an increasingly important role. Even the design of the Come Back looks like something from the future – with its curved and circular forms, the bench is futuristic in appearance, yet has a friendly look and feel.

The raised central section creates adequate distance to ensure privacy for users. On the other hand, the circular design of the bench means people can turn around to interact and use the raised section as a table.

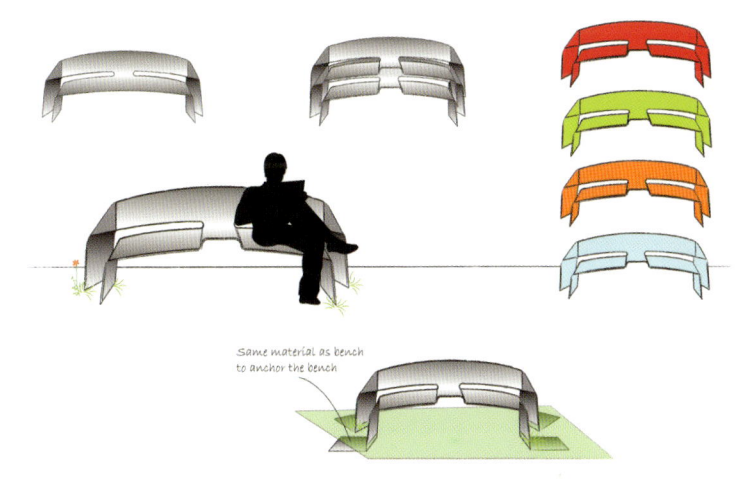

SEATS

Comunitario

Design: **Diana Cabeza** • Production: **Estudio Cabeza, Santa & Cole**

These benches were designed as an open and neutral support system catering for different use options. Their undefined nature allows the user the possibility of establishing a personal relationship with the bench.

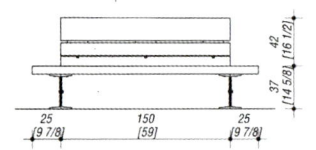

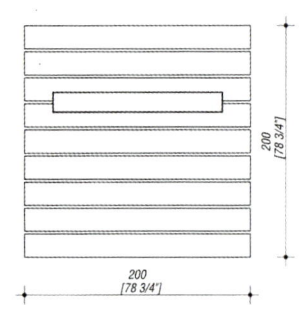

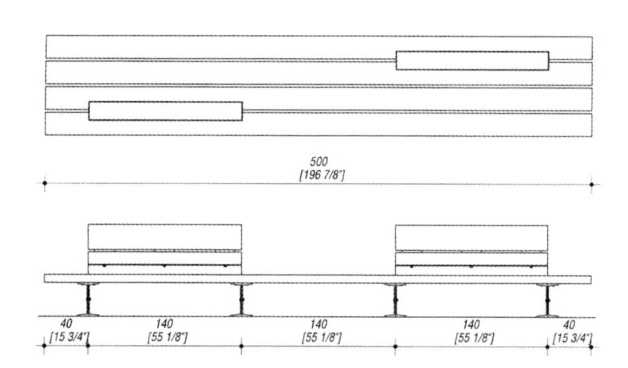

Cornamusa

Design: **Diana Cabeza** • Collaborators: **D. D'Andrea / A. Ferrugia** • Production: **Estudio Cabeza**

This bench, made of sandblasted reinforced concrete, weighs 250 Kg. It tries to answer a wide range of necessities with one single object that can be used in many different configurations by simply altering the direction in which it is facing. Suitable for plazas, promenades or pedestrian areas, the basic configuration of the bench is ergonomic, but used in an inverted position it can become a limit or a bollard.

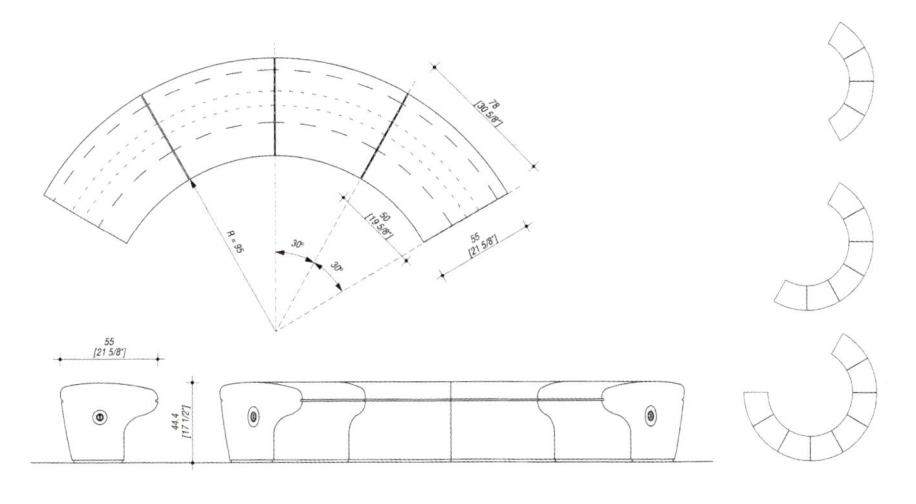

Crusöe

Design: **Roger Albero** • Production: **mago:urban**

Crusöe is a modular bench designed by Roger Albero. It is a hybrid design arising from the combination of three items as different as a bench, a stair and a basin in the ground around the base of a tree. Crusöe was conceived taking the image of a stair as a reference. It is a place to sit down and rest, of a type that invites group gatherings and conversation. Moreover, thanks to its dimensions it can contain plants, from flowers or shrubs, to trees of considerable size, capable of providing a large area of shade around them.
It consists of three symmetrical interlocked elements of concrete, stacked on top of each other. This modular element can be installed as a unit or as half a unit (for example placed against a wall), as a bench or as a container for plants, one, two or three elements high.

SEATS

Cube

Design: **Runge Design Team** • Production: **Runge**

With some influence of Far East calmness and concentration, Cube suites public outdoor areas. The pure beauty of the combined elements of granite, stainless steel and premium hardwood is combined with perfect craftsmanship and offers a meditative atmosphere. With its length of 218 cm (85.67 inches) and depth of 60 cm (23.58 inches) it easily offers seating for up to ten people sitting on both sides.
Cube impresses by its simple and clear design combined with selected premium materials.

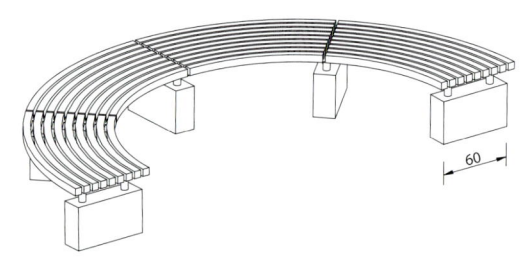

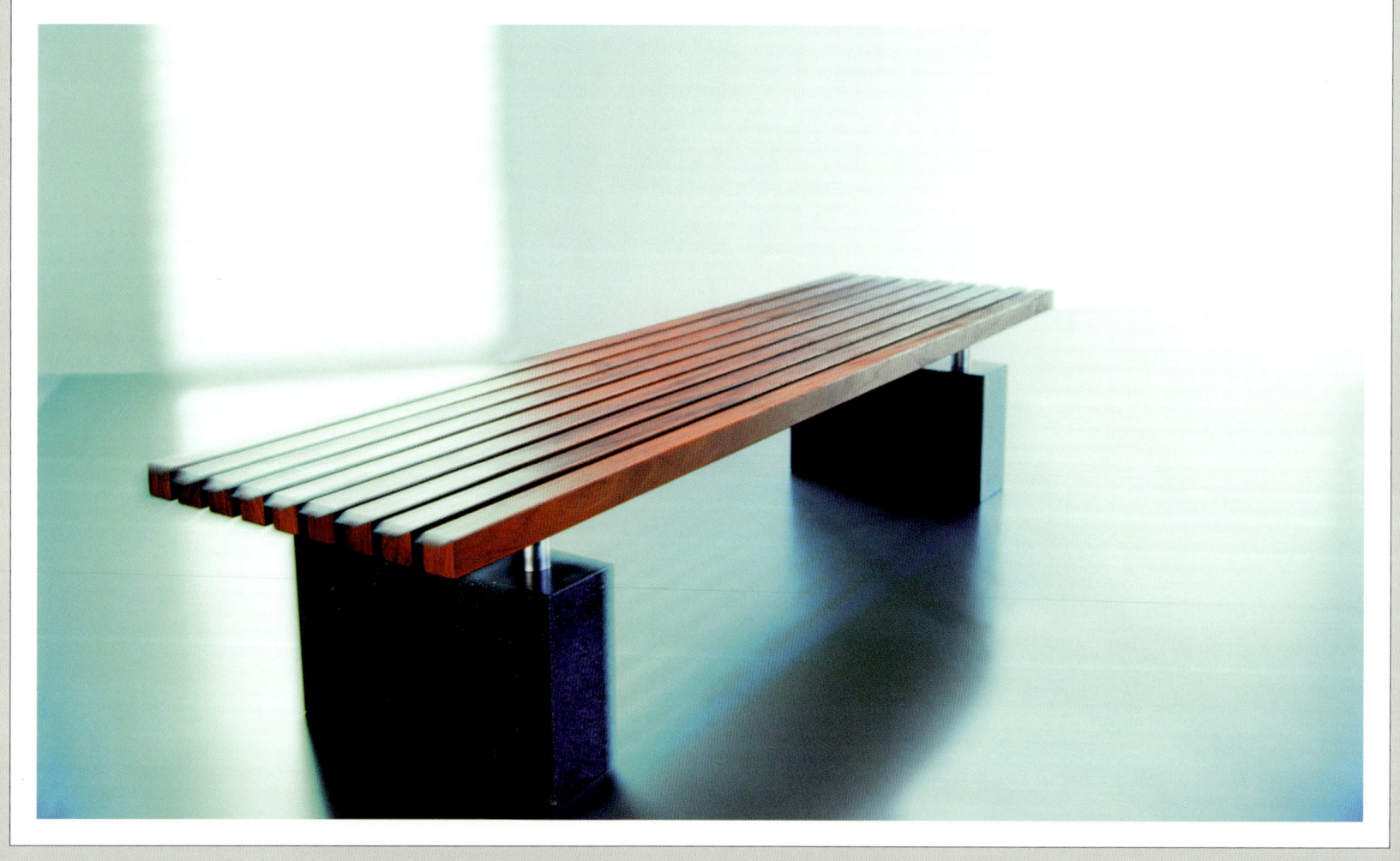

42 SEATS

Cuc

Design: **Foreign Office Architects - Farshid Moussavi & Alejandro Zaera Polo** • Production: **mago:urban**

The Cuc (worm) bench was designed to fit into and complement the paving system of the Auditoria of Barcelona Park, one of the emblematic spaces of the Forum of Cultures Area. This paving system consists of units that, placed one after the other and rotating on their own axes, allow it to adapt to any sort of terrain, however irregular. The bench could not conform to straight lines or Cartesian geometry, as the paving was designed to follow the sinuous profile of the dunes in the park. This was the idea behind the Cuc bench.

Made of concrete, the Cuc seat consists of a truncated cone that tapers away from its round seat towards the ground. It has a groove down one of its sides, which locks into the next unit, and so on. The surface of the seat curves up to provide a small, radial backrest. The Cuc bench is capable of multiple configurations simply by rotating each of the units that compose it. It is possible to construct straight or curved structures as further units are added to the chain, resulting in an increasingly flexible shape as the chain gets longer. The geometry can be re-altered even after being fitted. The Cuc units are made in three colours: white, granite grey and ochre.

SEATS

Daciano Da Costa

Design: **Daciano Da Costa** • Production: **Larus**

Daciano Da Costa directed this intervention, homage to Jorge Vieira (1926-1998), a sculptor in the Mediterranean tradition who gave his work a popular meaning while he resorted to an abstract expression of the human figure. His works mix well with the austere architecture of the city of Beja (Portugal). The benches make use of materials and solutions typical of Cor-ten steel and of wastebaskets with an angle-iron foot, all of which is reminiscent of the three typical supports used for the sculptures of Jorge Vieira.

Deca

Design: **Tobia Repossi** • Production: **Modo**

A relaxing seat like a chaise longue designed for urban parks and gardens. The structure is composed of two simple curved elements, each made out of six Fe 360 B steel tubes bolted together. The ends are fixed in position by a steel plate. The entire item is hot galvanized and powder coated for outdoor use. The structure has two plates at the base with holes for fixing the bench to the ground by means of M10 plugs, suitable for the paving.
The bench is available also in the AISI 304 stainless steel version.

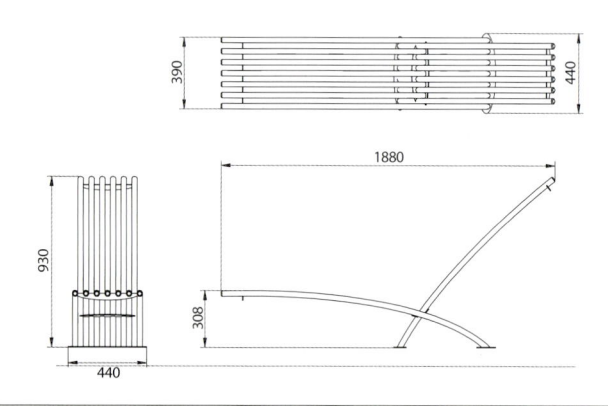

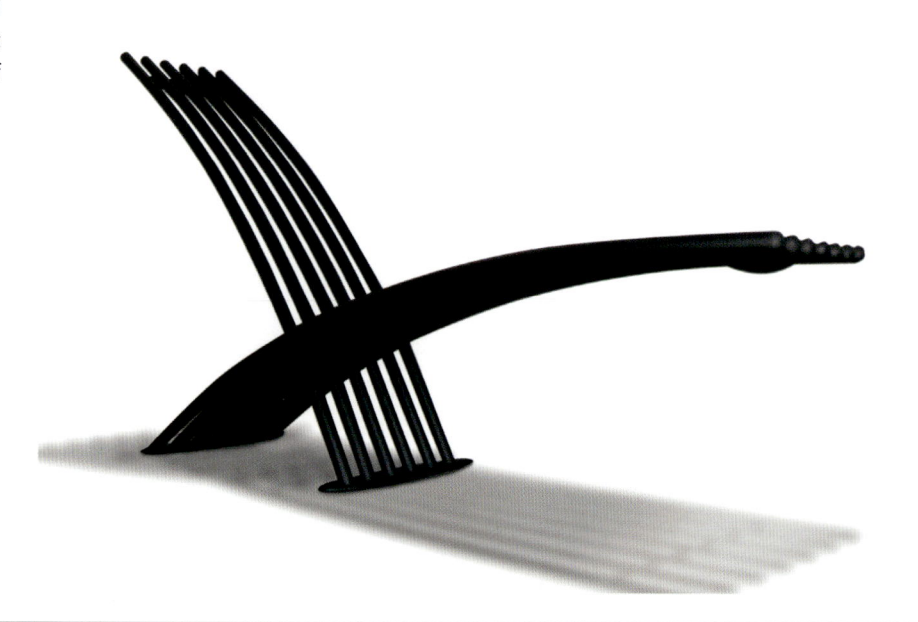

44 SEATS

Degrau

Design: **Inês Lobo** • Production: **Larus**

Degrau is a monolithic concrete design, the simple forms of which give it weight and solidity. Its shape makes it easily adaptable to sloped locations. From a distance, the sites where they have been installed look like an extension of a domestic living room into public space.

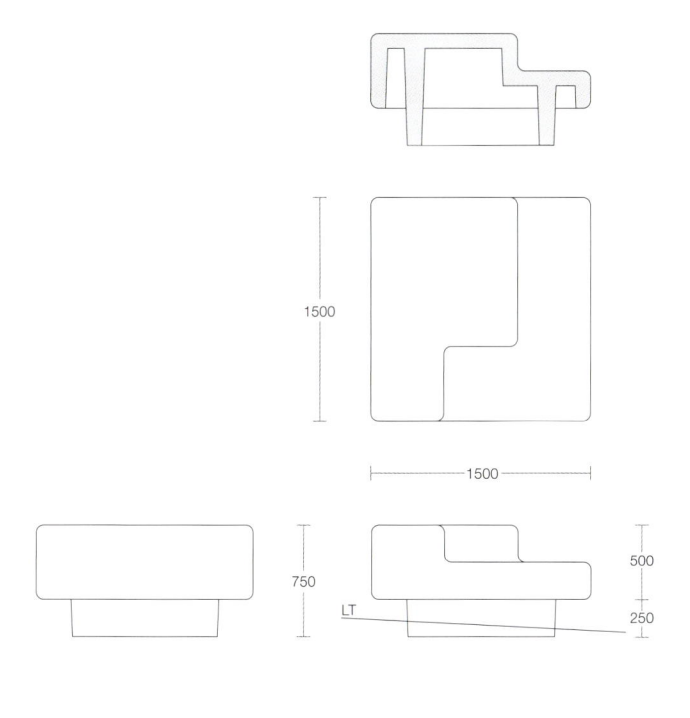

Divano

Design and production: **VelopA**

With its round lines and streamlined design, the Divano is an exceptional bench. The gently curving seat and backrest are made of durable wood and provide optimal comfort. The length gives a sense of allure as well as providing plenty of seating space.

SEATS

Dom

Design: **Sergio Fernández** • Production: **Tecam BCN**

The Dom bench comes in two forms, a simple backless bench and a complete bench with backrest and armrests. The backless Dom is a simple urban bench made of five pieces, which include the seat of four 30 mm (1.18 inches) thick planks and two legs of steel tubing, with optional armrests. The planks can be of Elondo wood or Flemish pine, autoclave treated and with two coats of a waterborne varnish. The legs are galvanized steel, fired with micro textured silver. The bench is mounted with stainless steel screws.

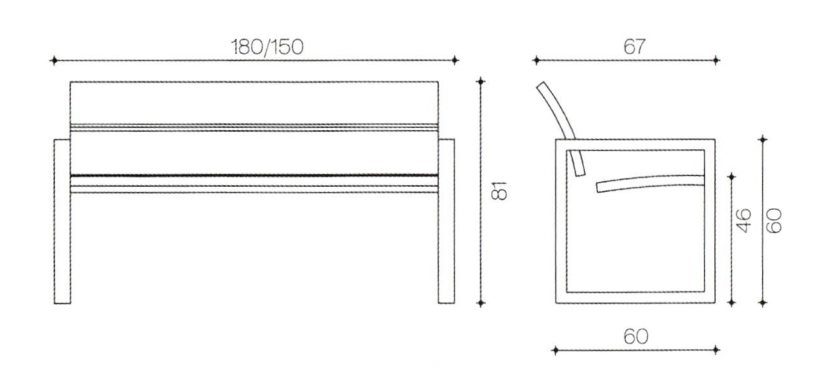

SEATS

Elemental

Design: **Juan Sádaba** • Production: **ONN Outside**

Elementary in its solid shape and conceptual simplicity, this bench leaves all the options open as to how it is positioned. The independent blocks can be grouped to allow the users to create their own unique formation.

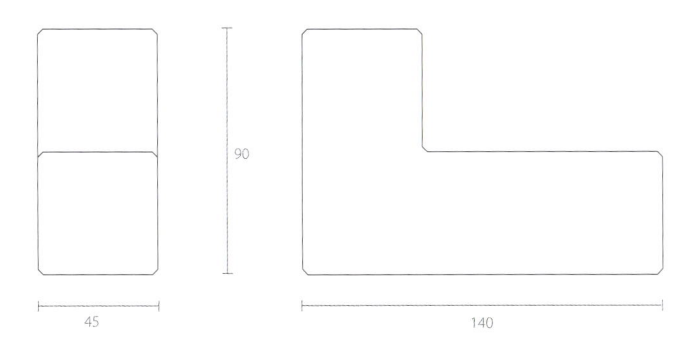

Elios

Design: **Tobia Repossi** • Production: **Modo**

This free-standing single seat in sandblasted concrete, treated to prevent deterioration, with an oval shape and a smooth surface, is usually supplied in a standard colour "grey", but is also available in different colours (according to order). Elios does not require fixing to the ground.

SEATS 47

Encuentros

Design: **Diana Cabeza** • Development: **Diana Cabeza, Alejandro Venturotti** • Production: **Estudio Cabeza**

"Encuentros" is inspired on the rocks of "Playa Negra", a black South Atlantic beach on the coast of Tierra del Fuego. It is a homage to the end of the world and a bridge to join distant places of Earth. "Encuentros" celebrates the encounter with Nature and the feeling of acknowledgement and delight given. It is a walk on a cold summer day and the possibility to warm our bodies on the rocks, or on a clear moonlit night observe the motion of the waves uncovering the rocks and exhibiting their brightness. "Encuentros" is a contact with textures which caress our bodies with messages of the past. "Encuentros" proposes an evocative encounter place, to wait, to rest, to see and be seen and eventually meet oneself and Nature. "Encuentros" is a useful sculpture formed by four units (1 square meter) of red and brown Sierra Chica Argentine granite. The units can be combined to form multiple configurations to compose a topographic site for encounter rituals.

Equal

Design: **Joseph Gascón** • Production: **Escofet**

Equal is an element that combines concrete and wood in a play of linear geometry, creating a place for repose for one or more people from a composition in delicate equilibrium: equilibrium between the masses which constitute the base of the bench and emerge to form the backrest; between two materials that in their combination each bring the other into relief - the cold finish of the concrete contrasting with the warmth of the wood; equilibrium between its modes of use, as it offers users the option of sitting with or without a backrest. Its weight means it does not need to be anchored to the ground and its nearly 3 meters of length offers a comfortable and attractive surface.

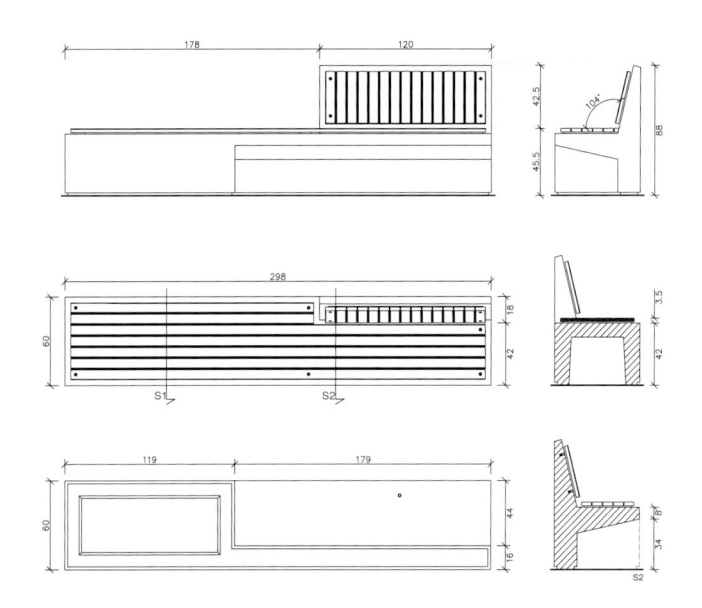

48 SEATS

Essen

Design: **Franc Dey** • Production: **Fundició Dúctil Benito**

Ensuring that it provides a high level of resistance, the Essen bench is a cast iron seat in a contemporary style. Finished in gray, the mixture of gaps and solid spaces in the backrest and the seat, as well as the purity of its lines, combine to achieve an element that is suitable for all kinds of urban spaces and even interiors.

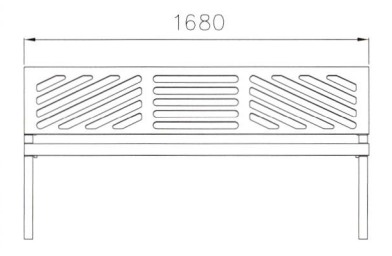

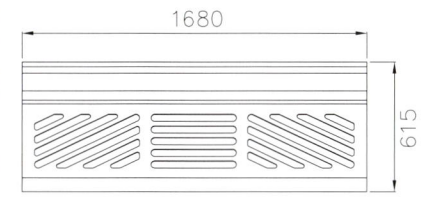

Fenicia

Design: **Luigi Ferrario** • Production: **Modo**

This winding and sinuous bench consists of modular elements that can be assembled to form different shapes according to customized radial outlines. The items that generate the outline of this bench are a series of identical strips of steel plate, 10 mm thick by 40 mm wide, bent into the section of the bench. They are placed next to each other according to the outline the project requires. The items need to be anchored solidly to the ground by fixing the feet in a concrete foundation, at least 120 mm deep. A possible alternative is the use of a base-plate, attached with bolts. Each item has a semicircular finishing piece on the end, to avoid sharp corners and edges, fulfilling the safety regulations without loosing its aesthetic characteristics. The solidity of the entire structure is guaranteed by a Ø 5 mm rod that is inserted through the axis of the individual pieces, locking them into a consistent whole. The bench is finished with an antioxidant treatment and powder coated for outdoor use.

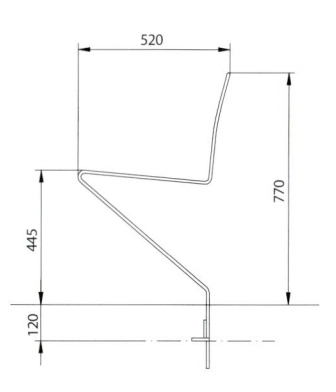

SEATS

Feris BK

Design: Rehwaldt Landschaftsarchitekten • Production: Richtscheid Metallbau

In the course of redesigning the market square of the city of Halle, a complete line of urban furniture was
Developed which includes bicycle racks, tree grates, trash receptacles as well as various benches and planters. The most prominent item is the "Feris BK" bench by Rehwaldt. The simple, timeless design of the bench smoothly integrates into the urban space. Powder coated steel cheeks combined with wooden battens give an example of how to offer a high-grade convenience and serve the needs of maintenance at once. A tiltable back is its main feature, making the bench a characteristic piece of urban furniture, accentuating the aspect of communication.

Finferlo

Design: Mitzi Bollani • Production: Modo

Finferlo is a small, coloured object with a safe, rounded, attractive shape, which offers help when needed.
It is quite difficult to put benches in certain urban areas because often there is not enough space, and yet they would be useful. This is where Finferlo comes in. Thanks to its small size it is functional and can ease the tiredness of the elderly, who often walk a long way without finding a place to have a rest.
How many times, on entering a shop, do you have to look for a safe place to tie up the dog or the bicycle? Finferlo meets these requirements.
How many times would you like to sit down and you find a bench that is already being used improperly? Finferlo can solve this problem! This is the sort of article that can satsfy different needs with a charming design which pleases the eye.

Flor

Design: **Mansilla+Tuñón** • Production: **Escofet**

Flor is based on research regarding the concepts of equality and diversity that are present throughout the work of Mansilla + Tuñón. In the case of this concrete "flower" they have implemented a subtle game of similitude and difference. The biomorphic and radial form permits it to be used by individuals or by couples with no loss of intimacy.

Flor has been installed in the courtyard of the Archivo Regional de la Comunidad de Madrid, situated in a complex architectural ambiance of different periods, styles, materials and uses. The "flowers" complete this public meeting space that welcomes visitors to the various institutions that share the location.

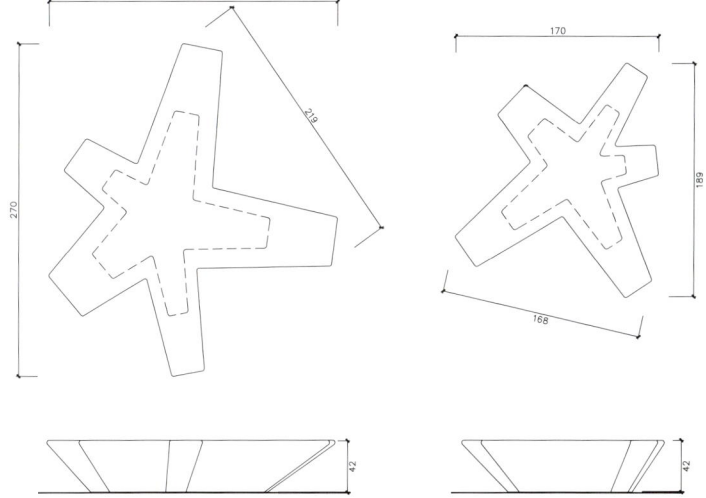

SEATS

Fun Bank

Design: **Bernhard Winkler** • Production: **Euroform**

Fun Bank is an unconventional bench for kids and teenagers. With its unusual shape and resulting seating position, Fun Bank speaks the language of children. Fun is the perfect solution for any place where kids play, do sport or wait.

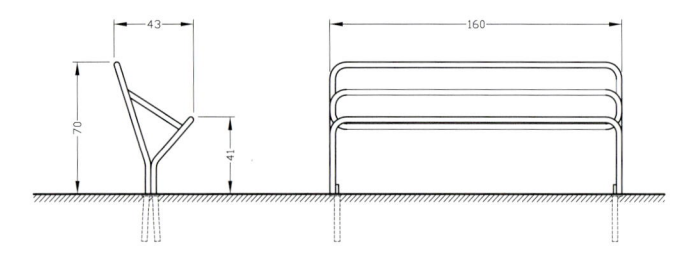

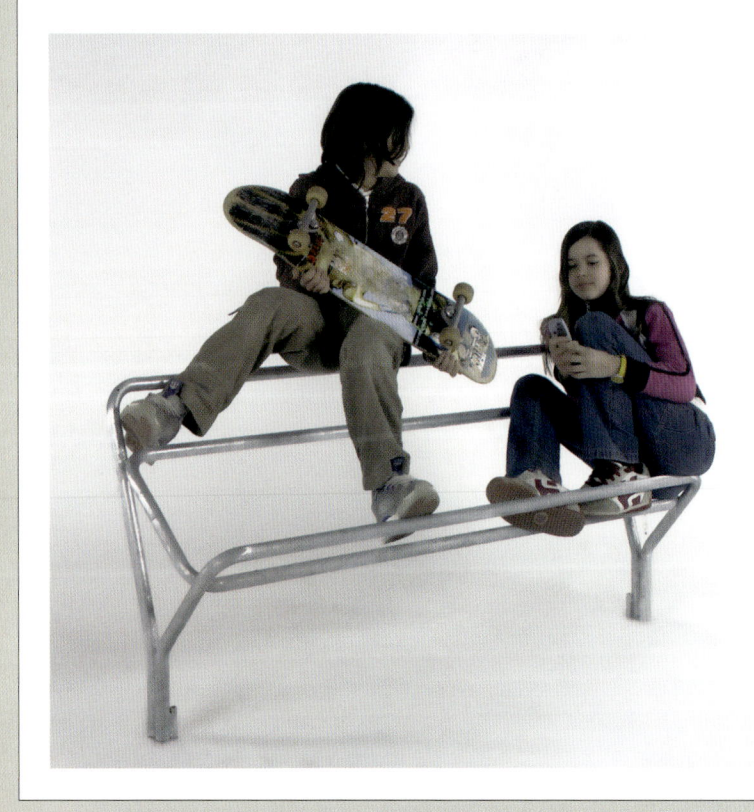

Godot

Design: **díez+díez diseño** • Production: **Escofet**

The design of the Godot bench is based on the idea of creating an element of street furniture that could be integrated into Samuel Beckett's stage-set for the play from which it has taken its name. The bench program consists of three prismatic-shaped units (single, double and triple), respectively measuring 92, 152 and 212 cm (37.33, 59.73 and 83.31 inches). These elements are made of concrete and all have a semi-circular hollow at one end. Assembled contiguously, they are designed to leave an empty space inside the module to be used as a planter. Godot can be installed around trees, forming a kind of pedestal that transforms and highlights the plant, while inviting passers-by to enjoy its shade.

Fun Bank

SEATS

Grindle

Design: **Greg Healey** • Production: **Street and Park Furniture**

After Greg Healey's recent trip through South Australia, the design of the Grindle Seat arose as his response to the extraordinary forms, textures and colors of the environment he experienced in the outback. The designer worked in collaboration with Street and Park Furniture to introduce this exciting new range to the market.
Greg Healey established Greg Healey Design in South Australia in 1995. Over time the practice has mainly worked in the realm of urban infrastructure projects with a strong contemporary arts focus. Each work is specifically designed incorporating the site's unique cultural and physical history, focusing on how the work and the materials selected relate to the surroundings on the micro and macro levels. The metal structure of the Grindle seat is of painted cast aluminum with a painted steel sub frame, which supports a seat and backrest of hardwood boards.

Harmony

Design: **Studio Ambrozus** • Production: **Runge**

A characteristic of the Harmony bench, designed by Studio Ambrozus and made by Runge, is the fitting of the wood, which seems to grow out of the cast aluminum, single-piece structure of the feet. The wooden slats are of premium hardwood with a smoothly sanded and varnished surface. A standard range of alternative varnish or paint finishes can be supplied on request. The superior quality of the wood enables it to remain exposed without any surface treatment, UV radiation rapidly providing it with a natural silver patina.

SEATS

Hebi

Design: J.A Martínez Lapeña / Elías Torres • Collaborator: Masahiro Harada • Production: Escofet

Hebi means snake in Japanese. This bench was designed to wriggle and curl freely through the trees. It can be used to organize concave or convex spaces, interior or exterior areas, public or private space. It comes in two versions, a solid and a floating one; these can be either straight or curved. The esplanade of the Barcelona Forum 2004 was the first location at which these modular benches were installed. The outline of this extruded reinforced concrete item can rest on its full length or on its two ends only, allowing the passage of light, air and water.

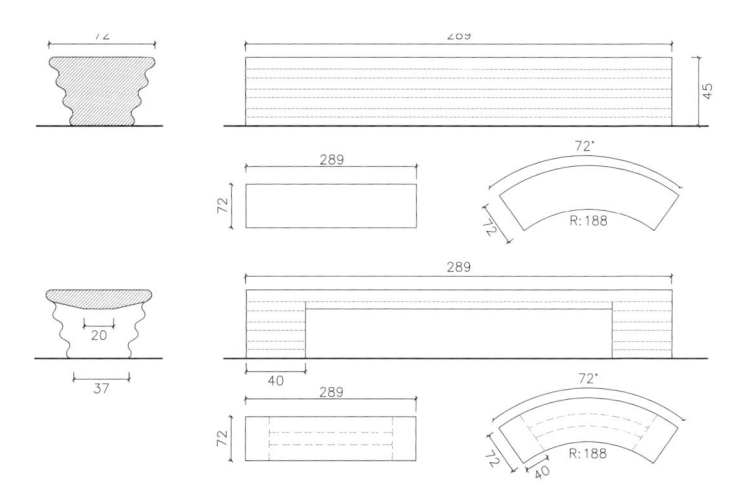

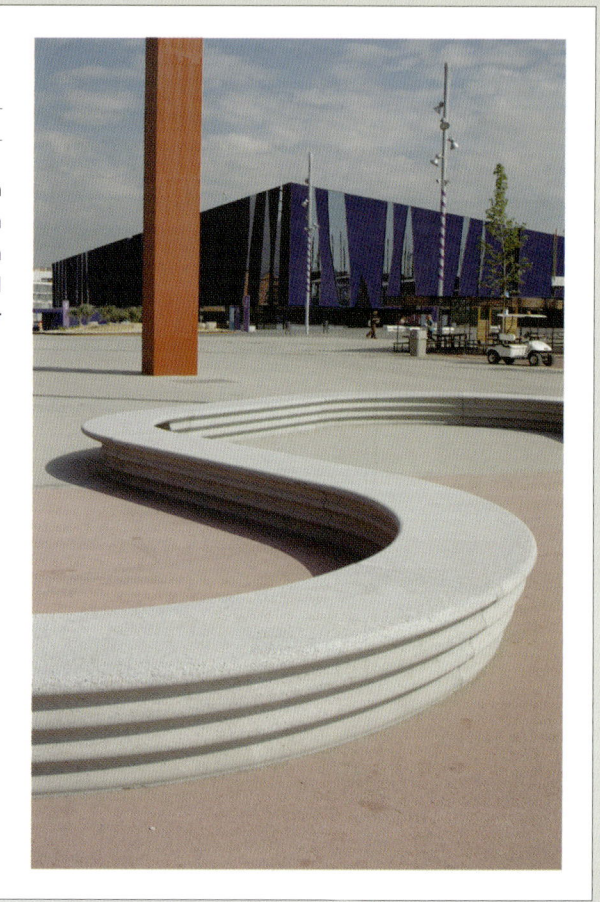

Hoja

Design: Diana Cabeza • Collaborators: L. Heine, A. Ferrugia • Production: Estudio Cabeza

This urban bench is specially designed for resting or reading in an open public space or a partially-roofed area, like a plaza, a patio or a gallery.
As a result of the distinct architectural independence between the seat and the backrest and the various lengths in which both units are available, the Hoja bench offers multiple options – as a large back support for someone sitting on the floor, as rest support for a standing person or as a space where a pram or a wheel chair can be placed. The back of this bench constitutes a large vertebrate surface, acting as an ergonomic support.

54 SEATS

Hop hop

Design and production: Miramondo

"hop hop" is a broad range of products that can be used in a variety of ways. Thanks to their straightforward design, they can be mounted on walls and external steps etc. By means of additional brackets, "hop hop" can be cemented into the ground, remain a freestanding element or be mounted on a wall. By combining differing lengths of wood with the corresponding sidepieces, a variety of arrangements is possible. A remarkable feature is the formal resolution of the intersection between the seat and the backrest. By means of the vertical wooden slat on the frontal edge of the seat, "hop hop" merges with the surface beneath and conceals sharp or unsightly wall edges. The seats are simple to mount on walls and other horizontal surfaces using four screws and four special raw plugs with internal metric coarse thread. The wooden slats are connected to the sidepieces by means of a special screw fastener that can only be taken apart with a specific tool, making it vandal-proof.

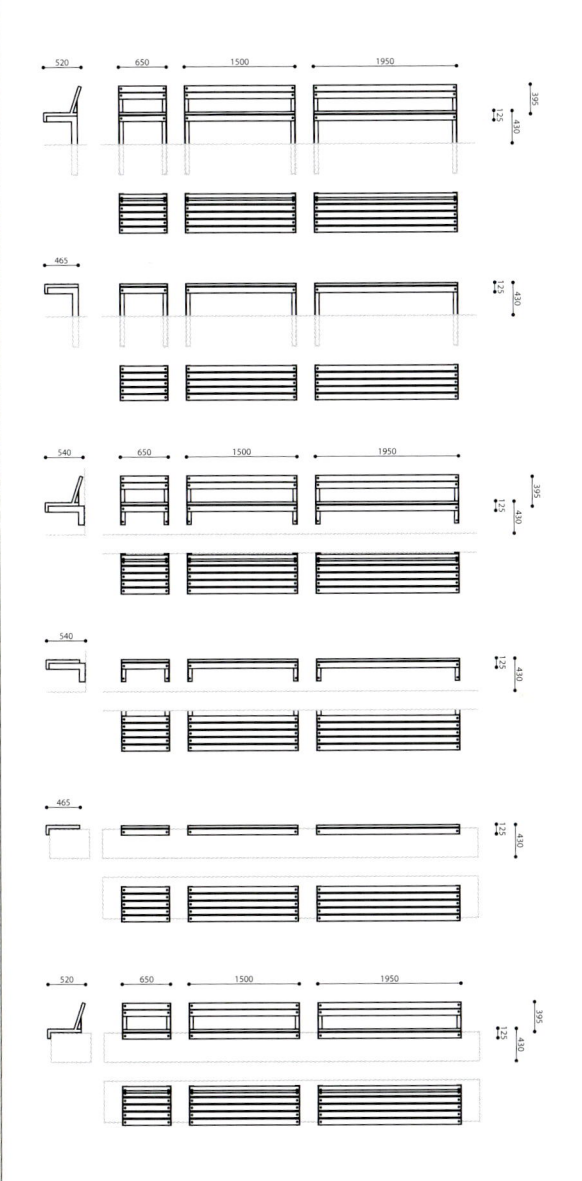

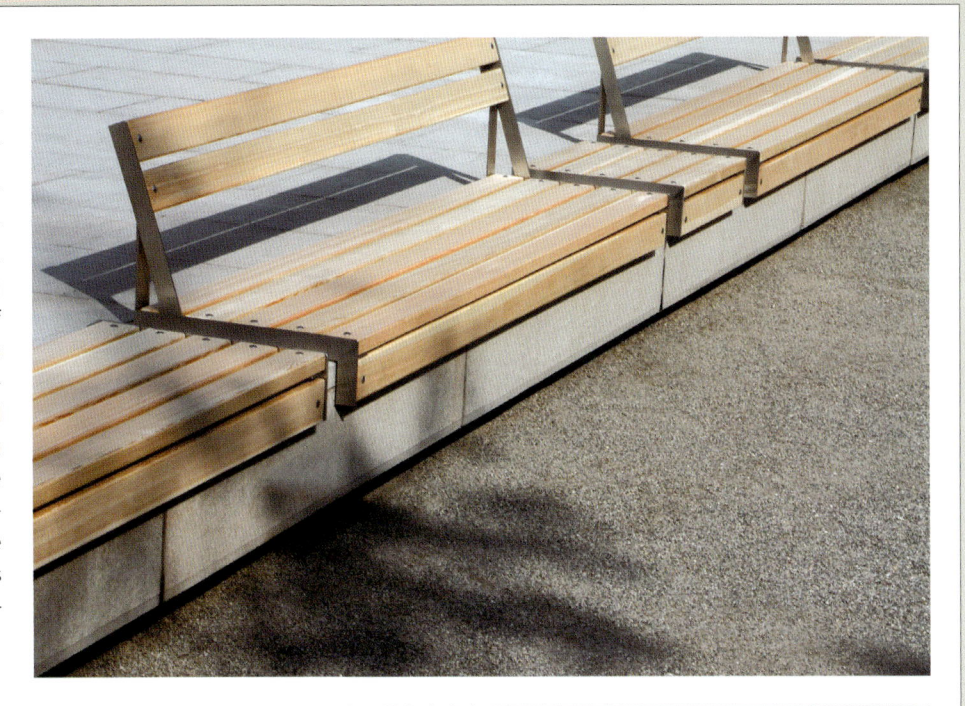

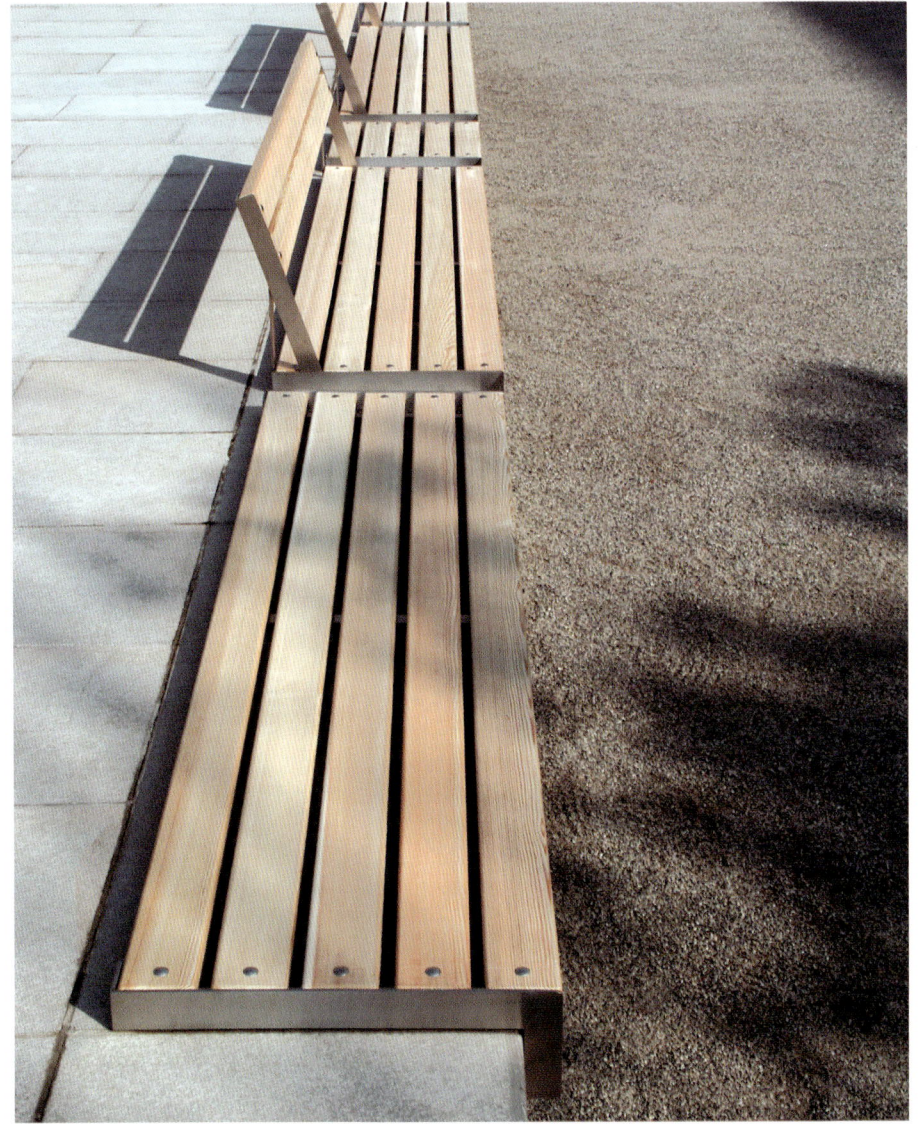

SEATS 55

Horse Shoe

Design and production: **Streetlife**

The Horse Shoe bench is minimal and distinctive. It consists of metal legs with rounded FSC Cumaru slats, a very elegant and hardwearing combination of materials that can withstand the ravages of time. The dark-red colour of the wood differs slightly in tint from slat to slat. The elevated seat with the round form of the horseshoe creates a surprisingly pleasant yet active seat. It adapts well to architectural plans, both in and out of doors. It is also available in a broader version that enables double-sided use. Leveling the bench is achieved by adjustable stainless-steel legs that end in studs to be simply embedded in the ground.

Hungaro

Design: **Equipo de Durban Studio** • Production: **Durban Studio**

Designing the Hungaro bench was preceded by a prolonged observation of the users and of the aging process of this type of structure. The design divides the surface and orders the space in a psychological way, offering more seating space than other benches of similar dimensions. The central trough prevents water from pooling on the top surface. The item is made of reinforced concrete, sandblasted, polished and water-proofed. Its weight makes any anchoring system superfluous.

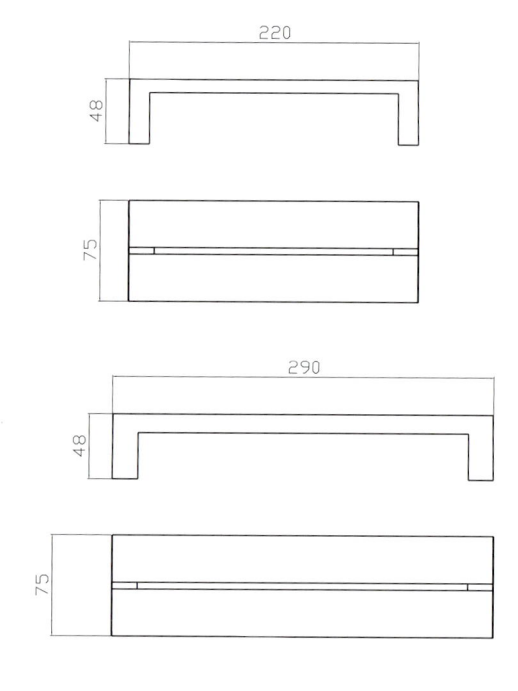

SEATS

lola

Design: RCR Arquitectes • Production: Santa & Cole

Over the past few years, RCR Arquitectes has become one of Spain's leading architectural practices. For the first time ever, they have dealt with the design of an urban element for its subsequent mass production: a bench made of artificial stone and coloured en masse, in white or black, similar to the aesthetic criteria that characterise their work. Simple, striking, versatile, ergonomic and, above all, capable of stirring up emotions in the urban environment.

Its organic simplicity allows for its integration in a number of settings, whether on surfaces, built-in to make steps or leaning against a small wall. Positioned in alignment, it becomes an axis or column that is able to articulate all of the elements in the space around it.

IP6

Design: Jesús Irisarri - Piñeda • Production: Larus

An ergonomic bench of roto-molded plastic for indoor and outdoor use. It features various possibilities of adaptation to different places. Its design includes drainage for any storm water that might gather. A specific anchoring system is provided to fix it onto the floor and it is illuminated inside. It can be supplied in various colours.

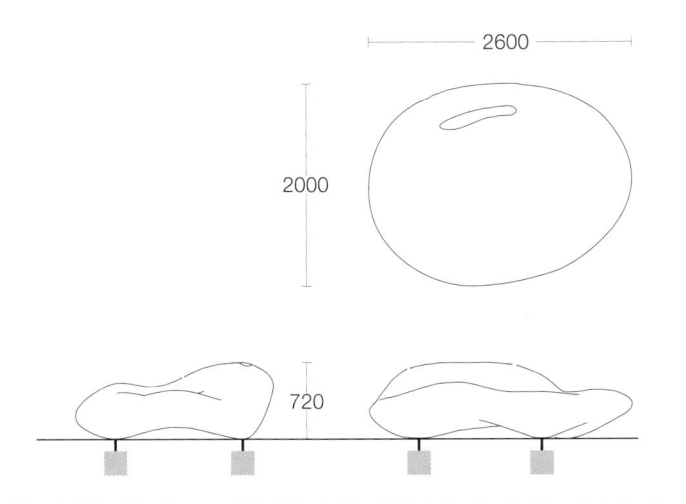

SEATS

Isi

Design: **Carme Pinós** • Production: **Escofet**

Isi is a modular bench built using a single 60 cm-wide piece which serves as both a seat and a backrest. The module can be positioned differently to create a succession of single or double benches, with and without backrests, or the joint combination of all these seat types.

Carmen Pinós' first installation in the outer lobby of the Torre Cube in the Mexican city of Guadalajara introduces a two-colour combination, black and white, adding a second degree of freedom to its forms.

The moulded concrete module with its lightly sandblasted surface is protected by an application of photocurable organic resin with water-repellent, oil-repellent, graffiti-proof and detergent- and solvent-resistant properties.

The elements are joined together with corrugated stainless steel pins, fixed to threaded bushings concealed in the concrete with structural silicone. It is installed on the ground using individual supports with metal spheres and rods threaded into bushings embedded in the concrete and anchored with epoxy resin.

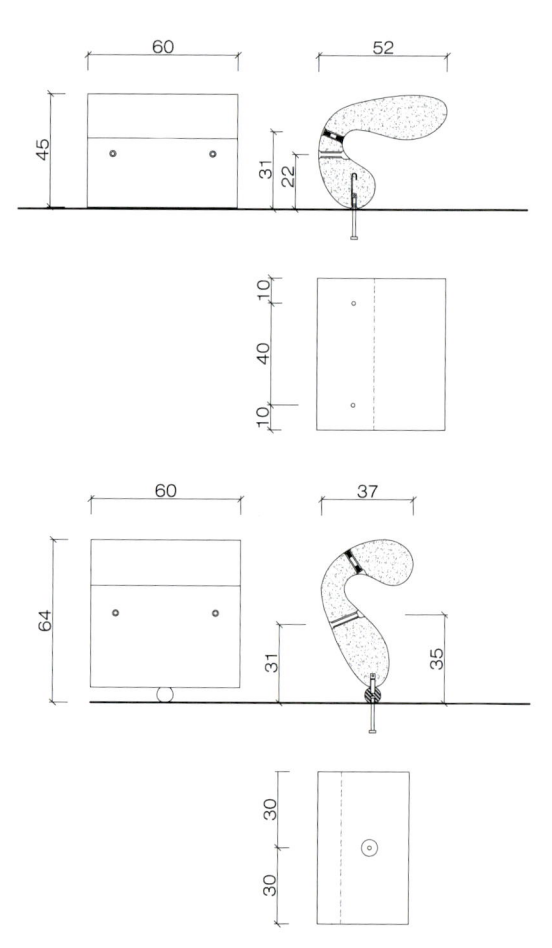

58   SEATS

Islero

Diseño: **Eduardo Arroyo** • Producción: **Escofet**

The Islero modular bench is a monolithic piece with several combination possibilities, filling the space open-endedly and generating new, usable floor space. Its geometry accentuates its light, airy nature, and the material seems to levitate, as an element that has mass but no gravity.

Its ergonomic nature allows for various different sitting positions and it can be used for a variety of leisure and work activities.

It is manufactured in moulded concrete and incorporates an exclusive, innovative Escofet system whereby sunlight or artificial light is reflected in a surprising, dynamic way as the viewer's gaze moves over it. The system is compatible with any shade of concrete, light or dark.

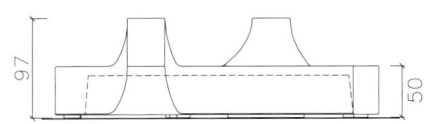

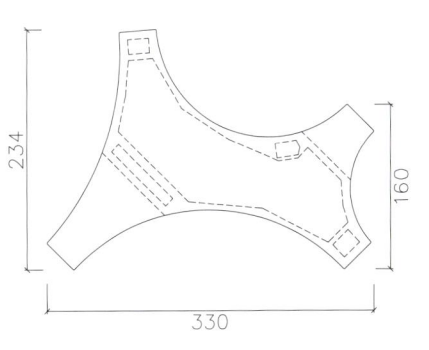

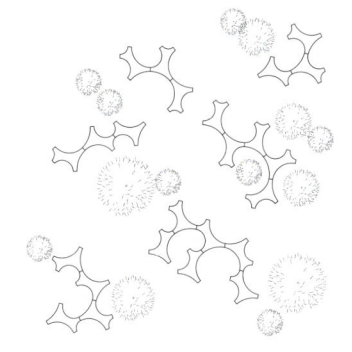

SEATS

Katia

Design: **David Karásek & Radek Hegmon** • Production: **mmcité**

A range of comfortable benches with high backrests to make it easier to rise from the seat. Transversally placed ergonomic lamellas as well as side supports made of bent strip steel create an extraordinary effect. Optional models have a sectioned seat to prevent people from lying on the bench. The galvanized steel frame comes painted in standard shades. The seat and backrest consist of transversal solid wood lamellas which are discreetly but securely joined to the supporting frame. The steel frame is easily fixed to the ground.

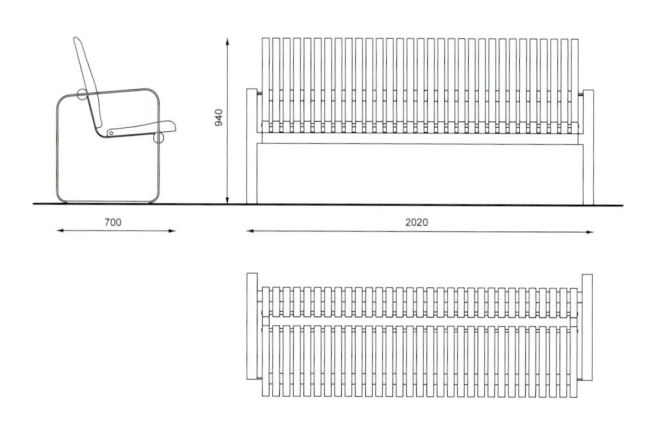

[K-BENCH]

Design: **Charles Kaisin** • Production: **Vange**

[K-BENCH] by Charles Kaisin, is an innovative combination of design and materials. This beehive structured extendable bench allows itself to be shaped according to the user's needs. The poetic of origami blends with modern materials in a perfect mix of tradition and modernity.

[K-BABY], has the same structure and is made of the same material as its big brother, the [K-BENCH]. It is a seat that can be used equally well as a low table. Its small diameter and light weight make it very easy to handle. The K-baby retains a circular shape at all times.

60 SEATS

Killy

Design: **Ton Riera Ubía** • Production: **mago:urban**

The Killy seat is surprisingly flexible in terms of its functionality, evocative lines and ergonomic capacity. With the Killy seat, mago : urban offer a seat that has an immediately noticeable purity of line, allowing it to be easily integrated into any urban environment. It won't take the limelight and can contribute to revitalising public space as an experiential space.
However, its main contribution, and the feature that has raised the most interest, is its capacity to transform. The Killy seat can be used as a single unit or in series, with or without a backrest. Without a backrest, its symmetrical action allows it to be used in two directions, as a double seat.
Two kinds of finishes are available, both with excellent thermal behaviour: one uses timber slats, and the other a special wood-resin conglomerate.

SEATS

Kimba

Design: **Ton Riera Ubía** • Production: **mago:urban**

The Kimba Terra series comprises three different benches and two corner seats. With these five pieces it is possible to create a modular sequence of infinite possibilities. They will adapt to any requirement and can also be used as individual items. The three benches are differentiated by their outline, straight, concave and convex. This multiplies the possible configurations with which to equip an urban space imaginatively. The two corner seats can turn around either way, adapting them to every layout and contour, however awkward this may be. When space permits, this characteristic can be implemented to alter the image of a location with a minimal investment.

Lancer

Design: **Equipo de Durban Studio** • Production: **Durban Studio**

The forms of Lancer are defined by lines that are simple yet firm. These are ergonomic items that have a neutral character, enabling them to combine well in the spatial configuration of any public space. The piece is made of an innovative type of concrete that is reinforced with fibre-glass (GRC, glass reinforced concrete), making a thickness of only 5.5 cm possible without loosing its solidity. This guarantees the concretes durability and resistance even in highly saline environments.

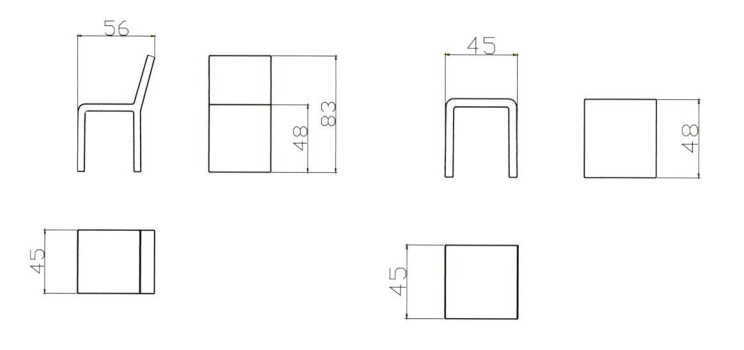

Laurede

Design: **Ruud van Eggelen** • Production: **mmcité**

This range offers robust outdoor furniture without neglecting a sophisticated design and optimum functionality. Its concise morphology will bring style to a wide range of different environments such as private gardens and parks. The structure of galvanized steel angle iron has been left without a surface finish, to weather naturally. The seat and backrest are made of solid wooden lamellas.

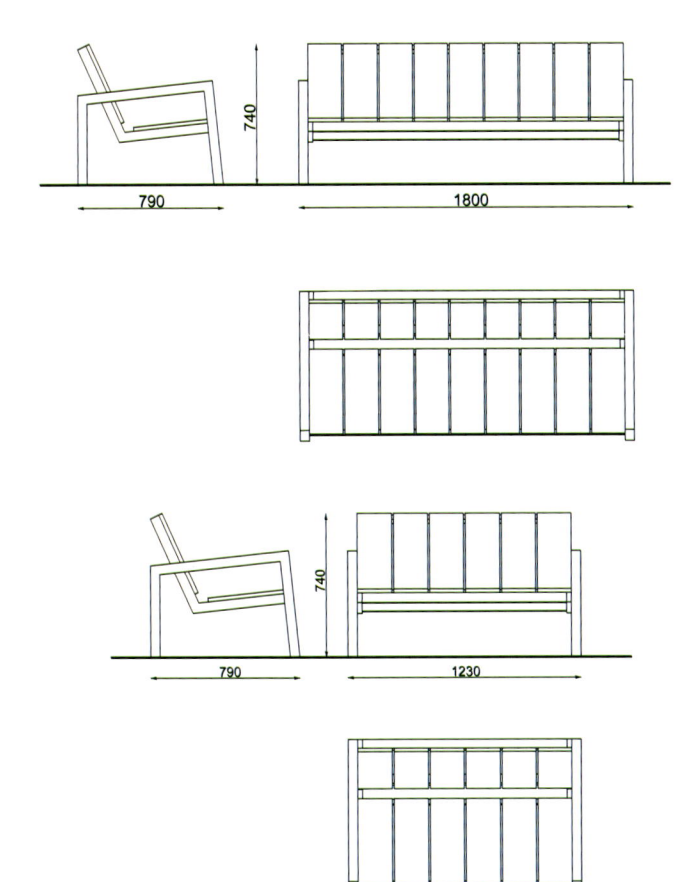

Leichtgewicht

Design: **Thesevenhints** • Production: **Miramondo**

"Leichtgewicht" - visually strong yet light in weight. At exterior construction sites, furniture is often the last thing to be put in place and the installation of heavy items of furniture is particularly problematic in areas that are difficult to access. Using modern fibre-concrete in combination with a supporting steel structure, makes the 135 kg, 115 kg or 60 kg of "Leichtgewicht" easy units to handle and can even be used in statically precarious situations such as roof gardens or underground car parks. The slight material thickness of these items has thermal benefits compared to massive concrete and stone pieces - this material gets less cold. The surface of the concrete is free of air inclusions and limestone edges, lending it an appearance of superior quality. The hollow space in "Leichtgewicht" can be provided with a lighting unit.

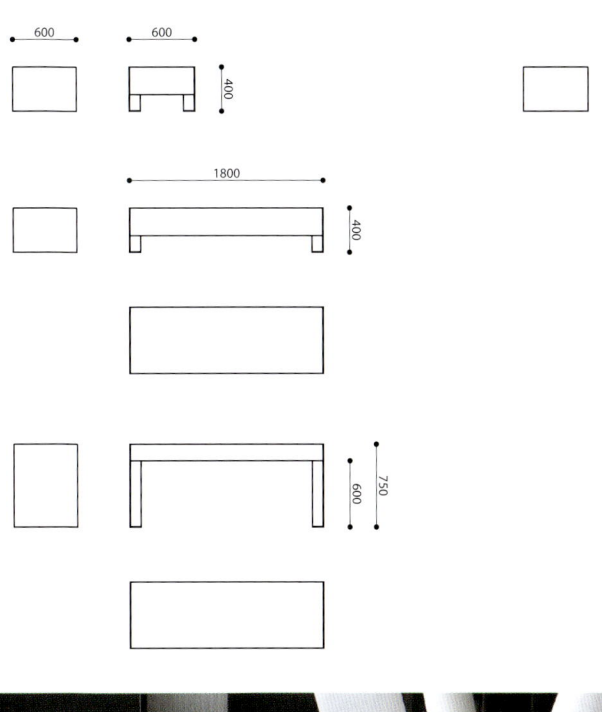

SEATS

Linea

Design: Thomas Winkler • Production: Euroform

Linea stands out for its clean geometry and lines. The main architectural element – a rectangular steel rod, is repeated in all the products of the entire range. In this new line, designer Thomas Winkler has used a new approach to robust, durable materials and the well-known "euroform w" machining techniques, reintroducing them in a new, modern design. Linea products fit in perfectly with any setting due to a design that is both strong and classical.

Link

Design: Nahtrang Design • Production: Escofet

Designed by Nahtrang Design, the Link bench is an extremely light, urban-style seating element, but with a high formal content. Essentially recalling the classic folding stool, its structure is simple, attractive and balanced, with echoes of the East. A modest little gem whose proportions make it easy to integrate with the environment.
LINK's subtlety of form and smart combination of materials – steel and concrete or steel and bamboo wood – make it a balanced element in the urban landscape or for contract furnishing. The series includes the LINK bench, LINK stool and LINK wall seat models, all with two seat options, concrete or bamboo.

SEATS

Literas Urbanas

Design: **Diana Cabeza** • Production: **Estudio Cabeza**

The intensity of urban life forces us to reformulate the idea of leisure for a better enjoyment of public space, reshaping the traditional park bench and re-thinking the concept of seating as an open support system with more neutrality and flexibility.
In this sense, these simple bunks constitute an ideal support for the new uses given to contemporary space and propose, in an ergonomic fashion, different situations: resting with the legs raised, sunbathing, reading, enjoying the scenery, etc.

Longlife

Design and production: **Streetlife**

The Longlife benches are the longest standard benches on the market, available in 2 lengths, as an 8 or 12-seater. They offer simple natural seating and enhance the linear dynamics of urban landscape. The FSC hardwood slats are laminated and finger jointed with a high-tec bonding system. The FSC hardwood is lively, durable, and will never rot. The slats are mounted in the patented Streetlock® comb system. The stainless steel mounting materials are theft-proof. The Streetlock® comb makes it easy to replace a slat. The slatted seat comes pre-assembled. The legs and brackets are galvanized.

SEATS

Longo

Design: Manuel Ruisanchez • **Production: Escofet**

The Longo series comprises six elements that make up four types of seats, a wastebasket and an ashtray. The bench is made of sandblasted and waterproofed reinforced concrete, in the colours beige and gray. It has a rectangular base that measures 400 × 100 × 45 cm. The seat of the bench, 2.8 m in length, is made of boards (section: 135 × 30 mm) of Bolondo wood. The bench has no back. The wood components are screwed onto three steel supports ready to be fixed onto the concrete bench.

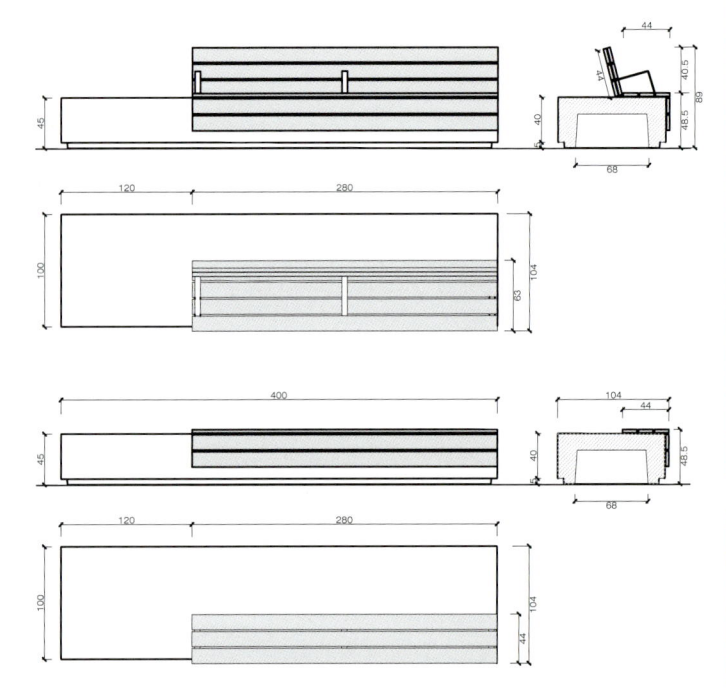

Loop

Design: Lucas Galán Lubascher, José Luis Galán Peña, Roberto Fernández Castro • Production: DAE

The body of Loop consists of 6 and 8 mm thick steel plate, folded and soldered, finished with corrosion-resistant powder-coated paint, over which powder-coated lead-free polyester steel-gray paint completes the necessary protection. Other colours can be provided on request. The seat is made of eight rods of tropical wood measuring 1852x40x25mm. The back has five rods 2000 mm in length. All the wooden parts are treated with tinted transparent oil that enhances the material's natural beauty and ensures maximum protection against the weather.

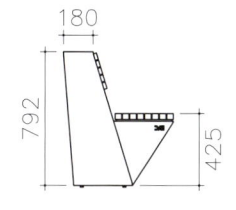

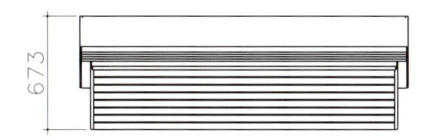

Lotus

Design: ImaginarQ • Production: Larus

Its particular construction and resultant color combination contribute to making Lotus a very special bench, in which neither of the materials plays a predominant role, either in the function it fulfills or in the aesthetic qualities it possesses. It comes in three formats, a single seat with a back, a double seat with a back in between the two, and a single seat without a back. The metal part folds back over itself, providing both the back and the support structure of the system. It consists of strips of galvanized steel plate, painted with a powder-coated wrought-iron-finish. The seat is made of Tali wood treated for outdoor use. A line of related urban furniture has been developed, following the trend of the Lotus bench, including tables, waste-baskets, flower pots, chairs, stools and bicycle racks.

SEATS

Lungo Mare

Design: **Enric Miralles & Benedetta Tagliabue** • Production: **Escofet**

Lungo Mare arose as a result of conversations that took place between Enric Miralles, Benedetta Tagliabue and Emili Farré-Escofet.

For Lungo Mare, the architects wanted a piece that would be as welcoming as a beach and as comfortable as the dunes or the waves of the sea. It is virtually a molded copy, in concrete, of the beach itself. The item looks a bit like a flying carpet. Thus, it will be able to fly to other places, landing in more urban situations, in parks, campus lawns... It took two years to design this item, spent in the workshop and in creative meetings with the technicians in charge of production.

Contemporary landscape is no longer only nature. Artificial objects are equivalent components of a single total landscape. Landscape is the object of a project and all sorts of hybrid forms are imaginable, halfway between nature and fabrication.

Lungo Mare was conceived as an item for public space, a transition between the sea and the beach, materializing the dream of making a metaphor of the waves or the dunes into a meeting place. An artificial space that imitates nature would make opposites meet: representation and abstraction, order and liberty; its shape welcomes the passer-by into the form of a body that is absent.

The item is made of reinforced cast concrete, with a soft surface finish. The stainless steel reinforcing structure is of B 500 S steel, adequately adapted to the structure of the piece, in a quantity of 60 kg per cubic meter of concrete, embedded at a minimum distance from the surface of 2, 5 cm.

The section is undulated and the perimeter is rectangular, measuring 2 x 4 meters (6.56 x 13.12 ft). It is provided with monolithic supports that keep it in a horizontal position.

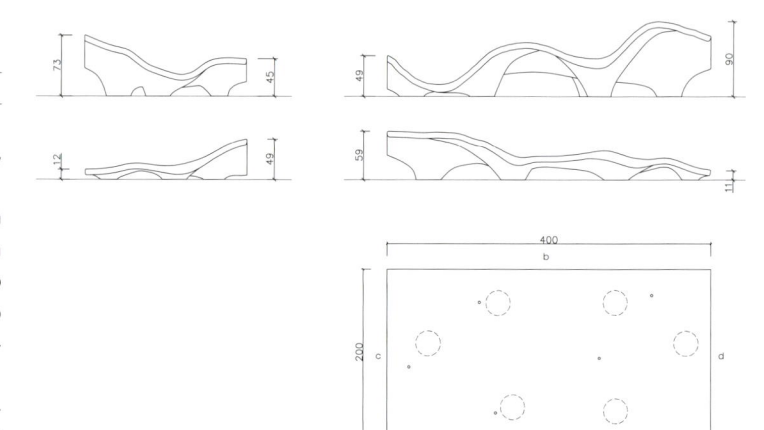

68   SEATS

Mateo

Design: **Josep Lluís Mateo** • Production: **Larus**

The support system is possibly the most characteristic aspect of these pieces of urban furniture designed by the architect Josep Lluís Mateo. The bench and the chair consist of a stainless steel tubular structure and seating platform of perforated stainless steel sheeting. The bench measures 2,160 mm in length and has 9 support points. The chair has 3 support points, one of which fits into a steel rail with a metalized enamel paint finish.

Metropol

Design: **Vilhelm Lauritzen** • Production: **GH form**

The bench ends are cast iron, the legs are steel piping. The seat surface is delivered in stainless steel or wood. The bench is mounted on an embedded pin or secured straight onto the existing paving. The Metropol Bench comes as a single bench or a double bench, with or without a backrest. The double bench is available in a variant with armrests.

The Metropol Bench won the Brunel Awards 2001 international railway design competition. Comments from the jury: Very comfortable, elegant, rigorous, easy to maintain. Museum quality brought into public transport.

SEATS

Mingle - Shade

Design: **Frog Design** • Production: **Landscape Forms**

Mingle is a carousel-style table with attached cantilevered seats that are easy to get in and out of. Asymmetric in shape, it imparts a sense of action and movement. The table surface and the chairs grow out of the same tubular steel supporting structure, an open-ended steel ring attached to the floor. There are two options for the chair components, with or without a backrest. The basic artifact measures 85" in diameter 32" in height. It weighs 75 lbs/per seat.
With the added option of mounting Shade, the sunscreen accessory, this piece of outdoor furniture consists of three functions rolled into one. Polycarbonate is used for the seating surfaces and shade wings. The tabletops are solid surfaces of compression-molded acrylic. All steel parts are primed with E-coat. All painted parts are polyester powdercoated.

Miriápodo

Design: **díez+díez diseño** • Production: **T&D Cabanes**

Miriápodo is a bench of infinite growth potential, with extraordinarily flexible compositional possibilities. Its articulated connecting system means it can acquire curved or straight lines, turning wide or narrow corners, and incorporating optional items like backrests or arms. This bench resulted from an analysis of the traditional long bench we can find in Central Park, the type used by Jack Lemon as an improvised bed in the movie "The Apartment"; the idea was to create an infinite bench that was not a part of a bigger one. Miriápodo is formed by equidistant modular bodies joined by a central axis, which is in turn formed of multiple elements, all of them identically constituted and having the same circular movement sequence. The bodies that form the seat can be exchanged at will with others that form the support members; otherwise there is no difference between the two, both consist of a single item.
Solid and firm, yet flexible, Miriapodo adapts and bends to fit any context, like a marvelous example of bio-sculpture. Chameleonic and sculptural, both prop and actor, the elements are made of cast aluminum, best suited for public interiors and controlled exteriors. There is no limit to its extension in length.

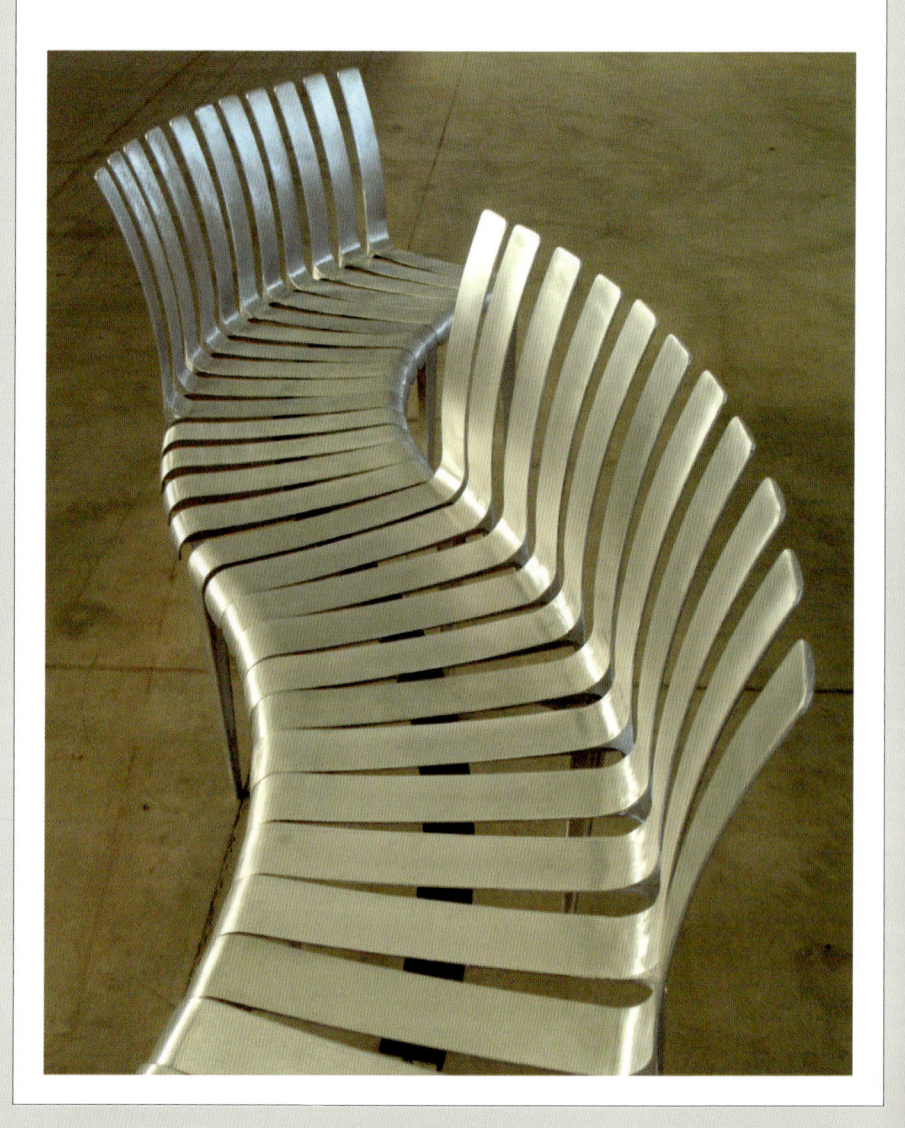

Mitrum

Design: **Rehwaldt Landschaftsarchitekten** • Production: **Kühn und Kirste**

Adjacent to a new research building and lecture hall in Dresden Technical University, two public squares were developed. The squares link the main axis of the building to the nearby streetscape. Sparingly arranged, but placed in a manner that is visually prominent, the site furnishing creates a sense of place and high-quality usability. Benches, bike racks and tree grates were especially designed for this site. The seats and benches have battens of wooden cubes. The warm coloured scumble leaves the material's texture visible in contrast to the concrete stand. Ruled by the grid, the design refers to the architecture around it and communicates the scientific purpose of the building.

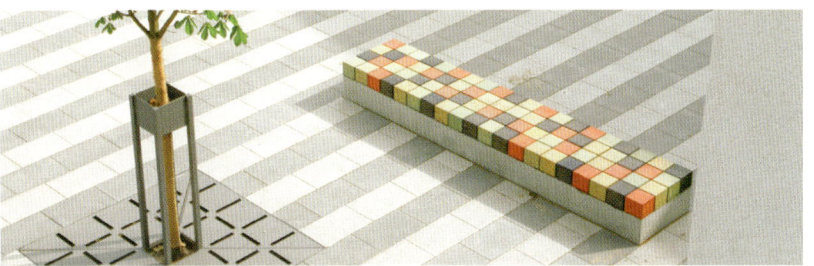

SEATS

Mix

Design: **Frog Design** • Production: **Landscape Forms**

Mix is a system of seats and wedge-shaped tables, an invitation to explore new possibilities in outdoor space. It takes planning beyond straight lines and simple curves to complex geometric configurations. Separate rail-mounted seats and tables delineate space, providing for one-on-one conversations or group interaction. Polycarbonate is used in the seating surfaces, which have a gently translucent quality. All castings are machined on CNC equipment and the components are subject to FEA specifications. All painted parts are polyester powdercoated.

The steel and aluminum used is over 60% recycled and recyclable. The dimensions vary slightly between the two different options, the straight run and the curved run. The straight run is 22" deep x 32" high; the lengths are: 46", 70", and 93". The curved run is 24" deep x 32" high; the lengths are: 58", 82", and 105". The items weigh approximately 50 lbs/per seat.

Mobilia

Design: **EBDNBA** • Production: **GH form**

The Mobilia collection is made up of a series of urban elements designed with a view to giving some personality and identity to the spaces where they are installed. The bench which is part of the series can be either straight or curved, thanks to the flexibility which comes from the separations between the wooden slats of the bench seat. The wastepaper basket visible at the end of the curved bench is partly buried in the ground so as to maximize its capacity while minimizing its volume. The materials used in the bench are steel, cast iron and wood. The basic model, measuring 2,000 mm in length and 600 mm in depth, can be put together repeatedly until the required length is reached.

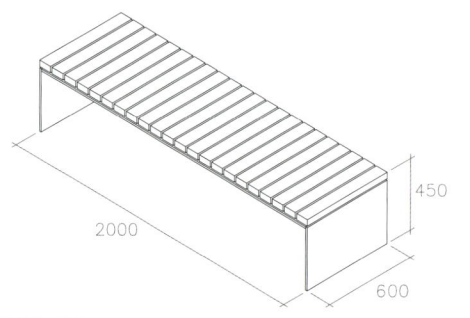

SEATS

Moiré

Design: **Alessandro Piaser** • Production: **Modo**

When a pattern of closely set parallel lines is superimposed on another such pattern aligned slightly differently, the interference pattern causes a visual effect similar to moiré silk. The Moiré bench is inspired in this effect. It consists of a seat and a backrest made of parallel stainless steel rods, Ø 10 mm and Ø 16 mm thick, fixed onto supports of the same material, laser-cut out of stainless steel plate in a shape that defines the outline of the bench. This is stabilized underneath by Ø 60 mm diameter steel tube that crosses the full length of the construction and rests on a base of Vicenza stone. An alternative anchoring system allows it to be fixed to a wall, or 100 x 100 mm legs that can be fixed to a concrete edge. The bench is available in 200 mm modules, with a straight or a curved outline that comes in two versions, concave or convex. The object's dimensions are 1,020 mm in height and 680 mm in width.

Moon

Design: **Enric Batlle - Joan Roig** • Production: **Santa & Cole**

Designed with a young and contemporary outlook, Moon can be used in different ways. The supporting structure connecting the wooden slats to the legs is made of cast iron, powder coated over a layer of rust proofing. The legs are of the same material.
Both the seat and the backrest are made of studs of solid tropical wood with a tannin blocking treatment, 45 x 45 mm (1.77 x 1.77 inches) in cross-section and of variable length, fixed to the frame with stainless steel screws. The back upper «shelf» and frontal «apron» are of 45 x 200 mm (1.76 x 7.86 inch) boards. It is the only bench with a backrest wide enough to sit on comfortably.
There are two galvanized bolts per leg, which fit into the previously made holes in the pavement, to be filled in with epoxy resin, quick drying cement or a similar material. No functional maintenance is required except to preserve the original wood color.

SEATS 73

Naguisa

Design: **Toyo Ito & Associates** • Production: **Escofet**

This modular bench was designed to be integrated into an urban environment or a large park. Made of concrete, its gentle curves are reminiscent of a meandering riverbed, simultaneously establishing a firm presence and requiring a perceptive eye from the beholder. As a piece of urban furniture, its singularity is that it is capable of transforming a large plaza or a park into a harmonious composition by merely being there.

The design of this bench is based on a four-meter-long sector of an arc, the curved and dugout surface of which generates a variety of different concavities, which consecutively and organically function as the seat. The raised center becomes a sinuous backrest or armrest, but the entire object can be utilized in multiple ways.

The curves can be added onto each other to create fully closed circles, measuring 11 or of 7.5 meters in diameter. Joining the items and altering the direction of the arcs generates a continuous curving bench, the effect of which can be increased if several groups are installed in a parallel pattern. It must be stressed that the bench was also thought of in terms of narrow pedestrian urban spaces and for small scale natural areas.

In interconnected groupings, the moderate height of the object doesn't impede the view, and the fact that the 'backrest' has a break approximately every 8 yards makes the interior of the rings accessible. The total height of the seat is 38 cm and the total height of the backrest reaches 63 cm. Thus, a person standing will find it the perfect height to lean on. The lower part of the body of the bench seems hollowed out in a natural way, so that, despite its being made of reinforced concrete, various effects of light coming through will enhance the perception of the item as a living organism.

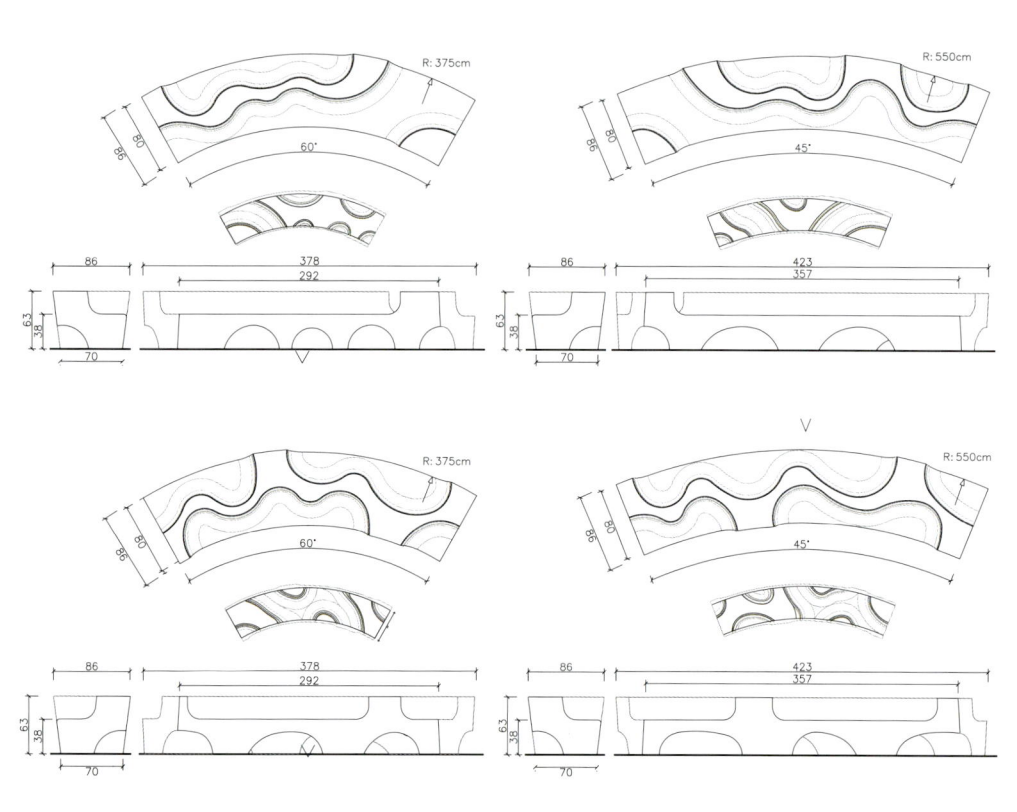

74 SEATS

Nastra

Design: **Outsign** • Production: **Concept Urbain**

The Nastra set of seats comprises an armchair and a bench. The skeleton of both pieces is made of ductile cast iron with a shot-blasted finish. The armchair has a seat of laminated wood or a laser-cut galvanized steel. Both pieces come originally in dark gray; however, it is possible to order them in other colours. They are delivered fully assembled and have to be fixed by bolts or threaded rods.

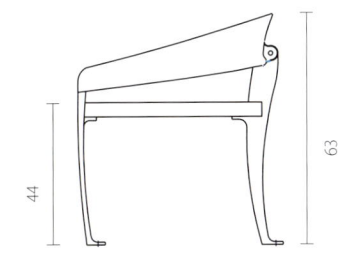

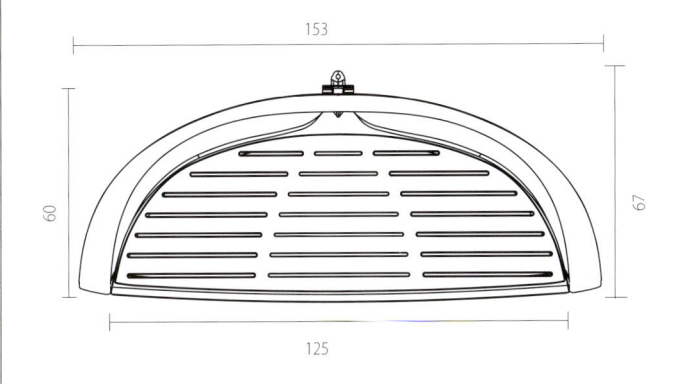

SEATS

NeoRomántico

Design: **Miguel Milá** • Production: **Santa & Cole**

This is an adaptation of what is now the classic NeoRomántico bench, with arms and a lighter structure. It is designed to complement urban or private areas needing an even more comfortable bench than its predecessor. Made of cast aluminium and wood, the bench arose from the need to update the NeoRomántico bench while adapting to the existing NeoRomántico market, thereby redesigning this romantic seat. The wide and rapid acceptance of the article in urban areas is the result of both its appearance and its comfort. Unlike its predecessor, its structure is more geometric and lighter. It is a unit designed for use in private areas and public or domestic use. It is remarkable because of its lightness and comfort. All the benches come with arms. It is solid, ergonomic, versatile and clean.

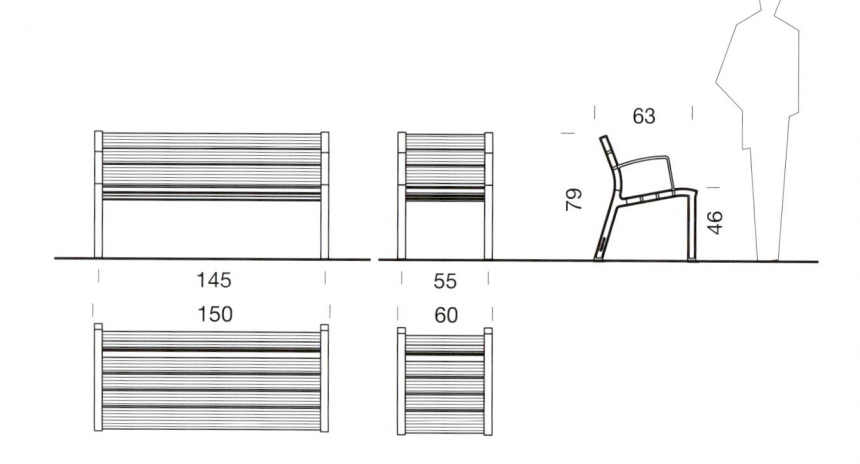

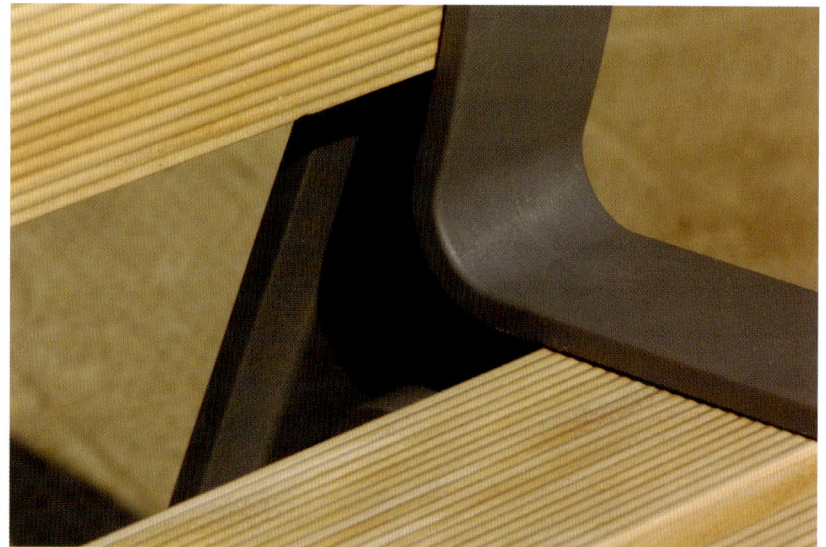

SEATS

Nigra

Design: **Marius Quintana / Montse Periel** • Production: **Escofet**

The Nigra Chair is single seat that has been conceived as an individual chair for informal gatherings and placements. These chairs can also be installed in a row next to each other in a line that may be straight, curved or crooked, and can even function as a low parapet or barrier.

It is made of cast reinforced concrete, molded in a single piece the cross-section of which is a broken line similar to a letter Z. The thickness of the folded sheet of reinforced concrete tapers down as it rises from its anchoring point upon the pavement. The base has a thickness of 18 cm. This is reduced to 10 cm at the seat and reaches its minimum thickness of 6.5 cm in the backrest of the element.

Its dimensions and the slight inclination of the seat and the backrest make it comfortable to sit on and loosen its formal rigidity and the perceivable hardness of the material.

The formal abstraction of the item, its black color and the great variety of possible groupings and combinations make this a versatile asset within a considerable number of different contexts and situations.

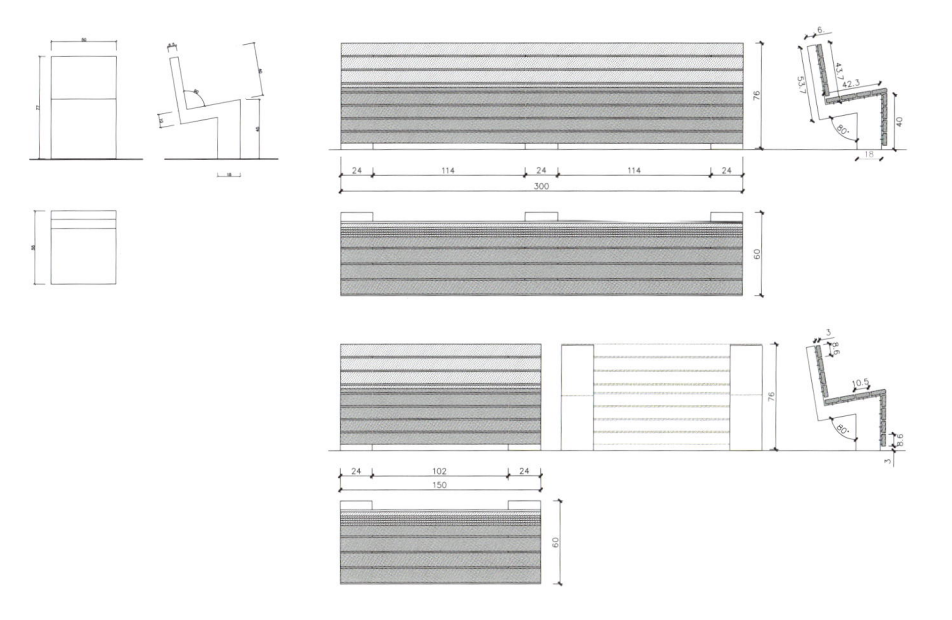

SEATS

Niu

Design: Daniel Vila y Esther Pujol (Nahtrang Disseny) • Production: Escofet

Niu is a multi-functional urban element. The apparent formal simplicity of a concrete ring 2.3 meters in diameter conceals great functional versatility. Niu is a planter, a seat, a tree protection element, a container for sand or a patch of lawn. Its gently sloping upper surface invites passersby to interact with it. The inclination of the elements constitutes a dynamic and intuitive compositional feature, which can be used to create a suggestive play of light and reflections. Like over-sized water lilies, the Nius seem to distribute themselves spontaneously through the space.

The Niu has arisen as a response to the idea of providing small oases of repose in hard landscapes, creating opportunities to relax on a patch of lawn or read in the shade of a tree without needing large-scale engineering interventions.s

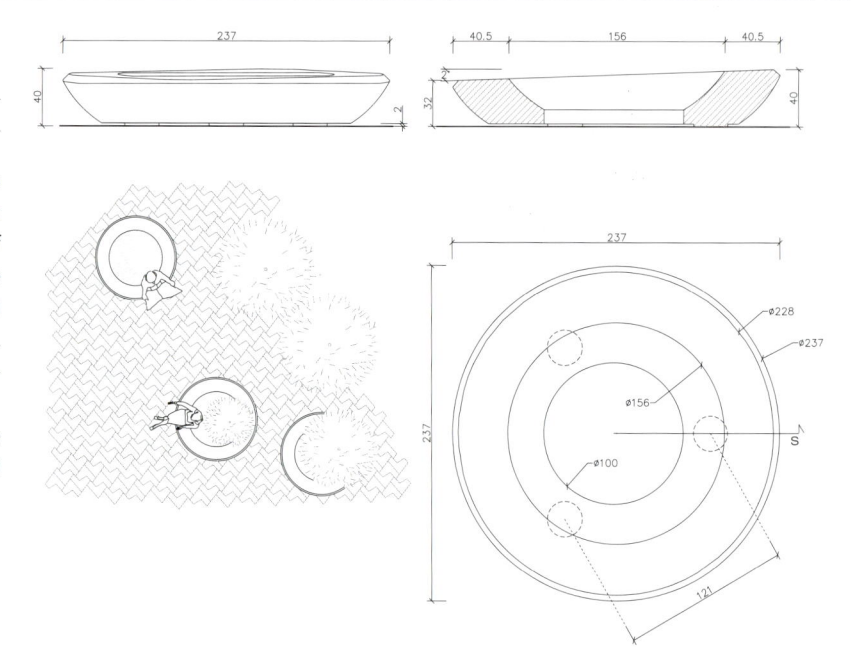

78 SEATS

Nu

Design: **Jordi Henrich & Olga Tarrasó** • Production: **Santa & Cole**

Nu is already a classic in the context of new urban furniture. Available with or without a backrest, it becomes a space for meeting and communicating, a surface to rest or work on. It can also be used to establish the limits between different functional areas. The structure –and in one of the models the backrest as well– is made of hot dip galvanized steel; it consists of tubular legs with disc-shaped feet and a longitudinal brace soldered to the upper part of the legs. The metal backrest is made of perforated steel sheet and the seat is made of solid wood square dowels of tannin-blocked tropical wood; in two other models the backrest is also made of wood, high-pressure impregnated red pine in one case, of tannin-blocked tropical wood in the other. The seat consists of 7 dowels or 8 dowels and the wooden backrest consists of 4 dowels of two optional lengths: 1.34 m y 2.58 m. It is fixed onto the pavement by means of 4 stainless steel screws on each foot. It requires no functional maintenance, unless the original color of the wood is to be maintained.

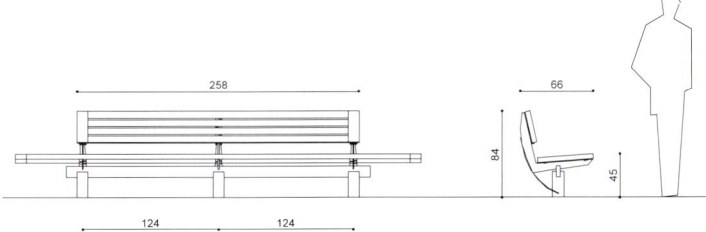

Onda

Design: **David Karásek & Radek Hegmon** • Production: **mmcité**

This is an original bench with separate seats, which prevents people from lounging in places where it is not appropriate. Purposeful and beautiful for both indoor and outdoor use, its design has been highly appreciated in the home market and abroad. The arched versions permit various attractive configurations. The Onda range also offers a single seat model which can be fixed onto the wall or a support post.

The structure is made of thick galvanized steel sheet. Separate seats are lightened by slotted linear perforations and fastened to the supporting frame. The range is supplied painted in a standard color.

Onda received the "Excellent Design 2003" award and selected into the Santa and Cole catalogue.

SEATS

Pacú

Design: **Diana Cabeza** • Production: **Estudio Cabeza** • Development team: **D.Cabeza, A. Venturotti, D. Jarczak**

This is an individual armchair. Interesting compositions can be achieved by combining several of them, thereby stimulating social interaction in public spaces in the city. The seat is made of cast reinforced concrete with a tinted aggregate in the mix for permanent body colour.

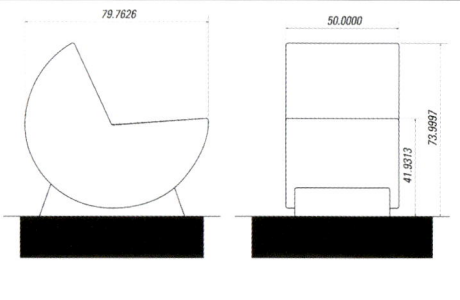

Pagoda

Design: **design-people** • Production: **Louis Poulsen**

The glowing street-chair emits light to both sides by means of its curved, white, inner surfaces. The duality of the chair makes it suitable for location in streets and squares, providing the area with low-level illumination and offering passers-by a place to rest. Pagoda is inspired in bollards but performs as an excellent part of outdoor urban furniture. The idea behind the product was to create an urban fixture with more than one function. Based on the Nimbus inground fixture, the Pagoda seat is a multipurpose lighting fixture suitable for all kinds of urban spaces. The design looks light but its construction is very sturdy as it consists of one single cast piece.

SEATS

Palazzo

Design: **Bernhard Winkler** • Production: **Euroform**

The design form of this new park bench by the company Euroform is particularly impressive. The homogeneous combination of frame and seating area results in the unusual visual appeal.
The refined rounded form can only be achieved by using a new material (grey cast iron). The extremely stable design is based on the highest quality standards. The bench can be used in many different areas thanks to its sturdy construction and blends in perfectly to any environment. The bench frame is available in powder-coated DB 703. The wooden seat is also protected by a high quality varnish.

Pancarè

Design: **Eugenio Cipollone** • Production: **Alis**

This four-seater bench has been designed by Italian architect Eugenio Cipollone. The seat measures 200x430 mm and consists of structural "T" and "L" shaped elements of steel, measuring 80x80x8 mm, soldered together, leaving an 8mm gap between the planks. The seat and the sides are made of the same structural "T" irons, finished in powder coated epoxy 80 micros thick, colour "sable noir". The Pancaré chair can be fixed by sinking the feet 200 mm in the ground or it can be anchored to the pavement with specific bolts. The version for sinking in the ground can include an "L" or a "T" shaped back. In either case, the separation between this and the rest of the chair is of 100 mm. The seat of the chair can include rectangular Teak or Bolondo wood pieces measuring 550x430x30mm, with longitudinal troughs for drainage. These pieces are held in place by a nylon knob designed to slide along the gaps in the bench.

SEATS

Patrimonial

Design: **Diana Cabeza** • Production: **Estudio Cabeza** • Development team: **D.Cabeza, A. Venturotti, D. Jarczak**

This urban element was designed specifically for the city of Buenos Aires. Both the version with a back and the version without it are made of cast reinforced concrete, with a tinted aggregate in the mix. The base is 1.20 m in length and permits the installation of individual armchairs or to place them in long rows, because they can lock onto each other. The possibility of facing them in opposite directions opens many opportunities of creating situations.

Pausa

Design: **Oriol Guimerà** • Production: **mago:urban**

The "Pausa" bench is a piece of urban furniture designed for mago:urban by Oriol Guimerà. This creative urban item, besides being a seat, tends to provoke an easy connection between people and an uninhibited use of public space. It is a refreshing and attractive answer, conceived to bring an innovative touch into those environments in which rigidity is weakened and freedom gains importance.

Regarding conventional outlines, its utterly alien shape suggests an undefined, different usage, which nonetheless doesn't establish any generational barriers. Thus, the "Pausa" bench is ideally suited to install along beaches, parks or other public areas, with the certainty that everyone will find the perfect place for the wanted rest.

SEATS

Perforano

Design: Óscar Tusquets Blanca & Lluís Clotet • Production: Bd

"We thought up the Catalano bench years ago, and it has since become a classic of the design of its time, and also one of the most extensively copied projects on the Spanish market. If we are now proposing a new solution, it is not so much to differentiate ourselves from all these poor-quality copies, as to rectify the shortcomings that we have become aware of over so many years of experience." Óscar Tusquets & Lluís Clotet

The fundamental change consists in replacing the deployé with perforated sheet steel. The bench thus loses elasticity and uses more material, but the seat gains a less aggressive texture and is much more resistant to corrosion and vandalism. On the basis of this change in the material, the structure and lenght of the module have also been modified, giving rise to a new handling of the aesthetic.

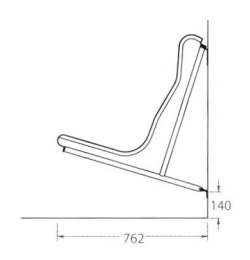

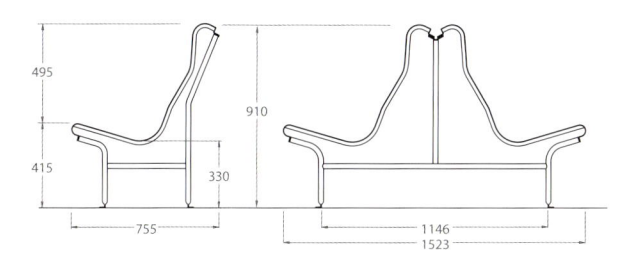

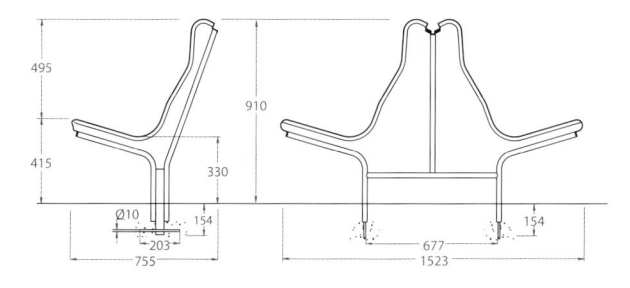

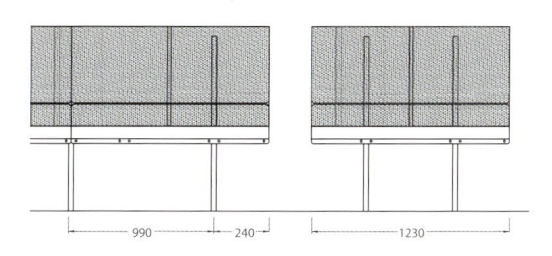

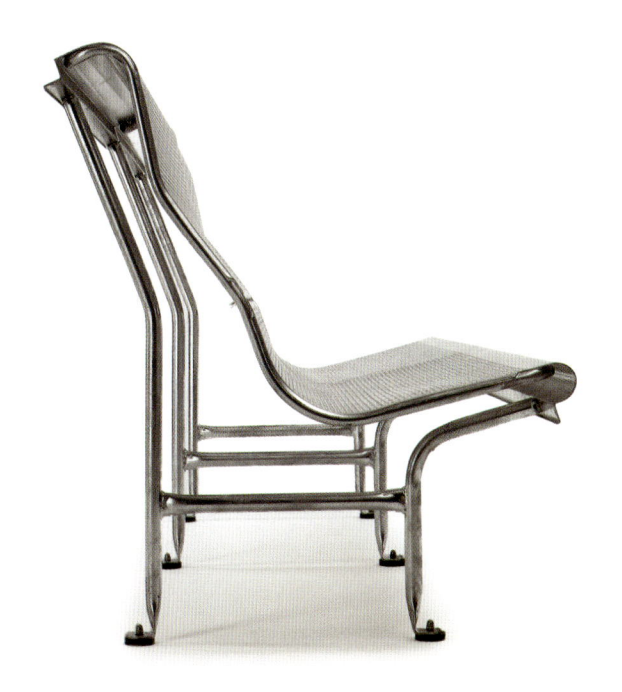

SEATS 83

Picapiedras

Design: **Diana Cabeza** • Production: **Estudio Cabeza**

Picapiedras is a series of useful sculptures. They propose communal intercourse and are to be placed in strategic positions for meeting and exchanging information. They were designed for people to gather around them. The nature of the raw material is manifested almost fiercely and technology plays almost no role whatsoever. The stone is cut and the timber is carved in the most traditional ways, defining a topographical ensemble that becomes useful according to its form and the disposition that arises as the parts are combined. It is not a seating system, it is a usable topography that enhances freedom of use or possession and stimulates a sensual understanding of the raw materials. It enables a new relation to arise between the user and the object, creating an unexpected intimacy. The user can make contact with the materials, feeling the timber, its temperature, its ruggedness, its texture.

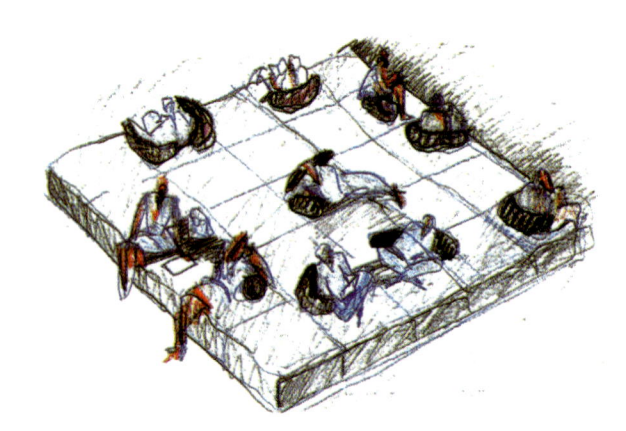

Picapiedras

84 SEATS

Pillet

Design: **Christophe Pillet** • Production: **JCDecaux**

Designed by Pillet and developed by JC Decaux, this bench seats three or four people. The designer has expressed his commitment to creating pieces aimed at groups of people or communities by explaining his belief that street furniture must avoid being bland or monotonous because it contributes to a city's image and is omnipresent in our surroundings. This philosophy is illustrated by the striking but also elegant appearance of this piece, which consists of four stabilised legs, a seat and a backrest. The legs and structure are made of cast iron, while the seat and backrest are made of tropical wood slats.

Pinxo

Design: **Coleman-Davis Pagan Architects** • Production: **Escofet**

Pinxo is a modular bench made of cast reinforced concrete. This item introduces a double purpose since it can be used to hang a hammock or as a conventional bench. It was Coleman Davis Pagan who first installed a version in dark red concrete as part of a project for public space on the island of Puerto Rico.

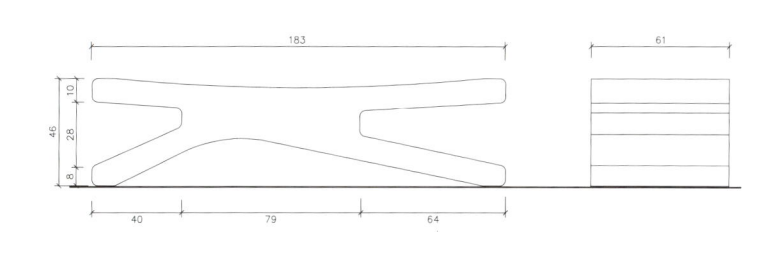

SEATS

Pleamar

Design: díez+díez diseño • Production: Gitma

The seminal idea for the design of this bench arose from an intention to continue the line initiated with the Zen bench, which was inspired in a rock, reintroducing the idea of nature into urban space; the reference we chose to achieve this was the poem "Marinero en tierra" ("seaman grounded") by Rafael Alberti. We worked on the idea of bringing the sea to the interior of any street or square, of any city, in which the sea is merely a dream, a wish, or a memory.

For the time being, two models exist, although the intention is to widen the number of Pleamar's available options to include various choices regarding length and use, such as the flower pot version; the bench is a rectilinear item, 2 meters in length by 80 cm in depth; the second is a curved volume that spans 45°, permitting the curve to be led to the right or to the left. The approximate weight of these two items is respectively 1500 and 1000 kg.

Manufactured in concrete, in a range of different colors.

They are both designed to be placed simply resting on the ground.

Pliegue

Design: Jose María Churtichaga & Cayetana de la Quadra-Salcedo • Production: DAE

The Pliegue chair is made of GG-20 cast iron, powder coated with polyester against corrosion. The item comes with a black wrought-iron-like finish but other colours and finishes can be supplied on request. The seat consists of eight rods of tropical wood, treated with translucent tinted oil to enhance the beauty of the wood and increase its resistance against the elements

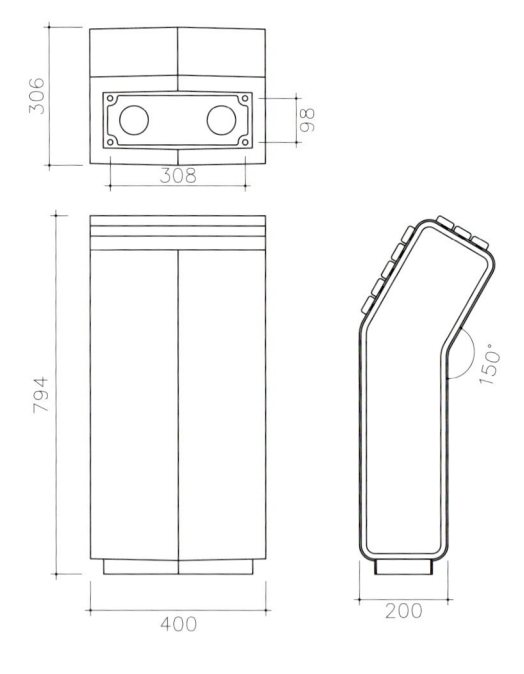

SEATS

Prat

Design: **Mercè Llopis Freixa** • Production: **Escofet**

This design aimed to provide a versatile table and stool set that could be easily integrated into all kinds of public spaces and would be suitable for performing, in an outdoor environment, the kinds of activities that are usually linked to indoor spaces: reading, playing board games, eating, or simply chatting or resting. The table consists of an empty cube, with the only essential parts cut out to allow people to sit opposite each other. The external parts of the cube, which are most likely to be touched, have been polished, and the inner parts have been left raw. The table is made of concrete because of its hardness, ease of maintenance and outstanding capacity to adapt to all kinds of landscapes. It also allows finishes in many kinds of colors, which extends its adaptability to different environments. The table and stool are modular elements that can form larger groups. A second mold provides a symmetrical version of the table, increasing possible configurations.

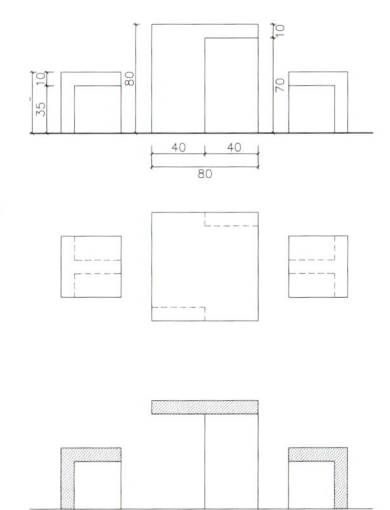

Pure

Design: **Runge Design Team** • Production: **Runge**

As its name indicates, Pure is a bench that attracts attention by its outstanding simplicity and a formal configuration that has been reduced to the minimal possible expression. The structure consists of 5 wooden battens of solid Niangon wood, the cross-section of which measures 55 x 100 mm. The surface texture is soft and smooth to the touch. A variety of finishes can be added to it according to the type of environment in which it will be expected to perform. Pure can be supplied varnished or painted in a series of standard colors; nevertheless, the high quality of the wood it is made of makes its natural finish quite sufficient, as its exposure to solar radiation and UV rays will give the wood a singularly attractive silvery patina in a short period of time.

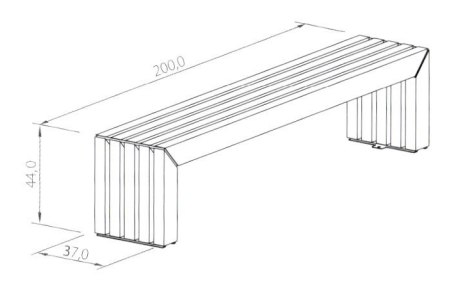

SEATS

Racional 2

Design: **Franc Fernández** • Production: **Tecam BCN**

Reducing the idea of a seat to the fundamental basics, this bench consists of a horizontal and a vertical component and two pressure-impregnated (autoclave treated) pinewood planks. These two main functional parts are supported by a hot-dip galvanized steel structure that provides the legs and the armrests. Only the two front legs and the armrests play an important visual role, as the two back legs are discreetly placed near the middle, where they prevent the seat from bending. The legs are connected and braced by the rest of the structure, which is concealed under the seat and behind the backrest. Racional 2 is 278 cm long. Taking the resistance of the materials to the limit and optimizing their performance was the motivation for this design brief.

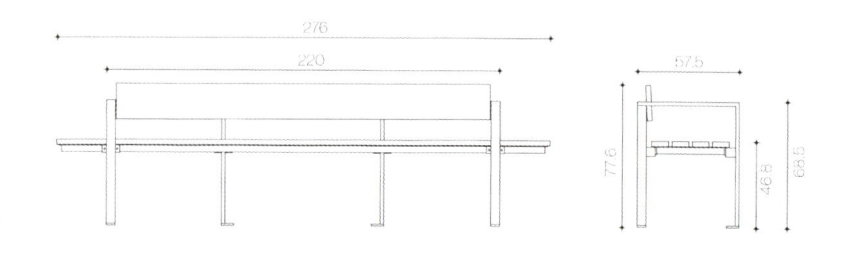

88 SEATS

Radium

Design: **David Karásek & Radek Hegmon** • Production: **mmcité**

This new product line derives its unique contemporary characteristics from the aesthetics of bent sheet steel. The optimal rigidity and excellent overall resistance of this steel bench is achieved thanks to the ingenious intersection of its walls. The version with a wooden seat presents a different visual aspect. The seat surfaces of both options have a rounded longitudinal slot to avoid lounging. The structure is made of galvanized steel sheet, painted in standard shades; the seat consists of metal sheet or solid wooden boards (optionally, round steel bars can be used). It is provided with an easy anchoring system for fixing to the concrete or pavement. This product line also includes new models of litterbins and bollards. A small stool extends the possible applications. The series was distinguished with the "Excellent Design 2005" award.

SEATS

Rambla

Design: **Diana Cabeza** • Production: **Estudio Cabeza**

This system of public benches offers great freedom. Organised in rows, the benches constitute a flexible support with log-like backrests. Randomly placed they are an invitation to multiple and varied uses.

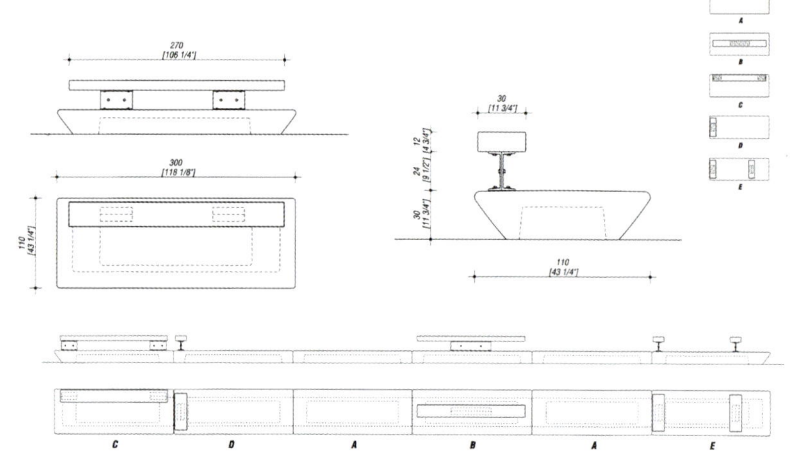

Recte

Design: **Ton Riera Ubia** • Production: **mago:urban**

The Recte is like an everyday sofa that you may find in anyone's home only in this case it happens to be in urban surroundings. It is a piece of furniture for the town which fulfils the objective of making public spaces more comfortable, but does not detract from its elegance and simplicity. The form is based on a slab of concrete with a backrest, two arms at either end and four stainless steel legs. This piece is obviously very tough and made from acid-etched concrete which hardly needs any maintenance. It measures 236 × 80 × 69 cm (92.74 × 31.44 × 27.11 inches).

Rehué

Design: **Diana Cabeza** • Production: **Estudio Cabeza**

Rehué is a set of seats and tables of two different sizes, which can be placed in multiple configurations, for outdoor or indoor use, for private or public space. The pieces are constructed of cast concrete using tinted aggregate. The standard choice of colours available is earth and black.

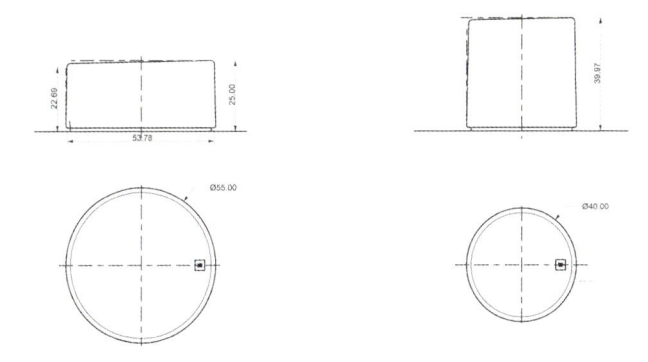

SEATS

Riddle Chair

Design: **Jean Nouvel** • Production: **Alis**

Riddle is an armchair designed by the Jean Nouvel workshop. Basically thought out in terms of use in the open air, this piece of furniture can equally well be installed indoors. It is entirely made of cast aluminium. The various parts are held together and onto the structure with security bolts. The chair can gyrate or be fixed according to the characteristics of the location where it will be emplaced. The arms and the back are held to the foot by two 90º curved aluminium bars 25 mm in diameter. This soldered structure is bolted onto the foot by a nut, soldered onto the 60mmØ tube. The chair leg is soldered to a 200x200x5 mm square base that is fixed to the ground by four M10 screws. The entire soldered base is to be sunken 10 cm below grade.

Rondine

Design and production: **Geohide**

Rondine is a circular bench ideal for placing around the foot of a tree, protecting them and allowing users to enjoy sitting in the shade. It consists of a seat and a backrest made of concentric rings made of wooden dowels and a support structure made of stainless steel with anchoring fixtures of the same material. The wood is treated for outdoor use including a coat of a fungicidal product and painted with a double coat of lightly tinted finish varnish, although other optional finishes are possible. The steel structure has been given a natural polished finish. It is provided with a variety of angular steel elements that allow it to adapt to a variety of grade slopes and permit the supports to be placed horizontally. The bench is designed to be installed on a firm foundation base.

Rough & Ready

Design and production: **Streetlife**

All Rough & Ready products are sturdy and robust. This unique program comprises: Straight benches, Linked benches, Curve benches, Circular benches, Topseats, R&R Bicycle Parking racks and Lineparking, Bollards, Tree tubs and Tree isles with R&R sitting rims. The All-Black beams of recycled agriculture plastics are another available option. The R&R Curve system, the R&R Circle benches and also the R&R topseats are designed for outstanding and natural spaces.
In conjunction, they form a coherent program for exceptional urban locations. They are fixed to the thermo-galvanized legs by means of the Streetlock® comb system, stainless steel and theft-proof. The optional backrests can be fixed in various positions.

SEATS 93

RS

Design: Jean-Marie Duthilleul • Production: Tecno

A waiting area seating system, with individual seats resting on a supporting beam, designed for indoor or outdoor use (aluminum seat version).
The various options regarding the seating are the following: injection-molded painted aluminum, aluminum and wooden slats, steel sheet, teakwood, wenge, black leather, black vinyl, or fabric. All other components (bases, brackets, beams and armrests) are either injection-molded or extruded aluminum, all powder coated. The system is also available with or without a backrest and with a perch. Bases are available for anchoring to the floor, to the wall, or remaining mobile. Other accessories include armrests, seat spacers, and a back-to-back beam.

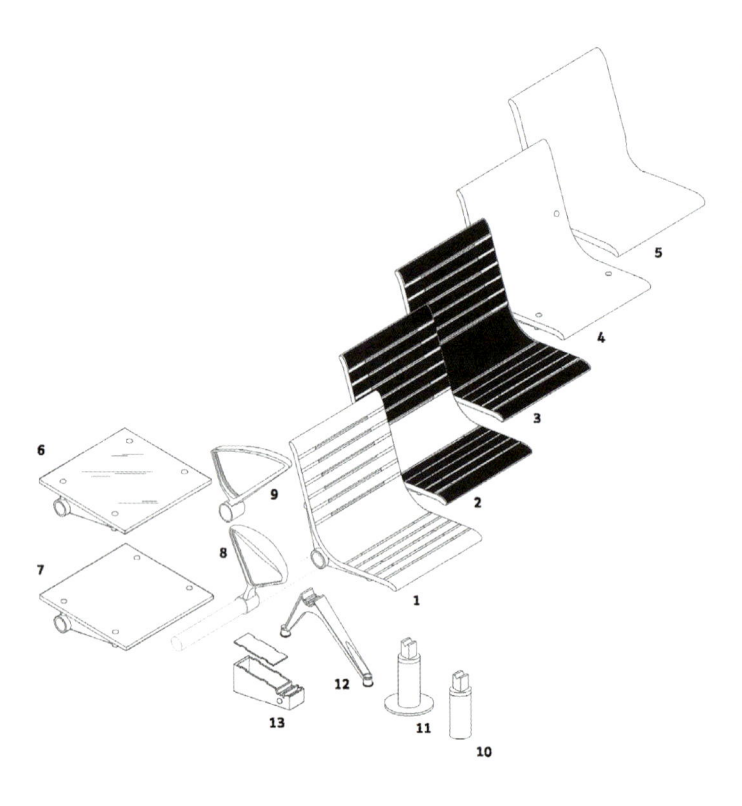

1. Bench seat in injection-molded painted aluminum or in steel sheet.
2. Bench seat with wooden slats.
3. Bench seat with wooden slats and a wooden curved part.
4. Bench seat shaped in plywood, veneered, edged and lipped in teak or wenge.
5. Bench seat finished in black leather, black vinyl or fabric.
6. Bench table in tinted toughened glass
7. Bench table in black laminate
8. Complete beam including sloped armrests
9. Complete beam including flat armrests
10. Base for fixing to the floor
11. Base for fixing to the floor by a disc
12. Mobile base
13. Wall-mounted support bracket

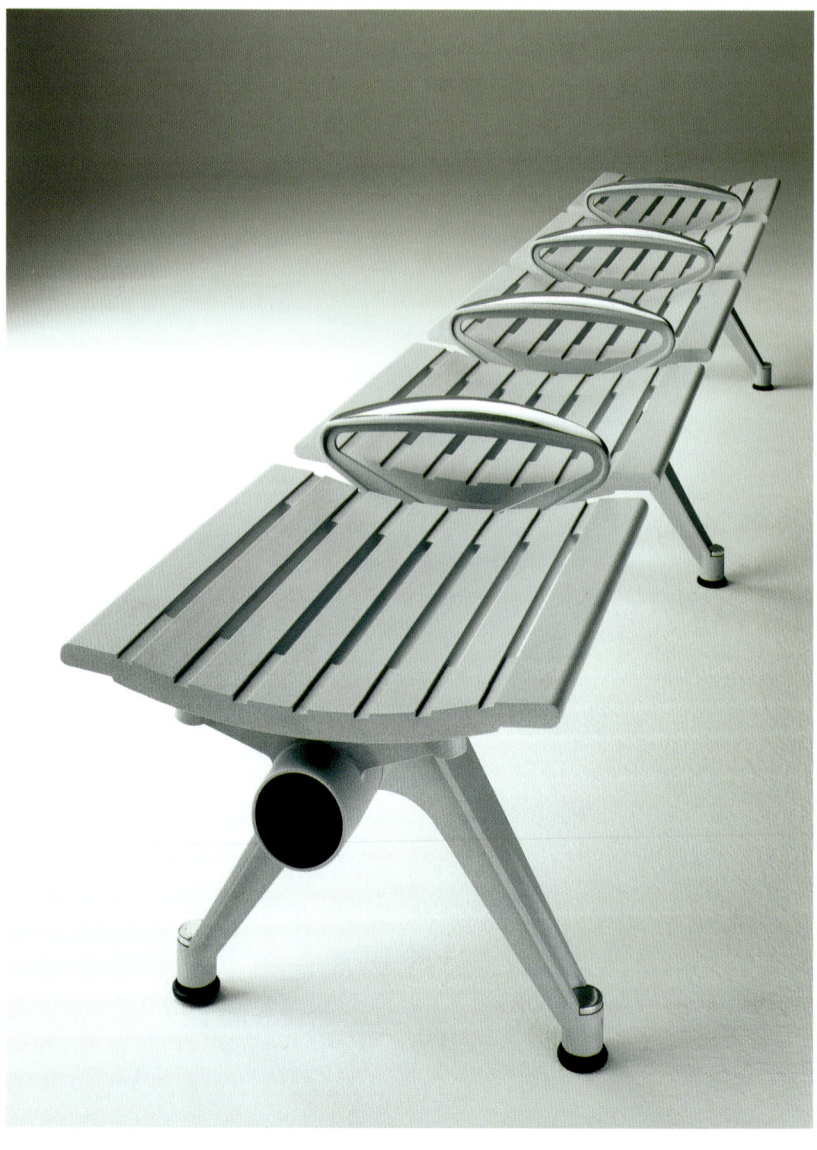

Rua

Design: **J.M.Carvalho de Araújo** • Production: **Larus**

The designers of Rua conceive of public space as a great sitting room, which should be comfortably furnished. It follows from this premise that urban furniture should be stable, fixed, oriented, vandalproof, repairable and changeable. It should not retain rainwater and should dry off quickly. Rua is a straightforward solution. A simple design could be the correct answer, with a neat and vigorous design susceptible of further adaptations. Moreover, it has a series of modular accessories to suit it to any space and type of configuration. Alternative thin films for the coating are being developed.

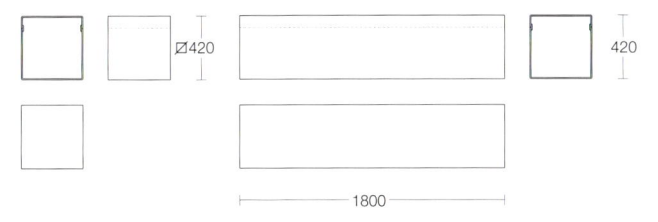

Shape

Design: **G&C Arquitectura y Urbanismo** • Production: **ONN Outside**

The SHAPE bench, highly architectural in its design, is available in two formats: with or without a backrest. The structure is realized in corten steel and the seat and backrest in tali wood treated with teak oil.

SEATS

Shoreline

Design and production: **Street and Park Furniture**

The full range of Shoreline furniture also comprises deck and cube style benches, a picnic setting, fencing, a custom-made wave-style cast bollard and a spiral bike rack. The furniture was designed to be very simple and streamlined. It was originally designed for a new foreshore development in South Australia. Since then it has been installed on neighbouring foreshores as well as being contracted for other coastal developments. It has taken over the coastline!

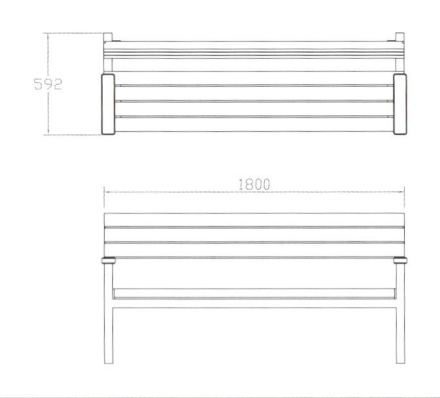

Sillarga

Design: **J.Carlos Inés, Gonzalo Milà** • Production: **Escofet**

Sillarga is a reclining chair made of reinforced concrete, constructed in one piece for a variety of use-oriented functional reasons, including its dimensions and weight. Coinciding with the idea of increasingly individualized urban furniture, this item presents itself to the user as a friendly invitation to relax, making the city a softer place. It responds particularly well to the problem of urban furniture in a harsh environment.

Severely punishing climate conditions, vandalism, and the possibility of theft (the item weighs 320 kg) (705.28 lb) are the circumstances this item was designed for. The length of the Sillarga bench allows for a multiplicity of uses. Its friendly shape requires a family and seems to ask for the company of a shorter version, the Sicurta chair.

The design of both of these chairs proposes a new manner of using and occupying urban space, changing the rigid linearity of traditional typologies for more open and flexible alternatives, to facilitate spontaneous communicative behavior.

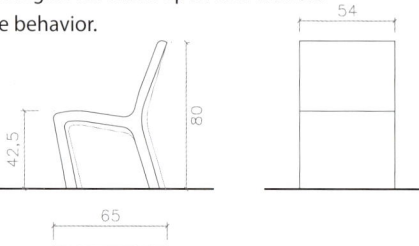

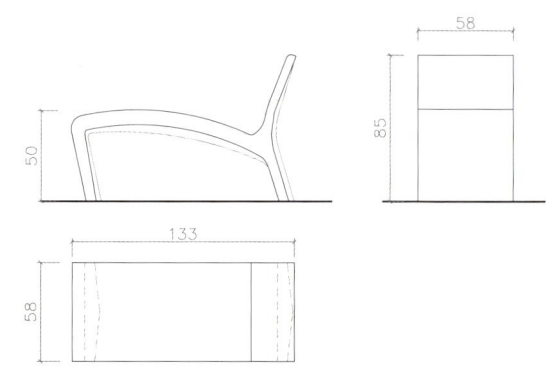

96 SEATS

Sit

Design: **Frog Design** • Production: **Landscape Forms**

Sit is a freestanding bench with four legs that suggest natural forms, like the branches of a tree. The section of the extruded cast aluminum support members is both visually satisfying and structurally rigid. The object combines the most rational use of the materials with a form that is reminiscent of quite traditional benches and historical styles, making the item capable of integrating into either contemporary or traditional settings. It is visually light, energetic, non-institutional and international in spirit. Its 3-dimensional aluminum castings look dynamic. The seating components lean in and away, gesture outward and around, creating an inviting presence. All steel parts are primed with E-coat. All painted parts are polyester powdercoated. The production process employs over 65% recycled and recyclable material. The piece measures 25" deep x 32" high x 74" long, and weighs 150 lbs.

Sitting-Around

Design: **Studio MAO - Emmeazero** • Production: **Modo**

This item consists of a structure in stainless steel and slats in mahogany wood, specifically treated for outdoor conditions. The main feature of this unusual bench is its capacity to rotate, by means of a pivot placed at one of the two ends. An unconventional, variable and amusing seating arrangement!

SEATS

Sit

Design: **Diego Fortunato** • Production: **Escofet**

Sit is based on the idea that urban furniture should be gentle, round, comfortable and non-identifiable with any particular historical period. It should be a type of object capable of blending naturally into any sort of environment.

The collection consists of two different sizes of rock-benches (or bench-rocks), made of concrete, measuring 240 cm (94.32 inches) and 75 cm (29.47 inches) in length, and 47 cm (18.47 inches) from the ground to the seating surface. The objects rest on a short, invisible rim underneath that anchors them to the ground, while keeping them from resting too firmly upon the earth, maintaining a subtle feeling of lightness, and avoiding the inevitable wobble that would result if the contact surface were a flat plane. Two different sizes of backrest-rocks can be added, making a comfortable and ergonomic piece of urban furniture. The backrest-rocks are held in position by countersunk stainless steel bolts. The different sizes, shapes and colors allow various configurations, enabling the landscape designer to compose his environment in a purely aesthetic manner, which simultaneously fulfills one the spaces requirements, inviting the passer by to sit down and enjoy a moment of relaxation.

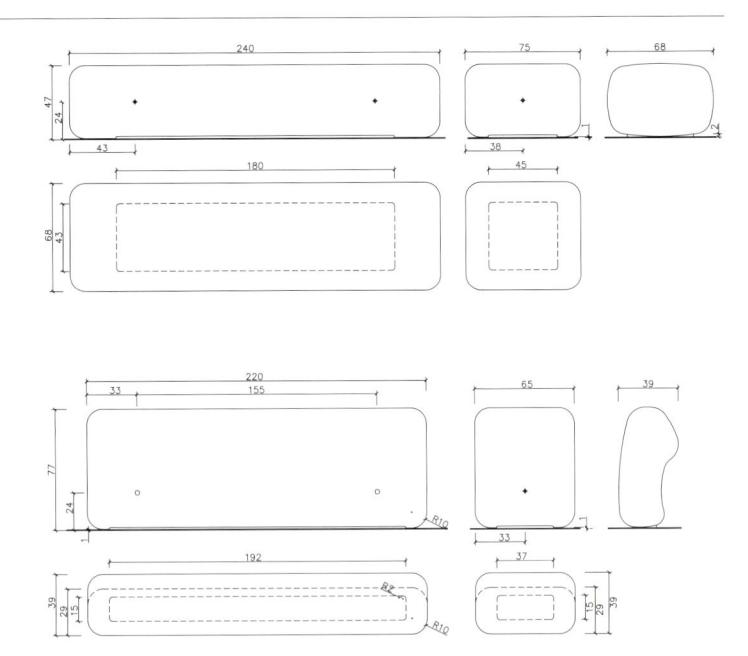

98 SEATS

Ska

Design: **Javier Machimbarrena** • Production: **ONN Outside**

The SKA bench is the outcome of the marriage of ergonomics with cutting edge design. The design of the piece was approached as a search for subtlety and modernity as if it were a car design project. An element which will sit as easily in the most innovative architectural project as in more classic contexts, the cast aluminum structure is available with or without armrests, with a tali wood seat and backrest and hidden fixings.
This bench is part of the SKA range which includes benches, a streetlamp, wastebasket, bollard, tree grid and cycle rack.

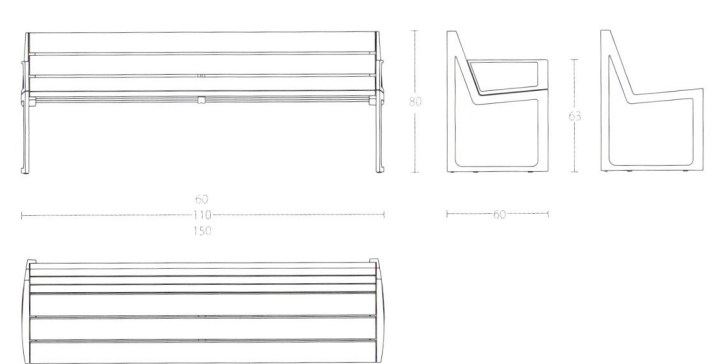

Slope

Design: **Pich-Aguilera Arquitectos** • Production: **Escofet**

The genesis and the final result of Slope are the outcome of a careful analysis of the tissues and organs of reptiles, how their scales overlap, how the structure changes at the transition points in which movement is required; The starting point was an isolated hexagon, which given its autonomous nature in generating surfaces, can be found as the basic unit of many cellular tissues, such as the shells of tortoises and the scales of many reptiles. In later phases of the process, more hexagons were added and their geometry was distorted, tensed and a curve was wrapped around them, always maintaining the criterion that the piece had to obey a logic of its own, both in isolation and in aggregation.
Once the design was ready, the production process was fairly complex, as the geometrical forms in question did not permit scale models to be produced by hand but directly by computer. A series of progressive steps were followed, from the physical models created by computer, which were then adjusted by hand, sanding and modeling the form; then it was reintroduced into the computer by scanning and a new model was produced, at a larger scale. This required the collaboration of professional model builders from the automobile industry, in which the bodywork of cars is created in the same way.
Slope is a piece of transition or infiltration which permits nature to be evoked within an urban context, while dissolving the urban in nature. Rather than a finished piece as such, it intends to be an instrument, the morphology of which speaks to the designer of the multiple structures and resources implemented in the piece, which will become the inspiration for the parameters of a new shell.

SEATS

So-ffa

Design: BCQ Arquitectos • Production: **Escofet**

Soffa is a bench that doubles as a piece of minimalist sculpture. Its dynamic form is made of reinforced concrete, coloured white or black. Its solidity makes it unnecessary to anchor it to the ground in any way.

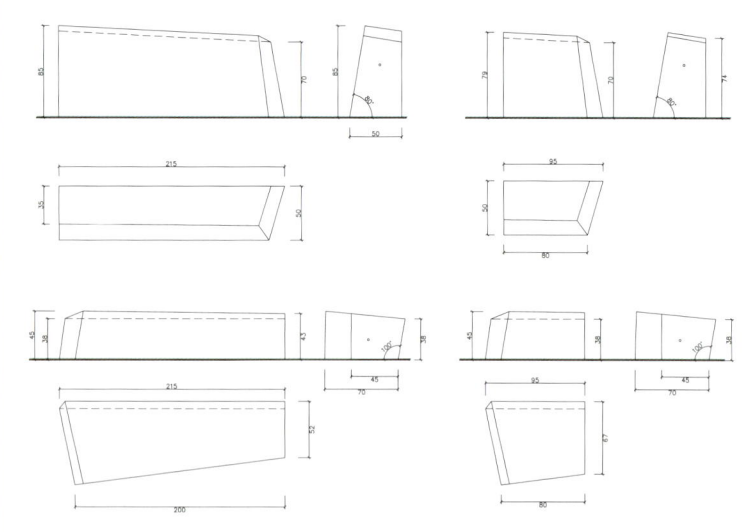

Sol y Luna

Design: **Fausta Stella** • Production: **Modo**

Structure in normal steel and slats of solid mahogany specifically treated for outdoor conditions. Two supporting cylinders whose bases respectively represent the sun and the moon characterize this bench.

SEATS

Sombra

Design: **Vicente Soto** • Production: **T&D Cabanes**

The Sombra benches combine compositional balance and formal lightness. They consist of a single support of carbon steel that performs as the main anchoring element with the ground and is the joining point of the thick wooden boards of tropical wood that make up the seat and the back.

Spring Seat

Design: **Greg Healey** • Production: **Street and Park Furniture**

Inspired by the form of a leaf spring on a truck's suspension system, designer Greg Healey wanted to provide the same gentle movement for his seat.
Street and Park Furniture and Greg Healey worked together to put this new range on the market. Greg Healey established Greg Healey Design in Southern Australia in 1995. Over time the practice has predominantly worked in the realm of urban infrastructure with a strong contemporary arts focus. Each work is specifically designed to incorporate the site's specific cultural and physical history, how the work relates to its surroundings at micro and macro levels.
Materials: Hardwood slats, Stainless Steel Spacers, Painted Cast Iron, Painted Steel

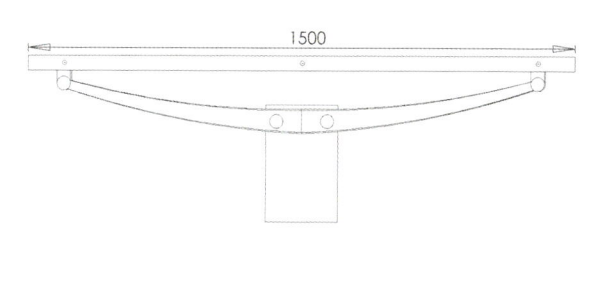

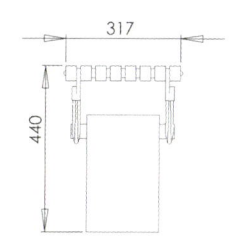

SEATS

Stay

Design: **Frog Design** • Production: **Landscape Forms**

Stay is an embedded bench: In the backless version, the beautifully minimal cantilever describes a wide, graceful arc. In the version with a back, the bench appears to spring from the ground, like a blade of grass. The materials used include aluminum castings, extrusions, perforated sheet, steel support members, and cast iron. Corrosion is prevented from attacking the steel components with E-coat primer. All the painted components are polyester powdercoated. Stay is 65% recycled and recyclable. Using local and regional suppliers allowed a reduction of the transport-related environmental impact. The products of this maker are built for longevity and durability; they can be repaired and refinished for extended life. The dimensions are 22" deep x 68" long. The item weighs about 150 lbs.

Sumo

Design: **Enric Pericas + Josep Muxart** • Production: **DAE**

This bench consists of a seating surface and a backrest made of composite pinewood planks, high pressure impregnated, sawn and glued, plus three hot-dip galvanized steel legs. The seat and the backrest are treated with a base coat of deep-penetrating tinted base varnish and two layers of semi-gloss, transparent, lightly tinted alkyd resin finish varnish. The cross-sectional dimensions of the seat are 442 × 140 mm, and the backrest measures 535 × 80 mm. The item is supplied in three standard lengths: 3000, 1750 and 750 mm. The legs are fixed to the ground by 10 mm expansion bolts.

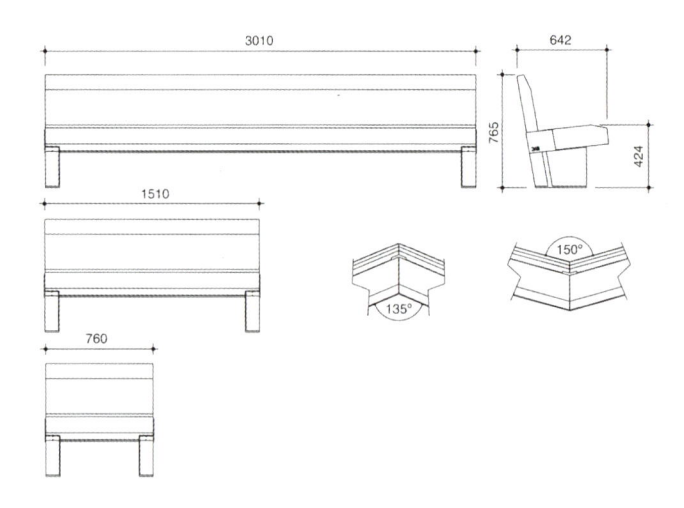

SEATS

STO

Design: **Daniel Nebot** • Production: **Macaedis**

The system consists of twelve different modules which can be combined in a great variety of different ways, satisfying the requirements of any project. Created for the achievement of harmonious compositions that will adapt to any space, introducing organic configurations into the urban environment. Its range of possibilities enhance the element of play and of social intercourse that is the very nature of a public bench, so certain modules include various hollows especially conceived to fit the younger users, or modules that include games, such as a chess-board, within the structure. The system includes tree basins, fresh water drinking fountains or ornamental fountains (module STV11), designed to provide the luxurious sound of water falling in spaces of all types.

The material is natural stone, in the colors of white limestone, creamy limestone, or grey agglomerate stone.

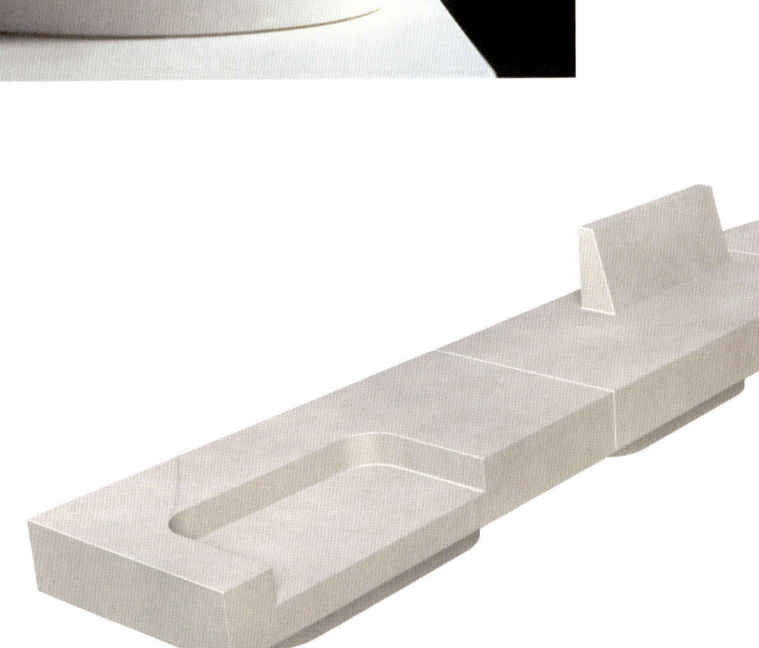

SEATS 103

The Swiss Benches

Design: Alfredo Häberli • **Production:** Bd

The Swiss Benches were created for Bd as a homage to the famous Banco Catalano. The outcome is a number of models of public benches that offer that extra function so typical of the designs of Alfredo Häberli. The Poet is a bench at which one can eat or write, with a table to rest on. The Banker is somewhat harder, The Philosopher is visually tranquil. Other suggestive options are The Loner, for lonely hearts, and The Couple. The toughness required of a public bench, which must resist corrosion and vandalism, need not be incompatible with aesthetic quality. The Swiss Benches are available in two optional finishes, hot-dip galvanized or painted with polyester resin. Both display all their beauty either indoors or in the open. (Translator's note: In several languages, the word bank indicates both a financial institution and an elongated seat).

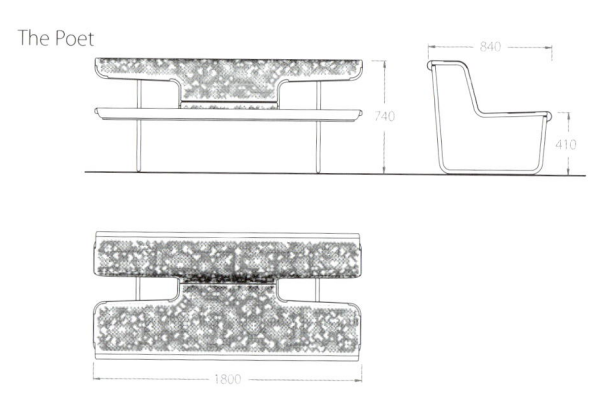

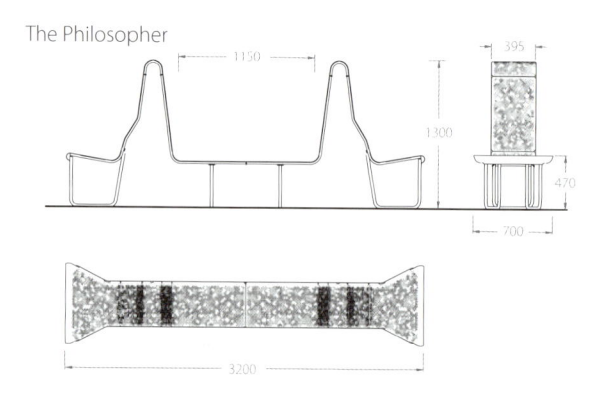

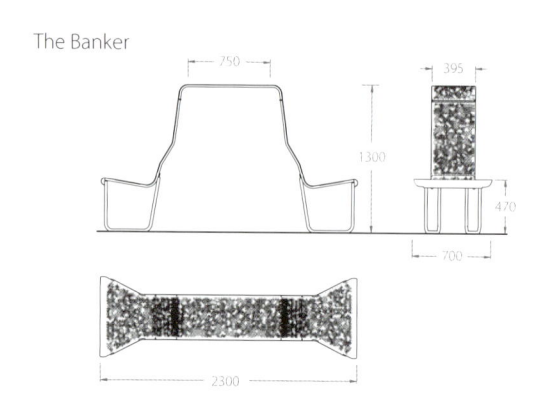

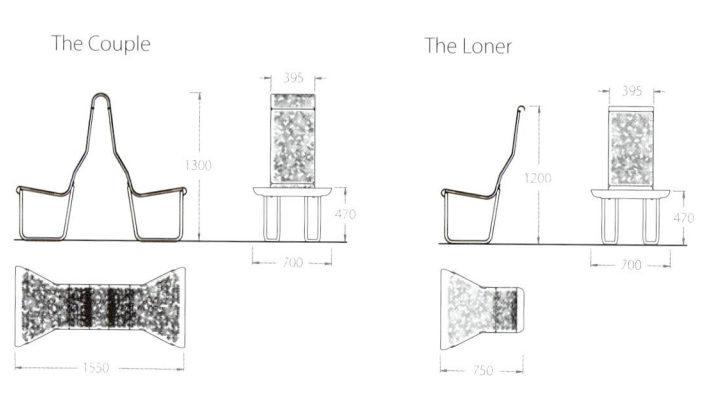

The Poet

The Philosopher

The Banker

The Couple

The Loner

104 SEATS

SEATS 105

Szekely

Design: **Martin Szekely** • Production: **JCDecaux**

Szekely is a bench with a capacity for six or seven people. It consists of a cast iron structure with two stylized central feet and a wooden seating surface on either side. This surface is made of wooden spars that are bolted onto the structure with screws protected with resin, creating a plane that seems to fold over the back of the seat. This determines a sober, symmetrical, minimalistic look, likely to enhance any natural or urban location.

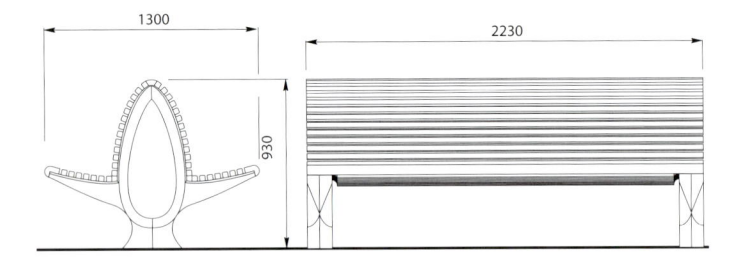

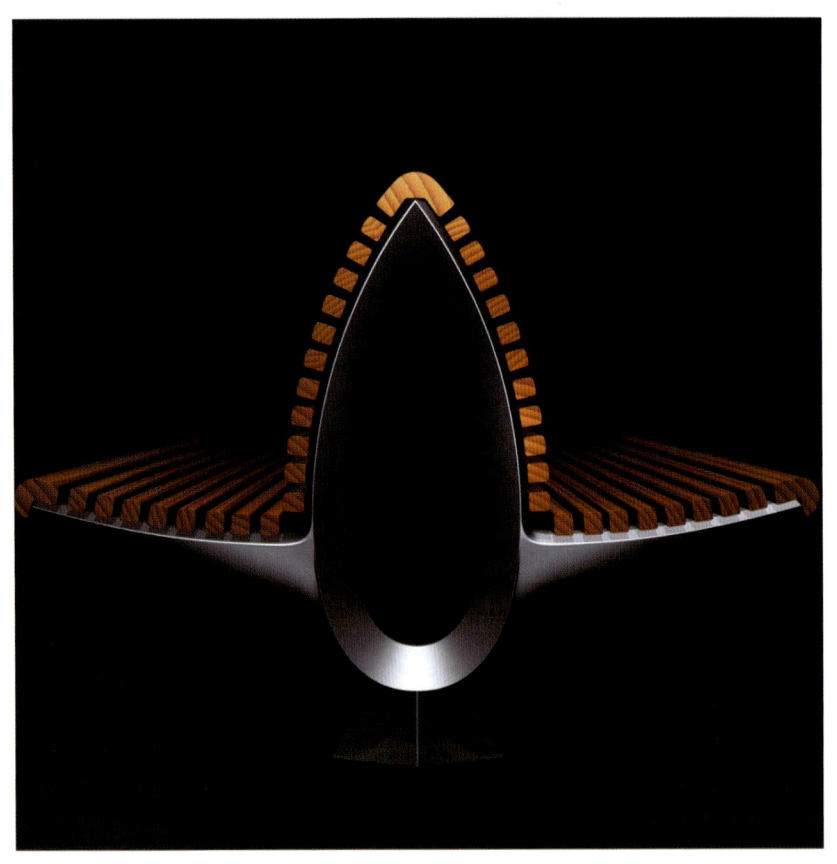

106   SEATS

Tauranga

Design: **Ted Smyth** • Production: **Woodform**

Designed by Ted Smyth for Tauranga, New Zealand, this bench is made of solid Kwila wood bent using the Woodform technology. Woodform Design has pioneered research into technology to develop systems for the bending and shaping of solid timber and MDF (Medium Density Fibreboard).

Tea Tree Gully

Design and production: **Street and Park Furniture**

The City of Tea Tree Gully is moving forward with dynamic developments. One of these developments was to create a visual impact with a uniquely designed range of street furniture, to introduce modern and innovative techniques into local construction and design. Street and Park Furniture worked in collaboration with a design firm to create a range of exciting urban furniture, including Seats, Tree Guards, Bins, Bollards, Fencing and Banner Poles. Street and Park Furniture aims to provide specifiers and customers with the convenience of a single supply source for projects involving street furniture, backed by specialist experience and support. Their philosophy since 1988 has been that, "better streets begin at street level".
Materials: Hardwood Timber, Cast Aluminium, Galvanized Mild Steel

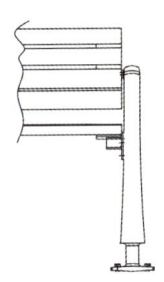

SEATS 107

Tens

Design: **Sergio Fernández** • Production: **Tecam BCN**

The 'Tens' bench is made of aluminum and autoclave impregnated aleppo pine. The wood comes from sustainable forestry resources. No sort of maintenance is required for its use outdoors, as it has been treated against ultraviolet radiation with acrylic water-born transparent lacquer.

The legs are made of anodized cast aluminum alloy AG3T. The structure is highly resistant. Two wooden boards of 35mm (1.37 inches) thickness provide the backrest and three boards provide the seat. Along the center of the bench runs a curved support member that prevents the boards from twisting or sagging.

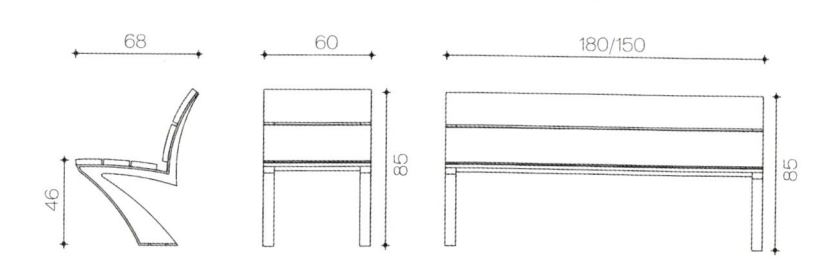

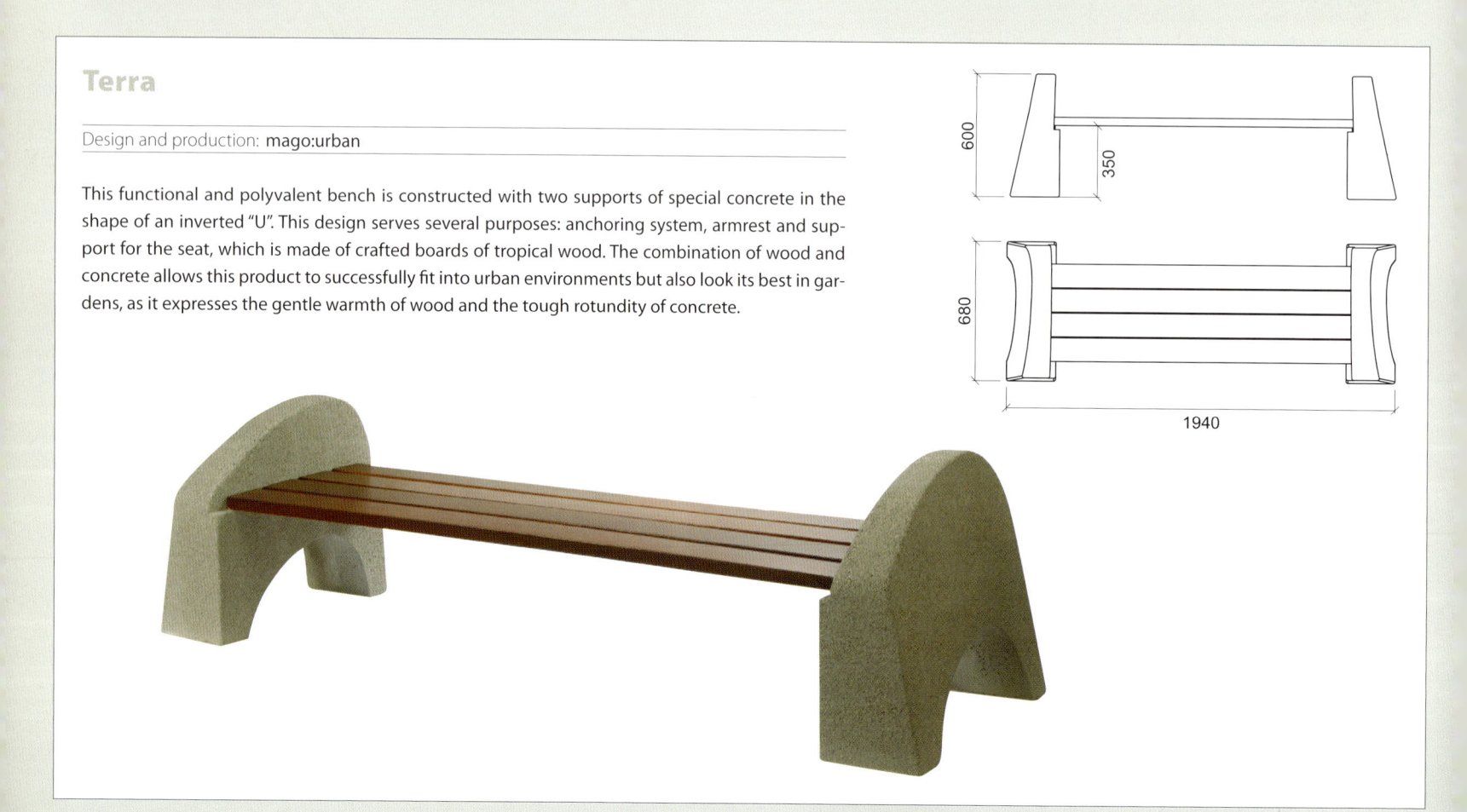

Terra

Design and production: **mago:urban**

This functional and polyvalent bench is constructed with two supports of special concrete in the shape of an inverted "U". This design serves several purposes: anchoring system, armrest and support for the seat, which is made of crafted boards of tropical wood. The combination of wood and concrete allows this product to successfully fit into urban environments but also look its best in gardens, as it expresses the gentle warmth of wood and the tough rotundity of concrete.

SEATS

Tetris

Design: **Roger Albero** • Production: **mago:urban**

Tetris is a new concept in urban furniture, created by mago:urban. The numerous possible combinations of the Tetris components respond to the needs of all sorts of spaces. Aiming at a versatile definition of space without forsaking rigorous linearity, designer Roger Albero based his proposal on logic, adapting the realization to the needs of each scenario, while maintaining the basic tenets of any urban project.

From modules as elementary as the sections of rectangular parallelograms, crosses, T forms, 90º angles or semicircular quadrants with various optional radii, an endless number of possible compositions arise, capable of adapting to any environment however unusual. This makes it easy not only to adapt in response, but often to actively modify the appearance of a place with only a modest investment. The various component modules perform both as a seat and a border. All the modules have the same height, length and width, making them easy to combine. A cube and a flowerpot module increase the system's versatility.

Technical characteristics:

Material: concrete

Optional finishes: exposed aggregate or polished

Colors: white, ochre, gray, black and deep magenta

SEATS

Topográfico

Design: Diana Cabeza • **Collaborators:** Martín Wolfson, Juan José Cano • **Production:** Estudio Cabeza

Sinuous, assimetrical and irregular, this bench's ondulating surface slides like the earth, glides like wet sand and draws watermarks as on a still damp surface.

Its topographic expression evoques subtle ergonomic qualities, and its concrete materiality is user-friendly. Can be configured in numerous and varied ways.

Precast concrete with color aggregate. Natural finish.

In versions with or without backrest. Can be matched side-to-side, back-to-back or combinations of both. Currently available in black and brown and grey. Simply placed or fixed with chemical or mechanical anchors.

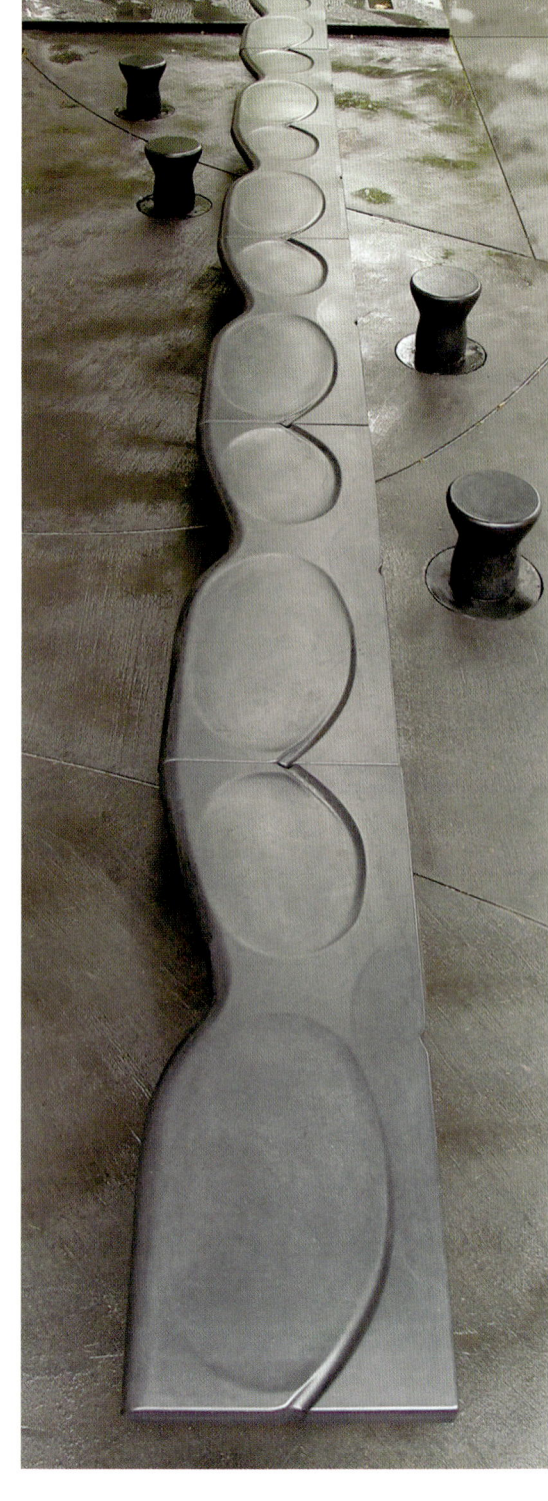

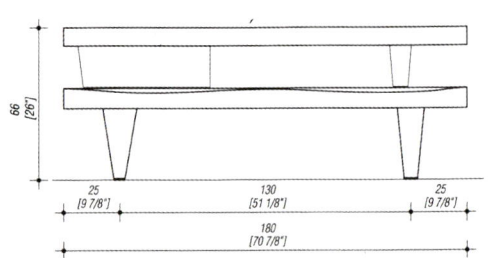

110 SEATS

Trapecio

Design: **Montse Periel-Antonio Montes** • Production: **Santa & Cole**

This bench is made of two elongated blocks of solid pine wood with a trapezoidal cross-section, which integrate naturally in parks and leisure spots in the city, introducing the formal geometry of a sculptural element that does not immediately bring to mind a bench, thereby facilitating a new reading of the surroundings and offering a multitude of possible uses. The two almost symmetrical bodies the bench consists of are staggered by a 90 cm difference along the longitudinal axis, creating the article's visual interest and opening a choice of exciting ways for Trapecio to enhance a sloping site by underlining its shape.

Two 450 cm (176.85 inches) long volumes are made of 20 × 40 cm (7.86 × 15.72 inches) thick structural wooden beams, composed of glued and shaped (lamelée collée) red pine, autoclaved laths. The two blocks are fixed to the supports, which are made of hot-galvanized steel, by means of rust-proof treated steel screws. Trapecio is fixed to the ground by mechanical blocks and two concrete cubes, 10cm (3.93 inches) below grade. No maintenance is required.

Trasluz

Design: **Francisco J. Mangado** • Production: **DAE**

The seat of this bench consists of eleven Iroko wood slats and a base formed by a box and lid in 10mm welded galvanized steel. The wooden slats which are 1,996 mm long and 40 mm wide by 25 mm are treated with a first coat of varnish primer and two coats of clear stained varnish with a satin-finish, based on acrylic resins in an aqueous phase emulsion. The box is finished with a coat of bi-component phosphate primer and a polyester resin based powder coating for outdoor performance. The standard colors are black and iron-effect steel grey. It weighs approximately 200 kg. The lighting comes from a 58 W fluorescent strip located inside the box which can be changed by lifting the seat.

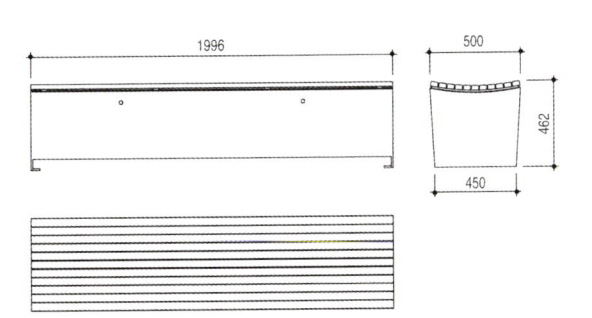

SEATS

Tubbo

Design: Paúl Basañez & Javier Machimbarrena • Production: Proiek Habita and Equipment

The Tubbo collection is a solution for public space that can be equally well integrated in an indoor or an outdoor environment. This design represents an evolution of the "Romantic Bench" by means of a see-through structure of stainless steel tubes, whereby different locations are equally suitable. Its permeable appearance reduces its barrier performance and makes it doubly versatile. The series consists of a long bench, a short bench and a long stool without a back, plus a railing that completes the set, which should be understood as a system whose simplicity guarantees multiple possibilities.

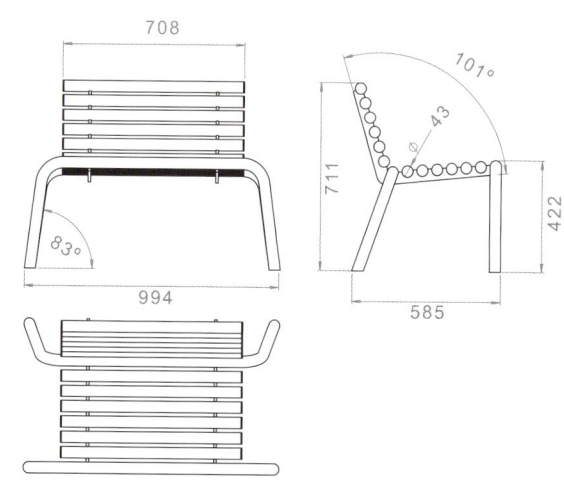

Tube

Design: **Roger Albero** • Production: **mago:urban**

The Tube series involves four bench models and an end-piece that goes with them, but they can be used individually. Tube Silla and Tube Siesta are two ergonomic models that are perfectly suited to receive the human body in a state of repose. The body of all the models consists of a strip of reinforced concrete that surrounds a characteristic hole that defines the series and gives the piece lightness without endangering the sturdiness of the sandblasted concrete they are made of.

SEATS

Twig

Design: **Alexander Lotersztain** • Production: **Escofet**

Twig is a system of benches based on the concept of modularity, interactivity and connectivity. With these ideas as the starting point, the intention is to enhance the diversity and fluidity of the users. The design's versatility permits a series of meeting points to arise in between, generating new uses of public space. The material used is cast reinforced concrete and gently sandblasted, creating slightly rounded edges and smooth surfaces that branch out under the shade of a tree or on a university campus lawn.

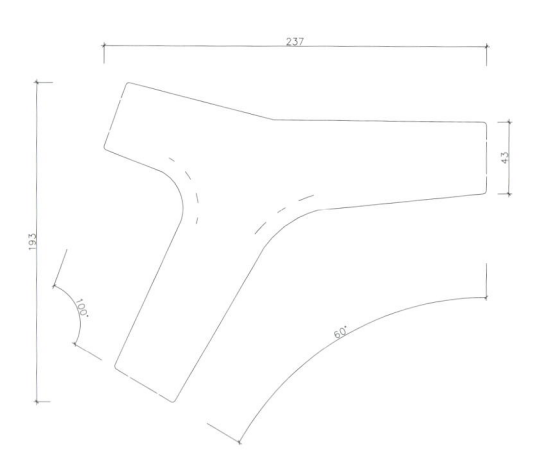

Vera

Design: **David Karásek & Radek Hegmon** • Production: **mmcité**

A smart bench presented in a wide range of options shows that advanced modern design does not always mean high price. Durability and toughness goes hand in hand with clean lines and shapes and remarkable lightness. Simply shaped table and park chairs enable to create original combinations in public and private environments.
Galvanized steel frame painted in standard shades. Seat and backrest made of steel round grid, stainless steel round grid or solid wooden boards which are firmly fixed to the supporting frame by concealed screws. All four legs can be easily fixed to the ground.

SEATS

Vesta

Design: **Jean-Luc Cortella** • Production: **Concept Urbain**

The Vesta bench has legs made of ductile cast iron with a shot-blasted finish. The seat and backrest are made of treated wood. The iron parts are available in any RAL colour. It is delivered fully assembled and has to be fixed by bolts or threaded rods.

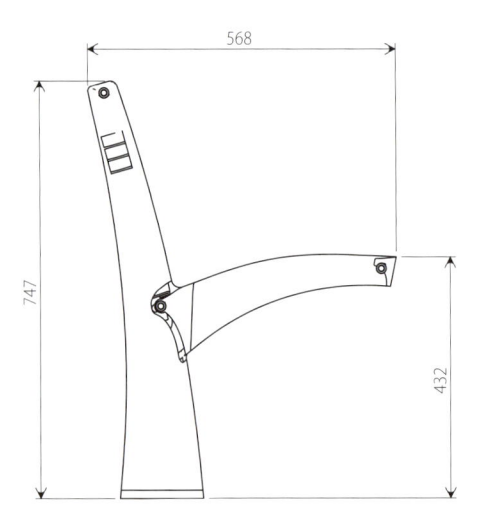

Via Augusta

Design: **Manel Castellnou** • Production: **Santa & Cole**

An outdoor sofa and an armchair made of wood are an inviting counterpoint to the city's accelerated pace. Its comfortably ergonomic design is an invitation to stop, have a rest, and watch things go by, a respite for the urban inhabitant.

The legs and the structural frame sustaining the wooden seat are made of zinc galvanized and oven painted steel angle irons.

The seat and the backrest are made of wooden slats. The armrest is a thicker piece of timber that goes all around the top of the back. All these parts are made of solid, autoclave treated red pine, fixed with stainless steel screws. The weight of the armchair is 42 kg (92.5 lb) and the sofa weighs 73 kg (160.9 lb).

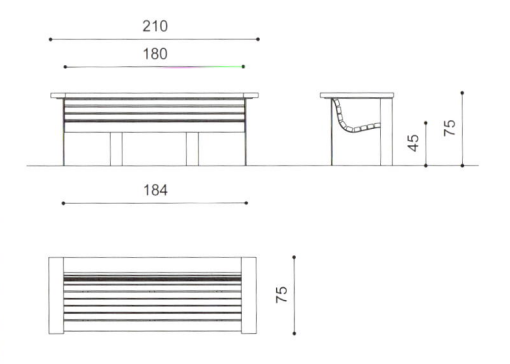

116   SEATS

Vivanti

Design: **Max Wehberg** • Production: **Westeifel Werke**

The Vivanti bench for the elderly provides more comfort and makes standing up easier due to its ergonomically designed backrest, armrests and footrest. Parking your own walking frame in the fitted parking facility creates a seat with a backrest. The Vivanti products can create a good walking route, for example from a residential area to a shopping centre, enhancing elderly people's mobility. The Vivanti benches are designed to create good resting places for the older shopper or walker. Both sides of the Vivanti bench can be put to use and it has supportive armrests and footrests.

Very suitable for a shopping street, the standing support with sturdy handgrips has been specially developed for use in locations with reduced space.

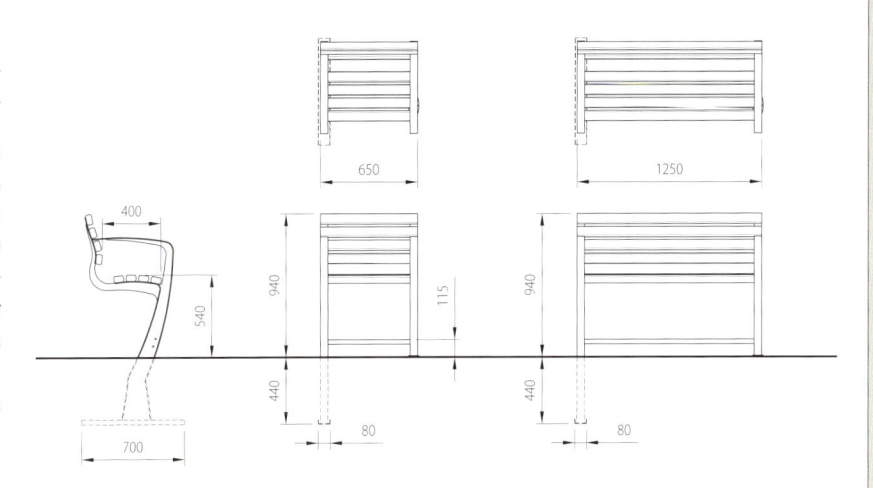

SEATS

Walden

Design: **díez+díez diseño** • Production: **Ecoralia**

The range of Walden products covers a wide series of options, from the simplest stool without a back, to the freestyle composition of an elongated seating system, which can extend to almost 6 meters in length; this is possible by the use of extruded Syntal plate and to the two-sided finish this design envisages; thus, it is fundamentally the clients who define the bench they wish to purchase.

The main environmental advantage of Walden is the exchange of the wooden parts of traditional benches for extruded boards of Syntal: This recycled material, obtained from the recovery of household refuse (RSU-Yellow container) and light-industry discards other than PVC, possesses a number of doubtless advantages; among them is its extraordinary durability, with no maintenance costs, an very satisfactory performance in outdoor conditions, including damp or even marine environments, as it is impervious to fungal or insect attack; it is easy to clean, even regarding graffiti; it is fire-resistant and self-extinguishing. The wide range of colors it comes in, added to its attractive visual and thermal qualities, warmer to the touch than metal benches, make it ideal to cover a long list of requirements.

The name Walden pays homage to the work of the North American philosopher Thoreau, who in a certain sense was the father of the science of ecology.

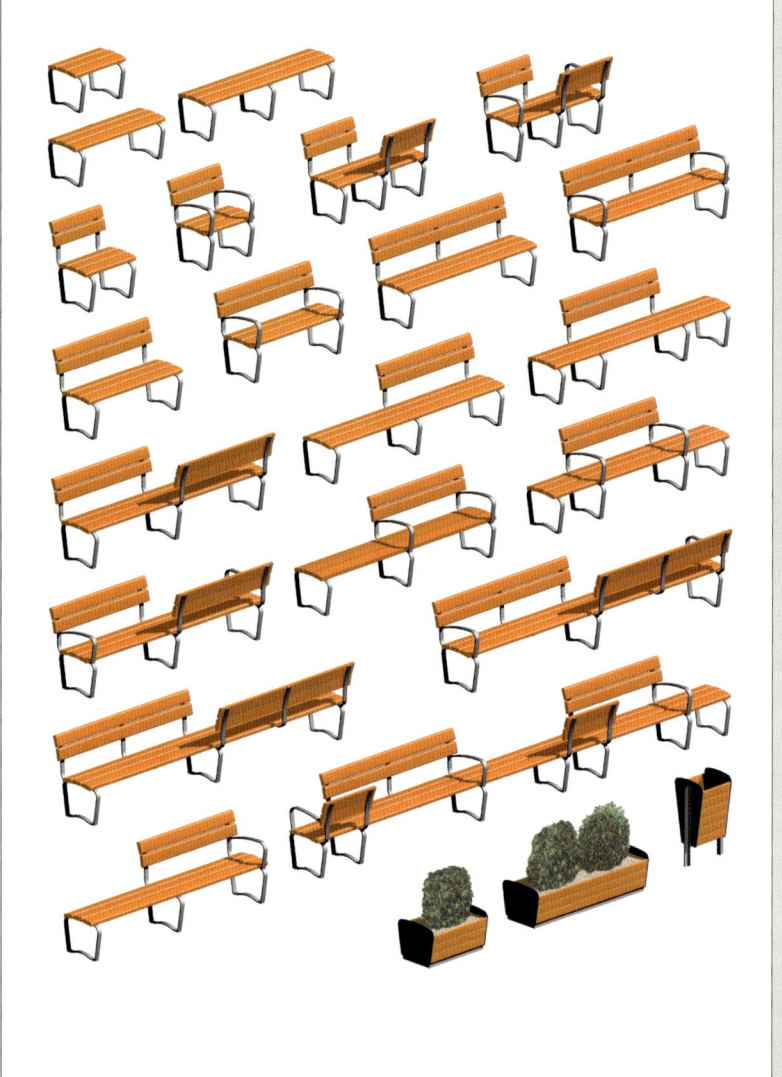

Wing Pedestal

Design: **Rud Thygesen** • Production: **GH form**

The Wing pedestal has a mahogany seat mounted on a steel structure. Wing was introduced at the Carpenters Fall Exhibition 2006, in Frederiksberg Garden.

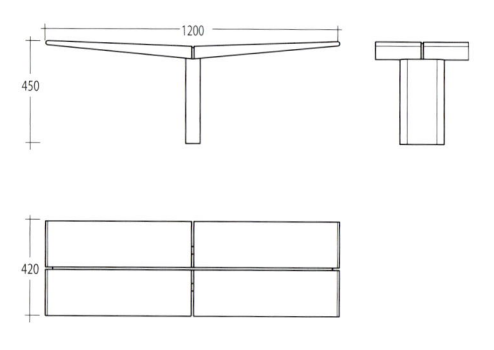

Xurret System

Design: **Ábalos & Herreros** • Production: **Escofet**

What do we do in public space? Basically we sit or stand, be still or in motion. If we see it in these terms, a bench is more than just a seat; it's an element that condenses the gaze and motion, an object that demands a form of construction that goes beyond the traditional fundamentals of ergonomics. A bench dictates how we seat and where we look, it doesn't prefigure our behaviour in a definitive way, it stands between us and the landscape ambiguously, with a degree of autonomy from both. This is why it can establish unforeseen dialogues, and seems to be an optimistic and exciting stimulus to create a relationship between the body and the external world. Xurret Sytem is a system for building points of reference, an open combination of five pieces and four colours that tries to trigger different ways of appropriating and activating places.

Main characteristics: A modular urban element, cast in plain concrete with a stripped finish. The Xurret system consists of five elements classified with the letters X, U, RR, E and T, which can form freestyle groups to shape urban or natural landscapes.

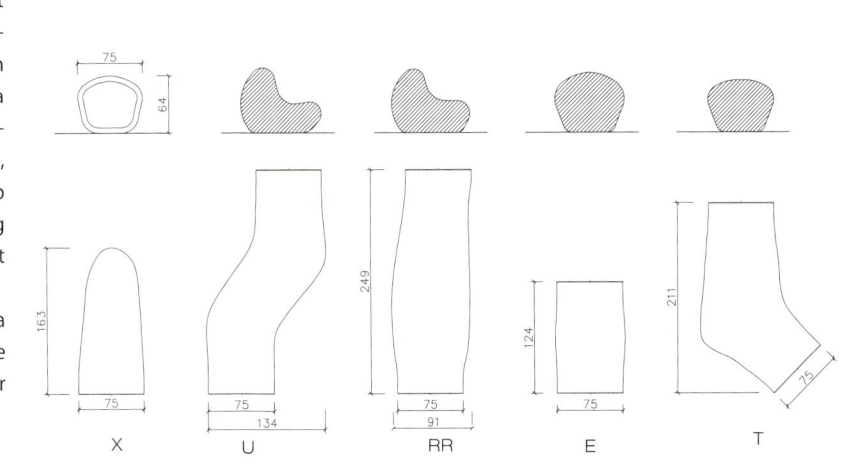

SEATS

Yin-Yang

Design: **Francisco Javier Rodríquez** • Production: **Escofet**

The Yin-Yang bench is basically a reinforced concrete monolith with corrugated steel and a double finish. This brings out a diagonal axe of symmetry that generates a dividing line between the finishes, half sandblasted, half polished. The item's abstract formalization resolves the points it rests upon by means of two folds of the upper surfaces which, cut diagonally, reach down to the ground. The item is installed by means of two M-16 steel rods, 180 mm in length. Total weight: 475 Kg.

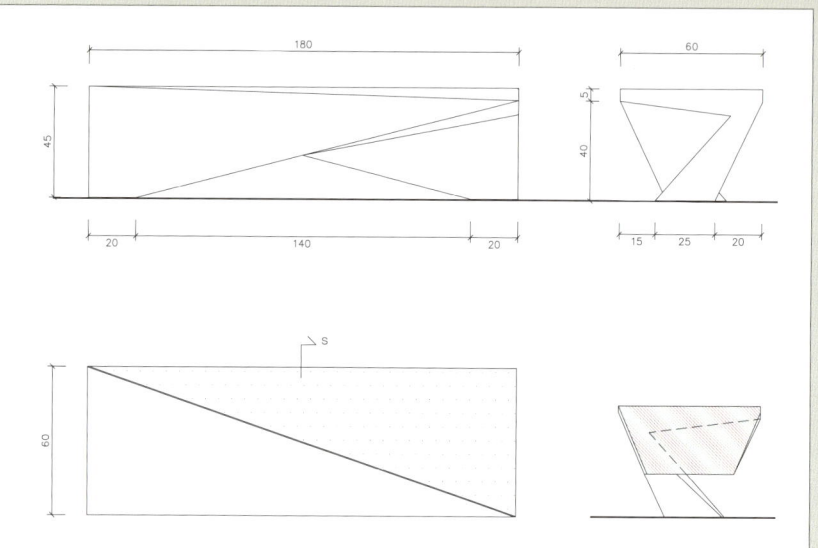

SEATS

Zen

Design: **díez+díez diseño** · Production: **mago:urban**

Besides their basic function as benches, these objects are web suited to environments for the very young, as they are completely devoid of corners or edges; likewise, this article's characteristically rounded and amiable forms blend well into the environment of nature. It is an object that can be used as an architectural boundary, in order to define or limit certain areas; its rounded form enables it to fit into many different situations with great compositional versatility.

The design arose from a visit to the Chillida Leku, the sculpture garden of the Basque artist Eduardo Chillida, in which the designers commissioned themselves to produce a type of seat that could be installed without clashing with the surroundings or the artworks in such a special place; the result was a bench that is simply an idealized rock, the thing most commonly sought for by anyone wishing to sit down in nature.

Manufactured out of concrete in a variety of colors. With a diameter of 65 cm and a height of 43 cm, the item has a weight of 260 kg. Installation is by simply placing the item on the ground.

SEATS

Planters

AJC

Design and production: Microarquitectura

Geometrical planter with highly distinctive feet, a composition which plays with volumes, light and shadow.
Of generous dimensions, it is available in two standard sizes for flowering plants or bushes and in customized sizes on request.
The elements in the AJC series: bench, wastebasket, street lamp, planter and boundary edges combine elegantly together when used in the same project.

Arcadia

Design: díez+díez diseño

This image corresponds to the award winning project in the First Public Space Design Competition organized by CTAP (Centro Tecnológico Andaluz de la Piedra: Andalusian Stonework Technological Center).
The project aimed to generate a program for the creation of urban spaces that go beyond the mere definition of the items of public furniture, to become a defining factor of the location. The image shows us an example of a tree planter that blends into the pavement which it is an integral part of. Emulating the typical protuberances of the terrain that arise around the foot of a tree, in this case a further protuberance appears in the form of a welcoming seat, which seems to be just another random incidental of the surrounding landscape.

Barcina

Design: Jaume Bach - Gabriel Mora • Production: Fundició Dúctil Benito

This planter has become established as a constant presence throughout the urban context of the city of Barcelona. It is a sturdy piece of public furniture conceived as a suitable inclusion into any sort of environment, with a formal appearance that makes a classical, deeply-rooted statement. The choice of an exceptionally durable material such as cast iron guarantees the "Barcina" planter its optimal resistance to any sort of erosion, thereby minimizing the maintenance budget correspondingly. The simple yet elegant circular bowl rests upon three spherical feet. One of these is perforated to drain away excess water while permitting the bowl's balance to be adjusted to the possible inclination of the pavement.

BdLove Planter

Design: Ross Lovegrove • Production: Bd

The BdLove Planter is made of medium density polyethylene, roto-molded and pigmented, containing five stainless steel reinforcement bars. It also has a self-watering system that consists of a circular disk with its capillary absorption cords, a water level indicator, a water supply pipe and three drainage bags. Non-slip EPDM rubber feet allow the water to drain correctly underneath the BdLove Planter, which is attached to the floor by means of stainless steel bolts. The planter comes in the following colours: fluorescent red (only for indoor use), beige, white, blue, green and sandstone (sand coloured granite) and millstone (dark coloured granite). It can also be custom made in special colours. The units are stackable and each unit measures 1.356 x 1.000 x 483 mm and weighs approximately 27 kg. The planter can be weighed down with water or clean sand, for extra stability.

PLANTERS 125

Bilbao

Design: Josep Muxart • **Production:** Escofet

The Bilbao series consists of a planter and a bench made of cast reinforced concrete. It has been designed to lend an organic and gentle look to the rigidity of the material. Thus, it features a mixture of curved lines and warped surfaces. The items are disquieting and seem to move discreetly. Their size makes them environmentally friendly. The concrete is sandblasted and waterproofed, which gives the material the appearance of natural stone. The pyramid shaped planter has a triangular base and the sides are slightly convex. The final shape is obtained by a circular torsion displacement of the upper plane in respective of the lower plane which generates arched surfaces. The angle of vision also influences it, creating a sequence of apparently different yet similar objects.

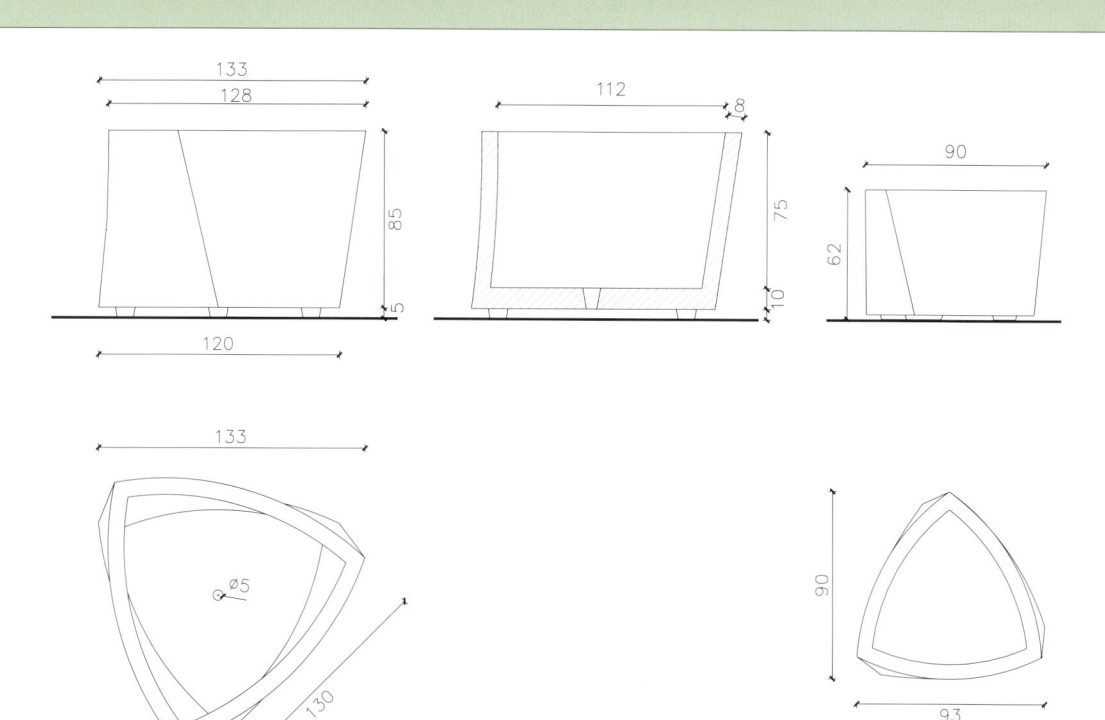

PLANTERS

Botánica

Design: **Gabriel Teixidó** • Production: **Macaedis**

This planter was conceived for the most favorable display of the natural qualities of stone. It consists of four blocks, which give it great stability. The treatment the material has undergone is such as to assure that the unavoidable contact with the vegetable soil in which the plants live will not alter the exterior appearance of the article. Its beveled corners allow it to be flexibly introduced in all sorts of placements. The item can be produced in Eneus marble, Iberian Cream, grey sandstone or white limestone, with a matt or medium-gloss finish texture. It is designed to be placed resting directly on the floor, and comes in three different sizes, which measure 1200 x 1200 x 500 mm, 1000 x 1000 x 450 mm or 800 x 800 x 400 mm; these options are respectively able to contain volumes of 440, 280 y 150 liters, and weights of 755, 450 y 280 kg.

Canasto

Design: **Diana Cabeza** • Colors: **Elisabet Cabeza** • Production: **Estudio Cabeza**

The Canasto planter is part of a product line that consists of a large planter, a medium planter and a basket, providing a coherently integrated solution for both indoor and outdoor public spaces of a municipal, institutional, commercial or corporate nature. With a range of eight intense and luminous colors inspired in the Pre-Columbian cultures of South America and a size and volume of considerable generosity, this alternative is well suited to the dimensions and scale of these spaces. Their form and color express both the traditions, the culture and the identity of that part of the world. The material is pigmented polyethylene, formed by roto-molding and finished with a sand-blasted surface texture. The dimensions of the large model are 114 × 83 cm (44.84 × 32.62 inches) and the medium sized item measures 92 × 76 cm (36.15 × 29.86 inches).

Botánica

Canasto

PLANTERS

Casicilíndrica

Design: Gonzalo Milà - Martina Zink • Production: Santa & Cole

Three plant stands with simple shapes to adorn urban sidewalks. Their different capacities allow for a wide variety of plantings.
Presented in three sizes with different diameters and heights. The plant stand is made of a single piece of cast iron with anti-rust protection, painted dark-grey. The element is simply positioned onto the ground. No maintenance required.

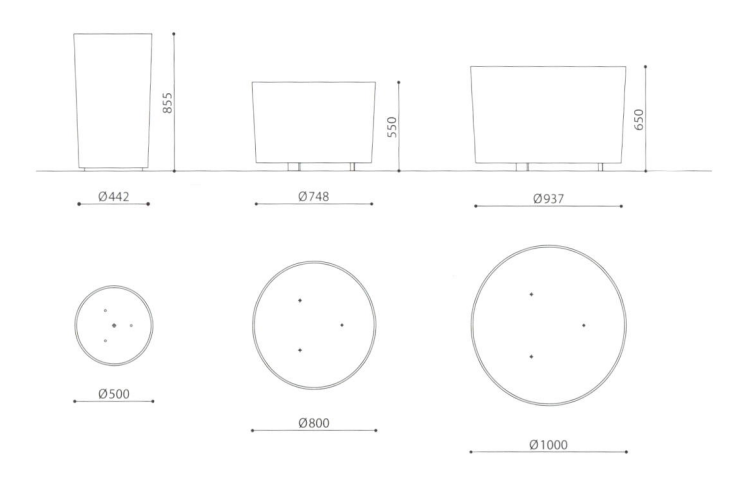

Cestae

Design: Silvia López • Production: Macaedis

Both the name and the physical appearance of this solidly constructed planter read as an allusion to the aesthetic ambiance of classical Rome.
Constructed out of four powerful slabs of stone, the item presents an image of unquestionable solidity within the urban context. The high quality resolution of the joins and the simplicity of the outline make this a pleasingly versatile item to choose, which can be fitted into traditional or more contemporary environments. The Cestae planters are available in the following types of fine marble: Alhambra Yellow, Eneus, White Macael, Green Macael, Golden Travertine, Iberian Cream, Marquina Black, as well as Capri Limestone. The article's dimensions are 600 × 600 × 550 mm (23.58 × 23.58 × 21.61 inches), with an interior capacity of 245 liters (8.65 ft3) and a total weight (when empty) of 160 kg (352.64 lb), due to which the only installation needed is to place it in the correct chosen location.

PLANTERS

Conical Tree Tubs

Design and production: **Streetlife**

These Conical Tree Tubs are available in various diameters, heights and material. They are made of CorTen steel or moulded in thick-walled, insulating synthetic material.
The CorTen steel makes the lifespan of the Conical Tubs almost unlimited (they will never rust through). If required, they can be finished in a RAL color and equipped with a municipal logo.
The standard version of the Syntetic Conical Tree Tub is mat, light grey or anthracite with a granite effect. The two available heights, 110 and 150 cm, permit light-footed layouts. The volume of 1.8 to 2.3 m3 is suited for trees and shrubs of up to 5-6 m tall. The tubs contain facilities to anchor the root ball, and to ensure insulation, good drainage, and the in-flow of air.

Cub

Design and production: **Tecam BCN**

This planter consists of an inner container and a galvanized steel structure with adjustable stainless steel legs. The wall cladding is of autoclave treated wooden boards of Dutch pine, measuring 140 x 35 mm. Another option is available for the lateral walls, consisting of 700 x 700 x 8 mm Trespa panels, an extremely environmentally friendly material patented by Hoechst; it is made of thermo-hardened resins resulting in a material the color of which is absolutely permanent due its particular resistance to ultraviolet radiation; Its resistance to fire or weather conditions is also notable; It requires no maintenance and comes already provided with two coats of water-born varnish.

PLANTERS

Dara

Design: **Josep Suriñach** • Production: **Fundició Dúctil Benito**

Dara is a planter of simple and elegant lines, designed for public spaces and pedestrian areas. It is made of iron which makes it highly resistant to corrosion, resisting up to 300 hours of saline fog. The finish is in RAL colours. Dara is inspired in the traditional garden flower pots, thereby giving an intimate touch to the spaces where they are installed, especially suited for quiet corners of the city.

Diogene

Design: **Alfredo Farnè** • Production: **Neri**

This galvanized steel planter designed by Alfredo Farné is conical in shape with a maximum diameter of 910 mm, a height of 490 mm and a capacity of 115 liters. It contains a polyethylene plant pot with the necessary drainage. The exterior is finished in Neri´s own dark gray paint.

Dish

Design: **Guido Marsille** • Production: **mago:urban**

Using clean lines and a clear-cut outline of the maximum simplicity as the main source of inspiration, this urban planter, shaped like a great, smooth cup in the form of a truncated cone, is well able to adapt to any environment in the city, such as plazas, pedestrian areas or others. The design's particular configuration avoids it being perceived as a visual obstacle. One of its greatest assets, the double function it fulfills as a tree-tub and as a bench, comes to the fore when it is installed in large areas with an important flow of people, or in dynamic or crowded situations like flower shows or commercial centers. As a planter, the smooth finish surface it displays adds a refreshing and elegant touch to its surroundings. As a bench, it is sufficiently wide to accommodate several people at the same time.

Fémina

Design: **Òscar Tusquets Blanca** • Production: **Macaedis**

The Femina planter is a sophisticated marble container out of which the plants emerge through an elegantly scrolled gap between the two halves of the top cover, allowing the necessary space for the stem or the trunk of the plant to grow. The independence between the exterior object and the container inside it make it easy to change or renovate the soil or the type of vegetation; maintenance is also reduced to the minimum. The Femina planter's cubical volume is available in three different sizes and in several varieties of marble, including Travertine Red, Travertine Cream, Macael White, Macael Yellow and Macael Cream.

PLANTERS

Gardel

Design: **Diana Cabeza** • Production: **Estudio Cabeza**

This oversized planter is ideal for squares and public spaces. It is a literal object: a huge plant pot (1100 mm in diameter) realized in pre-molded pigmented concrete, with an ergonomic upper rim, a clear reproduction of the classic ceramic pots so common in domestic gardens. The lower part of the piece has a bush-hammered textural finish. The planter is easily installed: it can be simply rested on the ground or fixed with anchoring bolts according to the tipping load.

Highlife Tree Tubs

Design and production: **Streetlife**

The Highlife tubs are part of the Highlife range, which includes benches and tree-grills. At ground level, these Highlife Tree Tubs can be easily relocated with a forklift truck. The tubs are equipped with FSC Cumaru wooden strips 25mm thick (highest durability class). They are suitable for trees of 12-14 meters. The tubs match perfectly with the Highlife benches.

Urbe

Design: **Joan Gaspar** • Production: **DAE**

The Urbe planter is made of 6 mm thick sheet iron, with a powder coated finish that makes it resistant to corrosion. Moreover, it comes powder-coated with lead-free polyester, which gives greater strength to the exterior finish, with a black wrought-iron effect. The boards are of tropical wood, treated with tinted transparent oil, to enhance the wood's natural beauty and give it maximum protection.

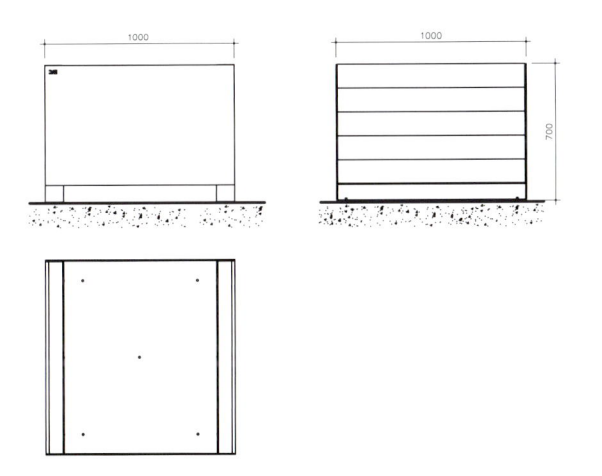

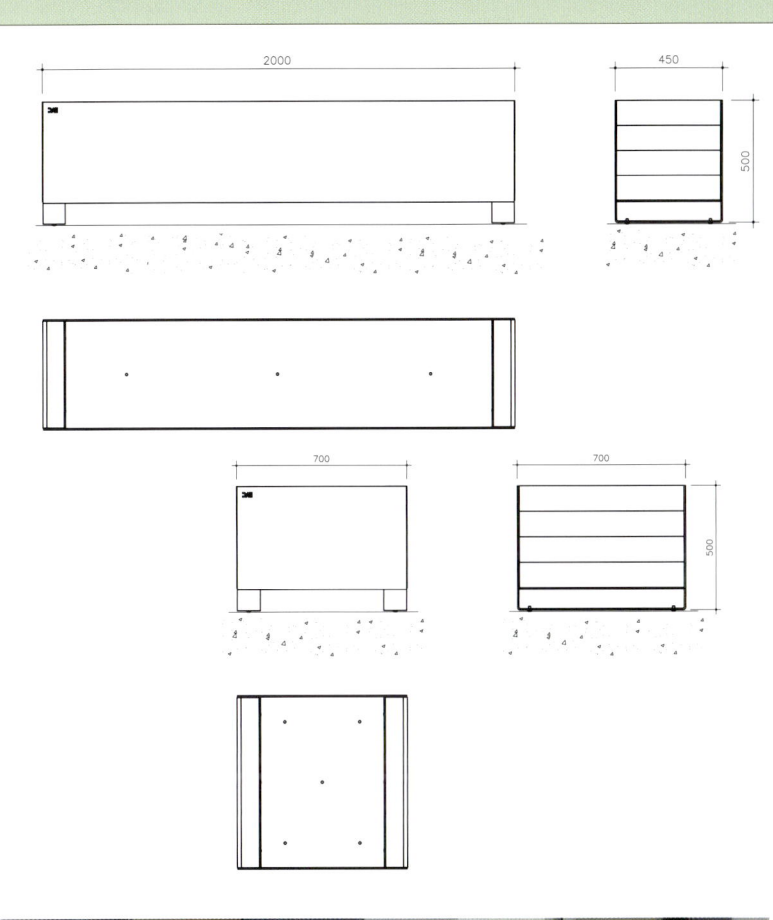

PLANTERS

Tree grids

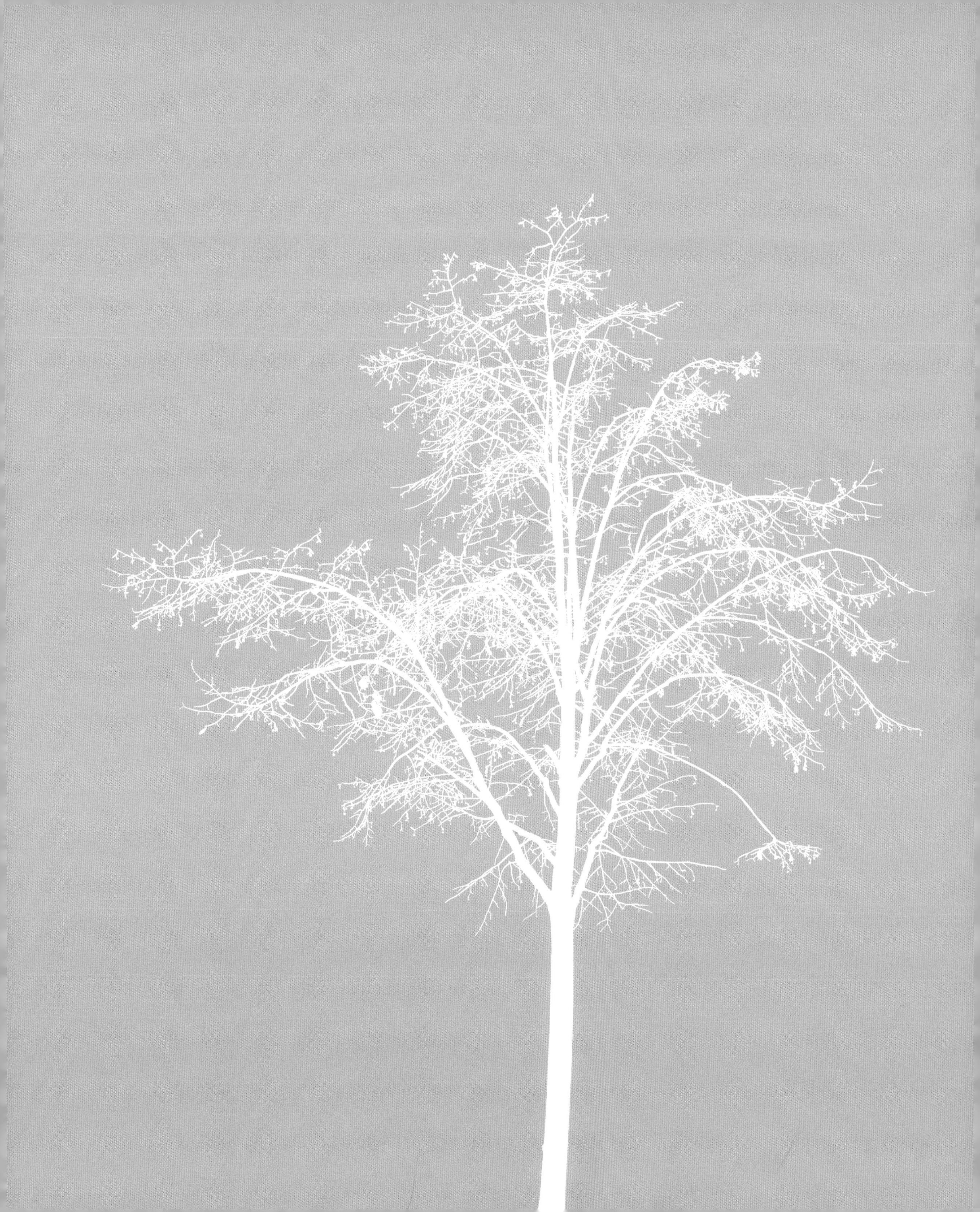

Arboré

Design: **Quim Larrea** • Production: **Macaedis**

Modular construction made of four rectangular elements creating a cross around the tree they surround. The elements are held in a steel structure built in L-shape to protect and solidify the whole set. The material is saw-cut. This process confers the necessary bumpy texture to make it nonslip.
Material: Natural stone and stainless steel. Size: 1000 × 1000 × 43 mm. Weight: 54 kg + 20 kg metal

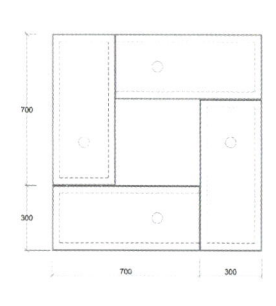

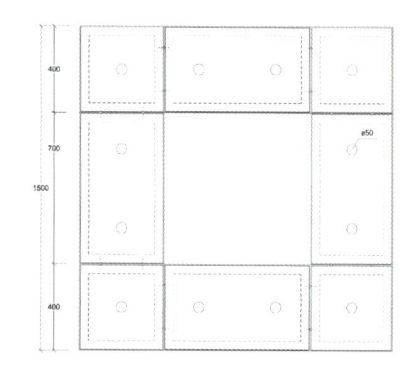

Beiramar

Design: **Guillermo Vázquez Consuegra** • Production: **DAE**

The Beiramar tree-grid consists of a modular piece made of cast aluminium. The perimeter is reinforced and it has radial reinforcement ribs. The object is pierced by a series of leaf-shaped drainage holes that spread outward from the central hollow.
The frame around the tree-hole is made of hot-dip galvanized steel plate, screwed onto the surrounding concrete pavement.

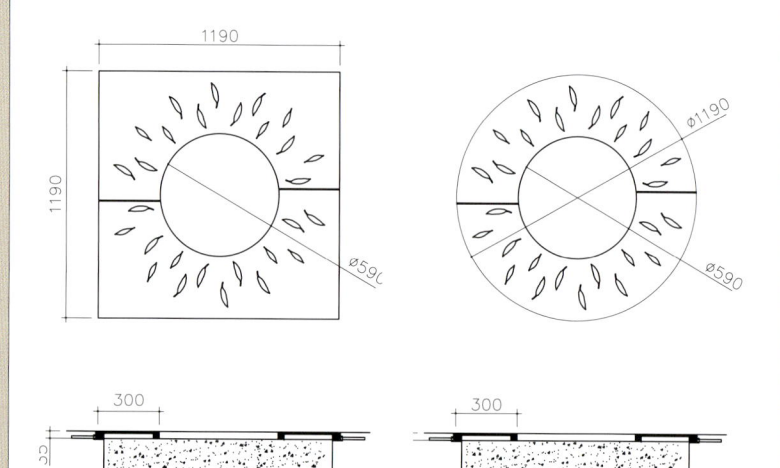

142   TREE GRIDS

Iona

Design: **Tobia Repossi** • Production: **Modo**

A circular planter made of two rounded sheets of Corten steel joined by means of a ring-shaped section in AISI 304
stainless steel. There is an "eight-shaped" hole for the flowers in the centre of the planter. When supplied, the planter doesn't have an oxidised surface, which will appear after a period of natural "aging", due to exposure to atmospheric agents. Iona is available both in the convex and concave version. It is a free-standing planter.

Las Tres Damas

Design: **Andreu Arriola / Carme Fiol** • Production: **Escofet**

These planters for public areas are part of a range of urban furniture called the "The Magic Flute", inspired in the characters and in the music of Mozart's famous opera. The different urban elements of which the series consists have a unique formal character and are made of noble materials; in combination with wood and steel, a harmonious counterpoint is created between the objects, while the melodious dialogue between the objects and the neighboring urban landscape is enhanced.
The entire range of "Las tres damas" (The Three Ladies) is particularly adaptable to all sorts of urban environments, due to the multiplicity of random patterns created by the different plant species they may contain. Despite the choice of Corten steel as the construction material, the shapes revert to the traditional forms of traditional pottery plant containers, to which toughness and wear-proof durability are added, as public urban furniture requires. These planters are the ideal containers for the floral tone of a musical dialogue that can be made to arise in the streets of the city.

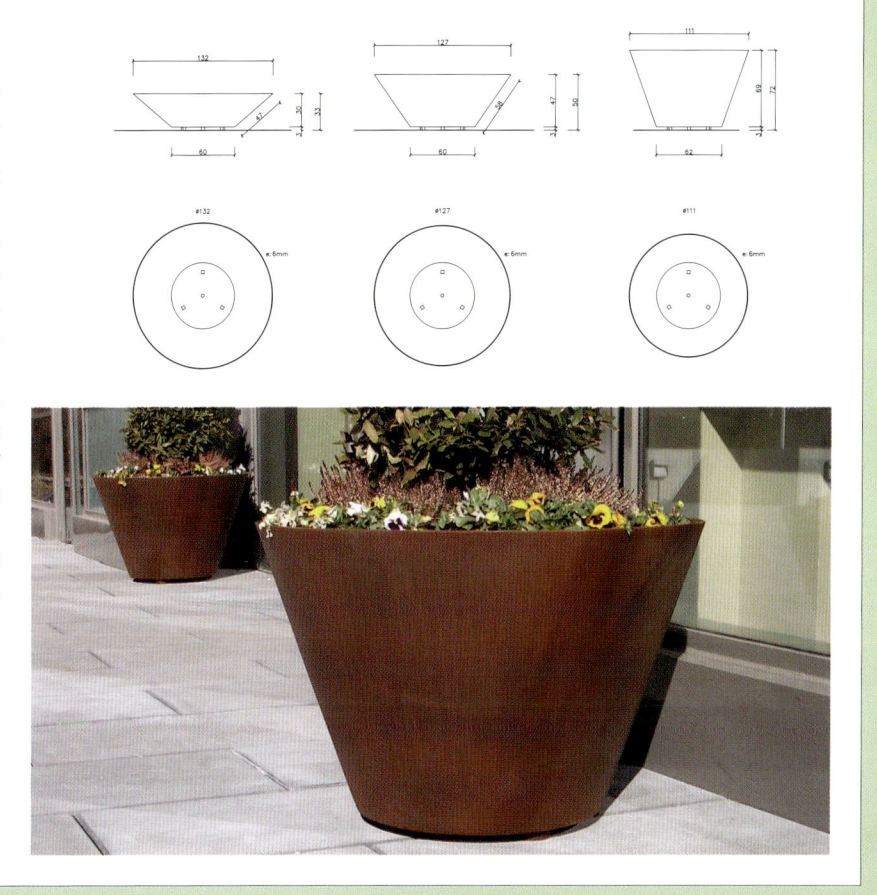

PLANTERS

Lineafiorne

Design: **Bernhard Winkler** • Production: **Euroform**

The Lineafiorne planter designed by professor Bernhard Winkler has a reservoir made of 2 mm metal sheet, hot-dip galvanized and powder coated with RAL colours. This reservoir is covered with untreated hardwood slats 30x59 mm, and finishing wooden slats 60x65 mm. It is a freestanding planter that does not require an anchoring system.

Lolium

Design: **Área de diseño Gitma y Chantilly design** • Production: **Gitma**

This is a modular planter made of Corten steel. It features a sharp slope that shows the flowers it contains to their best advantage. This is achieved by means of a straight piece placed at a 60º angle that permits a variety of combinations. It requires no special fixing to the ground as the weight of the earth prevents it from moving.

Marc

Design and production: **ONN Outside**

The Marc planter features an upper frame to enhance its decorative function and show off its contents to their best advantage. As it is available in two sizes and finishes, this planter covers the requirements of different plant types and is suitable for use in any urban environment. The structure is of Corten steel or zinc plated steel with a two-tone epoxy finish. The bolts and fixtures come in stainless steel.

Morella

Design: **Helio Piñón** • Production: **Escofet**

The name of the Morella series derives from a commission received from the urban planning office of that locality, and the brief to create a solvently constructed, formally coherent series of urban elements with a manifestly genuine character. To achieve the desired quality, resistance to wear and natural appearance, Corten steel was chosen as the main material: The series is made to last both visually and materially, making it a suitable choice to furnish public spaces with permanent facilities of an aesthetic nature, yet avoiding alien decorative statements that might disrupt the existing contextual environment. These items are well-suited to historic sites, where textures and atmospheres generated by superimposed cultures and periods cannot be interfered with lightly and where the placement of extraneous elements requires the conjunction of high quality and a low profile.

PLANTERS

Plaza

Design: J.A Martínez Lapeña / Elías Torres • Production: Santa & Cole

Plaza is a great planter for trees and arborescent vegetation, consisting of different panels of different materials and finishes for spaces in which traditional planting is not feasible. The structure is made of steel angle-irons with a powder coated anti-corrosive protection in a black, wrought-iron-like finish. This structure supports the panels, which are made of impact and damp resistant materials, such as stainless steel, polyester resin panels or tropical wood. The bottom is made of hot-dip galvanized steel mesh capable of supporting weights of up to 1.000 kg. The inner container is made of fiberglass. The item merely requires placing on its four adjustable stainless steel legs to achieve a perfectly level and stable installation. It requires zero maintenance.

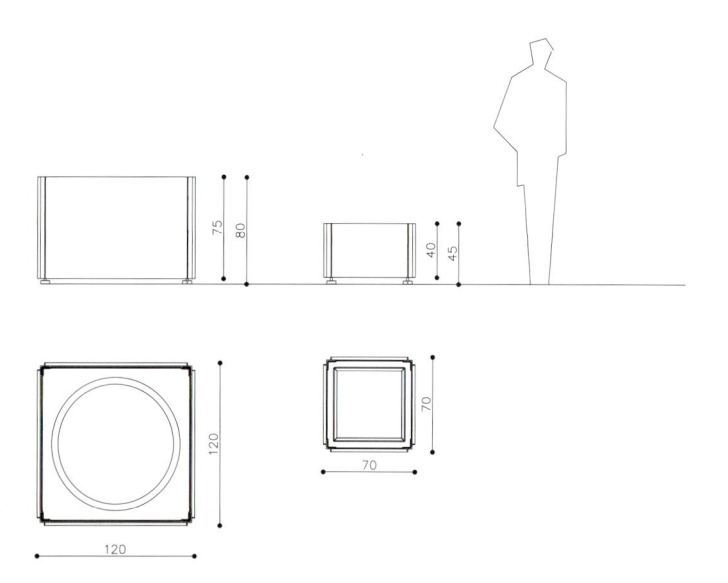

Shrubtub

Design and production: Streetlife

The Shrubtub are made of 4mm CorTen steel as standard. They contain a volume of growth medium up to 5 m3 and are suitable for shrubs, multi-stemmed trees and bigger city trees depending on the substrate volume. The Treetec nursing system is optional. The CorTen tub is well detailed, functional and deliverable with special double powder coating. The Shrubtubs are easy to move and anchoring of the root ball is possible. The single sides are strengthened to prevent bending by soil pressure. The bottom has special holes for water drainage and oxygen supply. The walls should be equipped with thick-walled geotextile for good insulation and oxygen distribution.

PLANTERS

Sputnik

Design and production: Colomer

This very robust circular container for plants has a clearly sculptural outline. It is made of grey coloured cast iron according to the quality norms UNE-EN-1561. The joints are sealed with zinc phosphate primer. The legs are available in a range of different finishes and materials. The entire item has received an anti-corrosive treatment and comes with a wrought iron finish. The various component parts are held together with zincified steel screws. The planter has the noteworthy capacity of 332 litres and its weight amounts to approximately 260 Kg. The only installation required is to place it on the ground in the desired location.

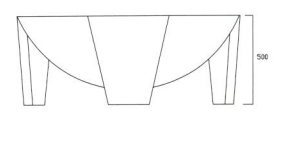

PLANTERS

Tanit L

Design: Ton Riera Ubía • Production: mago:urban

The most notable characteristic of this planter is its exceptionally large dimensions (190x190x115 cm) which make possibly the largest item of its kind available in the market of reinforced concrete garden accessories. Its great volume and the amount of earth it can contain allow for the cultivation of large bushes and even a great variety of tree species, making it the ideal choice for the installation gardens in space not initially planned for that purpose. In spite of the huge bulk of the object, its surface texture, which consists of an uninterrupted succession of horizontal lines on its four sides, manages to relieve the sensation of weight without being detrimental to its overall image of sobriety and elegance.

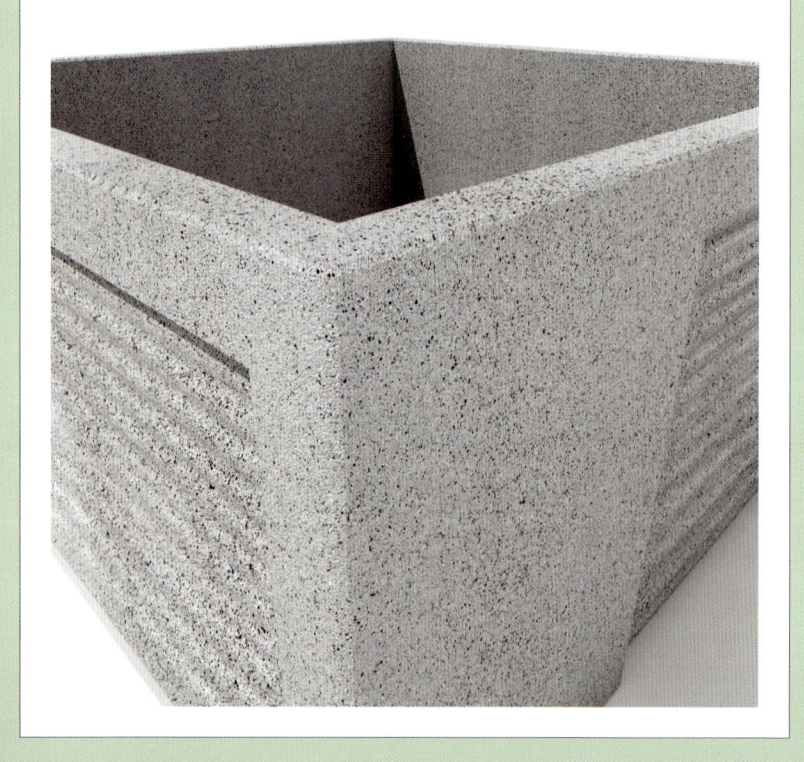

Tram

Design: Jaume Artigues, Miquel Roig • Production: Santa & Cole

Made out of cast iron, the assets this planter offers are its large capacity and a singularly ornamental value. It can be used to introduce vegetation into a domestic or a public and urban context, where it can even be implemented to create urban barriers and limits, aligned in a variety of configurations. It is available in three sizes, the dimensions of which are 2.00x0.45m, 1.00x0.45m, and 0.90x0.45m. Its height, 0.50m, remains the same in all three models. The article consists of one single element of cast iron, protected with an anti-corrosive treatment and painted with black 'wrought iron' finish paint. It includes a set of holes in the side for the installation of an automatic watering system. It is designed to be installed by simply placing it in the desired position. According to the model, the items weight varies between 172 kg and 190 kg.

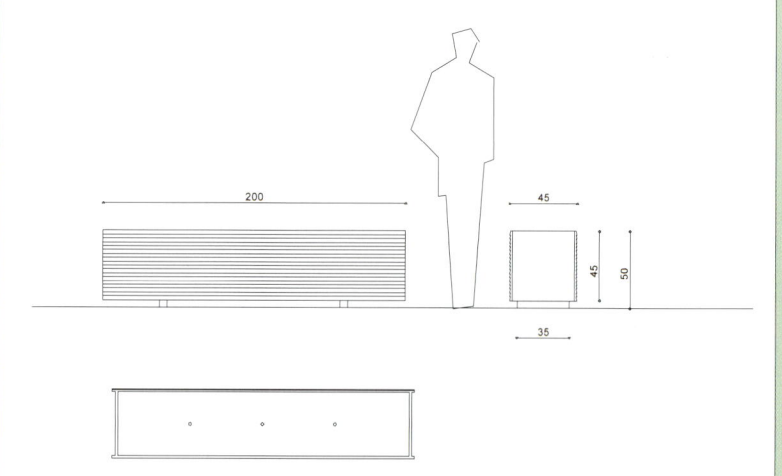

138 PLANTERS

Urbe

Design: **Joan Gaspar** • Production: **DAE**

The Urbe planter is made of 6 mm thick sheet iron, with a powder coated finish that makes it resistant to corrosion. Moreover, it comes powder-coated with lead-free polyester, which gives greater strength to the exterior finish, with a black wrought-iron effect. The boards are of tropical wood, treated with tinted transparent oil, to enhance the wood's natural beauty and give it maximum protection.

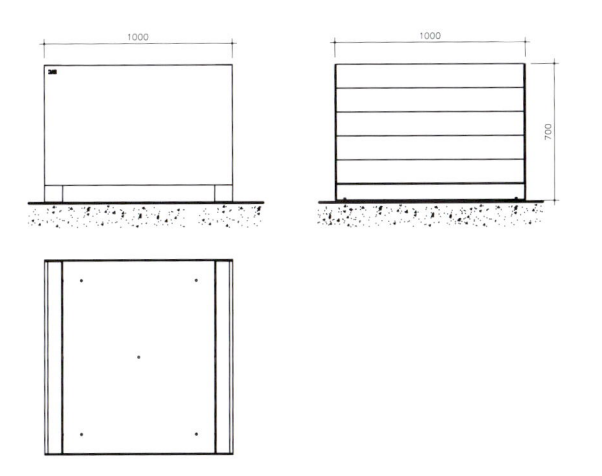

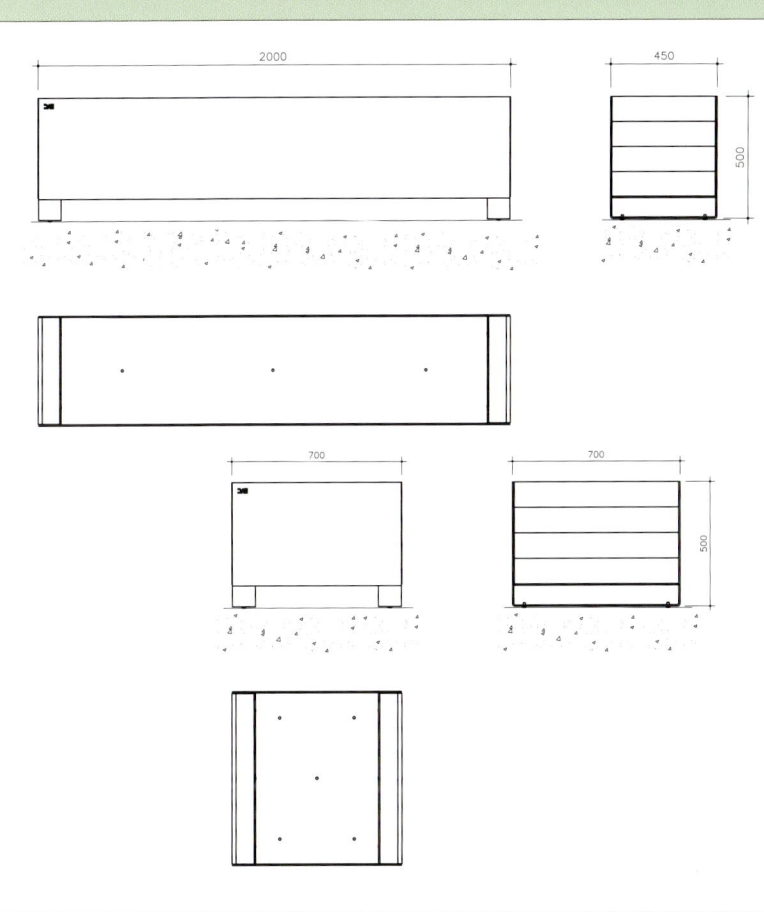

PLANTERS

Tree grids

Arboré

Design: **Quim Larrea** • Production: **Macaedis**

Modular construction made of four rectangular elements creating a cross around the tree they surround. The elements are held in a steel structure built in L-shape to protect and solidify the whole set. The material is saw-cut. This process confers the necessary bumpy texture to make it nonslip.
Material: Natural stone and stainless steel. Size: 1000 × 1000 × 43 mm. Weight: 54 kg + 20 kg metal

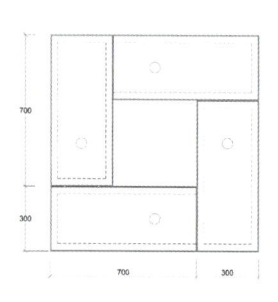

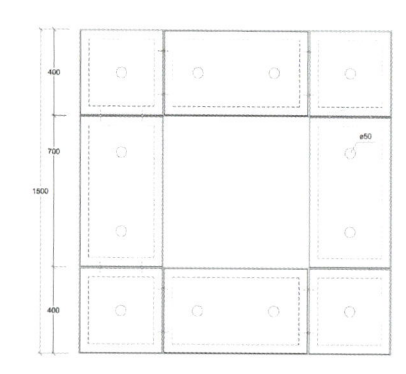

Beiramar

Design: **Guillermo Vázquez Consuegra** • Production: **DAE**

The Beiramar tree-grid consists of a modular piece made of cast aluminium. The perimeter is reinforced and it has radial reinforcement ribs. The object is pierced by a series of leaf-shaped drainage holes that spread outward from the central hollow.
The frame around the tree-hole is made of hot-dip galvanized steel plate, screwed onto the surrounding concrete pavement.

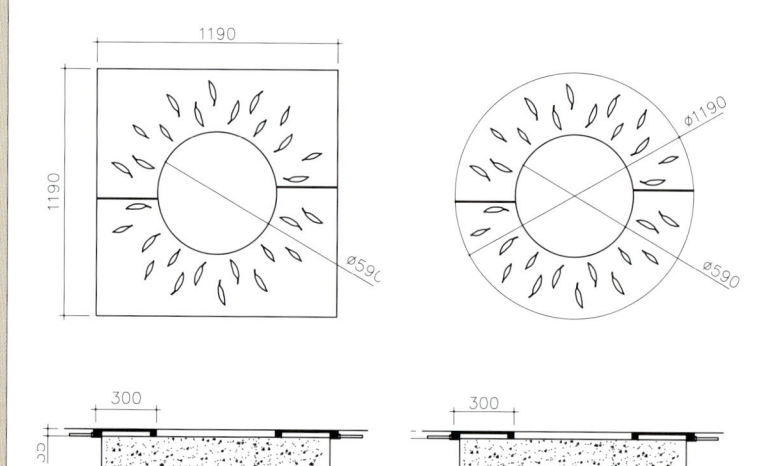

142   TREE GRIDS

Campus

Design: **SLA** • Production: **GH form**

Both types of tree grid come in untreated cast iron and consist of three sections. The rectangular grid has one continuous piece and two others with an identical semicircular hole that provides for flexible installation possibilities in relation to the surrounding pavement and asymmetrical placement around the tree. The grids are provided with a steel frame.

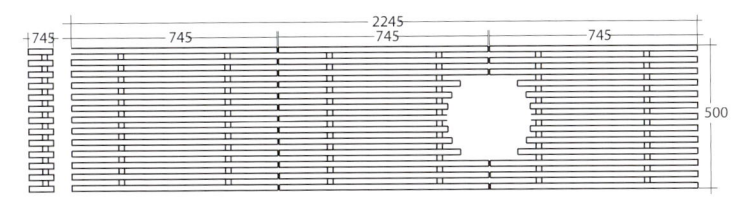

TREE GRIDS

Cap i Cua

Design: Juan Carlos Bolaños • Production: mago:urban

The Cap I Cua tree-grid consists of two identical elements made of structural concrete with a resistance of 400 Kg/cm2. The item is entirely self-supporting, resting directly upon the layer of concrete underneath the paving material, thereby making it very easy to install. Moreover, its dimensions are in accord with the various formats of industrially produced paving materials (20x20, 30x20, 30x30, 40x40, 60x40). It is very resistant: with a thickness of 8cm, it is guaranteed to support even vehicles with a load of up to 900 Kg per wheel.

CorTen Tree Grids

Design and production: Streetlife

The thick-walled CorTen steel Tree Grids are equipped with a random dot pattern. They are available in a round and a square variant, both with a tree hole of Ø 35 cm. Made-to-measure items can be customized in terms of dimensions and graphic pattern.

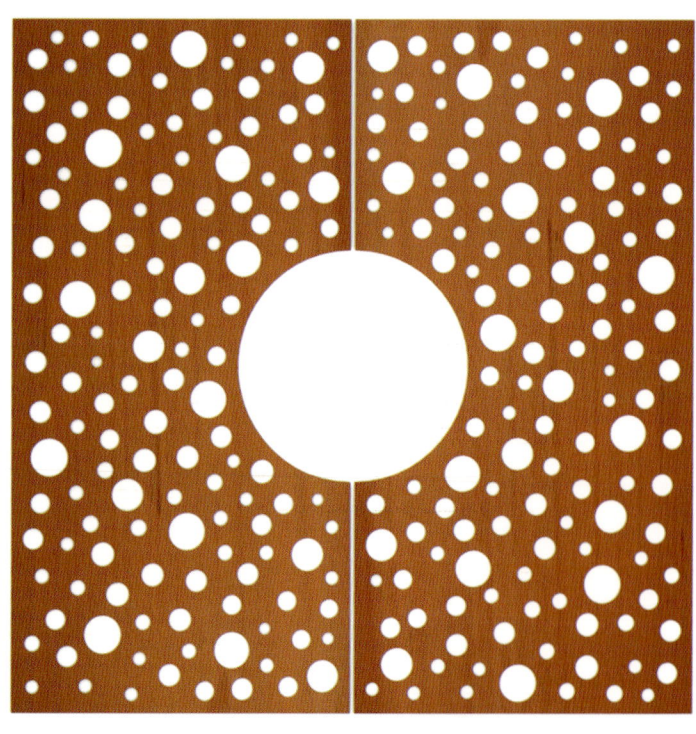

144 TREE GRIDS

Helix

Design: **Greg Healey** • Production: **Street and Park Furniture**

The impetus for this piece was a trip through South Australia's outback. Greg has responded to the forms, textures and colours of this extraordinary landscape in the realisation of much of this new range of urban street furniture. This adaptable range of furniture is particularly suitable for the use in contemporary streetscape design as it draws on Australian landscape forms in a unique and innovative way.

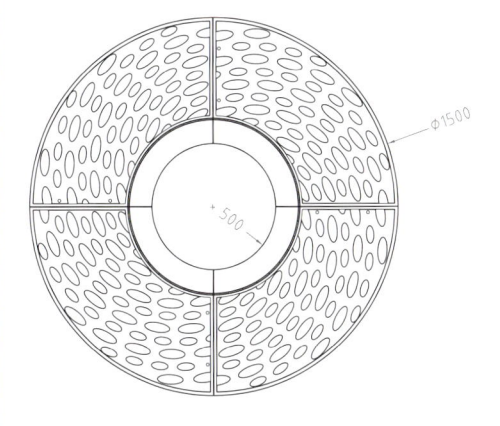

Iris

Design: **Roger Albero** • Production: **DAE**

Trees are an essential item in the urban landscape: the aesthetic reason is that they introduce a living element of significant dimensions to relieve the monotony of the predominantly orthogonal geometry of the prevailing architectural environment. The environmental reason is that they recycle the air we live on. Public urban space is characterized by its regular pavement almost more than by its buildings; thus, each tree-inhabited gap violates the nature of urban space. The problem addressed by the Iris Tree Grid is the following: how to create a gap large enough for the care and well-being of the tree, yet small enough to avoid a safety hazard. The Iris Tree Grid is a modular urban system designed to fit into a wide steel frame around a square tree planter, reducing the hole to little more than the diameter of the tree trunk. It consists of four right triangles made of painted cast iron, of a size and weight that makes them easy to remove and reinstall for maintenance work on the tree. Each modular element has a grid along one side to drain storm water into the tree-trough; the spikes of the grid adjust to the opposite side of the following module. The modules come in a range of sizes, making the system adaptable to a variety of different tree and tree-tub dimensions.

TREE GRIDS

Pictorial

Design: **Antoni Roselló Til** • Production: **Santa & Cole**

These four tree grids are inspired in the work of four of the crucial artists of the early twentieth century: Klee, with a pattern of spirals that refers to prehistoric inscriptions and evokes the mysteries of nature; Kandinsky and his very personal graphic vocabulary of symbols and signs; Matisse, and his characteristic arabesques of organic and vegetable motifs; and Mondriaan with his dynamically balanced rhythmic geometry spreading into space. Each of these compositions introduces art into the urban environment in a subtle manner and resolves the continuity between the tree and the sidewalk in a meaningful way. The grid consists of two or four identical modular components made of cast nodular iron with a granular finish and without any further treatment. The frame of the tree tub is made of hot-dip galvanized steel. The dimensions are 148 × 148 cm and 98 × 98 cm.

TREE GRIDS

Quadris

Design: **Martins Pereira** • Production: **Larus**

This luxurious tree grid is composed of four massive-looking surfaces of cast iron, designed to form two rectangular alignments on either side of the tree trunk. Two wooden surfaces bridge the gap, completing the composition of a square frame around the tree. At the same time, the two square wooden decks introduce a lighter element in weight, in color and in feeling. The different parts are joined by threaded bolts, with a series of tubular washers that maintain the distance between the parts. The cast iron elements are hot-dip galvanized and painted. The wooden decks are made of highly weather-resistant Ipê or Garapa wood, to which a weatherproofing treatment has been added. The cast iron elements measure 400 × 600 mm; the wooden decks measure 400 × 400 mm, as does the central hole. The entire object covers a square space of 1200 × 1200 mm.

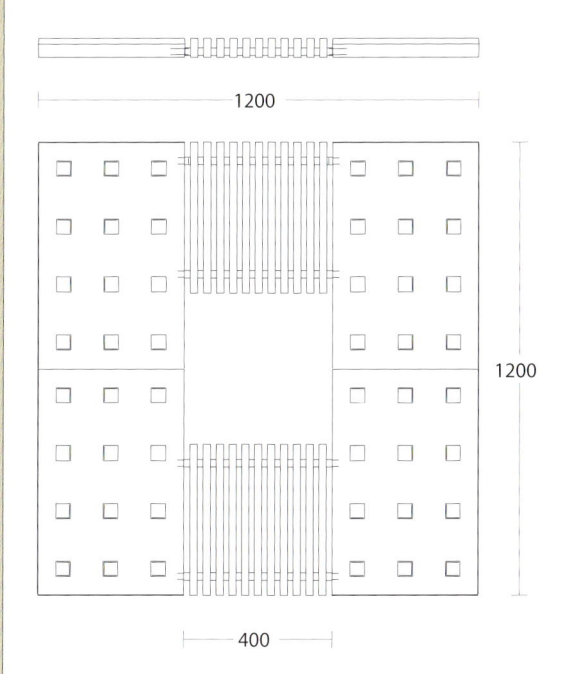

Rámla

Design: **Pere Cabrera & Jaume Artigues** • Production: **Escofet**

The name of this tree grid comes from the Arab term "ramla", meaning gravel or sand-pit, which later derived into the popular Latin term "Rambla", indicative of a torrent or dry river bed that only carries water after heavy rainfall. This item is designed for paved areas in the city, to distinguish or define the area the trees are planted in, and allows storm-water to flow in or out freely. In the Mediterranean area, the presence of torrential rains enables tree-holes to be virtually self-cleaning.

There are various different formats and accessories that allow a versatile adaptation of this item to existing trees: the tree grid can be enlarged or contracted as needed.

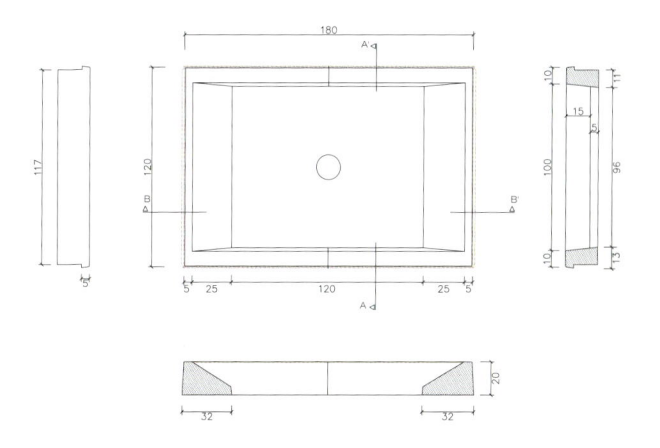

TREE GRIDS

Taulat

Design: **Bernat Matorell Pena** • Production: **Fundició Dúctil Benito**

This tree-grid has a simple and functional design that permits the tree to grow without bursting the tree-grid or the pavement. The arches can be cut out according to the girth of the tree, so this item can easily adapt to any tree and remain functional during the growth of its entire life-span.

Tree Isles

Design and production: **Streetlife**

The circular Tree Isles come in three sizes with diameters of 3, 4 or 5 meters. The tree isles consist of laser-cut CorTen steel sections whose edges can be set into a perimeter of FSC hardwood that functions as a seat. Tapered filling wedges between the beams seal the seating perimeter. The tree isles are completely freestanding on the concrete deck or other material. Streetlife also produces large Tree Isles in oval and free forms, thus converting hard urban locations into sympathetic sitting and resting places. A good reference point is the Bastiaansplein in Delft, with its three oval tree islands (9 × 4 m) with large pagoda trees above a car park.

148   TREE GRIDS

TV

Design: **Ernest Perera** • Production: **mago:urban**

This tree-grid consists of two identical parts made of structural concrete that has a shearing stress resistance of 83 kg per cm2 and withstands a compression stress of 350 Kg per cm^2. It is easy to install as it can be rested directly on the concrete slab beneath the pavement. It has a series of runnels all around the perimeter to enable the entrance or exit of water. Its dimensions are such as to make it compatible with a range of industrially produced paving materials (20 × 20, 30 × 20, 30 × 30, 40 × 40, and 60 × 40). Its thickness of 8cm is guaranteed to support even vehicles with a load of up to 900 Kg per wheel.

Yarg

Design: **Enric Pericas** • Production: **Escofet**

Yarg is a tree tub designed by the architect Enric Pericas and produced by Escofet, in fulfillment of a project commissioned by the City institute of parks and Gardens, requiring a tree tub design adjusted to the needs of medium sized trees to be planted along narrow sidewalks and the inner alleys within the blocks of buildings in Barcelona's Ensanche district. The exterior frame is a rectangular volume made of galvanized steel sheet, and measures 180 × 80 cm. Combining the upper components permits four different configurations according to the requirements, with one single blocking system and no screws. The lateral covers measure 80 × 51 cm; they are made of soft cast iron and have triangular ventilation holes and a lower surface reinforced with flanges.

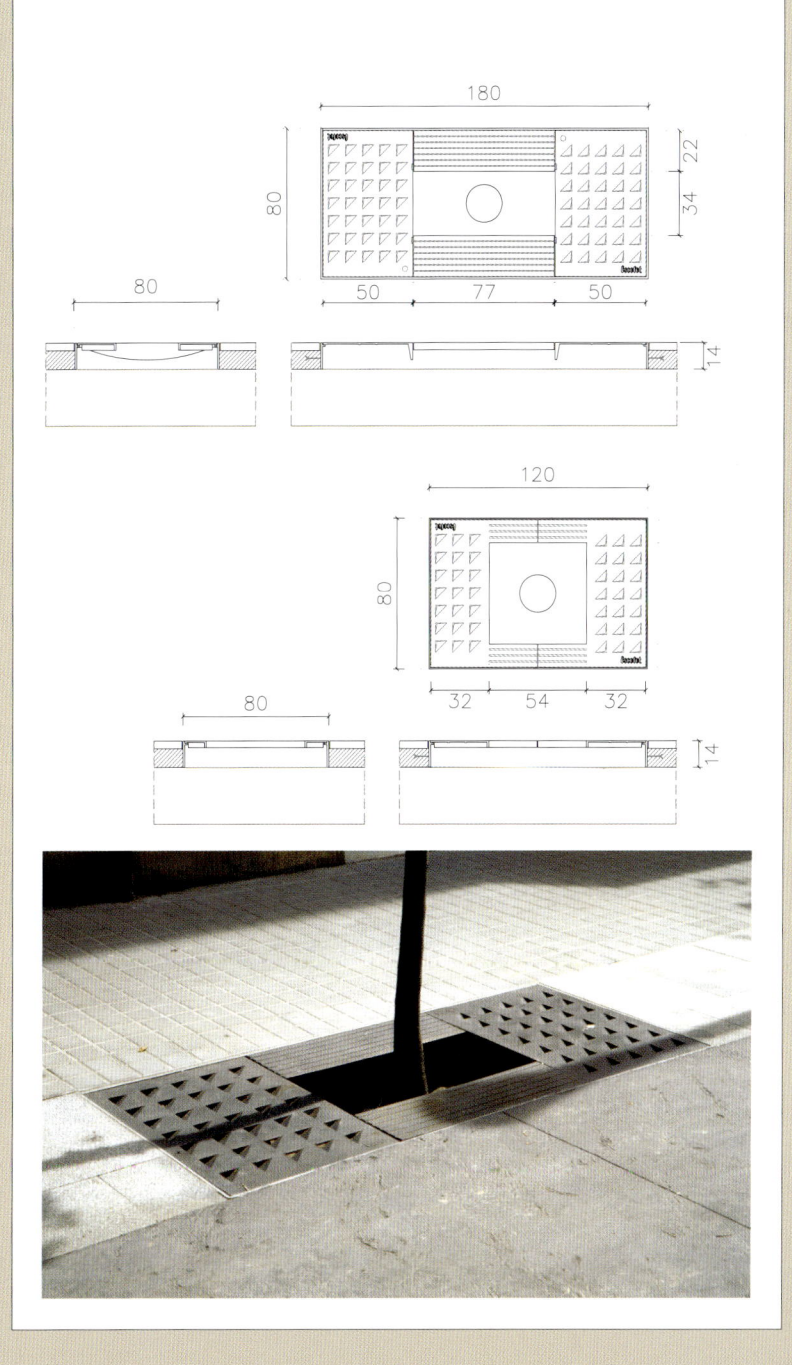

TREE GRIDS

Bicycle racks

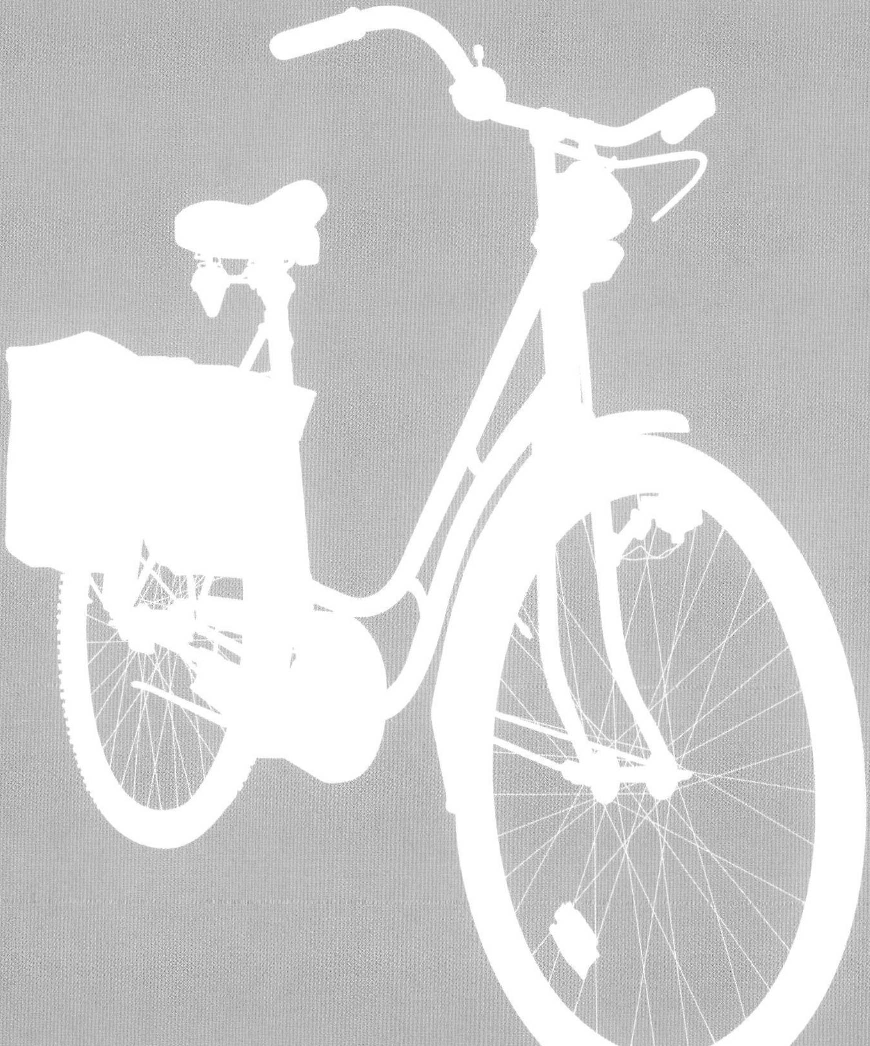

127

Design and production: **mago:urban**

The bike station 127, conceived and manufactured by mago:urban, features the possibility of parking three bikes at the same time. It also includes a ring that can be used with any kind of bike lock. The ends have been designed to allow more station 127s to be connected, as and when space for more bikes is needed.

Arca

Design: **Tobia Repossi** • Production: **Modo**

Steel bicycle rack, consisting of a basic element of 40 × 10 steel plate forming a spiral curve with an inner diameter of 850 mm. Arcas is supplied with a base, consisting of a press curved, 120 × 30 mm angle iron, to be fixed to the ground with M10 80 mm expansion screws.
The item is available in three versions: in FE 360 B steel, in stainless steel and in Cor-ten steel. The bicycle rack is hot-dip galvanized and powder coated, with thermo-hardened powders for outdoor use.
The structure is planned to hold up to 5 bicycles.
Dimensions: height 900 mm, length 1900 mm, depth 900 mm.
Bicycles held: 5

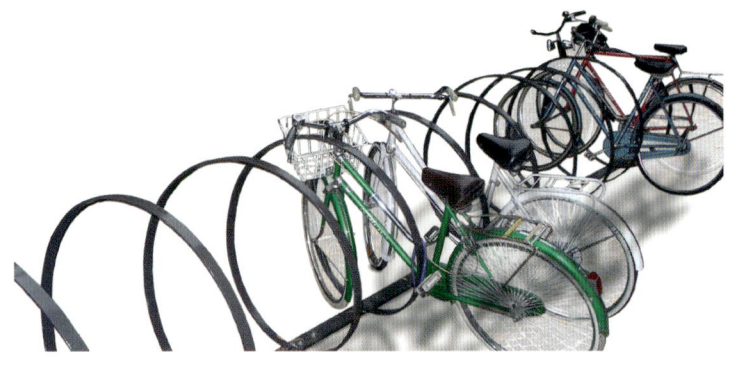

BICYCLE RACKS

Ba

Design: **Tobia Repossi** • Production: **Modo**

This unusually shaped rack for a single bicycle is a beautifully styled sculptural curve when not in use. It is made of a 30 mm Ø stainless steel tube (specification AISI 304) that is curved so that its shape permits a bicycle to be parked by simply positioning the wheel in the middle. It is supplied with a 150 mm Ø domed base-plate that keeps the wheel stationary. The optional finishes are glazed, polished or electropolished.
Installation requires the lower 200 mm of the tubes (up to the domed base-plate) buried in the ground.
The item measures 750 mm in height, 140 mm in width and 670 mm in length. The codification is 05BA600. It holds one bicycle.

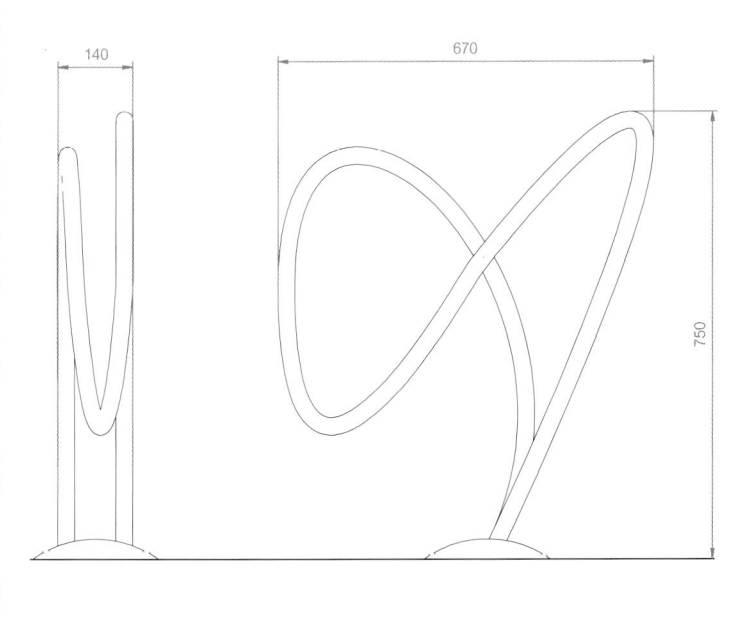

BCPark

Design: **Brunetti Filipponi Associati** • Production: **ORA Centurelli**

The BC Park is a bicycle rack with space for 5 bicycles, consisting of a structure made out of a single 6 mm thick sheet of metal. 5 slits for positioning the bicycle and 5 slits to attach the bicycle locks have been cut through the metal surface, using plasma or laser technology. The upper part is rounded, with a bending radius ideally suited to parking 5 bicycles. Metal plates are welded onto the two lower ends, with holes to introduce the anchoring system, fixing the item to the floor by means of bolts and expanding plugs in the introduced in the pavement. Holes and bushing are welded to the structure, which has a dowel for fitting the marker rod.
The marker rod is an iron tube with an external diameter of 21 mm. Welded at the top end is a rectangular sheet of metal banner with the perforated letters "B C PARK", cut using plasma or laser technology.

BICYCLE RACKS

Bicilínea

Design: **Beth Galí** • Production: **Santa & Cole**

For the realization of this bicycle rack, the designer modified the typical model of a linear railing, adding curved supports or braces that suit it perfectly to the function of holding bicycles, either leaned against it or firmly attached by their frame and a lock. The railing support consists of a stainless steel shoe or base, with a matt finish. The railing itself and the slanted extensions are made of stainless steel tubing, gauge Ø 84 and 51 × 2 mm wall-thickness, polished, and joined with stainless steel screws. Its modular character makes this item adaptable to multiple combinations. The supports are fixed by means of Ø 35 mm bolts for the feet and Ø 16 mm for the arms. The weight of each initial module with two risers is approximately 100 lb. It requires no maintenance.

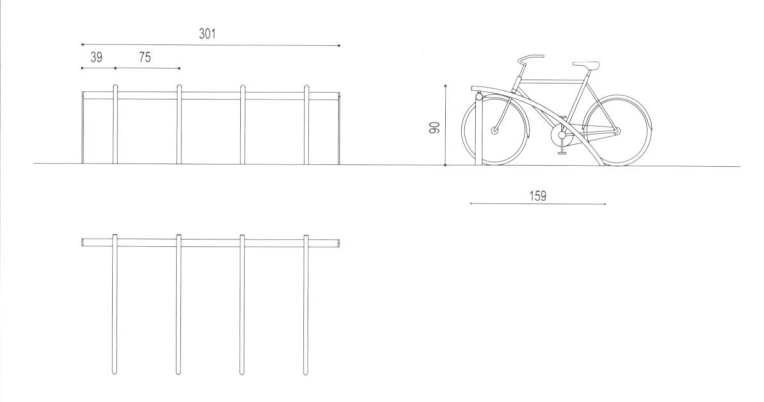

Bicipoda

Design: **Pete Sans** • Production: **DAE**

The body of the bicycle stand is made of hot-galvanized steel sheet, 5 mm thick. The base is made of steel sheet 8 mm thick. The item's full height is 850 mm. The four anchoring bolts are made of zincified steel, specification DIN 602 M-8, 100 mm in length. Its weight is approximately 17 kilograms (37.4 lb). The finish is galvanized.

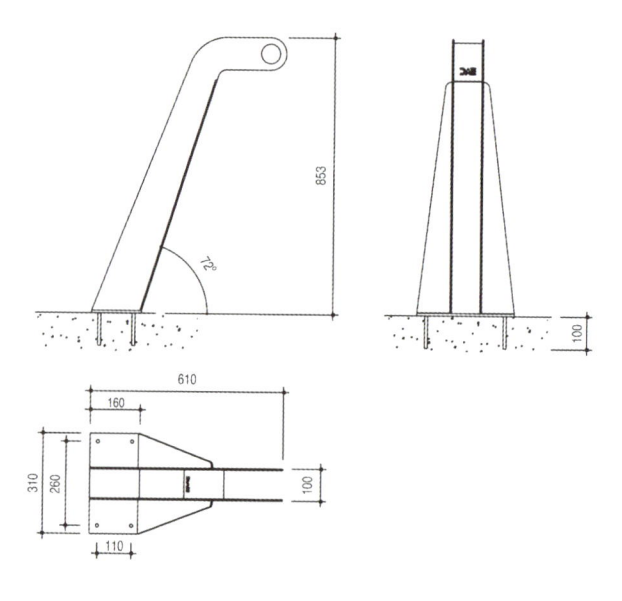

154 BICYCLE RACKS

Contínuo - Triângulo

Design: **Pedro Pereira and Francisco Providência** • Production: **Larus**

Contínuo - Triângulo are two models of bicycle rack made of galvanized and painted steel. They are held to the ground by means of their own specific anchoring system. The Contínuo model is fixed by means of a perforated steel base-rod. The Triângulo model is designed to hold the bicycle directly by the frame.

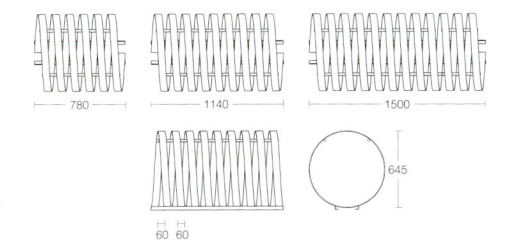

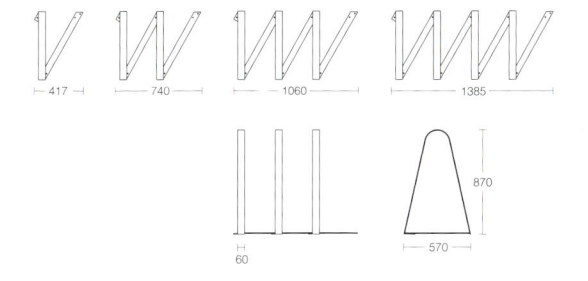

BICYCLE RACKS

Ezzo

Design: Tomas Ruzicka • Production: mmcité

The natural beauty of traditional terrazzo technology enhances the purist form of the Ezzo line of bicycle stands. The separate units can be assembled into endless lines. These bicycle stands are made of cast polished concrete containing tiny stones in a granite-like salt and pepper texture. The units are held together by a galvanized steel bar. The rack's solidity and weight allow it to be installed as a freestanding installation on the ground.

Flo

Design: Brian Cane • Production: Landscape Forms

Flo is a horizontal fluid spiral form of handsome and robust stainless steel tubing designed by Brian Kane to make a row of bicycles into a contribution to urban space while holding them securely and safely. All bike racks by Landscape Forms meet APBP (Association of Pedestrian and Bicycle Professionals) recommendations for supporting bicycles at two points and locking in at least one. All the racks are strong, durable, weather-resistant and tested to meet the quality standards requested by Landscape Forms, which led to awarding them the LEED credit for the encouragement of environment-friendly bicycle use.

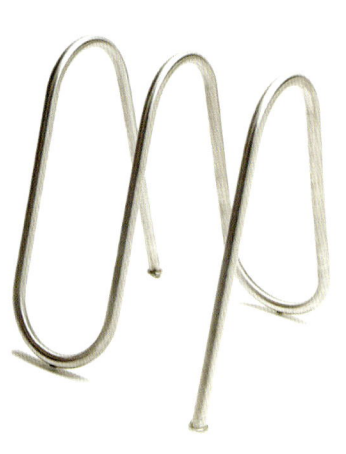

156 BICYCLE RACKS

Key

Design: **Lagranja** • Production: **Santa & Cole**

The design of this bicycle rack is based on agreeable, simple and dynamic lines. The idea was to revitalize a rather neglected an urban element. The structure is of high-density polyurethane and the base is of cast aluminium. It comes in two standard colours, anthracite gray and red.

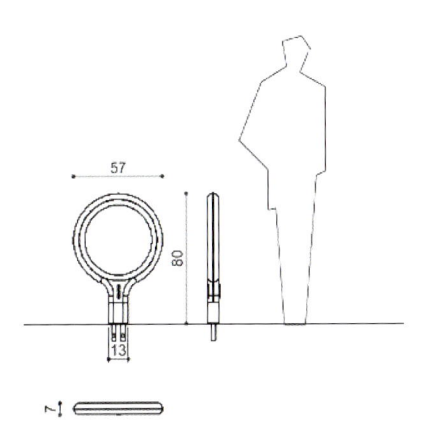

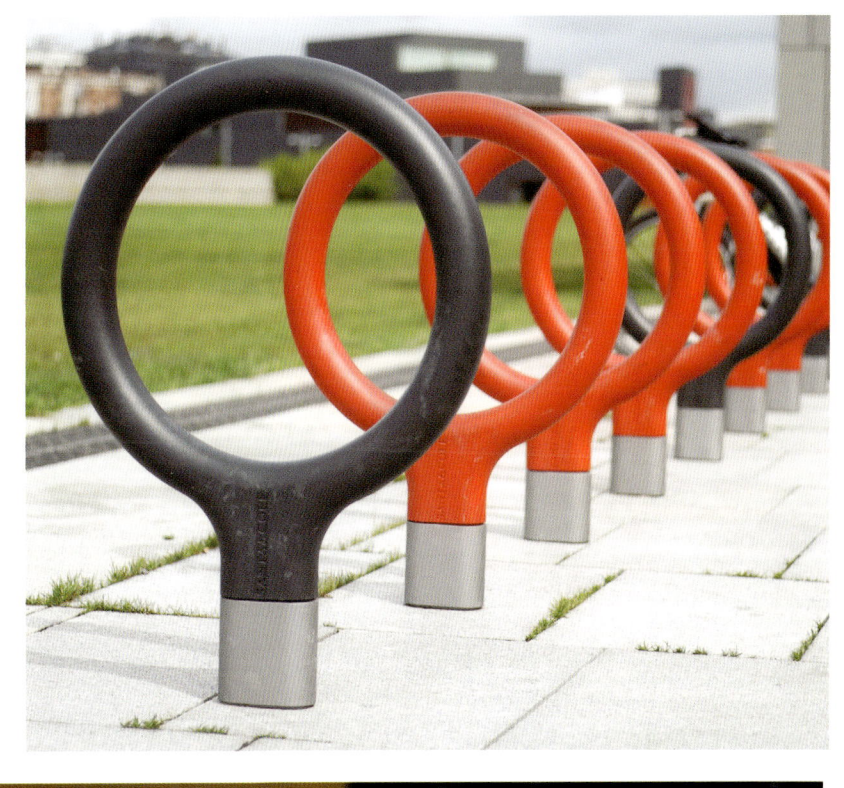

BICYCLE RACKS

Maia 360

Design: **Luigi Ferrario** • Production: **Modo**

Bicycle rack in Fe 360 B steel, made up of modular elements that are joined so that they form a semicircle with 1400 mm outer diameter. The main elements that characterize the bicycle rack shape are the 40 × 10 mm harmonized sections, which are identical and placed side by side.
Maia can lodge 14 or 7 bicycles (if they all are parked with the handlebar towards the centre). The structure is finished with thermosetting powder paint for outdoors.

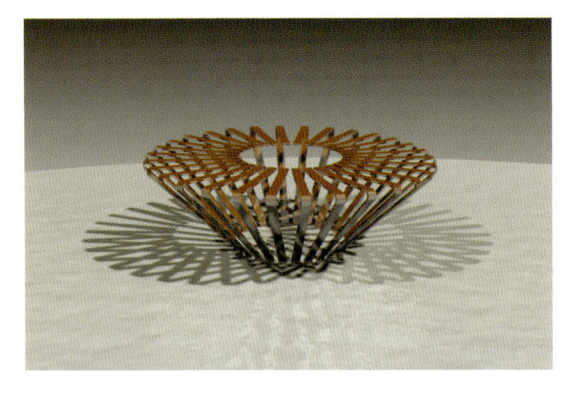

Meandre

Design and production: **mmcité**

This steel frame holds a sturdy ripple of rubber belt sinuously curved into a meandering shape for slipping up to five bicycles into the grooves resulting on either side. The horizontal bar at the top provides the element to which the bicycle can be chained and locked.

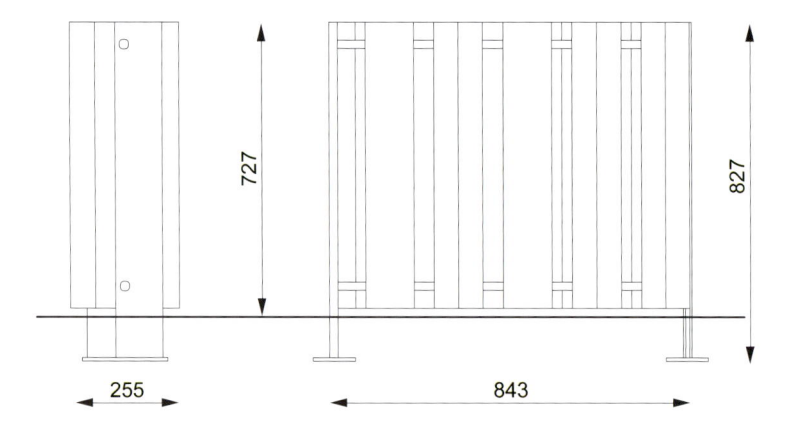

BICYCLE RACKS

Montana

Design: **Héctor Roqueta - Ferran Sesplugues** • Production: **Santa & Cole**

Montana is a safe, solid and modular bicycle rack for urban environments. The entire rack consists of a series of supports made of curved stainless steel pipe, Ø 33 mm in diameter, with a sanded finish, simply connected to each other by a clamp. There is a shoe at each end to fix the item to the pavement. Each shoe is fixed to the ground by means of two stainless steel screws. The connecting clamp is made of black polypropylene. The modular character of this secure piece of urban furniture allows it to be installed in a variety of ways. Its weight per unit is of 16 kg.

On

Design: **Ramos / Bassols** • Production: **Alis**

On performs as both bicycle rack and bollard. It is made of 5mm thick steel plate. Its circular base (220 mm diameter) permits it to be anchored to the pavement by a series of holes made for that purpose. The vertical part of the item is made of 15mm thick steel plate and measures 560x222 mm. The hole at the top has a diameter of 185mm that allows chains and rods to be passed through to lock bicycles to it. The various structural elements are arc-soldered together. The finish is galvanized by immersion in zinc, which is then dust sprayed in epoxy gauge 150 micros, giving it a smooth and even look. Colour can be customized.

BICYCLE RACKS

Quad bike

Design: **Ernest Perera** • Production: **mago:urban**

Quad bike, manufactured by mago:urban to an exclusive design by Ernest Perera, is a highly functional post, of simple lines and easily anchored to the ground which performs a double function: as a dissuasive element marking the limits of public spaces - squares, streets or gardens and at the same time serving to secure several bicycles thanks to the curved arms that are incorporated in two of its sides. Quad bike is realized in acid-etched reinforced concrete and weighs 54 kg.

Rough & Ready

Design and production: **Streetlife**

The Rough & Ready bicycle parking rack is a tough supporting and durable piece of urban furniture. The untreated and sustainable FSC hardwood (FSC controlled wood means it did not originate in protected zones or endangered species). The stand is designed not to damage the bicycles and creates a new and idiosyncratic image. For the first time, the street can feature a natural-looking, user-friendly yet robust stand. The hole in the steel leg is for securing the bikes to the stand with a chain lock.

BICYCLE RACKS

Sammy

Design: Oriol Guimerà • **Production:** Santa & Cole

A modular piece, at once bollard, containment rail, bicycle rack and potentially even a seat, made of cast iron and extruded aluminium. A good solution for defining functional boundaries of urban space and demarcating the city. The support is made of nodular cast iron with anti-rust protection and painted in black. The base is inserted 15 cm into the pavement into a previously drilled hole and filled with epoxy resin or fast-drying cement or such. No maintenance is required. Weight: 34 Kg.

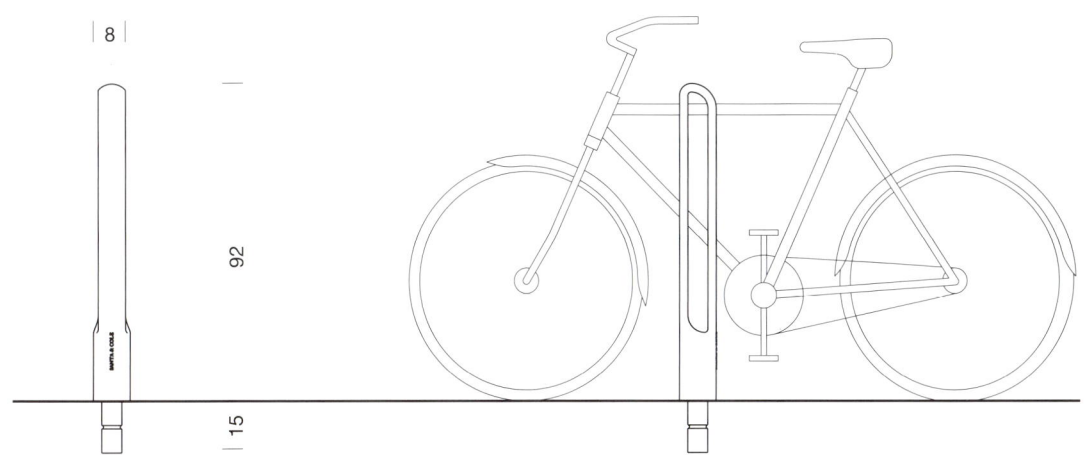

Tatanka

Design: Brunetti Filipponi Associati • **Production:** ORA Centurelli

Tatanka is a 5 space bicycle rack. There are two models, for a single or a double row of bicycles. To hold the bicycle wheels, there are 10 or 20 6 mm thick sheet metal plates, laterally fixed to the tubing with a double bend and welded in pairs to the side of the tubing. Each pair is positioned to form a cone shape (the narrow end is joined to the tubing) which is ideally-suited to holding a bicycle wheel in place. Two base plates are welded onto the two lower ends of the item, with holes for fixing to the floor by means of pressure plugs. The Single Tatanka also includes a pinewood plank as a wheel stop, measuring 95 × 35, treated in an autoclave. This component, which is fixed to the upper part of the tubing, can be alternatively used as a seat.
The Single Tatanka is 1600 mm (L), 500 mm (W), 420 mm (H) and weighs 54 kg.
The Double Tatanka is 1600 mm (L), 900 mm (W), 420 mm (H) and weighs 72 kg.

BICYCLE RACKS

Táctil

Design: Antonio de Marco • Production: Santa & Cole

A new kind of bike rack, a cheerful, uninhibited and very sturdy bollard, designed to cover the ever-increasing demand of parking space for city bicycles. Made of one single piece of sandblasted Corten steel sheet, silhouetted using an oxycutting process. The piece is delivered fully assembled and with anchoring instructions. The shaft is fixed into the ground with two bolts through the same piece, which go into holes previously filled with epoxy resin, or fast-drying cement or such. Maintenance is not required. Weight: 20 Kg.

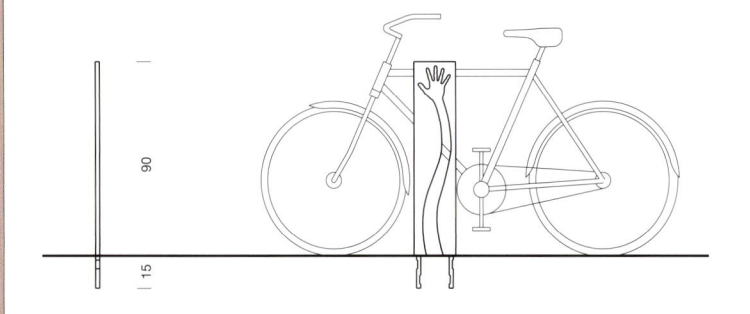

BICYCLE RACKS

Trian

Design: **Runge Designteam** • Production: **Runge**

Trian displays optically generated tension and dynamics. In addition to its characteristically dynamic shape, Trian is a safe cycle rack. The round tube made of electropolished stainless steel has a diameter of 60 mm. It is asymmetrically welded with mitre cuts of 45° and 29 °.

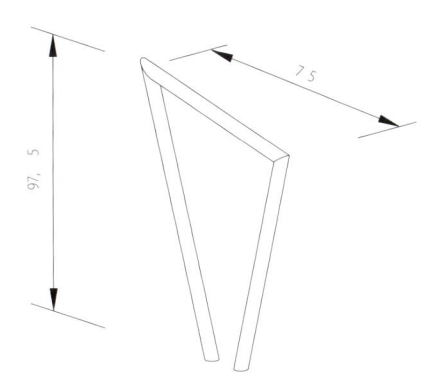

Velo

Design: **David Karásek & Radek Hegmon** • Production: **mmcité**

This highly practical and durable bicycle rack displays a sophisticated yet extremely unpretentious modern design. It is supplied in three different options, for one or for two rows of bicycles, and with or without an upper rail that serves as a stop and enables the locking chains a solid attachment. Moreover, these options are multiplied by two as there is a model with four or with six wheel-holding slots. The rack's elegant shape makes it suitable even for elegant and exclusive environments.

The body of the object is made of hot-dip galvanized steel. The item has a secure anchoring system for its installation in public spaces by means of concealed screws that fix it to the pavement. Nevertheless, Velo is perfectly stable and requires no extra support for use in a private context.

BICYCLE RACKS 163

Fountains

Agua

Design and production: Geohide

There is little doubt that this drinking fountain is eye-catching because of its elegant sculptural shape, which in fact is a result of its purpose. "Agua" is actually a double water fountain: an upper one which comes out of the very top of the structure itself, and a lower one which is plate-shaped and easily reached by people in wheel chairs or small children. It is made entirely out of a highly resistant kind of stainless steel unaffected by corrosion. It measures 0.90 × 0.15 m (2907 × 5.89 inches) and is just over one meter (3.28 ft) high. The total weight is 60 kg (132.24 lb).

Atlántida

Design: Enric Batlle - Joan Roig • Production: Santa & Cole

The Atlántida drinking fountain is good example of straightforwardly minimalistic urban design. It consists of a monolithic block of cast-iron, rust-protected and coated in black wrought-iron finish paint. The grid to collect the run-off water is made of the same material and rests within a frame made of corrosion-proof, hot-dip galvanized steel. The one-inch push-button spout is made of cast brass.

The item is supplied in two separate parts: firstly, the block with its spout, and secondly, the grid and the water collection receptacle to be sunk into the ground. This fountain can be installed on its own or in a row. Various distributions are possible. The base is buried 10 cm into the ground and fixed into position with four anchoring bolts. The grid over the water collection receptacle at the base is the same width as the front of the fountain.

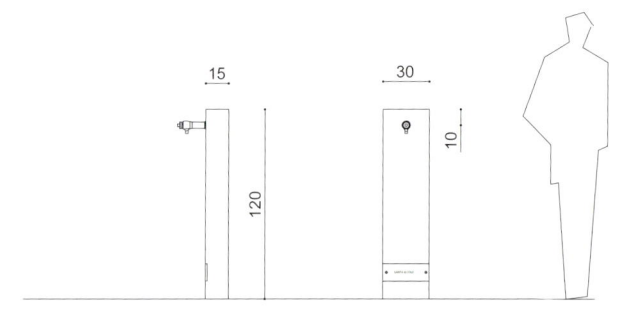

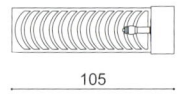

FOUNTAINS

Branca

Design: **Oscar Doll** • Production: **DAE**

This piece, created by the designer Oscar Doll, has been built in polished matt stainless steel, AISI 316L, with a 170mm diameter and a total height of 1400mm. The three fastening bolts are also made of the same material and a with a metrics of 14 and 130mm large.

The water duct has been made of polyurethane and reinforced with fiberglass. The grill, in galvanized steel heated by inmersion. it contains a nozzle of stainless steel AISI 316L, and screws in steel A4.

The whole set of the plumbing has been constructed with antitheft system, with an exchangeable brass head, and a chromatic pulsator. Inside, small pieces have been installed to resist possible corrosion, and a pressure reducer that leads the outflow of water stay always constant.

The piece weighs approximately 41 kg.

Chafariz

Design: **Diana Cabeza** • Collaborators: **L. Heine / M. Wolfson** • Production: **Estudio Cabeza**

As a recreation of the traditional neighbourhood water spout, this dispenser for drinking water (or refreshing feet or head) solves the issue of providing water in public spaces. Ideal for refreshment after park games, or cycling, or during summer walks, the "chafariz" stands proud waiting for thirsty adults and children. Both a totem and a user friendly play object, its steps and grab holes on the sides allow children to safely climb and drink.

The grate at the base is an embossed surface which, with little holes simulating water drops, contains water overflow. The lips of the spout keep the body dry.

Materials: Cast iron.

Finishing: Sand-blasted and color polyester thermosetting powder coated.

Size: body: 17 × 40 × 113.5 cm / base: 60 × 150 × 27 cm

FOUNTAINS

Caudal

Design: **Pau Roviras y Carlos Torrente** • Production: **Santa & Cole**

A public fountain based on geometric forms. Original, simple and pleasant, especially designed to be comfortably used by any citizen. Developed and improved in cooperation with Barcelona City Council and organisations of disabled people, it is accessible and suitable for everyone. Easy to operate, it was designed thinking of minimum consumption with an appropriate and constant flow to facilitate its use by people with motor disabilities.

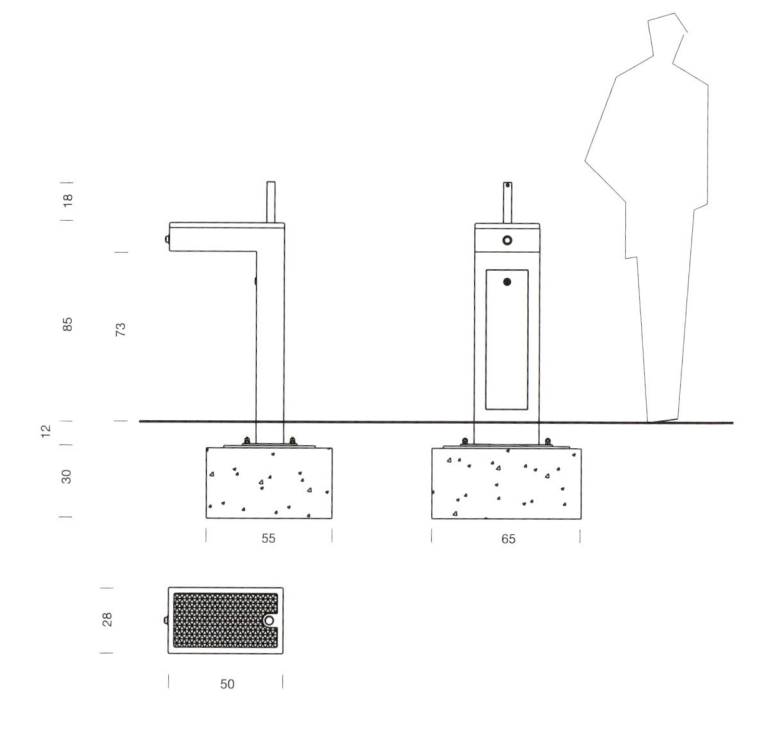

FOUNTAINS

Estena

Design and production: **T&D Cabanes**

The Estena drinking fountain is an example of perfect adaptation either to a fresh and modern context or to a site with important historical connotations. Its recycling capacity is of 30 litres. The base is made of stainless steel faced with Corten steel. The outer layer is of transparent paint.

FOUNTAINS

Fontfosa

Design: **Pep Bonet** • Production: **DAE**

Fontfosa is a notably sober-looking water fountain, made of cast iron with a black wrought-iron finish. The press-button is at the top and the stainless steel supply pipe is concealed under the fountain head, which has an inverted L-shaped cross section, avoiding anything that might disrupt the item's firm geometrical composition. The fountain drains directly into the base plate, where it is received by a grid installed flush with the pavement, thereby achieving a perfect integration with the surroundings it becomes part of. The article weighs 115 kg (253,46 lb), and is fixed in position by means of stainless steel anchoring bolts.

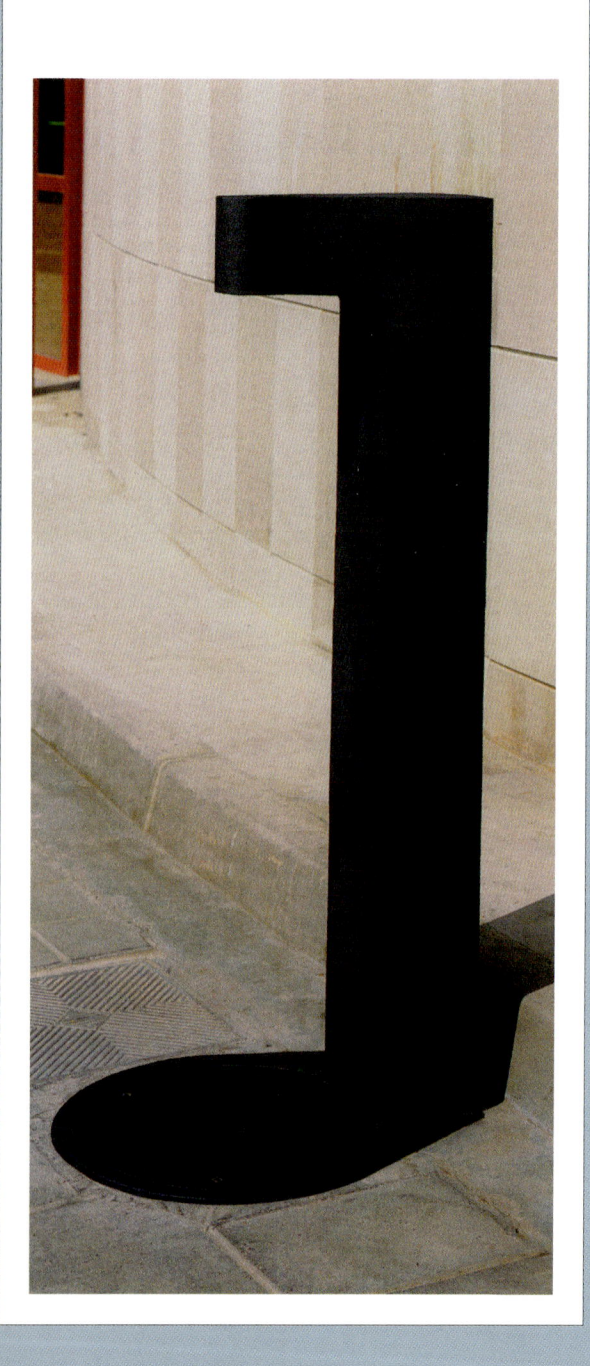

Georgina

Design and production: **Colomer**

This fountain, a piece designed by Colomer, has been built in in cast steel following the Steel Structure Basic Standards UNE-EN-1561. The height of the body would be about 1300 mm and 220 mm wide. An anticorrosion rubber-colour sealing primer has been used for the surface to be covered, also following the standard RD 1078/1993. Subsequently, a coat of finished anticorrosion that creates a forging effect.

This fountain is meant to be a very simple structure. The water tap is only composed by a stainless steel ball with a timer button and embedded cap.

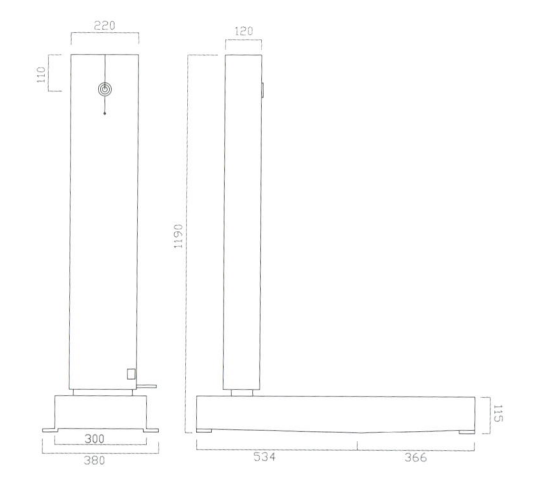

FOUNTAINS

Lama

Design: J.A Martínez Lapeña / Elías Torres • Production: Escofet

The spanish architects Elías Torres and José A. Martínez Lapeña created this fountain, a piece constructed on a reinforced waterproof concrete (cement in grey), on a sloppy in cast plan.

Embedded into the pavement, all the draining and intake elements are included: the shut-off-valve collection box and the optional pressure regulator, if necessary; water claim beaker and in cast grill.

The rod reinforcement is made in corrugated stainless steel, perfectly adapted to give the structure its shape in an amount of 60 kg/m^3 and a minimum distance of 2.5 cm.

The grifting contains a chromatic timer button and the jet of water is made of brass. The alignment tube is made of galvanized steel.

The in cast emerging plan has been given a shape for water conduction. Subsequently, the plan leans over a curved keel, also in in cast.

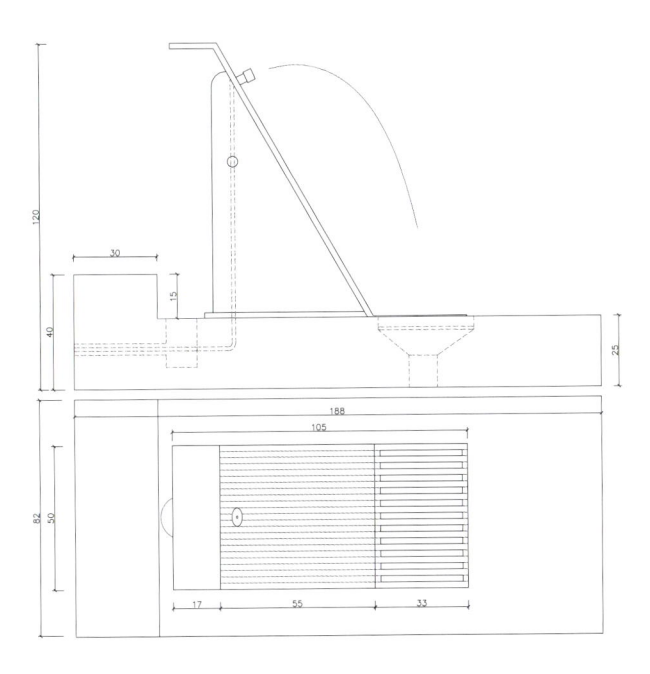

Lavapiés

Design: José Luis Camarasa • Production: Santa & Cole

The foot-shower designed by José Luis Camarasa has a system that works like a public drinking fountain, except that it flows downwards, through 10 independently worked outlets of needle-spray water nozzles. The structure consists of a polished stainless steel (AISI 316) tube, Ø 200 mm in diameter (7.86 inches), supported upon pillars of the same material but with a sandblasted finish. The internally concealed spray nozzles are made of brass and the press-button to release the flow is of stainless steel. The platform at the base of the structure is a galvanized steel grid that enables the water and the unwanted sand to drain away instantly and perfectly.

The article is connected to the mains through one of the supporting pillars. The body can be opened at both ends to facilitate maintenance work, which is minimal as the entire article is constructed using resistant, non-alterable materials. The foot-shower is ergonomically designed for people to clean the sand off their feet with the maximum comfort and security.

FOUNTAINS

Lilla

Design: **Tobia Repossi** • Production: **Modo**

The structure consists of 60 mm diam. stainless steel tube, sandblasted and shaped according to a parabolic curve. The fountain has a stainless steel supporting base plate, with laser carvings for water drainage; at the base it has a 250 mm diam. stainless steel bowl. Water outlet is available in the upper and in the lower part through a timer button at the final part of the tube. The bowl at the base can be used as a drinking trough for animals. Fixing to the ground requires sinking the drainage basin in a concrete foundation at a depth of 220 mm underground, which corresponds to the height of the basin.

Naia

Design: **Nuria Núñez** • Production: **DAE**

This sturdy and robust drinking fountain is designed for installation in public spaces and outdoor areas. It consists of a slightly tapering inverted conical body made of cast iron, anodized and painted. Its upper part finishes in a slanted transversal section that reveals the fountain itself, with a push-button tap and a blue drainage basin that suggests the presence of water but in fact is a reflection of the sky with a silver grey finish.

The item's approximate weight is 96 kg (211.58 lb) and it is designed to be anchored to the pavement with stainless steel screws.

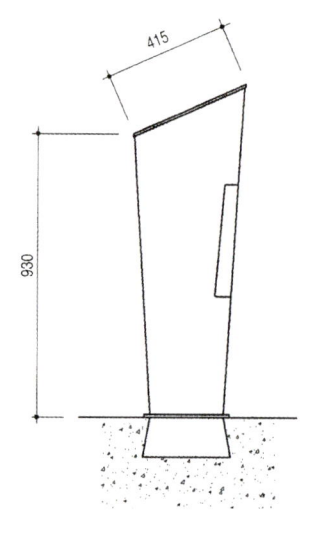

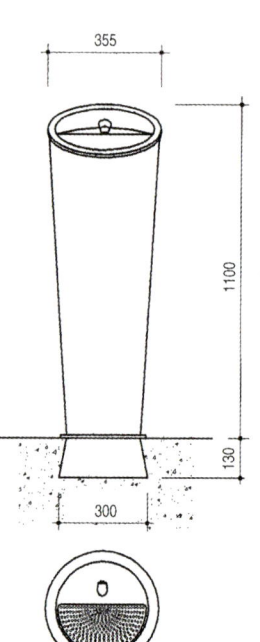

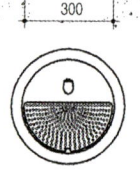

172 FOUNTAINS

Periscopio

Design: **Diana Cabeza** • Production: **Estudio Cabeza**
Development team: **D.Cabeza, A. Venturotti, D. Jarczak**

The Periscopio fountain is a water- dispenser with a grid and a drainage system, designed for public space in the city. It is designed to complement the Rehué benches, likewise created by Diana Cabeza. Periscopio is made of cast iron with a powder-coated finish of transparent thermo-convertible polyester. It is easy to install as it is simply inserted into the concrete floor

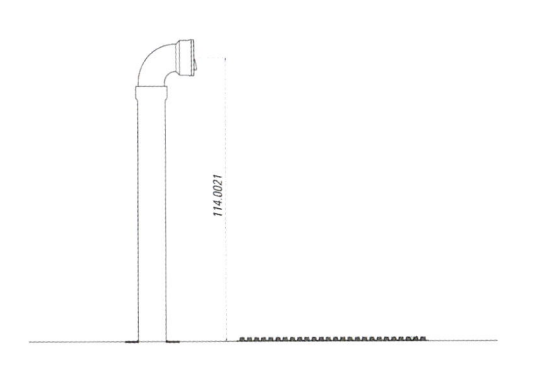

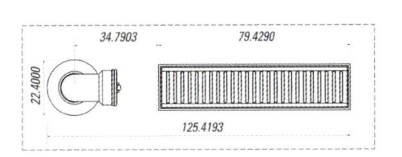

Tana

Design: **Francisco J. Mangado** • Production: **DAE**

The structure of this fountain, created by the architect Francisco Mangado, has been constructed by cast iron GG-20. The piece is supported by means of two fastening bolts of galvanized steel M-12, of 130 mm long. There is a back door made of galvanized steel, 2 mm thick.

The water tap contains a security system, with exchangeable head made of brass and it has also a water reducer for the water exit to be controlled and regulated and stay always constant. A round tap for flow regulation and a ½ gas connection.

A first priming coat has been taken, high adherence, with polyvinyl butyric and phenolic resin which contains zinc chromate to protect against corrosion. A second priming coat of epoxy made of two components; and a coat finishing of polyurethane enamel.

The standard colour of this fountain would be in black.

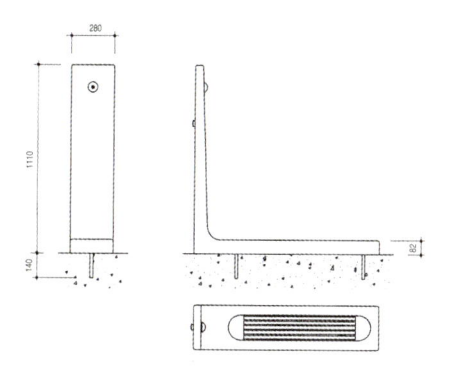

FOUNTAINS

Pavements

Ada

Design: **Enric Miralles & Benedetta Tagliabue** • Production: **Escofet**

ADA was designed by the architects Enric Miralles and Benedetta Tagliabue for paths in the Diagonal Mar park in Barcelona which they wanted to be finished in a sandy tone. Two sizes of colored concrete paving slabs, 120 mm in depth, conform this highly architectural paving, in which the paving layout is emphasized by open joints.

The rhomboidal pieces measure 900 x 700 mm and 500 x 300 mm.

Suitable for pedestrian areas with occasional transit of motor vehicles weighing up to 5 tons per wheel, the paving slabs are laid on a sand base 40 mm to 60 mm deep on compacted ground. Optionally, and as provision for vehicular traffic, they can be laid on a layer of sand over a sub-base of H-200 concrete 180 mm thick.

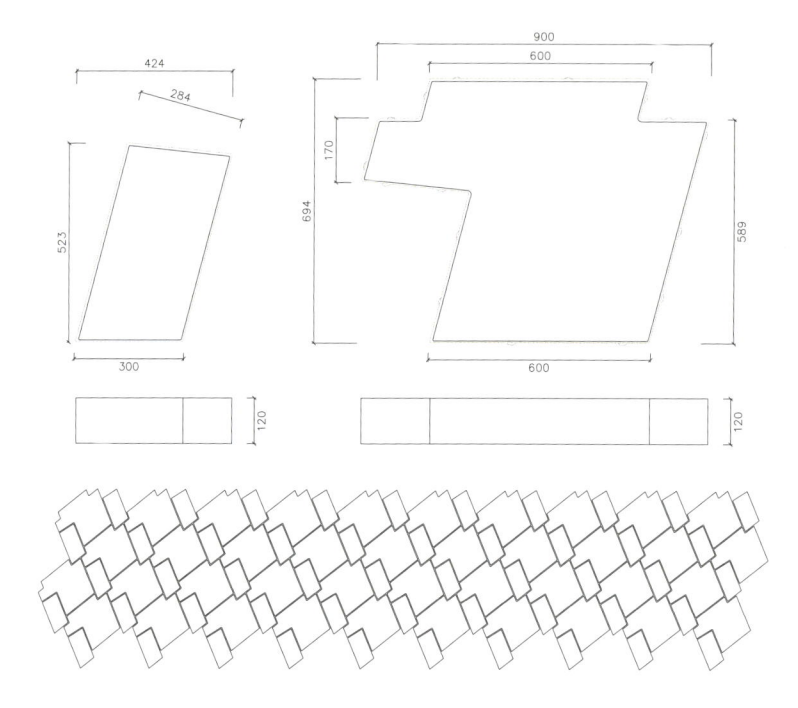

PAVEMENTS

Checkerblock

Design: **Hastings Pavement Company** • Production: **Escofet**

Checkerblock is a paving stone made out of vibrated and molded reinforced concrete in squares of 610 x 610 x 100 mm (24 x 24 x 3.93 inches). It is ideal for landscaping an area in concrete and grass, as it lets you shape the land and at the same time prevent erosion, performing like a reinforcement of vegetation and planted areas. The final appearance, with the grass growing between the gaps, is particularly attractive and visually pleasing. This combination of a green layer mixed with the solidity of a concrete surface is reassuring. The product comes in various colors, with a fine, smooth surface texture and it is laid over compacted sand. Each weighs 38 kg (83.75 lb).

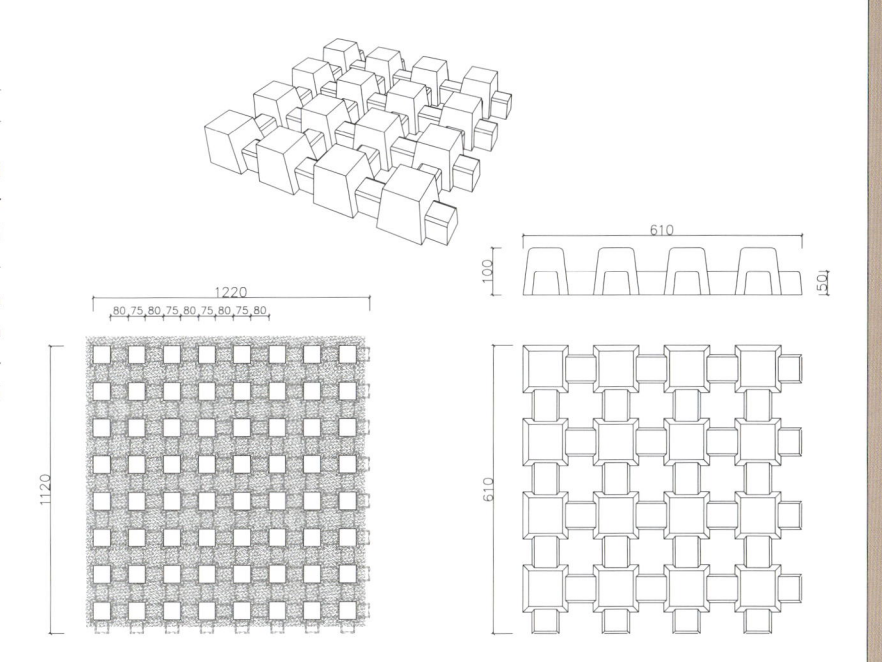

PAVEMENTS 177

Palma

Design: J.A Martínez Lapeña / Elías Torres • Production: Escofet

Palma paving stones are available in two formats that allow them to form different systems of drainage pavements, leaving the joints more or less open to silting with sand or to grasses appearing in the gaps.

The Palma x 2 is a piece that doubles the size of the original Palma paving stone, opening up the possibility of combinations forming endless compositions. The original paving will be defined by factors like the variations in the joints, the direction in which they are geometrically placed and the way the two sizes are set.

Suitable for zones with pedestrian traffic and the occasional vehicle, both formats are 10cm thick. When they are placed, the paving stones are pressed into a bed of sad with a granulation grading of 1-5 and a thickness of 3 to 5cm, laid over a base of compacted gravel or a 15cm concrete base with a characteristic resistance of 250 kg/cm2.

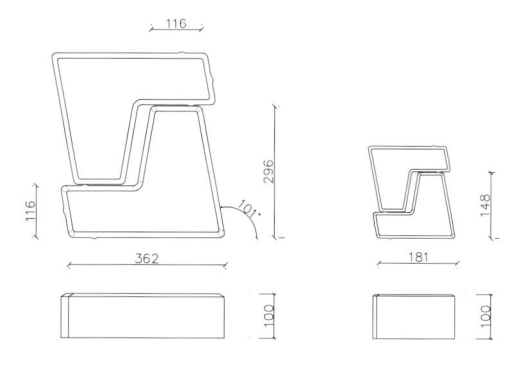

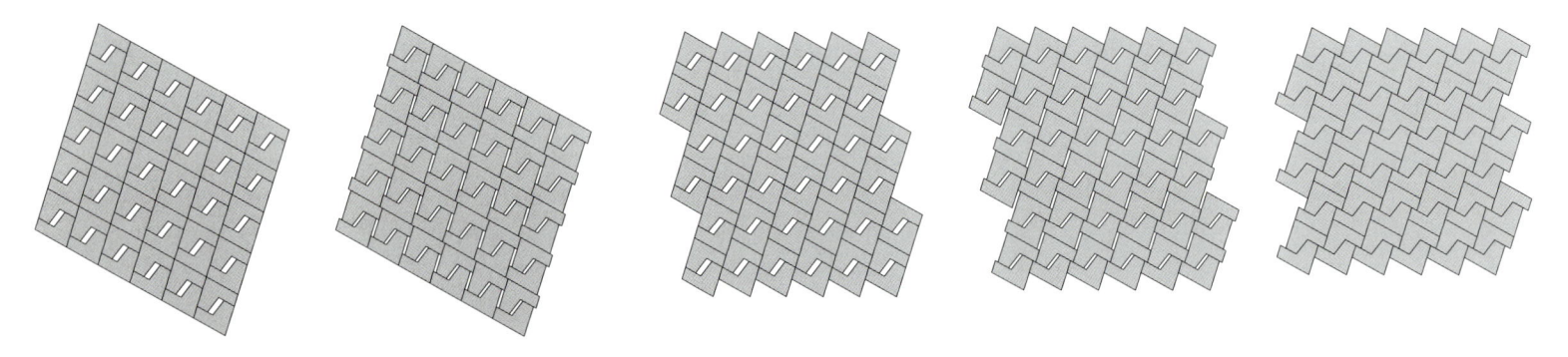

178 PAVEMENTS

Pass

Design: Jordi Miralles Tintoré, Jordi Miró Surroca • Production: mago:urban

Up until now, getting to the shore involved walking over the sand with no other protection than your sandals, or along a more or less irregular platform with a potential risk of falling. Moreover, the lack of an appropriate end made it difficult for people in wheelchairs or with limited mobility to get to the water.

To address these problems, mago: urban came up with the Pass platform, which consists of a line of juxtaposed modular slabs of reinforced concrete. The slabs are square, the upper side is flat and two of its sides are smooth; the third side has three convex teeth and two concave indentations, which permits the modules to be hooked onto each other.

The teeth and the indentations have a cylindrical perforation for the units to be locked together with a steel rod. This hinge mechanism allows the system enough flexibility to adapt to the terrain without affecting its smoothness and comfort.

The Pass module's upper face is entirely textured with anti-slip corrugations. Special modules are available for each end, where a smoothly tapered edge makes the platform easily accessible for all users.

An extra facility added by mago:urban to their Pass platform is the joining mechanism is functional on three sides, so a perpendicular platform may be connected to the main path. All the modules and the resulting walkway can be anchored to the ground, but only require their own weight and collective structure for stability.

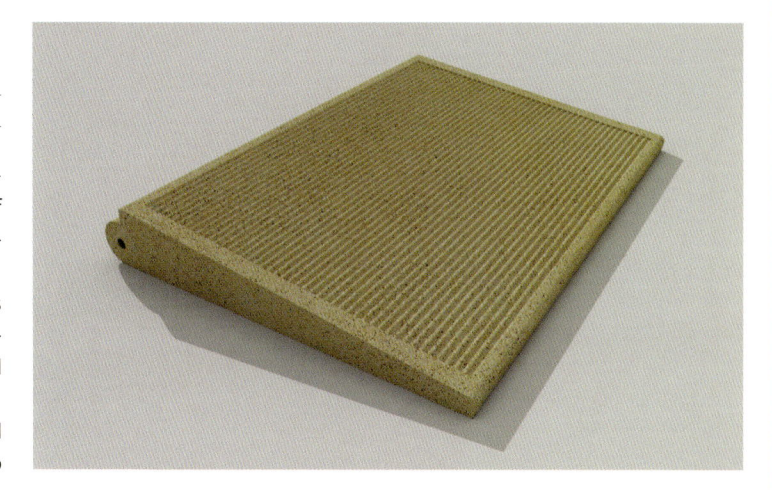

PAVEMENTS

Pictóricos

Design: Antoni Roselló Til • Production: Santa & Cole

The pictorial pavement series is a tribute to four artists who changed our perception of image: Henry Matisse, Piet Mondrian, Vassily Kandinsky and Paul Klee. They give art a functional urban use, applying it to pavements, an element remained unchanged since the XIX century. Inspired by pictorial tree-base grids, Antoni Roselló developed these pavings intending to integrate art into daily urban life environment, without troubling it, not as an alien but rather as a functional element. In a personal tribute to each painter, the elements of the series bear the name of each one of them, while the tree grids bear his family name; this allows for a great combination of pavements and tree-base grids. With these interesting pieces, Santa & Cole brings focus onto an element considered to be the skin of the city, the base of any future urban development. The concrete tiles take on the negative or positive image of each of the four painters, while functionally reinforcing the sidewalk. The pictorial pavement series satisfies the need to incorporate symbols into urban furniture, gives an iconographic value to urban space, and contributes to the city's identity.

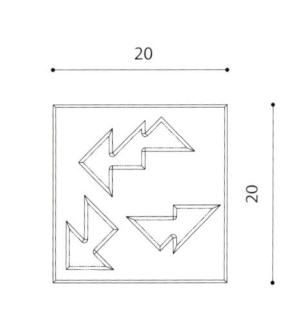

180 PAVEMENTS

Redes

Design: Alfredo Arribas • **Production:** Escofet

The Redes paving system has been designed by the architect Alfredo Arribas for the construction and consolidation of banks of earth in the project for the new corporate headquarters of Hermenegildo Zegna, in Sant Quirze del Vallès, in Catalonia, Spain.
The grid supports the soil and the grass which grows in its interstices, thus preventing erosion in various different situations in the project: in steep earth banks, pedestrian zones, and parking spaces with occasional vehicular transit.

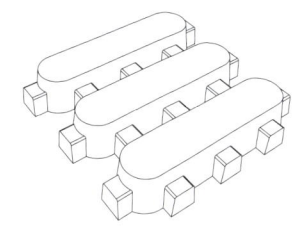

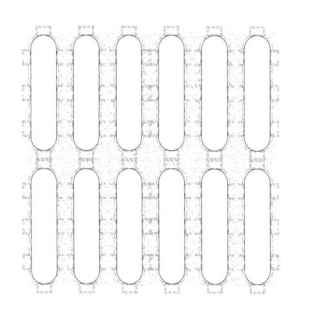

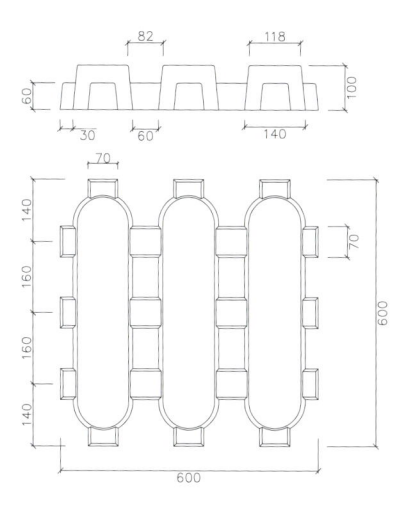

Wastebaskets

2278

Design: **Alfredo Farne** • Production: **Neri**

A conical steel column supports this litterbin made of hot-galvanised steel sheet. It has a terminal decorative element in steel. Its standard finish is dark gray. The internal bin is polythene. Dimensions: height 99 cm; width 39 cm; overhang 50.5 cm. Capacity 30 litres.

377

Design and production: **mago:urban**

The 377 waste bin is a piece of urban furniture designed and produced by mago:urban, characterized by its cylindrical shape and topped by a polyester lid that is also the mouth of the bin. The opening is fairly small to avoid the users depositing large garbage bags that would make it necessary to empty the bin with excessive frequency.

184 WASTEBASKETS

7kale

Design and production: ONN Outside

The 7 kale litterbin gives the impression of two asymmetrical bodies joining brusquely. This product has a distinctive, up-to-date feel, which can be appreciated from different angles. For better ergonomics in the cleaning process, this litterbin has been designed with a door at the front with a triangular lock making for easy access. The liner has two plastic handles for easy removal. It is suitable for use both outdoors and indoors and is available in two versions: wall-mounted (40 litre) or freestanding (70 litre), either fixed to the ground or on a pedestal with a steel counterweight hidden in the interior. A removable ashtray is included and the bin may be personalised with adhesive stickers or laser engraved with coats of arms or logos. The 7kale litterbin was selected in the 2003 ADI-FAD awards.

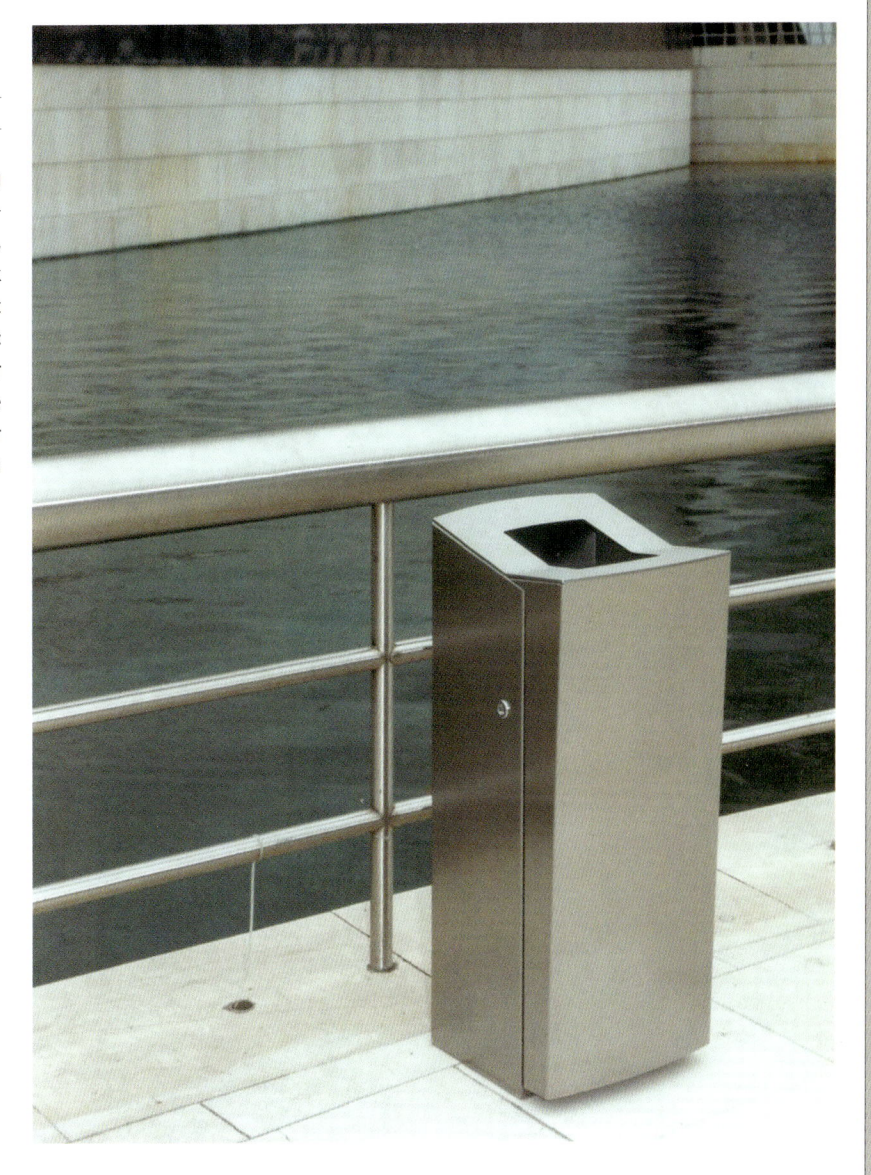

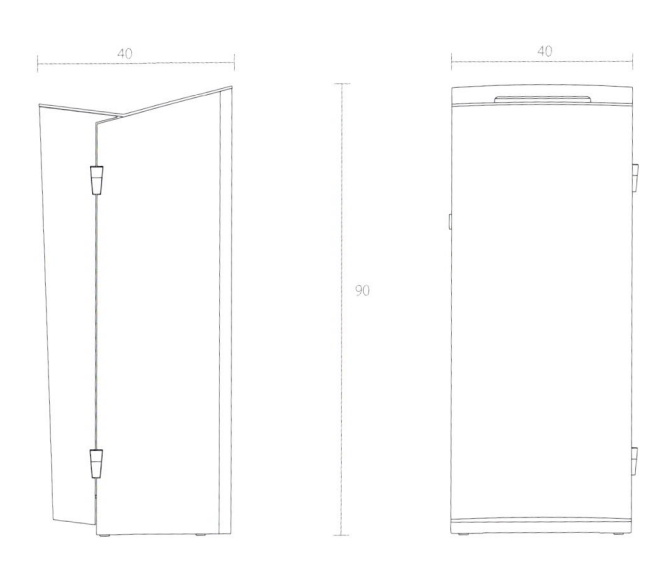

WASTEBASKETS

Argo

Design: Josep Suriñach • Production: Fundició Dúctil Benito

The Argo litter bin is triangular in plan, and consists of a reinforced steel sheet cube with laser-made holes. The cube element rests on a solid structure with a triangular base, which anchors it to the ground. The Argo litter bin looks exceedingly light, thanks to the texture of the cube and it's very fine legs. The structure is treated with the "Ferrus fdb" system, an iron protector process that guarantees a high resistance to rust. The main finish is Inde brown, but other options include oven-baked grey paint and stainless steel. A hinged grey cover is also available.

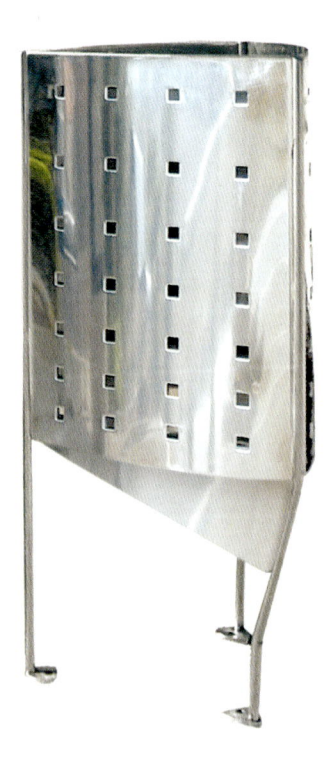

Arona

Design: Enrico Marforio • Production: Ghisamestieri

Litterbin realized in cast iron UNI EN 1561 consisting of a central body made in one single piece. The design includes the skeleton of the refuse container, the protection cover, the fixed wing and the anchor plates for ground fastening. The cast iron movable wing rotates on the central axle, allowing the wing to be opened to take out the garbage. The steel bottom is welded to the movable wing. The item has a bag-clip ring in galvanized steel. It has a 55-litre capacity.

WASTEBASKETS

Balia

Design and production: **Geohide**

In 1992-1995 the city of Lausanne (Switzerland) commissioned Chiché and the architecture and design office Synthèse to refurbish the Place de la Navigation. Given the lack of urban furniture that adequately fitted the brief and the urban context, the designers decided to create a number of items specifically for that project. This led to the consequent design of an entire range of items of urban furniture that addressed the local environment of Lake Leman, with its exquisite views of a landscape and a sky constantly reflected in the surface of the lake, its water birds, and its constant symmetry. Stainless steel is very frequently chosen by this design office, because of this material's durability, versatility, and capacity to mirror the colors of the surroundings, integrating the functionality of Lausanne's urban design into the Swiss city's natural environment. Site specific design is one of Chiche's objectives.

The 45 liter waste basket is easy to assemble, it can adapt to new or existing support poles of various diameters up to a maximum of 33 cm (13 inch). The item measures 35cm x 35 cm in width, has a height of 60 cm (13.75 x 13.75 x 27.51 inches) and weighs 8 kg (17.63 lb) (without the support structure). An aluminum alternative is available, as well as a grey chrome-plated and sprayed version.

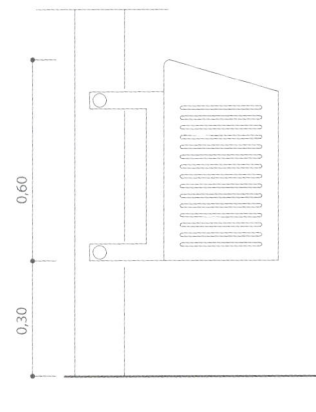

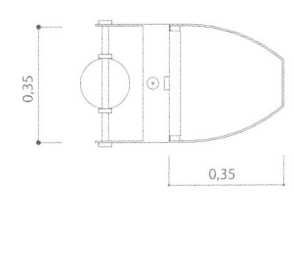

Banquina

Design: **Estudio Hampton / Rivoira y asociados** • Production: **Estudio Cabeza**

Trash, one of the lines designed by Estudio Cabeza, includes the Banquina waste bin. The item is made of 2mm thick perforated steel plate with a ½ " thick rim guard. The support posts are of solid, untreated, Quebracho wood. The object is finished with a coat of thermo-setting powder paint.

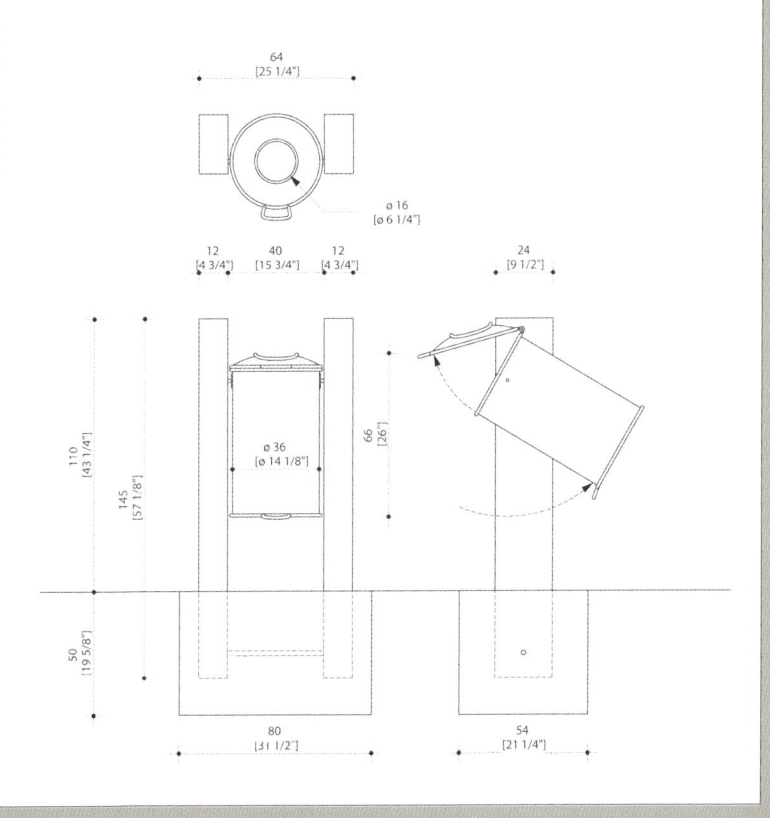

WASTEBASKETS

Bina

Design: **Gonzalo Milà - Martina Zink - Área Metropolitana de Barcelona** • Production: **Santa & Cole**

In collaboration with the MMAMB (Mancomunidad de Municipios del Área Metropolitana de Barcelona; Associated Municipalities of the Barcelona Metropolitan Area), Gonzalo Milà and Martina Zink designed this litter bin to solve the problem of litter-collection on the beach. Functional and elegant, it meets all the requirements of popular beach resorts: large capacity, low maintenance, quickly removable, a lock against vandalism and firm placement, as the lower 30 cm, buried in the sand, are filled with sand before the plastic bag is placed inside. The bins can be stacked for easy storage in the winter. The pigmented polypropylene body permits personalization or adaptation to the surroundings. The lid includes a space for a name, logo or municipal coat of arms to be engraved.

The body and lid are made of rotomolded pigmented polypropylene and weigh 10.40 kg (23 lb). The rounded lid has a central hole. The neck of the body is designed for easy placement of the bag, which remains concealed once the lid is closed. The bin has a capacity of 165 liters; it is 1.22 meters (4 ft) high but the lower 30 cm (1 ft) are buried in the sand, so it only stands 0.92 cm (3 ft.) high upon the sand. The upper diameter is 63 cm (2,06 ft) and the lower diameter, at sand level, measures 45 cm (1,47 ft.). A special lever to open it is provided with the bin, which is delivered fully assembled, but with assembly instructions. Zero maintenance is required.

Canasto

Design: **Diana Cabeza** • Production: **Estudio Cabeza**

Especially in the version presented with a natural coloring, the basket-like form of this litter-bin transports us back to our origins and the thousand-year-old craft of ceramics and basket-weaving. Its tall and upright, almost proud outline, gives it a singular character, making the basket into an adequate design element for interior or outdoor furniture.

The item is made of pigmented polyethylene, roto-molded and with a sandblasted surface finish. It is available in eight colors: red, tangerine, olive green, chlorophyll green, cobalt, sienna and purple. Designed to be merely rested on the ground without further anchoring devices, the Canasto litter-bin measures 440 mm (17.29 inches) in diameter and 850 mm (33.4 inches) in height.

WASTEBASKETS

Caos

Design: **Tobia Repossi** • Production: **Modo**

Litterbin is composed of a 22 mm gauge steel spring that spirals around the body of the bin, which it supports. The bin is made of metal plate. The item stands upon a sandblasted concrete base. It is easy to empty as the bucket is extractable.

Cinderello

Design and production: **Modo**

Ashtray and support post for outdoor use. The crossing of a curved plate with a 10 mm ø tube creates the main structure, which is fixed to the ground. The ashtray is a stainless steel moulded plate, with curved edges. The inner grating to put out the cigarettes is made of AISI 304 stainless steel punched plate, designed to be easily laid and inserted into the main structure.

WASTEBASKETS 189

Cordillo

Design: Greg Healey • Production: Street and Park Furniture

The impetus for this furniture was a trip through South Australia's outback. Greg has responded to the forms, textures and colours of this extraordinary landscape in the realisation of much of this new range of urban street furniture. This adaptable range of furniture is particularly suitable for the use in contemporary streetscape design as it draws on Australian landscape forms in a unique and innovative way.

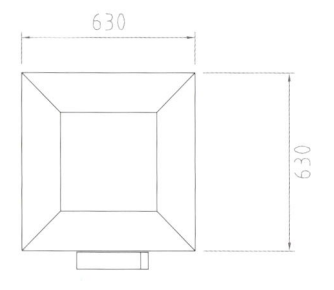

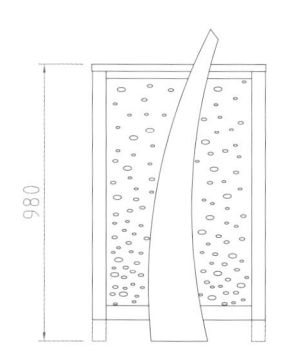

Cornet

Design: Hruša & Pelcák Architects • Production: mmcité

This distinctive conical litterbin appears to have been stuck into the ground. The original effect is effective on green, paved or even hillside localities. The galvanized steel inner bin is firmly attached to the supporting frame of the bin by a steel cable. The stainless steel body has a galvanized steel supporting structure. The inner bin is made of galvanized steel. The anchoring system remains entirely hidden under the ground.

190 WASTEBASKETS

Crystal

Design: **David Karásek & Radek Hegmon** • Production: **mmcité**

The geometrically closed design of this waste basket displays a stable and resistant construction, realized entirely in steel. The galvanized finish has been improved with an advanced painting technique, to give the body the maximum protection from corrosion. The version designed to gather the offal of dogs has an extra bucket for special plastic bags.

The steel structure has been painted in a single standard color. The ashtray, in the upper part of the waste basket, has a special stainless steel fixture on which the cigarette may be extinguished. The interior bucket is made of galvanized steel and the box opens frontally; it is provided with a lock. The item can be installed fixed onto a concrete base.

WASTEBASKETS

Cube

Design: **Studio Ambrozus** • Production: **Runge**

The two colors of this litterbin are characteristic of the design of studio Ambrozus. The combination of a plinth-like base, stainless steel side and top panels and a powder coated front and back add to the item's visual profile. The entire bin is made of stainless steel but the sides most exposed to wear are sandblasted and powder-coated. Stainless steel litterbins are seldom perfectly clean, and acquire a shabby, dirty look, especially the areas at the base and around the opening, which are exposed to more erosion and dirt. Smears are less visible on the powder-coated front than on an impeccable surface of stainless steel. Cube contains 80 liters of easy-to-empty capacity in the form of a lightweight plastic inner container or a plastic bag. Moreover, cube provides a large ashtray integrated into the design, which is pleasingly clear-cut and architectural, underlining its efficient functionality.

Cylindre

Design: **David Karásek & Radek Hegmon** • Production: **mmcité**

This cylindrical waste basket is constructed of strong corrugated plastic, reinforced with and interior nucleus made of steel. The interior container is made of galvanized steel and the base is made of fair-faced concrete. This is the basic item, from which a number of variations have been developed, some with a steel support, or with an accessory enabling it to be fixed onto vertical elements, such as lampposts. There is also a version clad in perforated steel sheet, which displays a different effect that is equally interesting. The cylindrical body of the wastebasket is firmly joined to the steel or concrete base. Its stability and structural composition make the complete object a highly resistant item against vandalism and regular wear and tear. Besides its concrete base, another option is available for it to be fixed to the pavement.

WASTEBASKETS

Diagonal

Design: **David Karásek & Radek Hegmon** • Production: **mmcité**

This series of multipurpose wastebaskets are made in a great variety of forms and materials. From the model made of wooden slats to the one made of steel sheet, all display a distinguished and elegant style. Designed to integrate well into the environment and highly resistant against vandalism, the range even supplies a triple wastebasket for the selective disposal of rubbish. The basic design is composed of a support structure of galvanized steel with alternative claddings of solid wooden slats, steel sheet with perforations, stainless steel sheet with slits, or expanded steel mesh. The covered models are available with a stainless steel ashtray accessory. The interior bucket is of galvanized steel and the whole item can be fixed to a concrete base or anchored to the pavement.

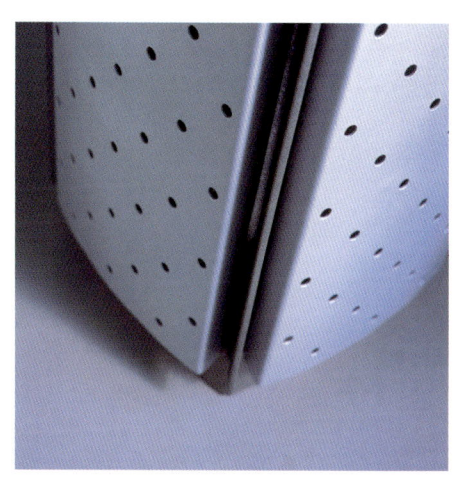

WASTEBASKETS 193

Ecclesia

Design: **Ergo - M. Pedemonte** • Production: **Ghisamestieri**

This wastebasket forms part of the Ecclesia street furniture series which incorporates traditional Christian symbols and iconography. The objective of the design is to reflect sacred values in exterior elements.

Ecology

Design: **Bernhard Winkler** • Production: **Euroform**

The Ecology wastebasket is a functional design conceived for places that require different wastebaskets for different kinds of waste. Its design allows three different types of waste to be collected in individual compartments.

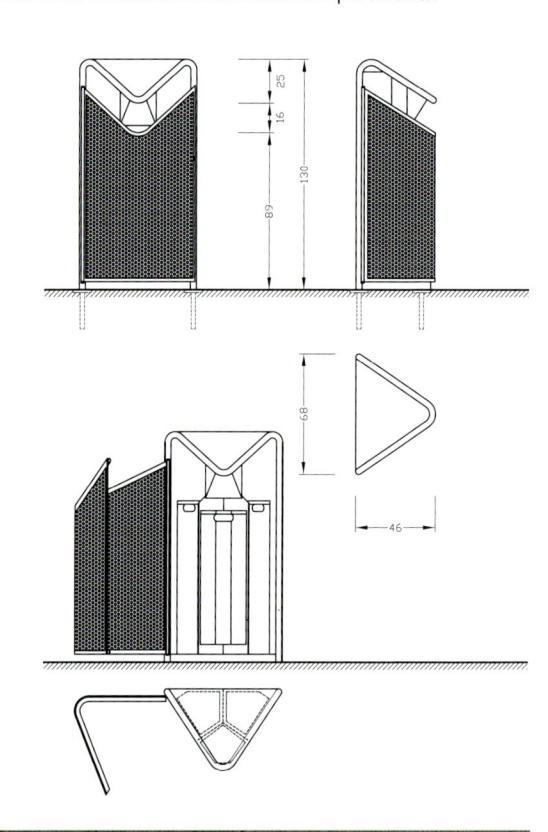

WASTEBASKETS

Fontana

Design: **Antoni Arola** • Production: **Santa & Cole**

A solid, ergonomically shaped litter bin with a large capacity (40 l). Its shape, an inverted cone with a very narrow base, has the advantage of optimising space and making leg supports unnecessary. The structure is made from stainless steel sheets, while the bin and (optional) lid are made of cast aluminium, powder painted, and the inner container is black polypropylene. The structure builds 9 cm into the pavement and anchors with 2 bolts per leg. The weight oscillates between 27 and 31 kg.

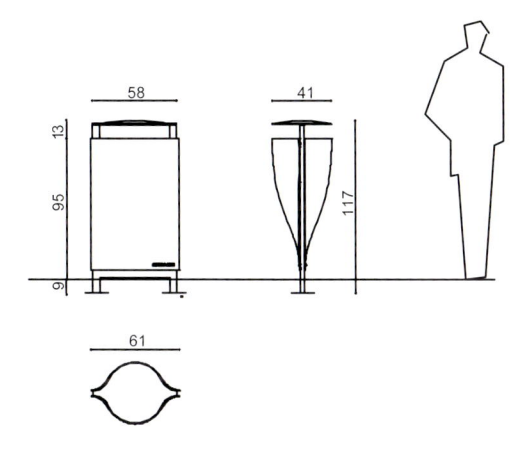

Grace

Design: **Sergio Fernández** • Production: **Tecam BCN**

This stylish, elliptically shaped wastepaper basket consists of a bin in 2mm steel plate with the ring of the opening made in polished cast aluminum. It stands on two trapezoidal shaped legs. Its design allows it to have two dimensions in one, combining sturdiness and capacity with a slim, vertical line making it suitable for indoor and outdoor use. It has a zinc coating fired in the oven to be oxyron grey or micro textured light grey.

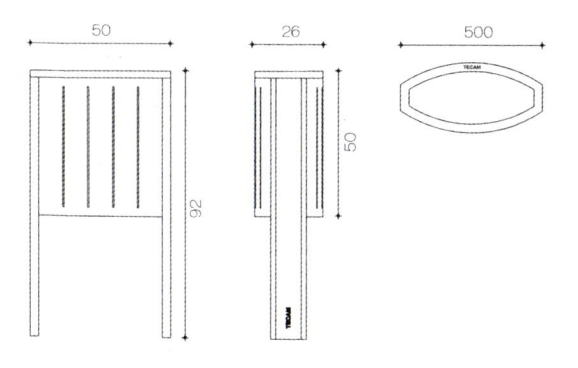

WASTEBASKETS

Imawa

Design: **Urbanica** • Production: **Concept Urbain**

The Imawa wastebasket is made of galvanized steel finished with RAL lacquer and has a stainless steel grill decoration. It has a sack holder or interior aluminium liner with a handle and a volume of 60 litres. Its front opening has a locking system with a special key and stainless steel lock.

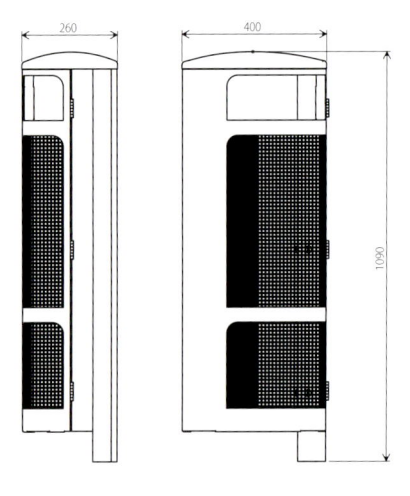

Lakeside

Design: **Margaret McCurry** • Production: **Landscape Forms**

The Lakeside wastebasket is part of the Landmark Collection of outdoor furniture created by distinguished architects and designers and inspired by familiar themes in nature, architecture and historic design. Lakeside litter receptacles are available in side or top-opening designs. The side-opening litter receptacle holds 30 gallons, the top-opening version holds 35 gallons. The steel panels are available plain or with plasma-cut decoration of grass or leaves. The standard litterbins come with a removable black polyethylene liner. Standard versions are freestanding or have a surface mounted support. Decorative motifs from nature inspired in trees and grasses are cut into the metal using state-of-the-art plasma-cutting technology. The new Landscape Forms colour palette provides fresh, out of the ordinary hues in powder coat finishes.

WASTEBASKETS

Laurel & Hardy

Design: Gonzalo Milà y Miguel Milà • Production: Escofet

The Laurel and Hardy waste disposal unit has a twofold function as ashtray and wastebasket, tasks that it can perform autonomously or together. It consists of artificial-stone cylinders finished off around the top with a ring of cast aluminium. These items can be installed in heavy duty locations, indoors or outside. The wastebasket has a lock to prevent vandalism and it should be used with a plastic garbage bag. The container of the ashtray can be taken out for it to be emptied into the wastebasket without disassembling it altogether. The two cylinders are fixed together by a threaded bolt and are likewise bolted to the pavement. It comes in two available finishes, gray concrete and smoke-black aluminium details or beige concrete with the aluminium details painted to look like Corten steel.

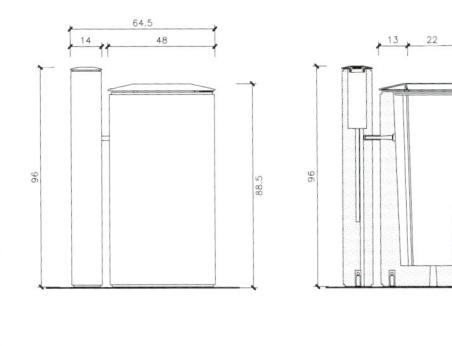

Lena

Design: David Karásek & Radek Hegmon • Production: mmcité

The articles from this range demonstrate that the need for large volume litter bins does not necessarily exclude stylish, modern design. The basic structure throughout the series consists of a thick, sheet steel envelope raised above the ground by a tubular leg that offers optimal stability and easy installation even on hillside locations. Its design, structure and optional finishes make this all-purpose litter bin suitable for any environment.

The galvanized steel supporting frame is painted in a standard color. The front comes in four versions: solid wooden lamellae, slotted or perforated galvanized steel sheet or stainless steel sheet. The lateral opening has a lockable door. The item is supplied with stainless steel cigarette extinguisher and ashtray. The inner bin is made of galvanized steel. The item is fixed to a concrete base under the pavement.

WASTEBASKETS

Linea

Design: **Bernhard Winkler** • Production: **Euroform**

Linea stands out for its clean geometry and unmistakable lines. Architectural design is revisited with linear, decisive shaping of bases and individual components. The main architectural element – a rectangular steel rod, is repeated in all the products in the entire range. In this new line, designer Thomas Winkler has used a new approach to robust, dura¬ble materials and the "euroform w" well-known machining techniques, reintroducing them in a new, modern design. Linea products fit in perfectly with any setting due to their design that is both strong and classical. The entire range produced offers designers a great deal of creative freedom in customising designs for parks, town squares, and streets.

Litos

Design: **Área de diseño Gitma** • Production: **Gitma**

Litos is a strong and solid cylindrical waste paper bin made of artificial stone. It is in fact a multi-purpose item as it can perform equally well as waste paper bin, flower pot or ash tray. It has a concealed system for emptying and is easy to maintain.

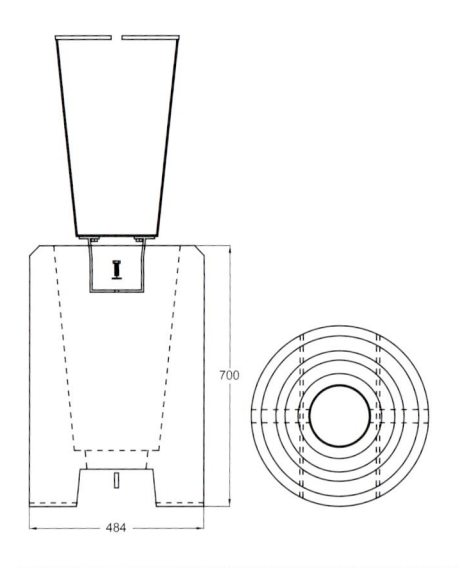

198 WASTEBASKETS

Mantel de Encaje

Design: **Diana Cabeza** • Developmet: **Diana Cabeza, Alejandro Venturotti, Diego Jarczak** • Production: **Estudio Cabeza**

The outer skin of this piece has a lacey quality, bringing to mind childhood memories of white lace tablecloths. This ethereal character lends great beauty to what is essentially a "container for waste".
Realized in punched aluminum sheet, roll-formed and soldered, with a white polyester thermo-convertible powder coating. It has a blasted concrete base which acts as a counterweight or as a fixing base if the piece is to installed sunken into the paving.

Marte

Design and production: **ORA Centurelli**

This item consists of a quadruple litterbin, supported above the ground on the time-tested old square pole. The walls of this item are made of perforated sheet metal, 2 mm thick, with square holes that measure 10 x 10 mm, or a 10mm round hole. The removable lid has an articulated hinge fixed to the pole. Using plasma or laser technology, cutouts through the lid are made in various shapes representing different types of refuse and simplifying differentiated waste collection. The available shapes are bottle, can, paper, battery, medicine, or others. Alternatively, the 3 mm thick sheet metal lid can be left entirely closed.
The 350 x 350 mm base-plate is perforated to take the anchoring bolts that will fix the item to the pavement. Hot-dip-galvanizing is available on request, according to UNI regulations. A choice of RAL paint coating can also be provided.The entire object measures 580 x 580 x 1020 (height) mm (22.80 x 22.80 x 40(height) inches. Each separate bin is 520 x 225 x 500 mm.

WASTEBASKETS

Maya

Design: Antoni Roselló Til • Production: Santa & Cole

The Maya litter bin is characterized by the way it spans the distance between opposite polarities: transparency and opacity, lightness and sturdiness, functional practicality and a refined aesthetic quality.

The item has a hinged and lockable top made of a stainless steel sheet AISI 304*, with a sandblasted finish. The body stands upon three legs and is made of pierced and stretched (deployé) stainless steel sheet mesh AISI 304* with an electro-polished finish. The article can be installed by permanently anchoring the legs into the concrete under the pavement or by simply placing it on the chosen location. The self-extinguishing interior bucket is made of black ABS.

The Maya litter bin, which weighs only 20 kg (44.08 lbs), can also be fixed to the ground with structural screws.

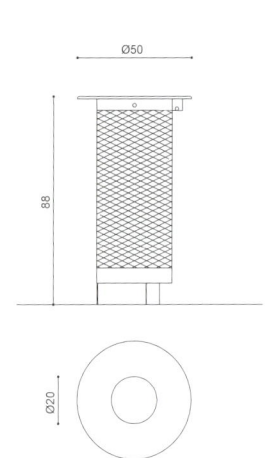

Mobilia

Design: Erik Brandt Dam • Production: GH form

The Mobilia dustbin has been developed emphasizing the expression of simplicity while setting new standards for the work environment regarding how efficiently it can be emptied. The dustbin respects the height and materials of the Mobilia bench, which underlines the wholeness of urban space. By developing the Mobilia series, GH form and Erik Brandt Dam have created an inventory of urban items developed as a set of building components that unify quality industrial products that leave room for individualized layouts according to the circumstances of each project. The Mobilia dustbin is partly buried due to the brief requesting both architectural expression and function; its lower emptying height makes the job easier for personnel. The dustbin's inner space is equivalent to an 80l standard plastic liner, the most commonly used type. The plastic liner is completely concealed in the body, which is easily opened for emptying. The Mobilia dustbin with the item number EBD.10.2022 is made of untreated cast iron. The container is also available with a surface treated design, corrosion class IV, in cast iron or steel.

200 WASTEBASKETS

Nastra

Design: **Outsign** • Production: **Concept Urbain**

Nastra has a body of cast aluminium, finished with RAL lacquer in the colour of choice. Its 85 litre interior is lined with aluminium. It has a locking system with triangular key. The stainless steel lock has a returning spring.

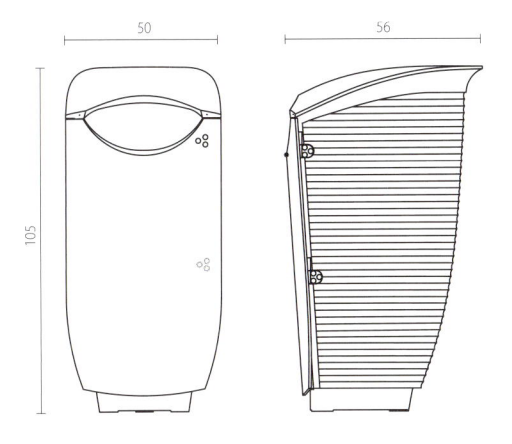

Net

Design: **Diego Fortunato** • Production: **Escofet**

Net is based on the idea of a line of urban furniture that is gently rounded and recalls no particular historical period. It is an attempt to address the sensual quality of cast concrete, enabling it to integrate well into any environment. Athough it comes in standard tones of black and white, it can be supplied on request in the full range of colours produced by Escofet. The surface texture has been gently sandblasted. Each item has a capacity of 40 litres and weighs 155 kg. It requires anchoring to the pavement for stability. The plastic container-bag is fixed by means of an articulated stainless steel ring. The compatible garbage-bag size is 575 x 1000mm.

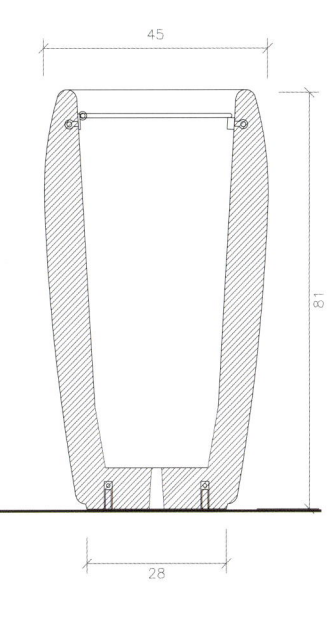

WASTEBASKETS

Pandora

Design: Alessandro Riberti - Studio Italo Rota & Partners • Production: Modo

A litterbin with a cast iron body (also available in aluminium on request), and a cast aluminium lid with three inlets, in this version with simple holes; it is provided with an inner stainless steel ring that blocks the liner, unlocked with a special safety key. Designed for use with an inner galvanised steel basket or dustbin liner. An inner stainless steel ashtray is available on request. The surface is treated with antirust protection and covering with thermosetting powders in silver, charcoal grey and metallic bronze.

Paralela

Design: Juan Cuenca Montilla • Production: T&D Cabanes

Paralela is a litterbin the support of which is constructed by means of a "U" shaped mounting bracket made of carbon steel. It has a capacity of 25 litres and can be adapted for use as an ashtray. It is made of galvanized steel plate with rows of perforations, the emptying system is gyratory and the basket is fixed in position with a slam-lock. The entire object is fixed to the ground with bolts and metal expansion-plugs. The finish is hot-dip galvanized, plus a layer of base paint and another of paint.

Pandora

Paralela

WASTEBASKETS

Pitch

Design: **Frog Design** • Production: **Landscape Forms**

Pitch is a trash receptacle in the shape of a flaring curve that rises out of the ground. Function drove the design of this simple form, whose widened top makes it easy to lift liners up and out, making it ideal from the maintenance point of view. From the point of view of the user, the object is easy, non-institutional in character, friendly and inviting. The full range of the «35» product line is engineered and BIFMA tested to ensure safety. This items dimensions are (Side Opening) 35" in height x 25" deep x 25" wide. The receptacle's total weight is 125 lbs.

Quattro

Design: **Bernhard Winkler** • Production: **Euroform**

The elegant, well designed Quattro litterbins always ensure a clean environment in their many designs, with or without a cover, fixed to the ground or mounted on a wall. It is available in two versions with or without the cover, which provides for an ashtray. It has a capacity of 50 litres

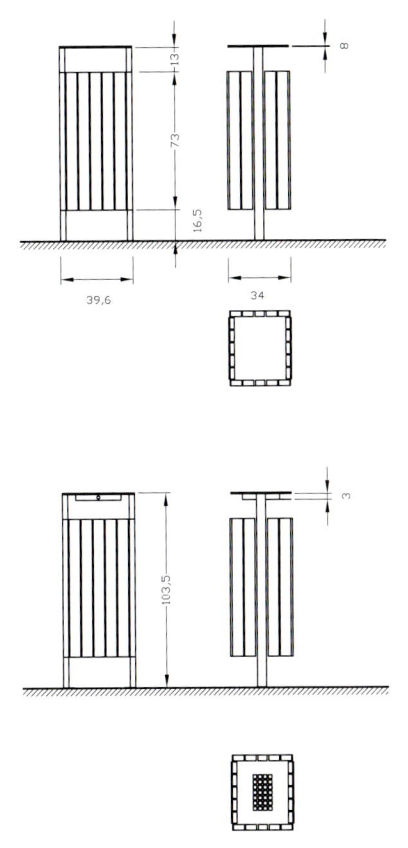

WASTEBASKETS

Racional

Design: **Franc Fernández** • Production: **Tecam BCN**

This wastebasket is made of extruded aluminum. The body consists of two cylinders, a mouth of cast aluminum and two intermediate rings of stainless steel. Its shape, the materials it is made of and the production method make this a very solid item. It represents an innovative concept in this field, by substituting the traditional tipping method by a system of swiveling on a hinge, making it incomparably more comfortable to work with. It is anchored to the ground by three expansion screws. It can be made case-specific for a type of floor. Colors: anodized aluminum.

Radium

Design: **David Karásek & Radek Hegmon** • Production: **mmcité**

The Radium litterbin is a geometrically styled body with softly rounded edges that is the direct result of the technology of bent steel sheet. The support structure is a rectangular ring with rounded edges that carries the inserted box, which in turn contains the galvanized steel inner bin. The complete piece is an elegant and durable example of public furniture. Its design establishes an associative link with the Radium benches and bollards. The supporting frame is made of galvanized steel, with a rustproof covering and painted in a standard shade. There is a forward opening lockable door and an ashtray with a stainless steel cigarette extinguisher integrated into the piece's top cover. The item is designed to be fixed to a concrete base or a pavement by means of stainless steel anchoring bolts.

WASTEBASKETS

Rambla

Design: **Guillermo Bertólez & Javier Ferrándiz** • Production: **Santa & Cole**

This is a robust, elliptical litterbin made of stainless steel, painted steel or galvanized steel. It is very practical and suitable for narrow streets. The urban Rambla litterbin, upright or attached to the wall, is a simple, economic and long-lasting product. It has an elliptical base and a simple, sober appearance and reasonable capacity. It is especially suitable for narrow pavements. Its opacity hides its contents and the unit has remarkable compositional possibilities when placed diagonally in groups, front to back or parallel, to reinforce any particular arrangement. The criteria that determined the design were comfortable use, easy handling and aesthetic appearance.

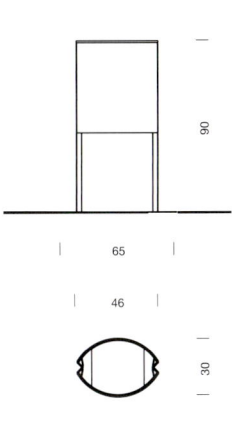

Rio

Design: **Juan Cuenca Montilla** • Production: **Tecam BCN**

This sturdily built wastebasket with an incorporated ashtray accessory and a capacity of 30 liters consists of an exterior body of galvanized carbon steel and an extractable interior container made of perforated galvanized steel sheet. The upper lid, which folds back, is of stainless steel and is fixed by a sliding bolt. The complete object is fixed to the ground by means of M10 steel bolts previously cemented into the pavement, for the base of the waste basket to be screwed onto. The unit is delivered with a hot-galvanized finish, a layer of base paint and one coat of paint, ready for an optional second coat in a color suited to the given project's requirements.

WASTEBASKETS

Rodes

Design: **José A. Martínez Lapeña & Elías Torres** • Production: **Santa & Cole**

The Rodes litterbin offers great durability and size, and is made of materials that require zero maintenance. The body is made of cast steel with a layer of anti-corrosive treatment and a coat of powder coated black paint. The upper part is of cast aluminium, powder painted in gray. The two pieces are fixed together with stainless steel screws. It has a stainless steel ring inside that holds the rubbish-bag. It is anchored to the ground with three stainless steel bolts that go into previously prepared drill-holes filled with quick-drying cement or epoxy resin or similar materials.

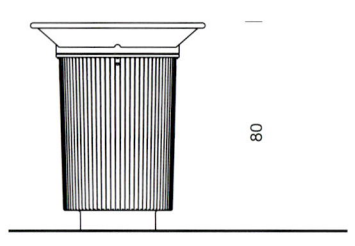

Sacharoff

Design: **Enric Pericas, Maria Luisa Aguado, Carles Casamor y Maria Gabás** • Production: **Fundició Dúctil Benito**

Sacharoff is a waste paper bin that combines design, functionality and toughness. The structure is made of cast aluminium with a grainy, matt finish. It consists of a bucket, a lock, and four MB expansion bolts. It can be locked with a key and can be turned around to make it easier to empty.

WASTEBASKETS

Saturno

Design: **Brunetti Filipponi Associati** • Production: **ORA Centurelli**

This square rubbish bin (single or double), which measures 300 x 300 mm (11,79 x 11,79 inches), is designed to be mounted on the Koh-JPost pole. It is made of perforated sheet metal on three sides, with square holes measuring 10 x 10 mm (0,4 x 0,4 inches) or rolled sheet metal 2 mm (0,783 inches) thick. The back is made of 2 mm (0,783 inches) thick sheet metal and has the attachments for hooking it onto the pole; there is also a plate with holes for the screws. The sheet metal lid is 3 mm (0,117 inches) thick. On request, cut-outs can be made through the lid using plasma or laser technology, in various shapes to make differentiated waste collection easier; the cut-outs can also be omitted. The available shapes are bottle, can, paper, battery, medicine; others can be requested. Hot-galvanizing according to UNI regulations and a choice of RAL paint coatings are available on request. The single waste bin dimensions are: Length, 780 mm (30,654 inches); Width, 290 mm (11,397 inches); Height, 900 mm (35,370 inches), with a capacity of 42 liters.

Sirio

Design: **Morandi & Citterio** • Production: **Modo**

Sirio is a program of litter bins and bollards all made of AISI 304 stainless steel plate or Corten steel. The geometrical development of the laser cut sheet steel creates a rotation effect (the object looks different, depending on the viewpoint).

WASTEBASKETS

Ska

Design: Javier Machimbarrena • Production: ONN Outside

The innovative design of the Ska wastebasket with its asymmetric, aerodynamic surfaces, reflects the aesthetic vanguard of the most advanced architectural projects. Realized in painted cast aluminum, the Ska wastebasket is fully resistant, with a capacity of 60 liters and an ashtray incorporated in the top of the element, it is available with just the top ring or complete with the internal bin. Also available with an anti-graffiti finish.

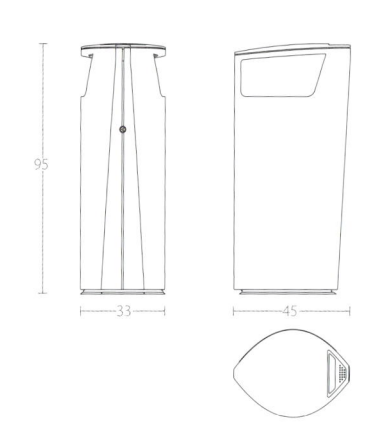

Sloper

Design: Luis Tabuenca • Production: ONN Outside

Sloper is a complete range of street furniture designed by Luis Tabuenca for the Tabuenca Saralegui and Associates studio and developed and manufactured by ONN Outside. Biomechanical research of the human body has established that an angle of 76º is the most suitable for the backrests on street seating. This angle has become a geometrical ruling criterion for a range of products that meet all the requirements of exterior environments. Sloper provides the solution to any urban project using the same aesthetic criteria of practicality and top quality materials. In addition, the flexibility of the lights, which allow for use and optimization of whatever light source is preferred, makes Sloper compatible with numerous street lighting projects.

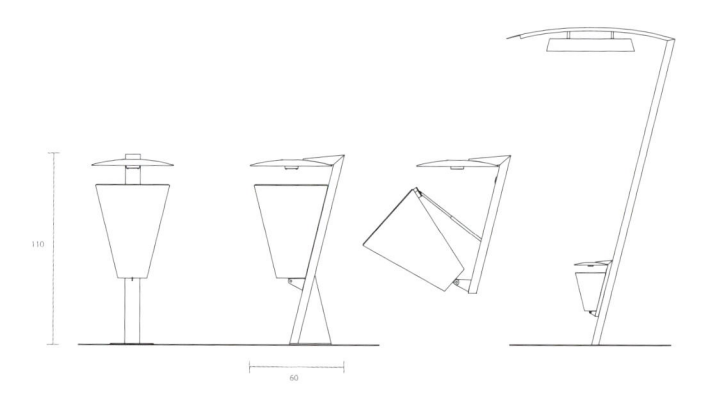

WASTEBASKETS

Socrates

Design: **Equipo Técnico Escofet** • Production: **Escofet**

The Socrates ashtray is an element in polished or acid-etched concrete which is available in the full range of standard colors. A small cube with a stainless steel cylinder inside for ash collection, it is available in two heights: 460 mm and 700 mm. It is installed resting directly on the ground on a rebated base which ensures the geometrical perfection of the piece while at the same time making it appear to float.

Starck

Design: **Philippe Starck** • Production: **JCDecaux**

This waste paper bin designed by Philippe Starck combines aesthetic values and functionality. The inverted elliptical body is made of cast iron, completed with a dome-shaped lid with three lateral openings. It is easy to empty thanks to the lightweight inner basket with anatomical handles. It is also easy to clean and remarkably vandal-proof, as it is entirely made of non igniting materials and the inside is only accessible by means of a special key.

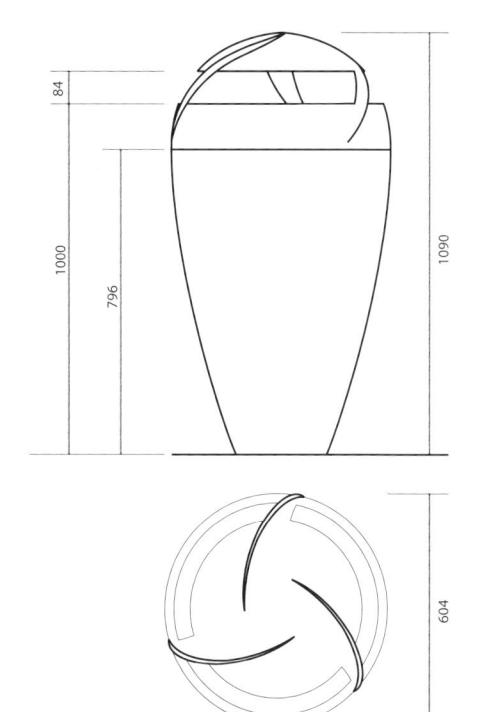

WASTEBASKETS

Trash

Design: **Diana Cabeza** • Production: **Estudio Cabeza**

A simple bin, with one, two or three mouths, and a flip top for removing the container bag and disposing of larger litter items. Optional hanging configuration from two hardwood posts, planed and natural finish, embedded into in-situ concrete block.

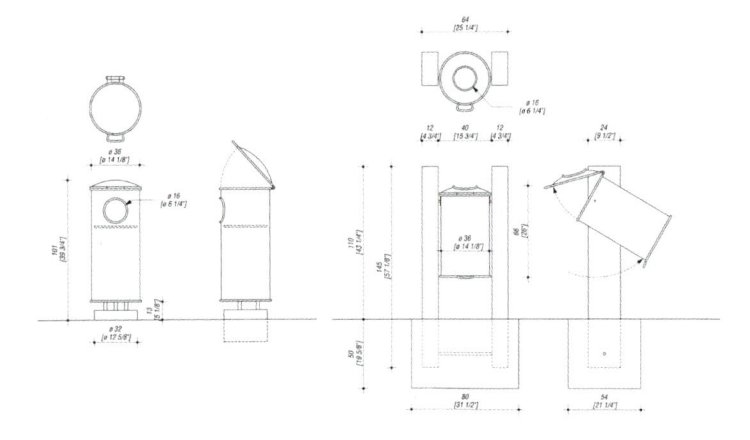

Urbana

Design: **Cristian Cirici** • Production: **Bd**

Making good use of these obstacles found scattered along our street represents a challenge: *"Our pavements are full of obstacles which are nevertheless necessary to provide the services we demand: lampposts to illuminate the streets, traffic lights... In view of the high number of obstacles already on the pavements the idea was to take advantage of these inevitable elements by using them as a support. To a certain degree this waste bin is rather like a parasite of these numerous urban obstacles. That is why the bin's fixture element comes in a wide variety of forms, with the only common feature being that no support of its own is required".* Fastening to the wall, lamppost and other urban furniture with Hälfen. To the floor with a built in support.

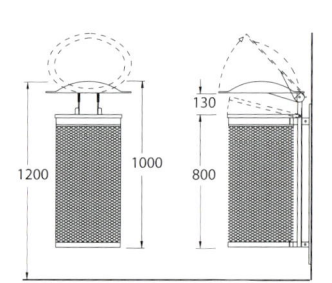

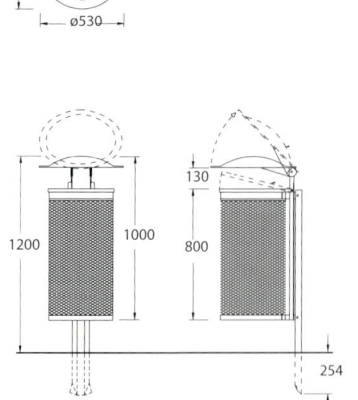

WASTEBASKETS

Valet

Design: **David Karásek & Radek Hegmon** • Production: **mmcité**

This slim and inconspicuous freestanding ashtray related to the SL bollards range is suitable for various localities. The article consists of a steel angle iron post that bears a lockable stainless steel box for cigarette ash or plastic bags for dog excrements. Its function is made identifiable by a cigarette symbol, engraved on the steel and enamelled red to increase its visibility. Another model serves as a support of the plastic bags for dog excrements. The galvanized and powder coated steel body rises 1000 mm (39,3 inches) over the pavement. Two widths are available, to gain adaptability to the proportions of a given installation: L 60 mm (2,358 inches) and L 80 mm (3,144 inches). Its robust structure and easy manipulation are the major advantages of this modern element of street furniture. It has a baseplate designed to be fixed in the concrete under the pavement, guaranteeing the object's stability.

Vega

Design: **Alessandro Riberti** • Production: **Modo**

A litterbin consisting of a 3 mm steel plate skeleton with a bin liner ring and a 1.5 mm turned steel plate frontal case lined with 70x28 mm impregnated iroko or pine wood slats. The openable hatch has revolving bodywork to facilitate removing the liner. The key closure is triangular.

Shelters

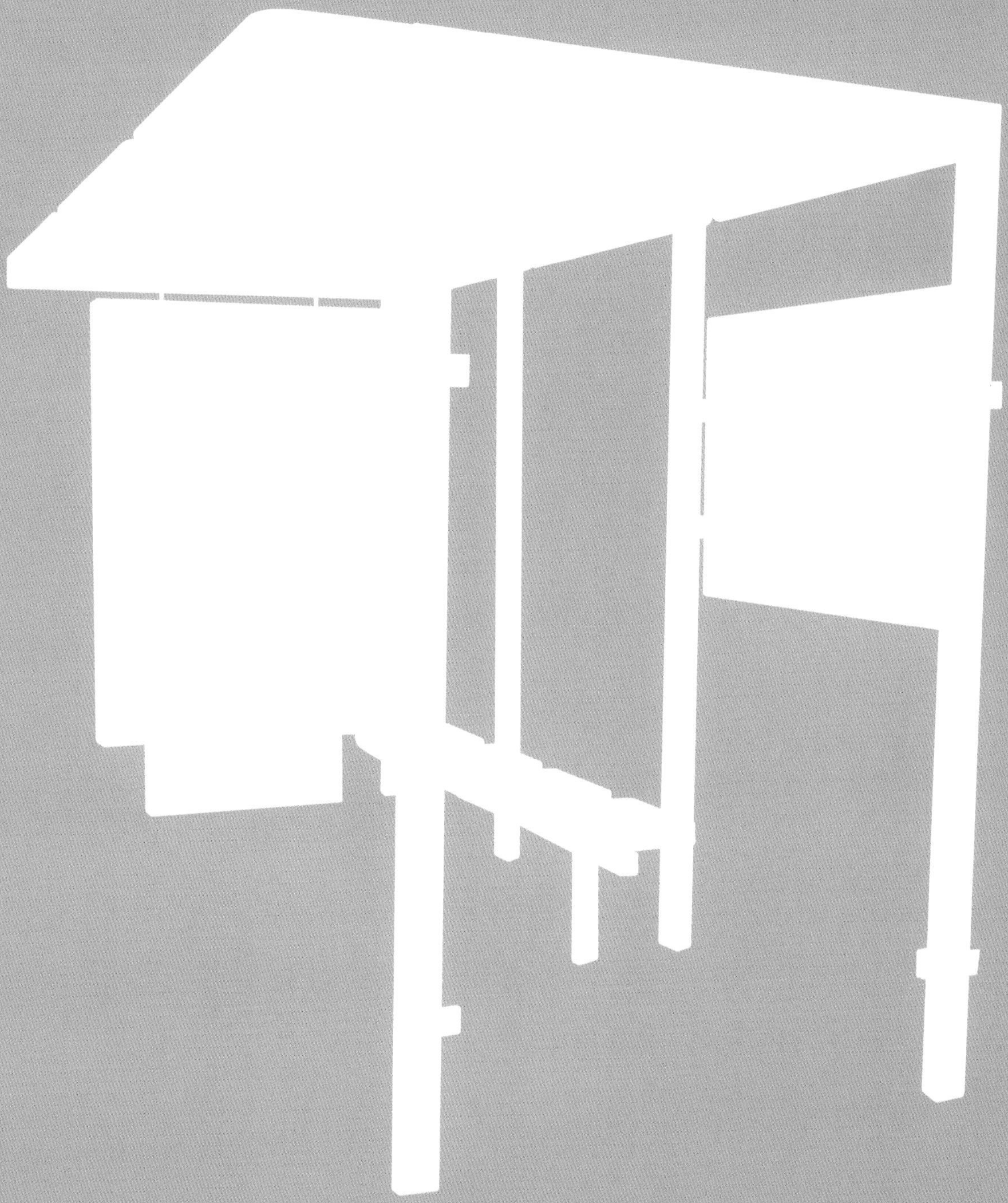

Andromeda

Design: **Studio Rota & Partners** • Production: **Modo**

The contemporary shape of this bus shelter creates a charming aesthetic impact. The inner structure is made of Fe 360 B steel, covered with panels of decorative laminated plastic suitable for outdoor use. The bus stop shelter is available with or without plate glass sides, with wooden seats and a lighting system.

APCD

Design: **APCD** • Production: **Larus**

The structure and the material for the roof of this straight planed marquee with a minimalist air is Zincor steel. The benches are also built of Zincor, perforated sheet in this case. Both the structure and the benches are painted with a dark anthracite-toned metallic paint, while the other components can be painted in different optional colors. Tempered glass completes the list of materials. Storm-water run-off is channeled towards the drains that are concealed inside the supporting pillars.

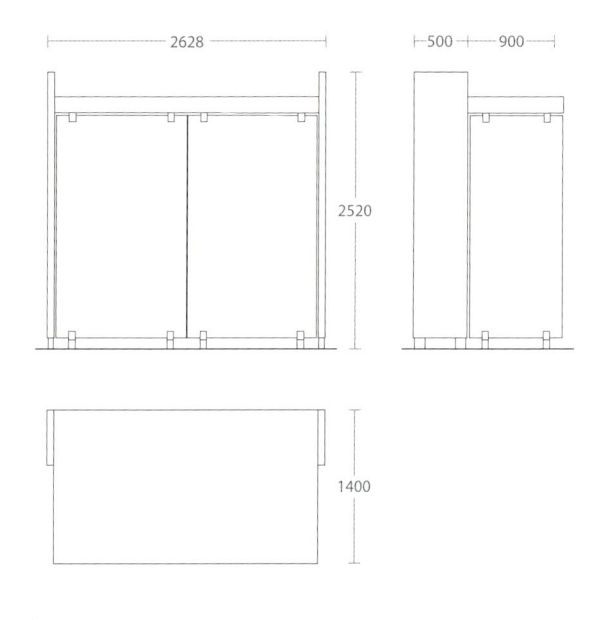

214 SHELTERS

Apoios de Praia

Design: **Alcino Soutinho** • Production: **Larus**

These pieces are intended for the catering industry, to support activities on the beach during the summer season. They are modular elements which provide a bar unit complete with its counter, a unisex bathroom with access for the disabled and a third module for a medical service. The main structure and the roof are constructed in marine board coated on both sides with fiberglass reinforced polyester resin, and include a thermal insulation of polyurethane foam. The ensemble sits on a stainless steel structure. The flooring consists of a non-slip plywood board in the bar area and a non-slip aluminum overlay in the bathroom and medical area.

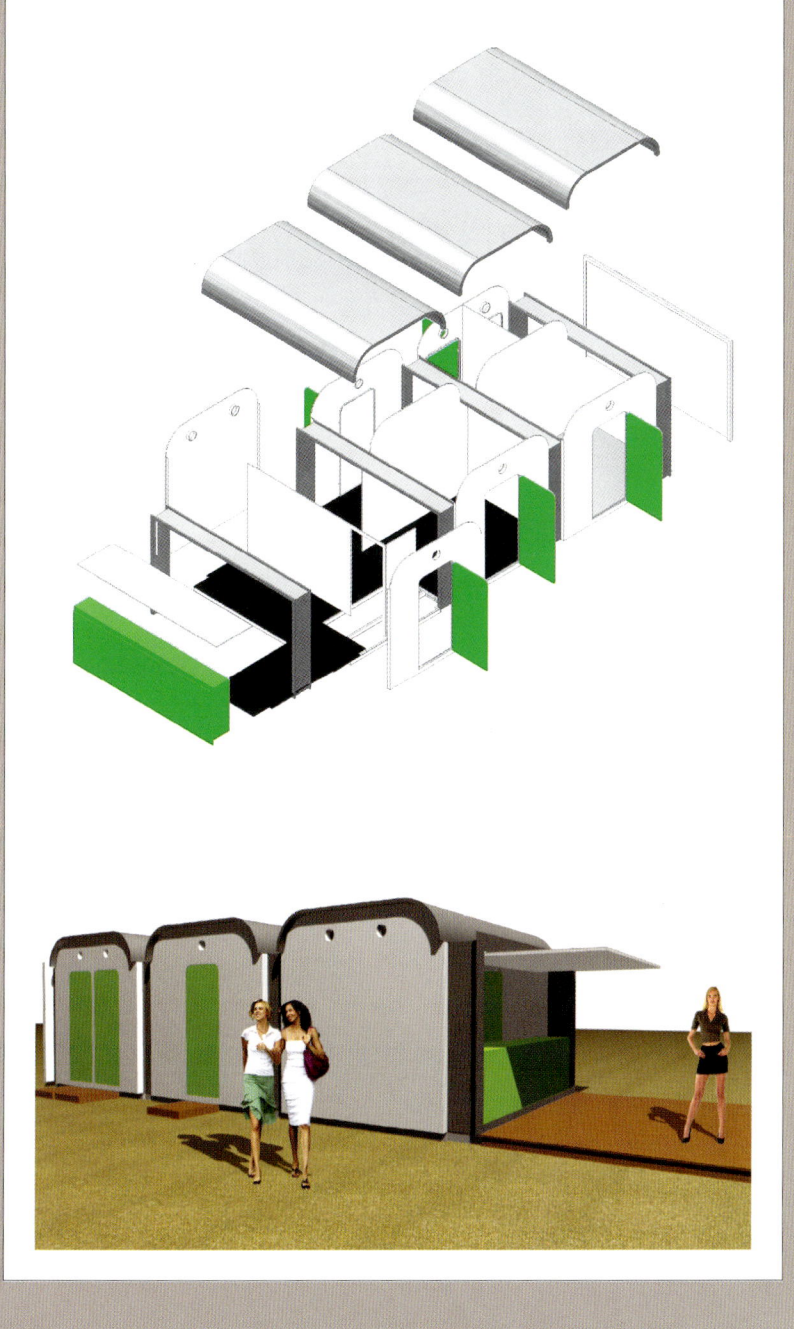

Arqui

Design: **Jorge Trindade / Larus - Aveiro** • Production: **Larus**

The compact volume of this kiosk or vending stand is defined by a variety of modular elevation walls that come in standard sizes, the dimensions of which are of 2 × 2 m, 2 × 3 m, 3 × 3 m, 3 × 4 m, 4 × 4 m, 5 × 5 m, etc. The body consists of a galvanized and painted tubular steel structure, which supports a roof of polyester resin reinforced with fiberglass and a finish layer of phenol resin. The kiosk has glass eaves around the upper perimeter, which are held by a succession of T shaped angle-iron frames. The interior cladding can make use of thermo-lacquered metal sheeting or other sheathing material. The ceiling consists of a galvanized and painted steel structure, to support particle board panels dressed with melamine. The functional elements and ventilation frames are made of thermo-lacquered aluminum.

The configuration of the elevations allows for a variable distribution of opaque and transparent vertical surfaces, making use of the availability of sliding doors and windows. Besides the possibility of interior partitions, this vending and display system allows for the installation of electrical supply systems, running water and air conditioning. The floor can be paved or a raised floor platform can be included.

SHELTERS

Aureo

Design: **David Karásek & Radek Hegmon** • Production: **mmcité**

This range of marquees comes in two different cover options and a great variety of materials, which permit the implementation of the most adequate choice regarding the characteristics of a particular location. The shelter can be arched or flat, made out of polycarbonate or of glass, and its sleek, clean structure has a number of interesting details. The support system is embodied in the rear screen, which enables it to be used without lateral panels, an option that is ideal for places where space is limited. The structure is made of galvanized steel painted in standard colors and is highly satisfactory level of resistance to vandalism and corrosion. The rear panel and the sides consist of tempered glass and wooden slats, the seat is made of solid wood, treated for outdoor use, and the roof installation can be realized in alveolar polycarbonate or in tempered glass. The storm water is drained through a support pillar. One or two advertising screens can be fitted, as well as a panel containing timetables or other public information.

BMG

Design: **David Karásek & Radek Hegmon** • Production: **mmcité**

With the supporting structure situated in the rear wall, the simple and clear design of this bus stop shelter is based on the combination of big glass areas, the coarse galvanized surfaces of the supporting steel parts and the powder coated frame details. The glass roof is provided with sand stripes, to filter the direct sunlight inside the shelter. The rear wall is hung on the frame from outside. The side walls can perform as backlit show-cases (CLV) to carry advertising, maps of the city or any other graphic information. They can also be enclosed in clear or mirror glass. This modern shelter designed for the city of Brno certifies its qualities in all types of city areas including historic centers.

The structure consists of rough finished galvanized steel with powder coated details. Tempered glass encloses the roof, back wall and sides. Rain water drains through one of the pillars. The solid wooden seat is treated for outdoor use. For narrow locations, an optional model with no side walls is also available.

SHELTERS

Buenos Aires

Design: **Diana Cabeza, Leandro Heine, Martín Wolfson**
Graphic Design: **Osvaldo Ortiz, Gabriela Falgione, Pablo Cosgaya y Marcela Romero**
Technology: **Santiago Herrera** • Lighting: **Pablo Pizarro**

We believe that the urban elements must respond to the geographical and cultural environments that surround them, being able to blend with the general disposition and particularities.

The elements to be placed on the sidewalks are endowed with a front and a back part, enabling people to walk throughout their perimeter and use them in different ways and from different directions.

This creates continuity between the private realm and the open public space and confers a more dynamic perception of the city avoiding the "urban pathways" that these elements usually generate.

The project focuses on preserving the historical heritage of the city, while providing modern urban elements life.

The "barrio" or neighborhood is the basis of the urban identity, the context of our history, and primary link to our social rites and life within the community.

The whole system of urban elements was with the idea of a city accessible to everyone.

218 SHELTERS

City 90

Design and production: Microarquitectura / Team Tejbrant

This timeless design harmonizes perfectly with any context. The pergola does not dominate the urban landscape, rather it completes it. Built in extruded aluminum, this product is light, aesthetically elegant and almost maintenance free.

It is available in a range of sizes, which flexibility makes it adaptable to the client's needs in each case allowing the ideal model and size to be chosen for each setting while ensuring a unified global image.

Eco

Design: Brunetti Filipponi Associati • Production: ORA Centurelli

This structure consists of a structural frame made of four tubular hot-galvanized steel support members 100 × 100 × 2 mm in section. These members are fixed to the ground by means of 8 mm thick anchoring shoes held by 8 mm expansion bolts. The roof is of galvanized steel sheet, 10 × 10 mm thick. As for the wall panels, the various options they are available in are: 6 mm thick methacrylate, 4 + 4 mm thick laminated tinted security glass, 8 mm thick laminated and tinted plastic, or corrugated galvanized steel sheet. It is also available with a two side panel to house advertising or another special lighting requirement. Other additional accessories are a 1700 × 400 mm bench and a waste basket. All the metal components are hot-dip galvanized and can be delivered ready-painted in the colors of the RAL catalogue. The model can be custom built to specified dimensions.

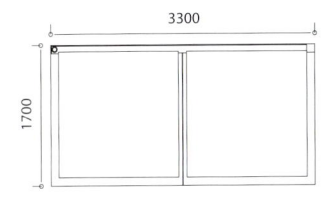

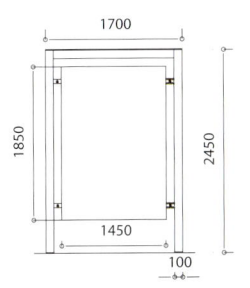

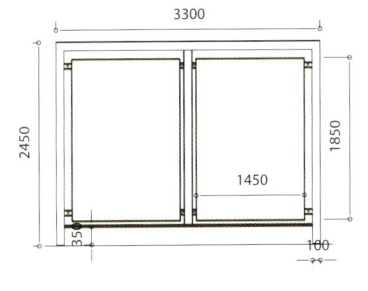

SHELTERS

Edge

Design: **David Karásek & Radek Hegmon** • Production: **mmcité**

The Edge bicycle shelter has a radial dynamic shape that combines a robust supporting structure with fine glass walls held up by sturdy stainless steel holders. The bicycle wheels are held in grooves that pierce the building's distinctly slanting plastic rear wall, the shelter's most characteristic feature. The frames can be chain locked to the tubular steel bars that separate the bicycles. The steel structure is hot dip galvanized or powder coated in any RAL colour. The roof and sidewalls are made of tempered glass. Optionally it can be provided with a corrugated roof of zincified sheet-steel.

Erandio

Design and production: **ONN Outside**

The Erandio shelter, manufactured in stainless steel and laminated glass, offers a wide range of possible combinations thanks to its modular design. Bench, perch, side enclosure, decoration of the glass with vinyl or glass fiber are some of the options for personalizing the shelter which can be manufactured in 3, 4 or 5 modules. The 54 possible combinations all lead to the same result – an elegant and understated space.

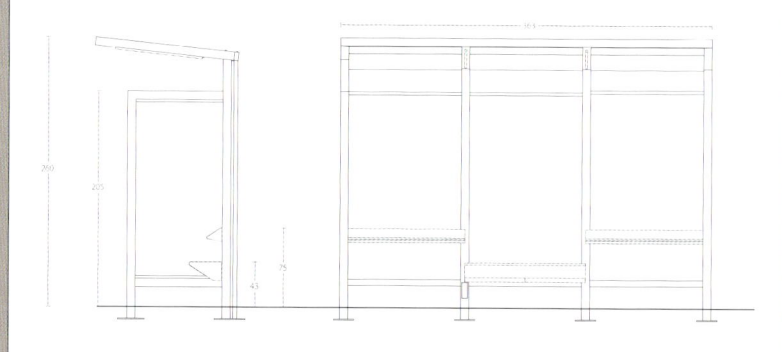

Foster

Design: **Norman Foster** • Production: **JC Decaux**

This bus shelter has been chosen for the Champs Elyseés in Paris. With a double sided lateral enclosure, it has a capacity for eighteen people, including seating for five or six. The overall design combines glass and steel for maximum visual and formal lightness, while also offering maximum protection from meteorological elements at either end. The vertical structure has been reduced to its most essential elements, and the design of the roof support elements, as well as the suspended bench, seem to follow the designer's high tech aesthetic.

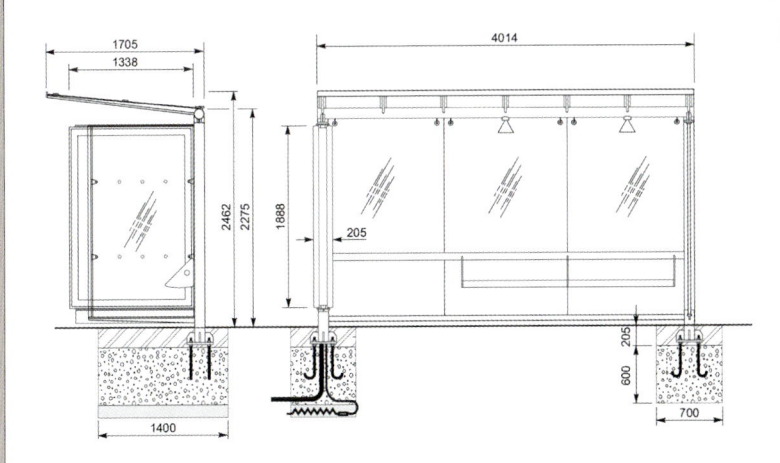

Gull Wing

Design: **Brunetti Filipponi Associati** • Production: **ORA Centurelli**

The supporting structure of the Gullwing bus stop shelter consists of 2 hot-galvanized steel tubular bars, with a round cross-section of 100 × 2 mm (3.93 × 0.08 inches). There are base-plates and backing plates at each end, provided with log bolts to bury in the reinforced concrete foundation slab.
The item comes complete with a roof shelter of galvanized steel sheet (thickness 10/10). (0.39 × 0.39 inches).
Double walls are available on request for advertising and/or lighting purposes. There are provisions for a bench (size 1700 × 400 mm) (67.49 × 15.88 inch) and a litter bin. All iron parts are hot-galvanized, according to UNI regulations. RAL paint coating is an optional choice. This prestigious product is ideal for any environment.

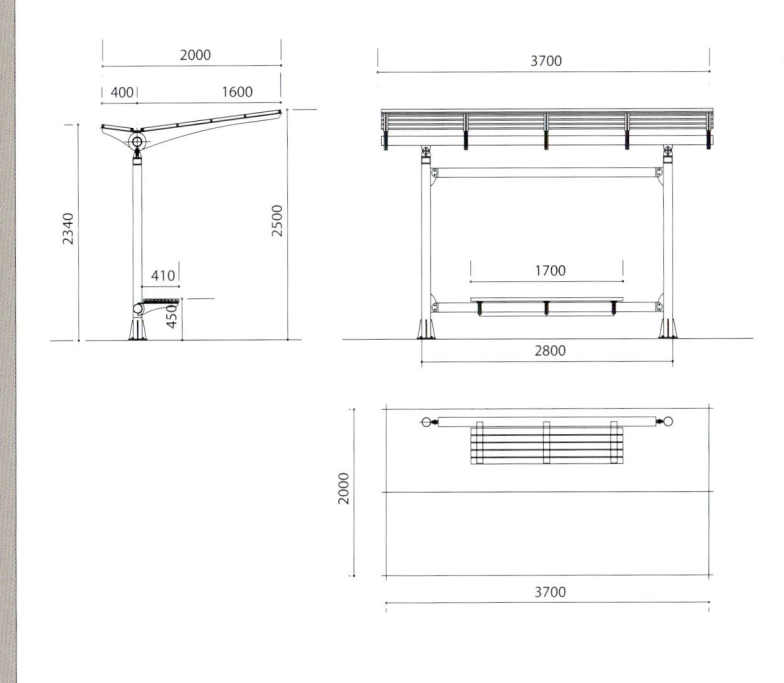

SHELTERS

Habana

Design: Màrius Quintana • Production: Microarquitectura

Microarquitectura has installed the Habana kiosks in parks and development projects in Barcelona and neighbouring towns such as Terrassa, Sabadell, Sant Adrià, Badalona, Ripollet, Santa Coloma, El Prat de Llobregat, Sant Boi, Vilanova i la Geltrú, Cambrils, el Vendrell, Lloret de Mar and all the way to Valencia, Cáceres and Ibiza. The kiosks have been approved by the Barcelona Town Hall, Barcelona Institute of Parks and Gardens, Collserola Consortium, Barcelona Metropolitan District, Cambrils Board of Tourism, The Sagrada Familia Board of trustees, and others. Microarquitectura regularly carries out signaling projects or sculptural installations. As for the urban furniture they develop, the ADA series is a relevant example of beach facilities (shower, foot shower, fountain and litterbin) or the AJC series of streetlamps, benches and litterbins. The enterprise is experienced in working jointly with institutions in a context of research, to provide items of tested quality in which performance and sustainability meet. Designed to fulfil the requirements of seaside, park or urban environments, Habana is a module that can be installed with or without the pergola. The two items, module and pergola, have been separately designed to enhance their adaptability to any situation. The pergola can be extended indefinitely or even be installed on its own; the sunscreen roof of wooden slats can become an awning if replaced by weatherproof glass. The underlying idea is to implement the maximum respect for urban locations through unobtrusive, timeless design. The unconcealed metal structure can accommodate a variety of wall panels, fixed or sliding, opaque or clear. When closed it becomes a vandal-discouraging compact volume, which unfolds into a welcoming open space during working hours. This tightly measured object allows transportation and assembly to be executed with no complications beyond connecting it to the power and supply line. Built according to accessibility requirements for the disabled, it can house a cafeteria, a vending stand, a first-aid centre or a dressing room.

Heritage

Design and production: JCDecaux

Heritage is a shelter with a capacity for 15 persons, six of them seated. The structure is supported by four cast iron posts. The roof measures 5 m2 and the information box comes as a separate accessory. The glazing consists of three separate sheets of glass at the back and one at the side. The materials chosen for this item provide maximum durability and resistance, and its design is vandal-proof.

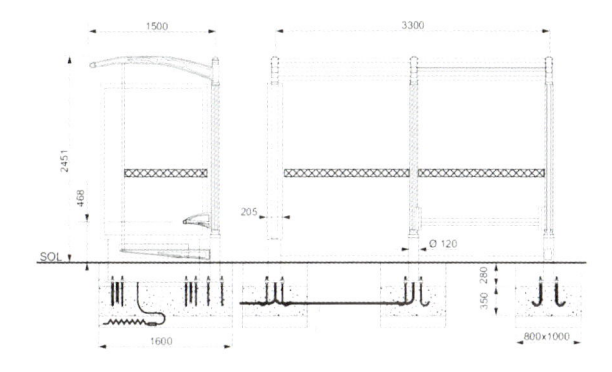

Kaleidoscope

Design and production: Landscape Forms

Kaleidoscope is a series of parts designed to create a sense of place. The basic structure consists of a post and a canopy. These can work on their own or with the optional addition of seating and lighting to make handsome gateways, transit stops on city streets, valet parking stations, bike rack shelters, break areas on corporate campuses and covered seating in malls, parks and zoos. Kaleidoscope is modular and has replaceable parts. It is assembled, not constructed, and can be removed and relocated. It meets demanding wind force and snow load testing.

Smart Shelter is an outdoor transit shelter that integrates the Kaleidoscope canopy and structure by Landscape Forms with solar powered lighting and advanced light-emitting diode (LED) technology.

Smart Shelter was developed in response to customer requests for an illuminated transportation shelter requiring no external power and reliably meeting the tough demands of urban environments, a rugged, durable, cost-effective and low maintenance solution for cities and transit agencies that enhances safety, security and service.

Nimbus

Design: **David Karásek & Radek Hegmon** • Production: **mmcité**

The stable and time-tested structure of this range of all-purpose shelters enjoys a visually light appearance. Its smartly supported arched roof seems to hover over the glass walls and the slender steel pillars. The shelter is available in a wide selection of dimensions. The galvanized steel structure is painted in a standard shade. The rear and side walls are made of tempered glass, the roof consists of twin-wall polycarbonate. Rain water drains through the pillars. The shelter has a solid wooden seat treated for outdoor use. A timetable holder is optional.

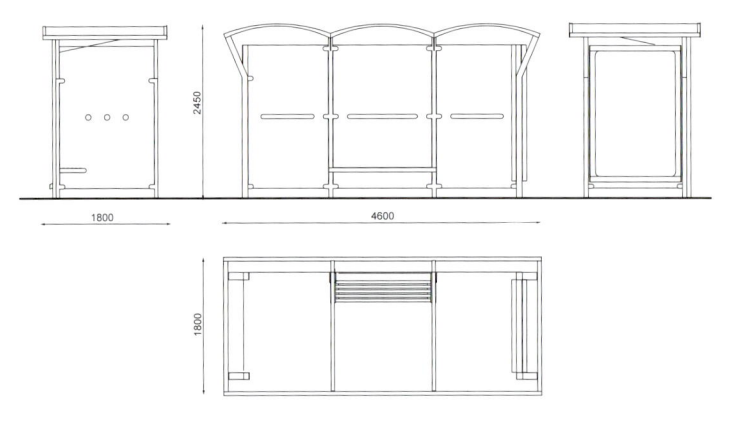

SHELTERS

Pausanias

Design: **Antoni Roselló Til** • Production: **Santa & Cole**

Available in different sizes for different functions, this modular micro-architectural kiosk is accessible to the passer-by, yet provides a totally-sealed and robust box for roadside trade in the city. The anthropologist James Frazer said of Pausanias: «without him, the ruins of Greece would be an insoluble enigma». Pausanias was a traveler and geographer who, in his "Description of Greece" recorded what he saw with outstanding documentary sense. Antoni Roselló pays homage to this 2nd-century AD chronicler who gathered information, shared it with his contemporaries, enabling us today to know what ancient Greece was like.

In contemporary urban design, the kiosk spans a gap between the modern-day chroniclers and the users of information. Daily information requires support and organization. Roselló has responded to this making it totally accessible to passers-by without invading public space, but adding a technological air. Its formal simplicity and clear-cut shapes resolve all the needs of this complex functional unit in the minimum space, dignifying this often over designed item. It invites as many functions as can be demanded of a self-financing, autonomous urban commercial unit, selling press, sweets or lottery. The back and sides can support standardized advertising panels.

Its main structure consists of sandblasted stainless steel sections and an exterior finish of grey-pigmented reinforced fiberglass panels. It has an automatic opening system, operated by activating the sandblasted stainless steel sash blind and the subsequent stainless steel and glass counter manually. Finally the upper canopy is raised, creating a show-window and an intermediate space between the vendor and his customers. Optionally, the display can be placed in the sides. Inside the kiosk is a storage area, an electrical installation space and a hatch for deliveries. The storage cupboard has room for an air-conditioning system. The interior is illuminated by 6 large translucent Macaya wall lamps equipped with LED's. The unit is delivered fully assembled, leveled in position by manipulation of its four adjustable legs.

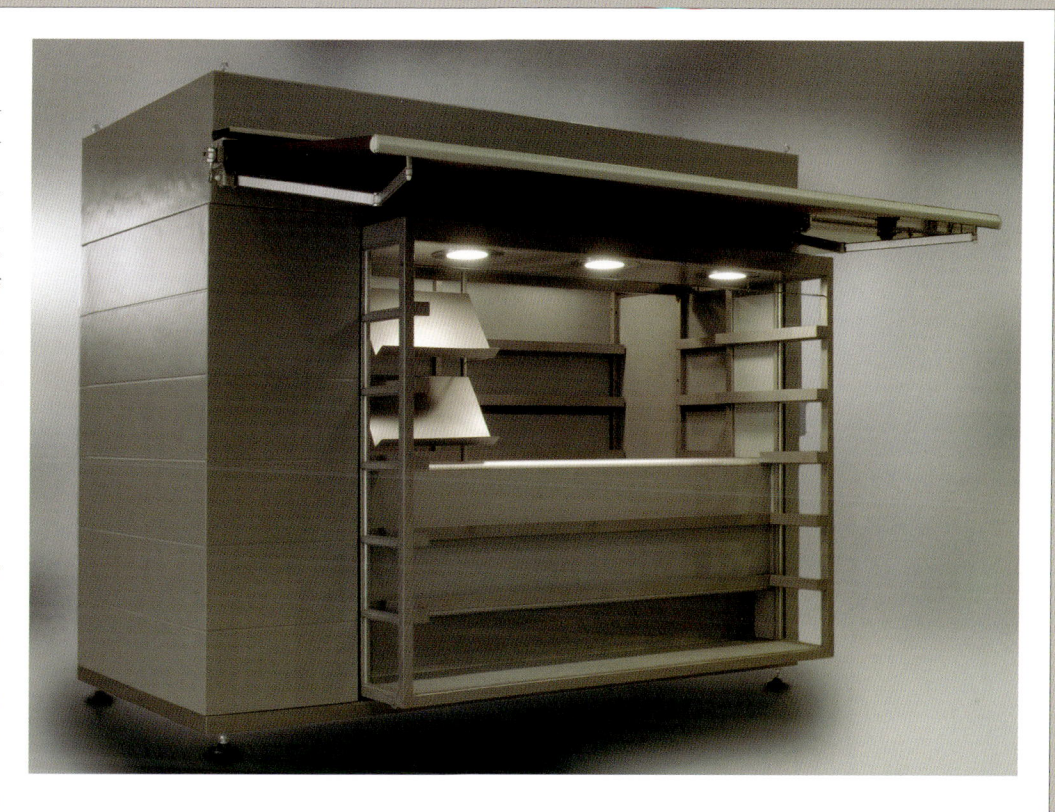

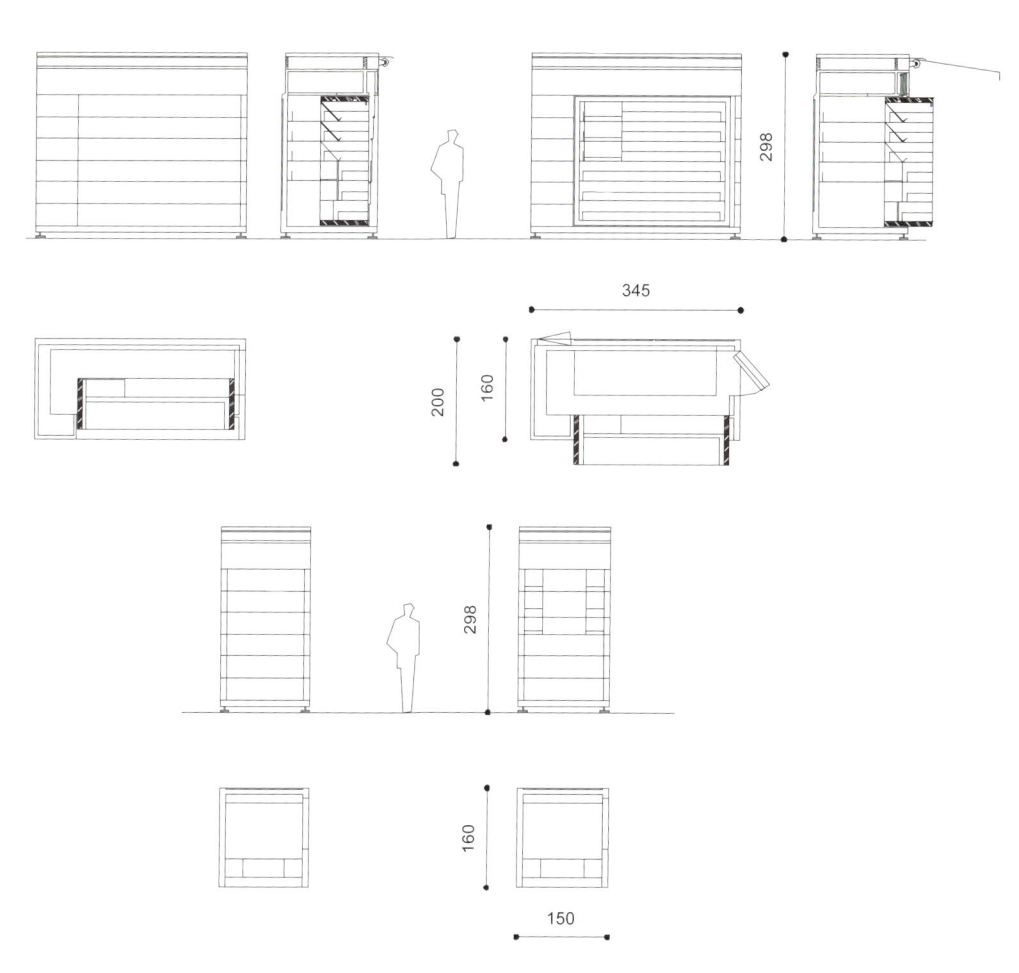

SHELTERS

Pórtico

Design: Jorge Alves • Production: Larus

As the name of this article suggests the main element of this marquee is the diagonal structural frame from which the roof is suspended. This frame is reinforced by a lower structure that is fixed to the seat through the glass. One of the pillars houses the electrical wiring, while the other is used as the stormwater drainage pipe. Its particular structure allows several units to be installed in a row, giving the group a unitary and continuous appearance. The material used throughout the whole of the structure, the roof and the bench is Zincor steel sheet, perforated for the bench accessory. Both the vertical structure and the bench are finished in anthracite colored metallic paint, and the remaining members can be custom finished. The transparent panels are made of tempered glass.

Refugio Verde

Design: Diana Cabeza & Martín Wolfson • Production: Estudio Cabeza

Refugio Verde shelters a bus stop in Puerto Madero (Buenos Aires). The roof is of laminated security glass with an inner layer of green PVE, designed to act as a green filter onto which the leaves seem to have dropped after a strong gust of wind, creating a sort of green canopy. In the summertime the users find shade here, and for a while their skin is tinted a beautiful shade of green. The structure is made of steel, protected from corrosion with polyurethane paint.

Regio

Design: **David Karásek & Radek Hegmon** • Production: **mmcité**

This structure combines galvanized steel with components of wood and of tempered glass. The very unusual choice of wood for the support structure of the roof underlines the organic expression of this model of marquee. In fact, it is an elegant solution that guarantees an appropriate level of resistance to vandalism and to the most adverse weather conditions. The structure is made of galvanized steel painted in a range of standard colors, supporting components of marine laminated wood weatherproofed for outdoor use. Tempered glass has been used for the rear and side panels, and the roof can be realized in alveolar polycarbonate plastic or in security glass. One of the support pillars at the back serves as the drainage outlet for stormwater. The bench is made of solid wood, treated for outdoor use. Conceived for use in areas with a limited amount of free space, models without the side panels are also available.

SHELTERS 227

Rural

Design: Jorge Trindade • **Production:** Larus

This marquee displays a metal body, enclosed on three of its sides, with a structural frame that supports the roof and provides the object with the required stability. The roof is made of sandwich-type paneling, the exterior face of which has a sheet of polyester resin reinforced with fiberglass. The interior side of the roof consists of tubular panels and polyurethane foam. The body of the marquee itself can be made of tempered glass or of pattern-embossed metal sheet to make it an unsuitable surface for advertising.

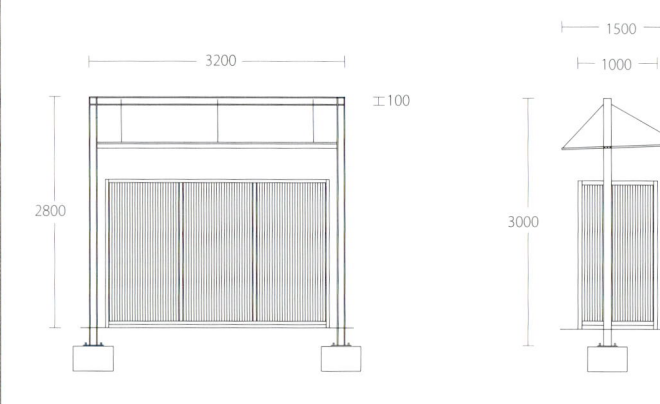

Skandum

Design: David Karásek & Radek Hegmon • **Production:** mmcité

A simple but elegant structure that fulfils all the requirements on cost-effective terms. The heat-galvanised steel structure comes painted in a standard shade. The rear and side walls are of toughened glass. The roof is of chamber polycarbonate. Rainwater drains through the pillars. The shelter has a solid wooden seat treated for outdoor use. A timetable holder is optional.

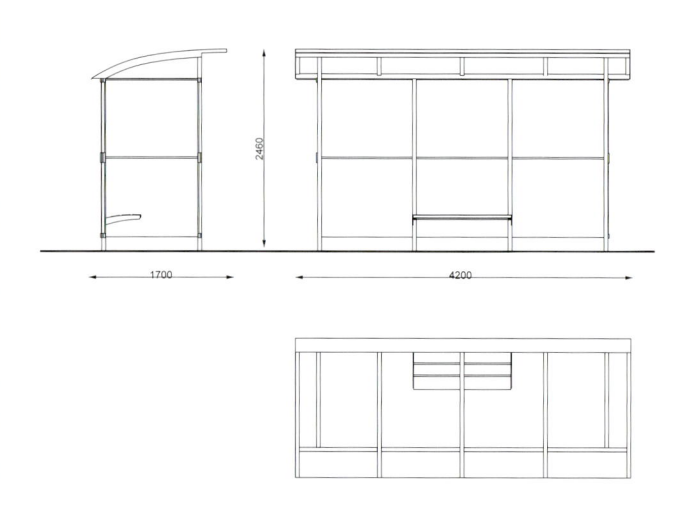

T Bus

Design: FromAtoB Public Design

The T Bus busstops have been designed for the city of Tilburg. The design consists of a range of products: busstops in different arrangements, benches, lightposts, garbage bins, poster-frames and passenger information units - that can be combined in many ways, to create small or large busstops. All elements have a strip of stainless steel cladding that can be connected to form one continuous line along the platform, out of which the different elements arise. The busshelter itself is a modular design, that can be made in single and double versions. It has a glass roof that can be outfitted with solar panels, and a glass wall with a fog-effect. The openness and curved shapes create a spacious and inviting busstop, even in the smallest configuration. In the double-sided configuration there will, even in very bad weather, always be a dry side to shelter.

SHELTERS

Terminal

Design: **David Karásek & Radek Hegmon** • Production: **mmcité**

The roof of this bus stop shelter consists of two wings that hover above cylindrical supporting poles, which they are joined to by a light structural framework. It can be supplied in a choice of different materials, and the special combination of tempered safety glass and galvanized sheet metal profiles suspended under the supporting frame produces a striking effect.

Terminal consists of a galvanized steel structure that comes painted in a range of standard shades. The roofing combines safety glass and profiled (trapezoidal) metal sheeting with an Aluzinc surface. Rainwater collects in the gutter situated under the central beam and drains through the pillars. The facility can be completed with an integrated lighting system, benches, litter bins and timetable holders. It is possible to extend the shelter by the addition of individual modules.

Tokay

Design: **Lisa Segatori** • Production: **ORA Centurelli**

The main structural frame of the Tokay bus stop shelter is made of n°2 galvanized steel sheet sides with a thickness of 3 mm, made by plasma technology. The pierced decoration can be customized, thereby adapting the character of the item to different architectural contexts, from the classical to the severely contemporary. The whole skeleton is made of electrically welded square steel tubing with a cross section 60 x 60 mm (2,358 x 2,358 inches). The steel tubing is perforated to attach the lateral surfaces or to add on another shelter. The side surfaces consist of a frame of galvanized steel tubing with a sheet of 4+4 mm (0,15+0,15 inch) laminated safety glass, fixed onto the main frame by galvanized screws.

SHELTERS

Tramvia

Design: Rafael Cáceres Zurita / Antoni Roselló Til

The idea behind these shelters is to offer a neutral design to counteract the surrounding urban complexity, with simple forms and clean lines, and materials which fit in with the city's collection of street furniture. In addition the aim was to produce a design that could be modular and serialized, so as to construct single or double platforms, different level safety barriers, and so on. The ticket machines, information panels and equipment are all featured in one compact unit so as to avoid the different elements being stretched out all along the platform. The structural approach is fundamental in achieving the essentially light appearance of the shelter: the supports and side enclosures of the equipment unit are set up in the hidden supports of the shelter; the barrier is the most minimal expression of a pedestrian safety barrier; the wind protection is made of glass. The supports which stand at 8 meters above the platform level also feature lighting for the platform and the public way and are an essential part of the structural concept of the shelter. They also act as support elements for the tram's overhead power cables.

UMD

Design: **Antoni Roselló Til** • Production: **Esteva**

This project sets out to create a series of component modules to be assembled into first aid centers in busy public areas like beaches, concerts or other situation congregating large numbers of people. One of its characteristics is that its dimensions are adapted to the inside of a transport container (6m x 2'40m x 2'60m). Once its has reached its destination, a very short time is needed to convert it into a fully equipped first aid facility, by means of efficient but simplified assembly systems. The complete object consists of two modules: the first contains a toilet, a changing room and a store room; the second contains a surgery and a waiting room, which have been distributed to make optimal use of the space available. A traditional entrance area has been omitted by vertically raising a part of the module to create a sort of entrance porch, resolving the entrance area to the waiting room and to the surgery, as well as the connection to the roof, generating a space for a lookout platform, which is reached by a small ladder. This is partly covered by a semicircular sun screen; the entire volume of the watch-tower serves as a support for the Red Cross logo and first-aid sign. The porch also resolves the connection to the other module; either at an angle or in a straight line, this volume functions as the hinge that permits the expansion or rational extension of the unit. A horizontal extension of the surgery room is also foreseen, which will generate a space that can be perceived as the waiting room. This module foresees various openings (skylights and windows) that will be concealed when the unit is closed, making it sight proof and discouraging to vandals. Conceptually, the design has two movements, two actions, a vertical mode related to vigilance, action and control, a horizontal mode akin to consultation, cure and rest.

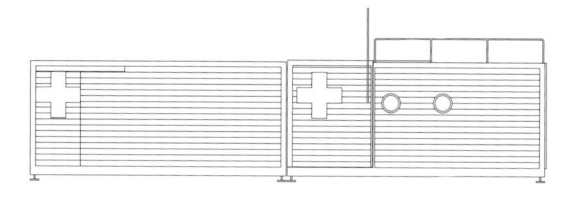

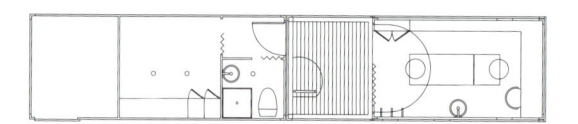

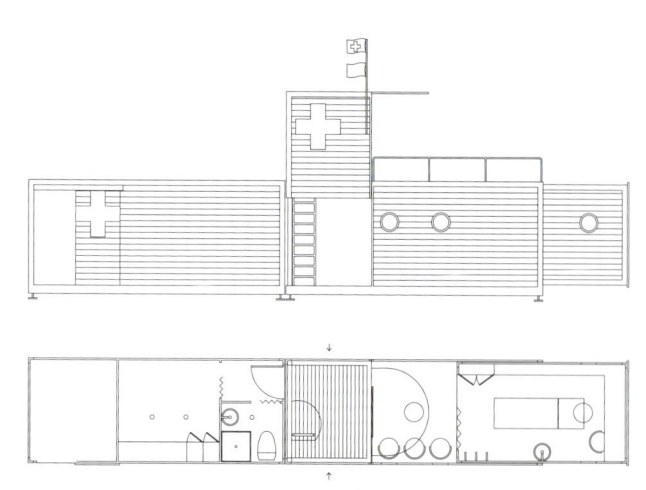

232   SHELTERS

UMP

Design: **Antoni Roselló Til** • Production: **Esteva**

A volume, an impenetrable prism, a mechanism, a movement, the apparition of an empty box, a small architecture, a possibility of service.

With its dynamic opening system and its adaptability to multiple uses (box office, information, bar, etc.), this item is adjusted to the dimensions of a standard transport container. Easy transport is one of its defining characteristics. The hydraulic movement system converts the module into a closed and vandal proof box, but reveals the nature of its functions when it opens and becomes a support for a raised sign or other defining announcement.

This construction expresses flexibility, resistance and durability, so a stainless steel structural frame of high quality was chosen, with open flanges to avoid condensation in hidden areas that are impossible to maintain. Polyester finishes have been applied due to their proven resistance to urban environments and easy cleaning of human aggressions. As it is a compact item devoid of accessories, it is immediately operative and requires no other assembly tasks in order to function besides being connected to the mains.

The particular case illustrated houses an Information Booth and Ticket Vending Office as part of the cultural activities of Barcelona Promoció (Barcelona Teatre Musical). Initially the brief contemplated four fully independent booths, each of them with its own logistical equipment, despite which, the decision was made to centralize all the facilities within a single volume, reducing construction costs and enhancing the enterprise's image of integration and functionality.

SHELTERS

Limits

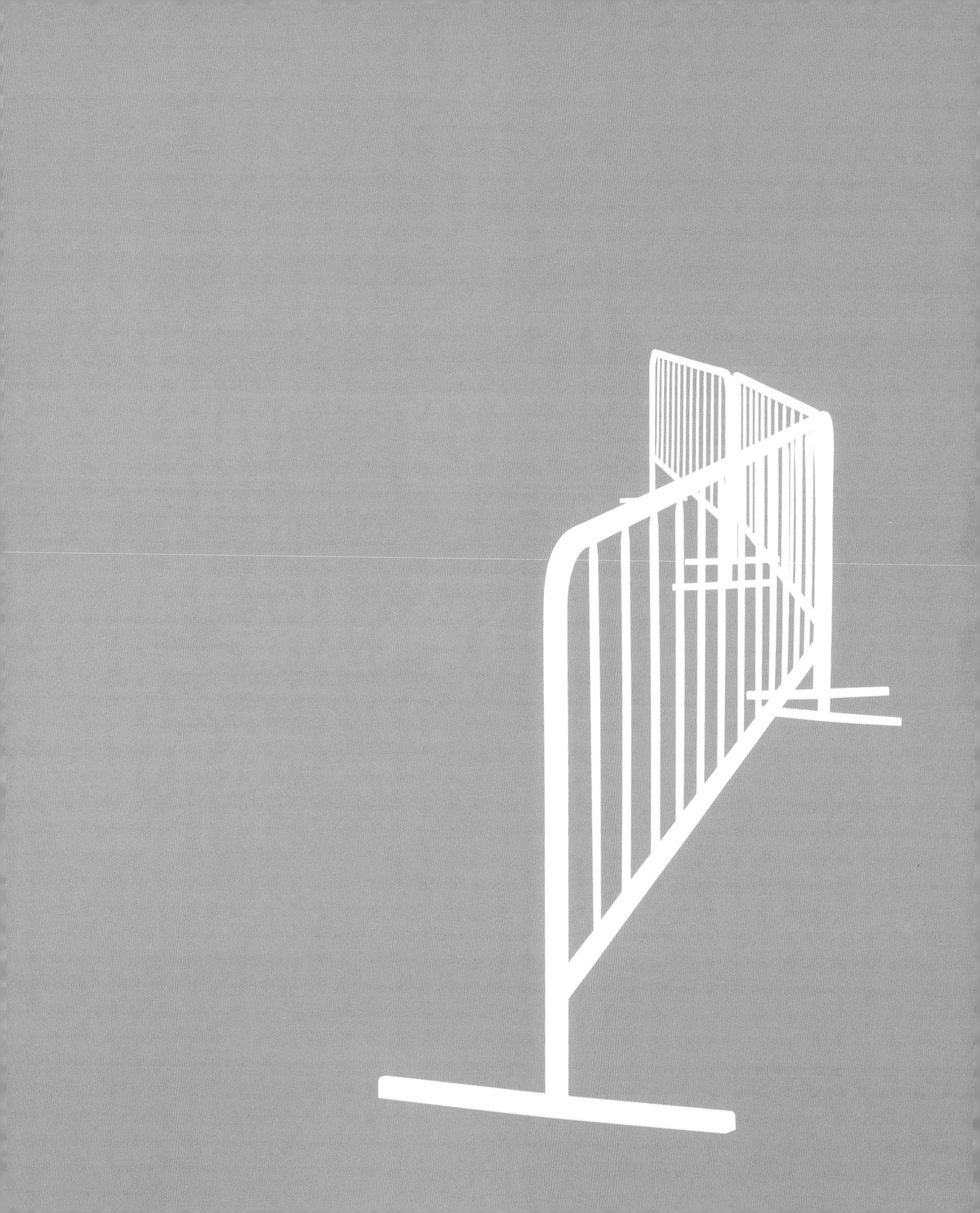

2994

Design and production: **Neri**

Bollard made in UNI EN 1563 nodular cast iron. The bollard is composed of a helical cast iron column with a rotation of 63° around its vertical axis. The base of the column has a flange. The bollard's height above ground is 95 cm.
The bollard is fitted with a cast iron fixing lug cast together with the bollard, for cementing into the foundation plinth.

Bamboo

Design: **Barbato e Garzotto** • Production: **Modo**

Fence system for public and private parks, characterised by a series of vertical elements in non-continuous succession. It consists of a 3 mm thick base in Fe 360 B steel sheet angle. The wings at the base allow for an easier fixing into a pre-existing foundation. This base has 14 round tubes of Fe 360 B steel, 50 mm Ø, to be inserted sequentially: they all follow a progressive variation of the centre-to-centre distance, while maintaining their proper role as a fence. The final height of the fence can be individualized, ranging between 1280 mm to 1780 mm. The item comes finished with a hot-dip galvanising process overlaid with a coat of thermo-hardened powder-paint for outdoors. The fence is delivered in single panels of 1.5 linear metres each, which are to be placed side by side and locked together by a tongue-and-groove system.

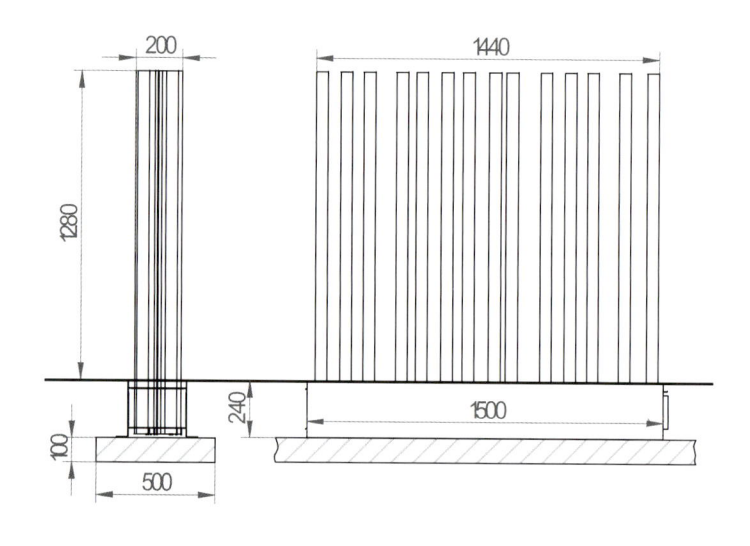

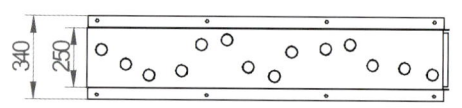

Barriers

Design: **Lisa Segatori** • Production: **ORA Centurelli**

These barriers were designed with the idea of making the city more accessible for everyone. Their visual impact makes them easily identifiable by all kinds of passers-by, and indicates the presence of services in the vicinity, such as swimming pools, sports grounds, pedestrian areas, parking lots, etc. In contrast to typical, anodyne urban barriers that simply state what is "not permitted", these barriers are pleasant and expressive, providing information and at the same time furnishing the area where they are installed.

Campus

Design and production: **GH form**

The Campus linear drainage is produced in untreated cast iron. Its dimensions are 260 × 500; it is also available in the width 140 mm. The drainage can resist weight from heavy vehicles. The standard production of this drainage unit is intended for straight lines, but can also be provided to fit the given radius of a particular project.

The design has "ears" that cover the edges of the subjacent water channel so that the drainages can be placed against surrounding pavements and in continuation of each other.

LIMITS

Cilíndrico

Design: **Albert Viaplana / Helio Piñón** • Production: **Escofet**

This modular item has been conceived to outline flower-beds and gardens or to separate pedestrian pathways from a road. The 4 cm separation produced between the cylinders allows for the escape of excess storm-water not absorbed into the ground.

Consentido

Design: **Área de diseño Gitma and Chantilly design** • Production: **Gitma**

The Consentido border post offers a new variable form concept for these items, which project there interesting shadows upon the pavement and are intended as border beacons that actually indicate the direction of traffic flow. It consists of a cut out sheet of carbon steel lacquered in different colours according to the function to be fulfilled.

LIMITS

Haiku

Design: **díez+díez diseño** • Production: **T&D Cabanes**

The cast iron 80cm high bollard Haiku has elegant, slender lines. The fluidity and lightness of its design is a far cry from the usual monotonous heavy bollards. Its shape is based on a triangular cross section which rotates lightly on its axis.

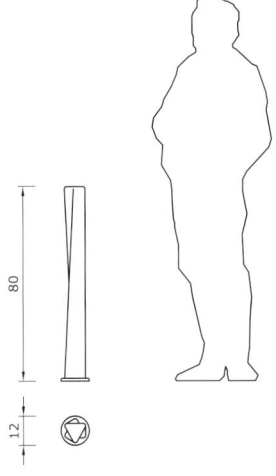

Imawa

Design: **Urbanica** • Production: **Concept Urbain**

The Imawa series consists of a single post and a barrier composed of two joined posts. The posts are 110 or 120 cm in height and are made of profiled aluminium with a factory-machined head in cast aluminium. The post is finished in powder-coated RAL colours.

LIMITS

Limitot

Design: **Ton Riera Ubía** • Production: **mago:urban**

Limitot is an element of street furniture designed to demarcate and protect private spaces in urban environments. This original model by the designer Ton Riera Ubía is manufactured and sold exclusively by the company mago:urban.

The barrier perfectly combines two indispensable aspects: it is strong enough to resist all kinds of aggressions or attempts to move it, and its aesthetic design allows it to soften the impact of garbage containers and other necessary urban elements on one hand, and to make the outdoor areas of sidewalk cafes and restaurants safer and more intimate on the other.

Limitot is held in place by gravity, so there is no need for an additional anchorage system.

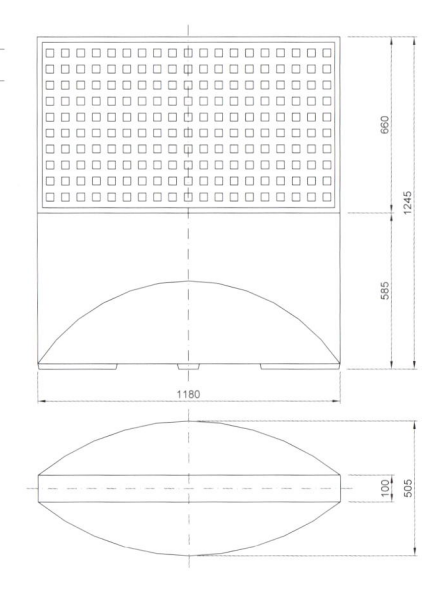

Linea

Design: **Montse Periel** • Production: **Santa & Cole**

This is a stainless steel line; it is a limit and a place to rest. In just one item, it provides a solution to the problems of coordinating urban space. This linear handrail acts as a barrier to pedestrians and as a place to lean on. It restricts access, marks out areas, acts as protection against falls, or subtly accommodates the public. It is a minimum formal expression and offers many functions without being a visual barrier. The single material it is manufactured in, stainless steel, provides a light appearance and is essentially hardwearing. It is very sturdy and all its parts may be easily changed. Its modular design means it can be installed in continuous sequences, according to the need.

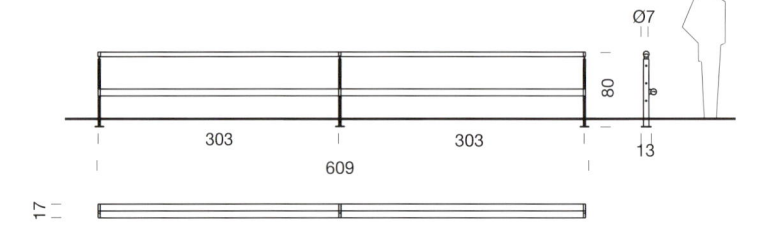

LIMITS

Lineapalo - Linealuce

Design: **Bernhard Winkler** • Production: **Euroform**

Lineapalo has been designed by Bernhard Winkler, professor at Munich's University of Technology. This pair of objects constitutes a simple bollard, while Linealuce follows the same design but incorporates a light.

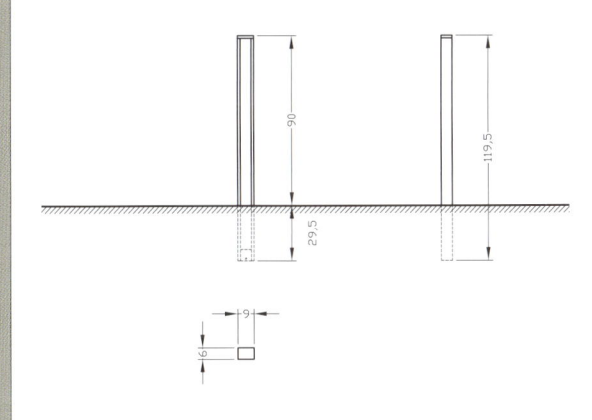

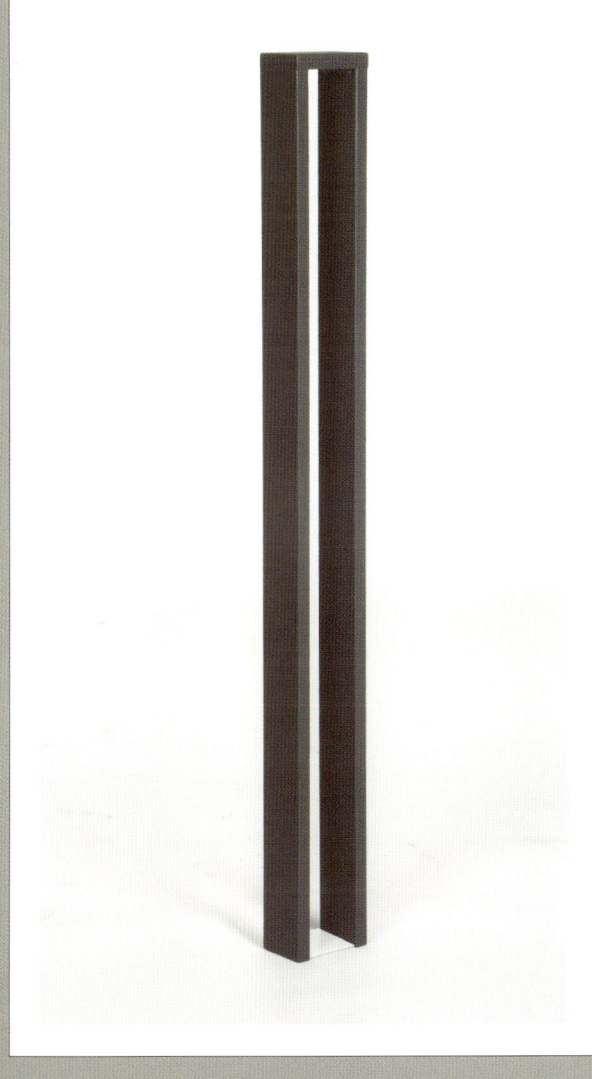

Luco Mojón

Design: **Helio Piñón** • Production: **Escofet**

This landmark has more image than body, more appearance than volume. Seen from the front it shows its larger size, like a cat wanting to intimidate an intruder; as you move past the object it gradually vanishes. The intention was to create an item that would naturally integrate into the city landscape without the violence generated by a new arrival, always perceived as a stranger. The object was not to be diminished but to be given a likeable configuration. Instead of the fully three-dimensional cylinder, the flatness of a spade offers the maximum visible surface to those approaching by car or on foot, but smoothly disappears as one drives or walks onward down the street. The longitudinal slot that lightens the upper half of the element provides it with an expressive gesture while providing an attaching facility for bicycles, motorcycles or dogs.

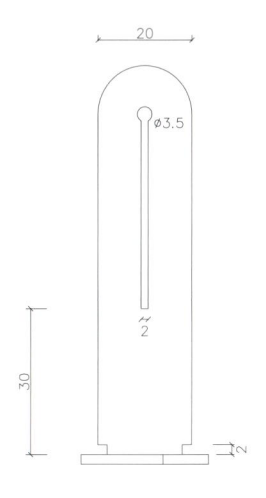

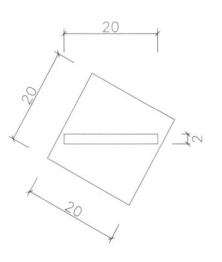

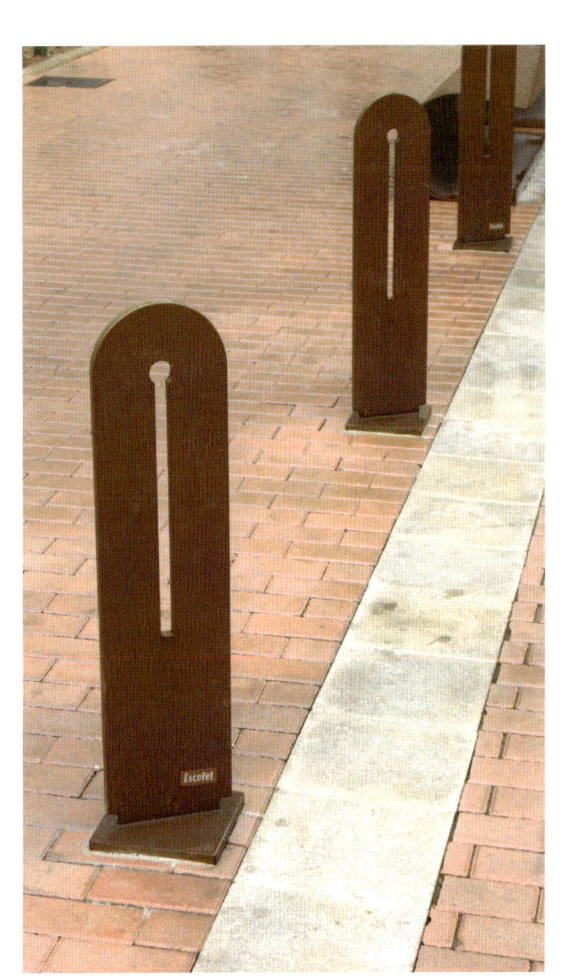

LIMITS 241

Marioska

Design: Área de diseño Gitma and Chantilly design • Production: Gitma

The organic looking Marioska pylon consists of a cut-out of carbon steel, lacquered in different colours according to the use it will be put to. Its shape changes the conventional appearance of a dissuasive urban item and offers the stroller a new way to visually enjoy the street. It comes prepared for two alternative types of anchoring: a base to be embedded in the concrete or with a folded plate foot, for fixing to the ground with bolts.

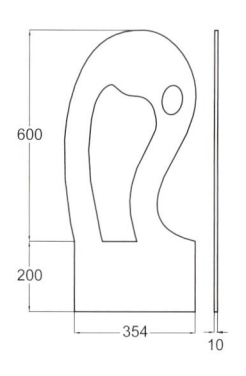

Morella

Design: Helio Piñón • Production: Escofet

This boundary post designed by Helio Piñon takes its form from two cylindrical surfaces of different radii which flow into each other, producing an object which is precise yet complex, with a misleading appearance that is visually reversible, according to whether it is hit by sunlight or whether, from twilight onwards, it is itself the projection of a low beam of light.

The Morella is much more than a boundary post and reference: it also accompanies the pedestrian. In its natural habitat in the town this is undeniably an urban piece, perhaps because of a certain complicity it has with the passers-by. Built in rust color corten steel plate each piece weighs 28 kg (61.71 lb).

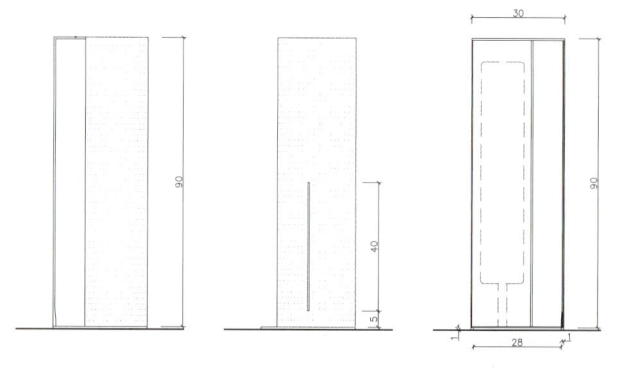

LIMITS

Murllum

Design: J.A Martínez Lapeña / Elías Torres • Production: Escofet

Murllum is a dual-purpose street furniture element: it forms an enclosure that conceals water-treatment infrastructure on an urban site, and it also serves as a continuous bench providing seating along its length.
It consists of two elements, a modular screen with built-in circular glass 'lenses' and a bench that acts as a support. When several of these elements are joined together, it creates a wall-bench with a modulation of 3 m and a height of 9 m. It is portable and self-contained, so it doesn't need to be fixed to the ground, and its base is designed so that it can be easily moved with a forklift truck. The bench is made of granite grey concrete, with an acid-etched and waterproofed finish, and the screen is granite grey stainless steel-reinforced concrete, with acid-etched and waterproofed glass lenses.

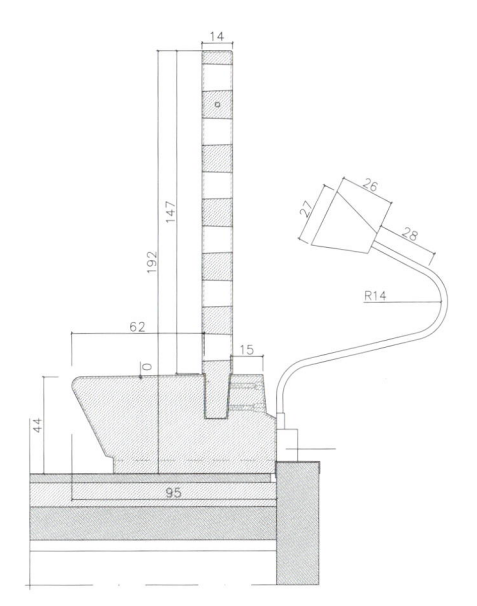

Nastra

Design: Outsign • Production: Concept Urbain

The Nastra bollard has a height of 85 cm and is made of ductile cast iron. The finish is shot-blasted and metallised with oven-hardened polyurethane paint in RAL colours.

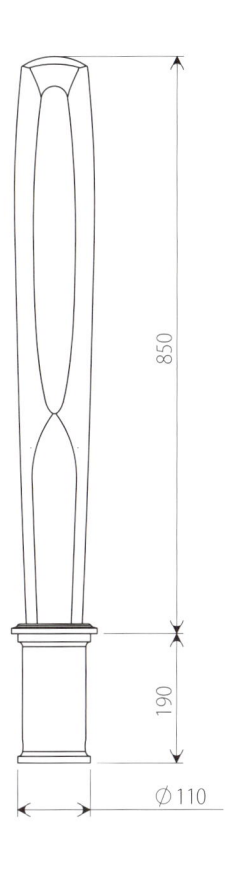

LIMITS

Neobarcino

Design: **Joaquim Carandell** • Production: **Fundició Dúctil Benito**

Neobarcino is a pylon for the outlining of pedestrian areas. The items are made of cast iron which gives them a character of strength and resistance. Their unusual and organic form will adapt well to any urban environment.

On

Design: **Ramos / Bassols** • Production: **Alis**

The exterior railing, On, 1, 2 or 3 meters long, can be used to delimit any space. The 400 mm high supporting bars are realized in 10 mm steel plate and finished with matt silver epoxy paint. Anchoring elements are fixed to the top of the supporting bars to receive the handrails formed of steel tubing 104 mm in diameter and 2 mm thick.

The base plates of the element, soldered to the supporting bars, are 104 mm diameter circular pieces and can be placed below or on the paving.

Stainless steel caps close the ends of the handrail tube, using the same fixing system as is used for the union of the handrail with the supporting bars.

Onda

Design: Atelier Mendini • Production: Ghisamesteri

Bollard in cast iron, UNI EN 1561, consisting of a decorative column realized in a single cast piece supplied with an anchoring extension to be secured to the ground; cast-iron cover fixed to the body by stainless steel dowels.

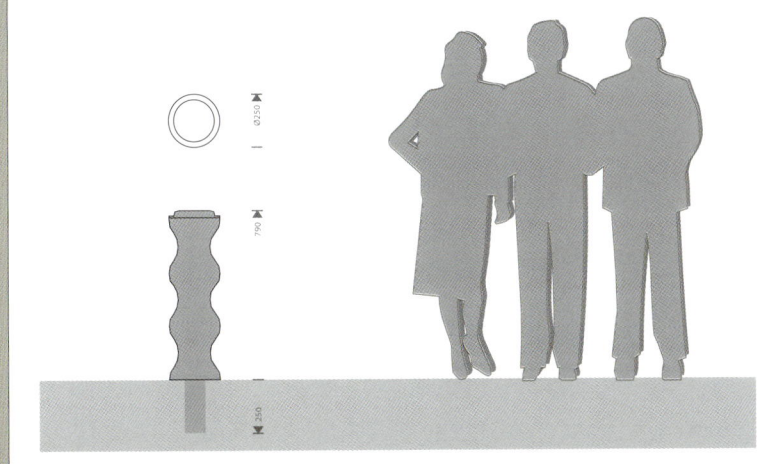

Paracelso

Design: Adolfo Ruiz de Castañeda • Production: Tecam BCN

Valla Paracelso is a railing that spans lengths of 2.13m. It consists of a square vertical post with a 135mm. The post has a series of square perforations of 20x20mm, through which light shines out. Its horizontal part is formed by an oval handrail, and four cylindrical tubes below, with a 220mm gap between them; it can also be supplied to order with only two tubes. The distance of 2 m between posts can vary according to the requirements. The materials used for the item are cold galvanized carbon steel, or stainless steel, or the combination of both. It can be paint finished or semi-gloss finished if it is the stainless steel model. The fence can be leaned towards the pavement or the other way round. It is fixed with metallic M10 raw plugs. The electrical equipment consists of a compact Ip 67 lamp with an 18-watt fluorescent tube.

LIMITS

Pausita

Design: Oriol Guimerà • Production: mago:urban

Pausita, the bollard exclusively designed by Oriol Guimerà and manufactured by mango:urban is a small pylon that plays with the same designer's bench 'Pausa'. It's an innovative street furniture element designed to suggest communicative connections among its users. As well as fulfilling its dissuasive function by perfectly delimiting spaces or areas like squares, streets and gardens, the Pausita boundary marker stands as a decorative and unusually evocative diaphanous sculpture.

Petrelli

Design: Área de diseño Gitma y Chantilly design • Production: Gitma

Petrelli is a simple dissuasive pylon; despite its straightforward and static nature, it manages to look alive. It can be placed in a row, obliquely or in a parallel distribution. It consists of a cutout sheet of Corten steel. There are two systems of fixing it to the ground, by embedding it into the pavement or with a folded foot to be bolted down.

246   LIMITS

Pisolo

Design: **Tobia Repossi** • Production: **Modo**

Bollard in sandblasted concrete, oval shaped, treated with an anti-erosion additive, with a covering cap in stainless steel. Free standing bollard.

Propeller

Design: **Greg Healey** • Production: **Street and Park Furniture**

Greg Healey worked together with Street and Park Furniture to put this new range on the market. The impetus for this furniture was a trip through the South Australian outback. Much of the realisation of this new range of urban street furniture is Greg's response to the forms, textures and colours of this extraordinary landscape. This adaptable range of furniture is particularly suitable for use in the design of contemporary streetscapes as it draws on Australian landscape forms in a unique and innovative way. Materials: painted cast aluminium with a steel internal spigot. Heavy-duty impact malleable cast iron version also available.

LIMITS

Rampante

Design: Òscar Tusquets Blanca • Production: Escofet

Rampante railings, designed by Oscar Tusquets, is a modular urban element in colored reinforced concrete with an acid-etched and water repellant finish. The 640 kg modules are installed in trenches 30 mm deep and 100 mm wide which are then filled with concrete and the surface leveled with the paving.

Robert

Design: Miguel Milá, Bet Figueras • Production: Santa & Cole

Along there usual design lines, this garden fence by Miguel Milá and Bet Figueras bears three main features: functionality, simplicity, timelessness. Derived from the classic traditional fence we used to protect our gardens, Miguel Milá and Bet Figueras have developed a new light, long-lasting fence, noticeable for its great resistance and easy platen replacement. Made of only two elements a cylindrical support and a double-platen sheet this sober yet, at the same time, functional piece easily adapts to any garden type or city ground. Designed as a modular piece, it can be used in different ways (fits any surface) and installed in open or closed sequences. Made of laminated sheets and stainless steel rails, the Robert fence is a versatile and resistant piece that will remain in its place for an unlimited time.

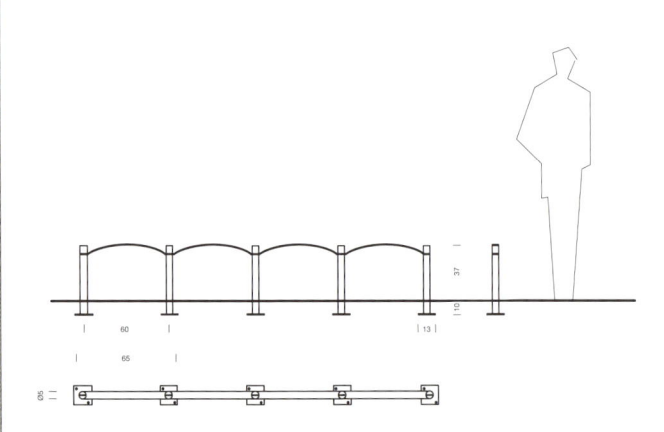

LIMITS

Rodas

Design: **Ton Riera Ubia** • Production: **mago:urban**

The Rodas pylon is a dissuasive module that is highly acceptable to municipal employees responsible for the management of public space, as it will easily adapt to all sorts of urban environments. Its size and shape are also praiseworthy. Rodas is an effective solution for the purpose of controlling or directing traffic, temporarily or permanently. Suitable for pedestrian zones, garden areas, zebra-crossings or the zoning of events in public space. These circumstances require an element like this: easy to move with a fork-lift, a crane can pick it up by the ring at the top. Once it is placed on the ground it is unbreakable and unmovable.

Rough & Ready

Design and production: **Streetlife**

The robust beams in FSC Hardwood or in All Black (see p. 14A) are combined with a solid galvanized steel or Corten steel frame. With the standard version (BOLS) the frame extends 40 cm into the ground. The floor version (BOLV) can be easily anchored on a smooth surface or substratum. The beams are covered on the top and are mounted by means of stainless-steel theft-proof flange nuts. The bollards are also available with low-energy LED beacon lighting. Available in 2 heights: 45 and 75 cm. The diameter is about 15 x 15 cm.

LIMITS

Rondo

Design: **Bernhard Winkler** • Production: **Euroform**

The universal frame has a classic, aesthetic shape although it is contemporary in design. With a height of 89 cm, it is ideal for fencing areas off. Rondo is also well suited for parking bicycles.

Sagrera

Design: **Josep Muxart** • Production: **Escofet**

Sagrera is a modular fence designed to limit areas in the manner of a palisade. It is made of cast reinforced concrete and has no particular surface finish. Installation involves planting the modules in a running foundation trench of 60x60cm, and then filled in with "in-situ" concrete in the customary way. Reflected light gives the items a variety of tones that play with the folds on the vertical posts, which produces an effect of light and of movement.

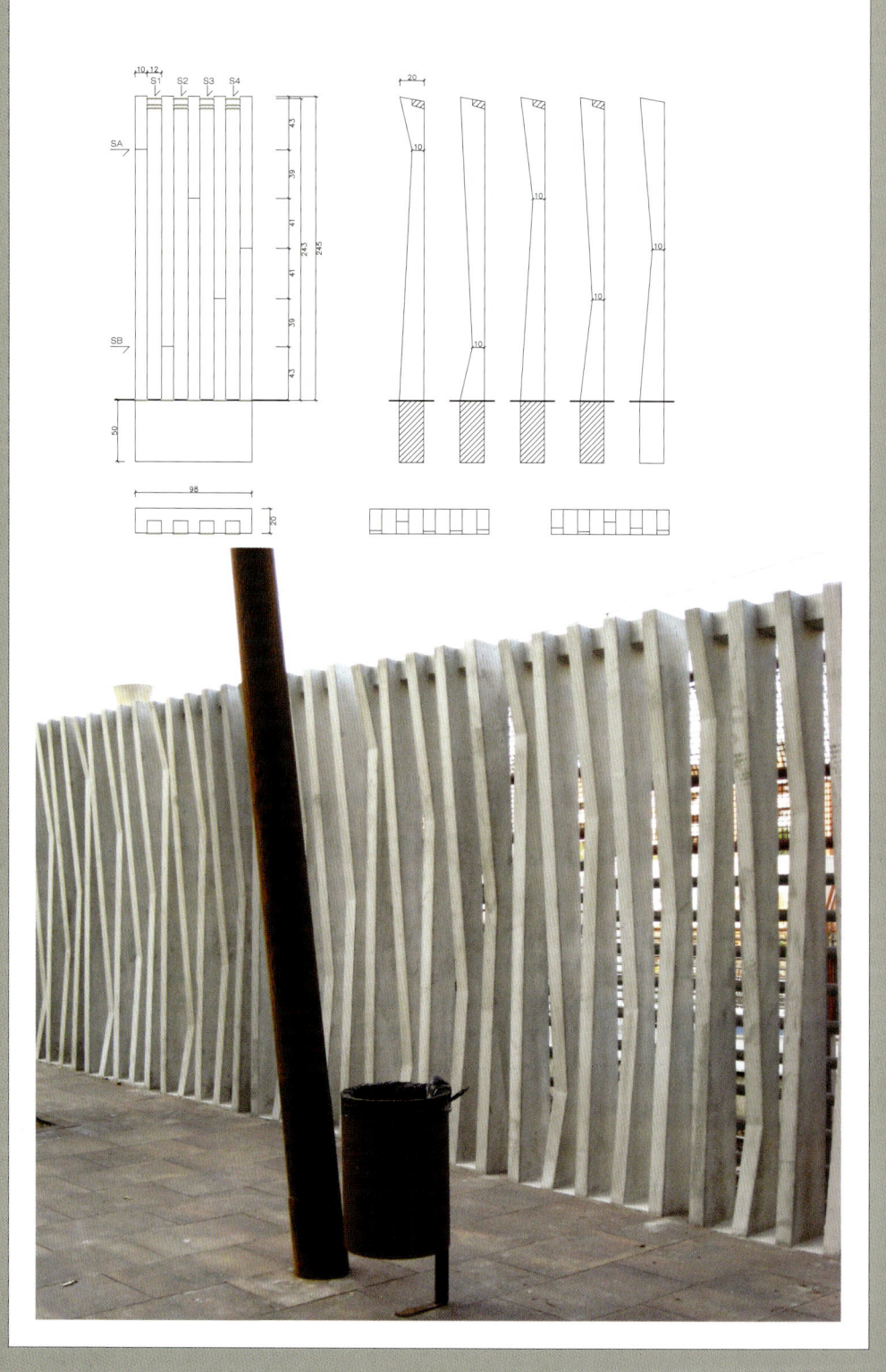

LIMITS

SD

Design: **David Karásek & Radek Hegmon** • Production: **mmcité**

A simple and geometric bollard made entirely from steel, consisting of a single tube that also acts as a base. The upper part of the end of the tube contains a cylindrical hollow lid.
The body of each bollard is made from steel with a galvanized steel powder coating. The lid is usually made from aluminum, depending on the model within this line, and finished with a coating of metallic paint. The total height of each element is 1000mm, and two bollard sizes are available: one with a 114mm diameter and a smaller one measuring 76mm.
These elements are usually placed side by side, in pairs. It is possible to join them using a chain, and they are anchored to the floor with screws. These S-line elements clearly demonstrate that maximum attention to detail is possible in a city's urban furnishing elements.

SE

Design: **David Karásek & Radek Hegmon** • Production: **mmcité**

The SE Line bollard is based on an ingenious design that joins two L-shapes facing each other in different directions. Rather than creating a visual obstruction, when it is in place it is a pure and simple presence that appears to be even slighter because it is partly see-through. It is made from galvanised steel finished with a powder coating, and it stands 1 m above ground level. It can be fastened either above or below ground level with concealed anchorage bolts.

LIMITS

SH

Design: David Karásek & Radek Hegmon • Production: mmcité

This radically geometrical all-steel bollard is based on a standard steel H profile, with a purely shaped top consisting of a recessed square plate.
The item consists of a galvanized steel, powder-coated body that rises 1000 mm (39,3 inches) over the pavement. It can be anchored to or under the pavement with screws.

Ska

Design: Javier Machimbarrena • Production: ONN Outside

The SKA bollard, manufactured in painted cast aluminum, exudes robustness and a vanguard aesthetic, qualities which make it a very attractive piece.

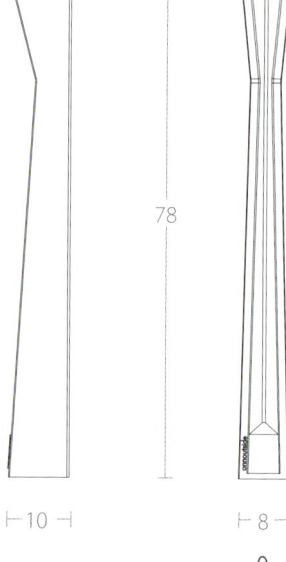

252   LIMITS

SL

Design: **David Karásek & Radek Hegmon** • Production: **mmcité**

This all-steel bollard has the most lapidary shape, which is nevertheless of notable elegance. It has been created by the simple expedient of adding a horizontal square top ending onto a standard angle-iron. This solution enables the range to include other versions of railings and even an innovative ashtray. Two dimensions are available, which can alter all the proportions of an installation: L 60 mm and L 80 mm (2.36 and 3.14 inches).
The item consists of a galvanized and powder coated steel body, which rises 1000 mm (39,3 inches) over the pavement.

LIMITS

Sloper

Design: **Luis Tabuenca** • Production: **ONN Outside**

SLOPER railings are available in two heights: 900 and 1100 mm. They comprise floor-mounted rails in painted cast aluminum and a stainless steel tube handrail. The space between rails can be filled with laminated glass. The design and aesthetic of the railing makes it ideal for urban environments as well as homes.

Solid

Design: **Tomas Ruzicka** • Production: **mmcité**

Despite its clean geometrical shape there is no lack of gentleness, enhanced by the terrazzo effect. A traditional material in a fresh, new form. An interesting detail is the system of fixing it to the pavement. High resistance and durability. The body of the bollard is made of cast polished concrete with tiny stones in a salt and pepper finish.

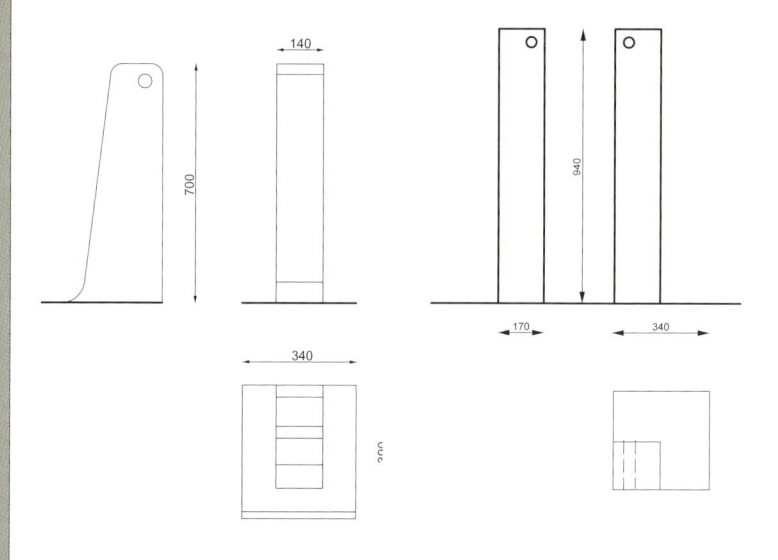

SR

Design: David Karásek & Radek Hegmon • **Production:** mmcité

This all-steel bollard is associated through its design and structure with the Radium benches and bin, as it works with the same see-through supporting frame made of bent steel sheet. The body is raised above the pavement upon a short leg with a base-plate.

Each bollard has a galvanized steel, powder coated body that rises 1000 mm (39,3 inches) over the pavement. It is designed to be anchored to or under the pavement with anchoring screws.

Tente

Design: Leopoldo Milà • **Production:** DAE

The idea here is to have a flexible bollard consisting of a top, a base and a box embedded in the ground, manufactured as one piece in GG-20 pearlite cast iron. The piece can be in either polished shiny stainless steel or hot-dip galvanized steel, with a coat of high-adhesive primer, phosphocromate of polyvinyl butyral, phenoplast with rust-proof pigments, and finished with a polyester resin-based powder coating, especially for outdoor use. The standard color for this second option is wrought-iron. The approximate weight is 23.2 kg (51.13 lb). The mechanism works when the spring located in the embedded box is compressed, going into action when the piece is subjected to a pressure of 60kg (132.24 lb) or more.

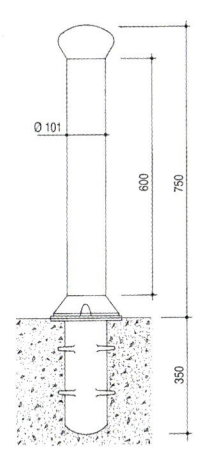

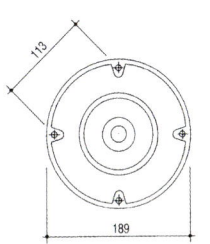

LIMITS 255

Tona

Design: **Daniel Nebot** • Production: **Macaedis**

Developed from the eccentric revolution of a truncated conoid, this piece functions as an easily visible marker for localization, contention and signaling purposes. The elimination of edges provided by this system makes this marker a very resistant element to possible aggressions. Fixing the item to the ground is achieved by a steel ring, which is anchored to the pavement and provides the cone with an elegantly finished base.
Materials: Natural stone and stainless steel.
Placing: Anchored to the ground with corrugated bars (rebars)
Size: 220 × 220 × 400 / 650 mm (8.64 × 8.64 × 15.72 / 25.54 inches)
Weight: 30 / 47 kg (66.12 / 103.58 lb)

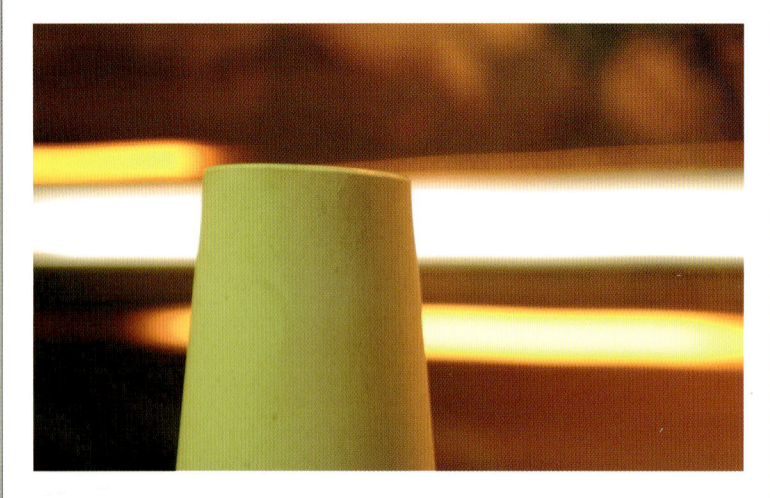

Topino

Design and production: **Geohide**

Topino is a robust box-shaped pass marker designed to be used on streets and roadways, which includes a lighting system built into one of its sides. The body is formed by a prefabricated white reinforced concrete element, with a sandblasted finish and smooth corners and sides, although other finishes are also possible. It measures 0.30 x 0.30 m, with a height of 0.60 m, and its total weight is 155kg.

Tube

Design: Roger Albero • Production: mago:urban

The Tube series comprises four different bench models and one railings model which complements the other elements. These five elements permit the generation of infinite spatial possibilities as they adapt to every requirement. They can also be used individually.

The essential characteristic of the series is that all the elements are hollow. In spite of their size, this gives them a visual lightness which contrasts with the robustness of the acid-etched reinforced concrete from which they are made.

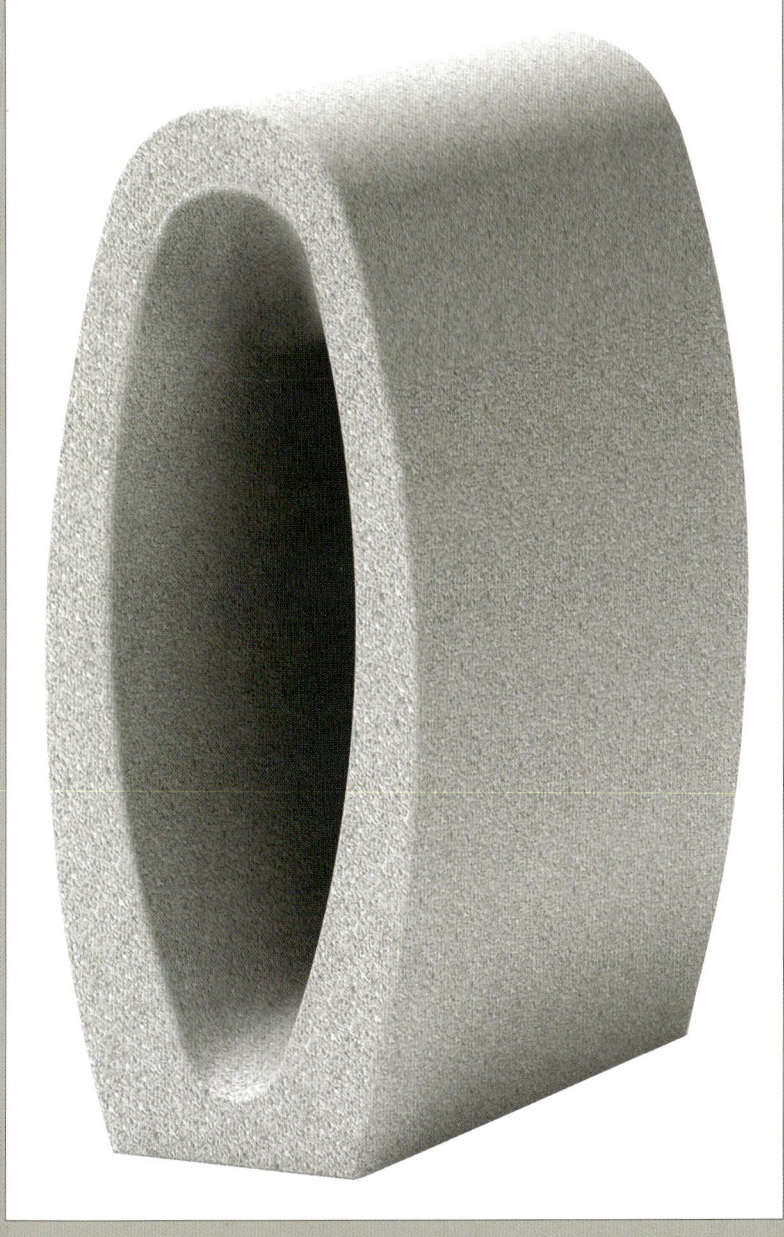

Vento

Design: Roger Albero • Production: DAE

The body and top of this beacon is made of cast aluminum while the shade is made of a translucent methacrylate with an outer diameter of 200mm (7.86 inches). It has a sandblasted matt anodized finish. The piece is embedded in the ground and weighs 23 kg (50.7 lb).

LIMITS

Lighting

108

Design: **Enric Batlle - Joan Roig** • Production: **Santa & Cole**

A simple and functional street lamp, which arises at an angle. Its shaft has a continuous rectangular cross-section, designed to be useful without prominence. The tubular element has a rectangular cross-section, finished in hot-galvanized steel. The hot-galvanized steel tube column and arm have a continuous cross-section of 120 × 280 mm for the 4.7 m lamp, and 150 × 300 mm for the 7.5 m lamp. The arm leans 15 degrees in relation to the horizontal. Optionally, they can be delivered painted. Optical unit and extrusion reflector in high gloss anodized aluminium and tempered glass diffuser, equipped for discharge lamps, metal halides or high pressure sodium vapour (max. 150 W). Optionally, double level equipments can be included for the command line.

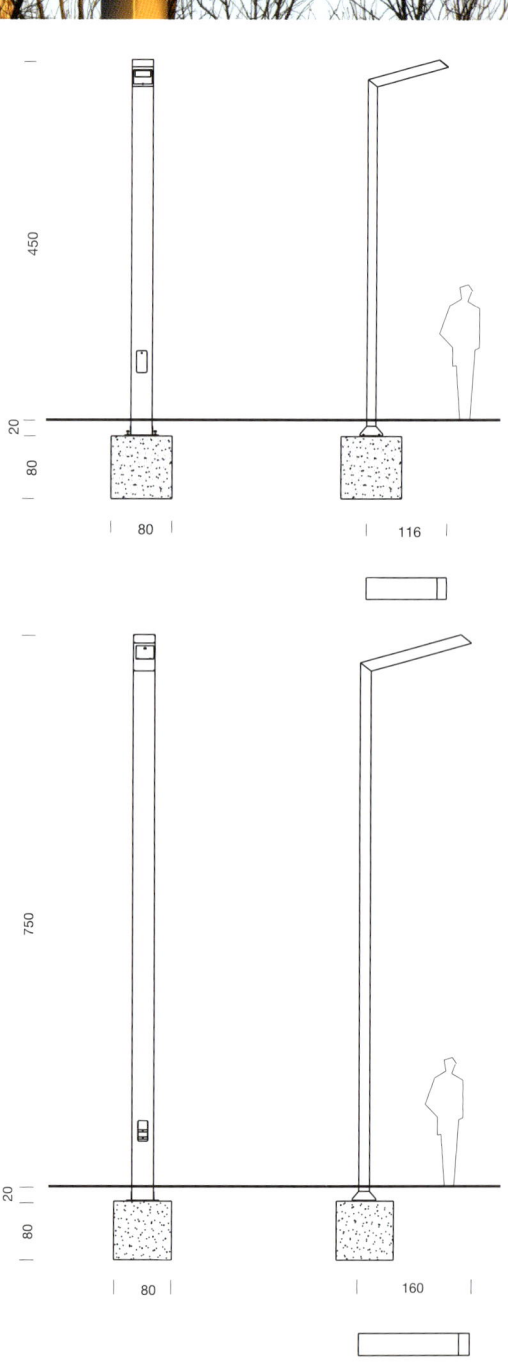

LIGHTING

17°

Design: **Francisco Providência** • Production: **Larus**

The angle of inclination gathers the components of the lighting device: the vertical elevation of the pole and the arm with horizontal projection. The illumination is housed inside the tube and projects light vertically. The tube features a cut-out where the cylinder is joined to the illumination cone. The design is inspired in a reductive and laconic expression, suggestive of freedom. The body of the element is made of stainless steel and it carries a 150W metal halide lamp, colour 3000 k, 1531 lux and 13 500 lumens.

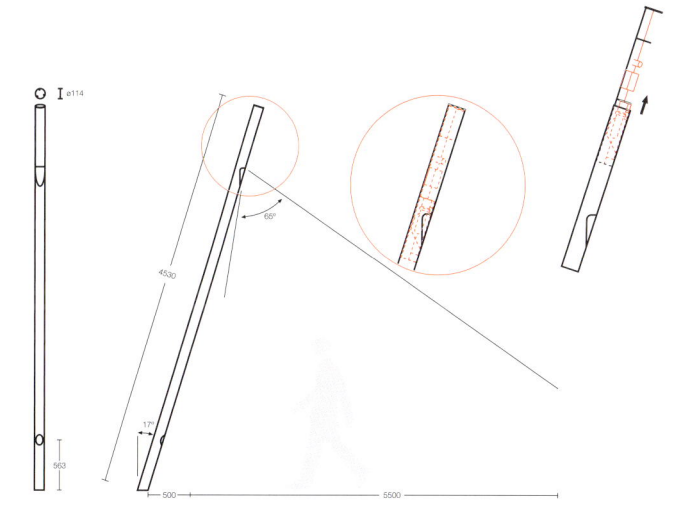

LIGHTING

AJC

Design and production: Microarquitectura

This streetlamp with projected lighting is built like a telescope with the upper part emerging from a square casing.

The AJC light embodies the contemporary style of floodlight often seen today, but is a far cry from the cold, technical image which has a tendency to be too simplistic.

Its elegant appearance comes partly from the materials used – the effective combination of painted iron with stainless steel, and partly because of the lamp's sleek, geometric lines.

The range of models offers versatility with two heights as well as the option of hanging varied combinations of lights at different heights. This makes it possible to illuminate different kinds of areas, whether they be roads, pedestrian zones, town squares or open spaces.

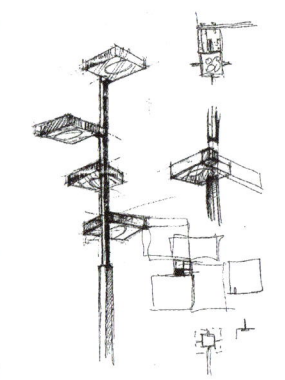

Andrea

Design: MBM Arquitectes, Martorell, Bohigas, Mackay, Puigdomènech • Production: DAE

The standard version of this lighting column consists of a base, a blind element, a semi-blind element, 6 meters of open truss modules and a 9550 mm cast iron lamp carrier of perlitic steel GG-20. The upper part of the lamp holder is finished with a fiberglass reinforced polyester hat. The luminaire includes a methacrylate gradable light diffuser, reinforced at both ends and measuring 4 mm in thickness, 600 mm in diameter y 1000 mm in length. The item is finished with a first coat of maximum adherence polyvinyl butyric base paint of zinc phosphate with anti-corrosive pigments, plus two coats of two-component polyurethane aliphatic enamel paint. The standard color is matt black with a wrought iron effect.

If necessary, a ventilation grid can be supplied, made of steel sheet protected with an anticorrosive dip. The height of the column is variable, according to the number of modules installed and the requirements of the client. The item is anchored to the ground by means of 12 zincified steel M-24 anchoring bolts, 1000 mm long. The approximate weight of the complete fixture is approximately 4625 kg.

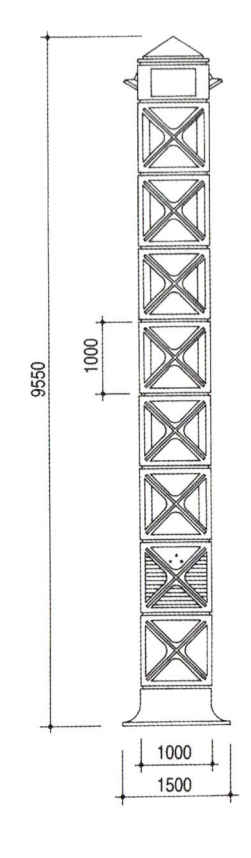

262 LIGHTING

Arken

Design: **Office of City Architecture Copenhagen** • Production: **Philips**

Arken is a streetlight with an integrated system that allows it to be installed on all kinds of columns and wall brackets. It provides 350° symmetrical lighting thanks to its top reflector and opal glass cone diffuser, which also creates a soft, glare-free lighting effect. Arken has been designed to be used in contemporary urban environments, from residential zones to pedestrian areas and commercial centres. It can either have an anodised or cast aluminium structure, and the diffuser is made from polycarbonate, making it resistant to impacts and UV rays. The screen can be made from polycarbonate or compound polyester, which is also UV ray-resistant. It can be mounted on columns up to a maximum height of 4.5m.

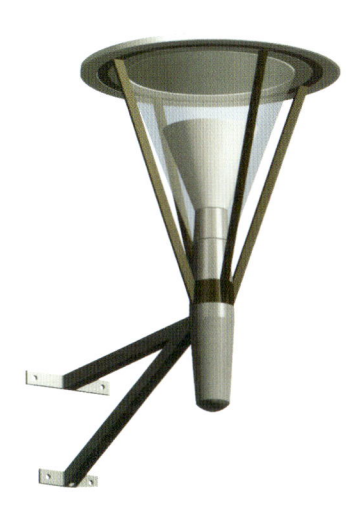

Ballerina

Design and production: **Geohide**

Ballerina is a symmetrical street lighting fixture designed for pedestrian areas. It consists of two main components, the support post and the luminaire. The support post consists of a hollow steel cylinder, 130 mm in diameter, rising 3.30 meters (10.82 ft) above the ground, galvanized and painted. Other finishes can be supplied on demand.
The lamp sheds a warm indirect light which is evenly distributed around the post, avoiding the discomfort and harsh visual effect of directly seeing the light source. It is possible to adapt the luminaire onto new or existing poles of variable diameters (max. 0.34 m / 13.36 inches). The fixture has a self-stabilized fastening by means of two transoms. As it is entirely made of stainless steel, it is highly resistant and unalterable. The system can be easily and swiftly assembled. The surface finish is sandblasted (other finishes are available upon request).

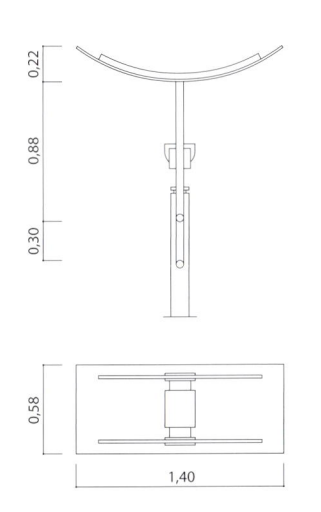

LIGHTING

Balta

Design: **Patxi Mangado** • Production: **Santa & Cole**

Balta is a simple, orthogonal-profile street lamp with a triangular section. It has been specially designed to "dress" urban spaces, and its shape and originality make it unique. The hot galvanized steel column and bracket are painted grey, and a weatherproof stainless steel box houses the lamp and an aluminum reflector. The diffuser is made from tempered glass. It uses discharge lamps (high-pressure sodium vapor or metal halide), up to a maximum of 150W. The column is fixed with a reinforced concrete cube made on site, and anchor bolts.

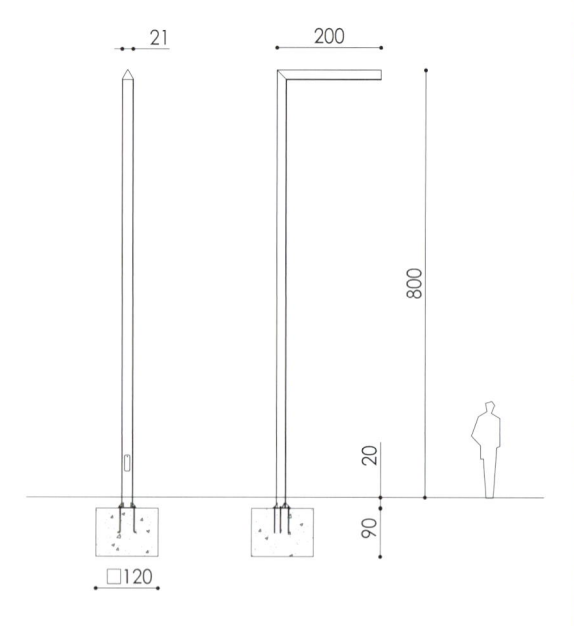

Bd Love lamp

Design: **Ross Lovegrove** • Production: **Bd**

This luminaire-bench is made of medium density polyethylene, rotomolded and pigmented in a range of different colors and with 8 stainless steel inserts at the base. The item can seat 3 people. The light diffuser screen is made of natural tone polyethylene of medium density with an additive against ultra violet rays. It is easy to disassemble for repair or changing the light source. There is a semi-gloss finished, cast aluminum (Al 2560) connection ring between the base and the diffuser screen. The piece contains the light source, a 230V 100W halogen lamp.

The luminaire-bench is available in the following colors: fluorescent red (only for indoor use), beige, white, blue, green, sandstone and millstone. It can also be supplied in special colors. The bases, each one of which measures 1410 × 1200 mm, can be stacked. Each unit has a height of 3000 mm (9.84') and weighs approximately 52 kg.

264 LIGHTING

Calaf

Design: **Josep Bosch** • Production: **Tecam BCN**

The support column of this 6 meter tall street lamp is made of steel sheet. The design is based on the achievement of an increased rigidity of a laminar surface by means of a series of folds or corrugations. This is a functional physical principle that can be widely perceived in the vegetable world, among the reed and grass family in particular. The result is a tapered lamp stand, lightweight yet strong and stable, the six meters of which lean outward at an angle of 8 degrees. The luminaire is by Roura, with a booster mechanism for lighting up. The structure of the lamp is constructed of hot-dip galvanized steel sheet.

Camelot

Design: **DA2** • Production: **Ghisamestieri**

Camelot is a street lamp designed to add a familiar touch to urban spaces, with a typically interior decoration look that contrasts with its effective outdoor luminous performance. It is available in several heights and with different diffusers. These consist of an opaque anodized aluminum top designed to avoid luminous contamination, and a variety of translucent "veils" in different colors, which show up clearly in wide open spaces. The modular system allows these veils to be changed very easily, besides the possibility of using urban symmetrical or non-symmetrical luminaires. Its only support has been carefully designed so as not to interfere in the light beam at all. The available "veils" allow the most adequate style to be found for any given occasion. Camelot can be installed in any urban context, either of a contemporary or of a historical nature.

LIGHTING 265

Dinosaurio

Design: **Alessandro Caviasca** • Production: **SIARQ**

Beyond the function of illuminating the public space in which it is located, this street lamp incorporates the task of being a solar energy power plant producing photovoltaic energy. With a maximum height of 13 meters (42.64 ft), it carries two projectors of 250W and 400W, besides its 18 solar panels with a photovoltaic surface of 25 sqm (269 sqft). The system is capable of generating up to 3800 kWh per year. All the energy captured this way is fed directly into the power supply system; likewise, the energy consumed by the light projectors –about half of the amount that the system generates- is acquired from the regular supply line. The electrical bill amounts to the difference between the energy provided and the energy consumed. The item itself is an innovative piece of public sculpture in which the solar panels are an added part of the design. Their inclination and the sculpture's curves instill a dynamic sensation to the composition; likewise, the colorful combination of materials, Corten steel and the techno-bluish panels create an exciting vibration between the sculpture and the environment.

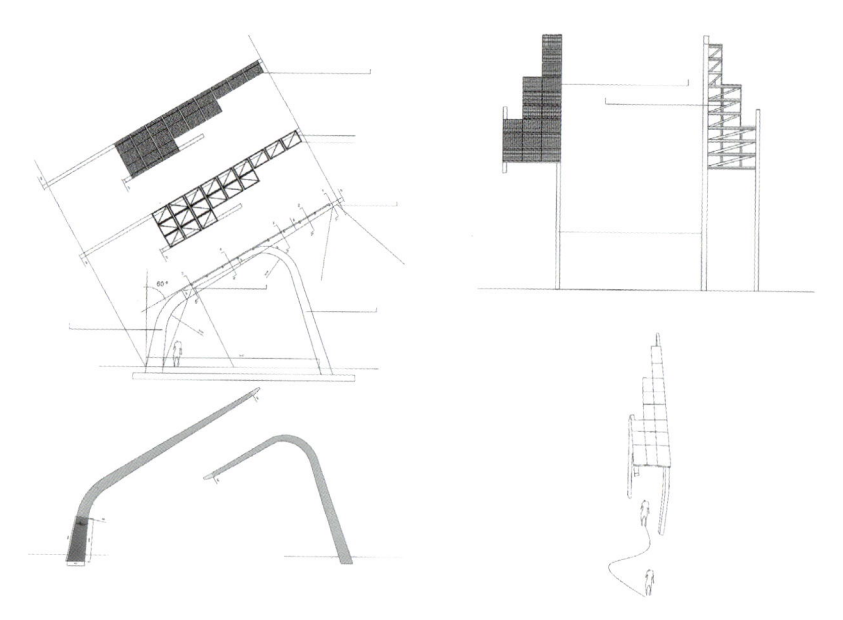

266   LIGHTING

Diogene

Design: **Studioata** • Production: **Neri**

This street lamp designed by Neri comprises a transparent suspended light fixture which complies with all the relevant light pollution regulations. The base is made of galvanized steel, polished stainless steel and cast iron. The Diogene streetlamp is available in various different sizes – 6.7 or 8 meters high and with 1, 2 or 3 arms.

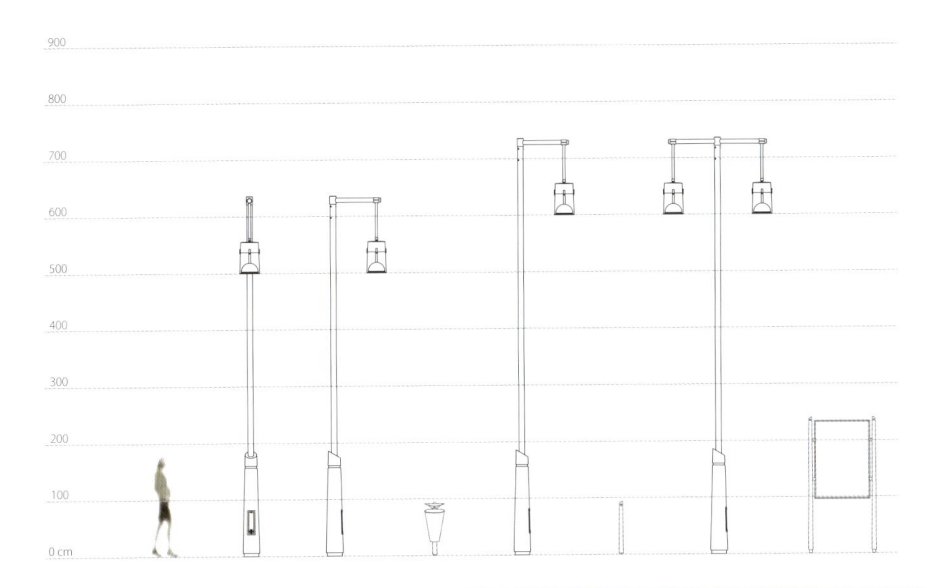

LIGHTING 267

Diorama

Design: **Ramón Benedito** • Production: **Santa & Cole**

Ramon Benedito has created an attractively-shaped lighting unit, inspired on traditional lines but made with modern-day materials and technology and destined to last because of its pleasant shape. A highly familiar street lamp that looks as if it had always been around while at the same time telling us something new. It is made of cast aluminium, has a plastic diffuser and is equipped with compact fluorescent lights. It is mounted on a cone-shaped matt aluminium column. The light projection angle reduces its light pollution ratio to zero.

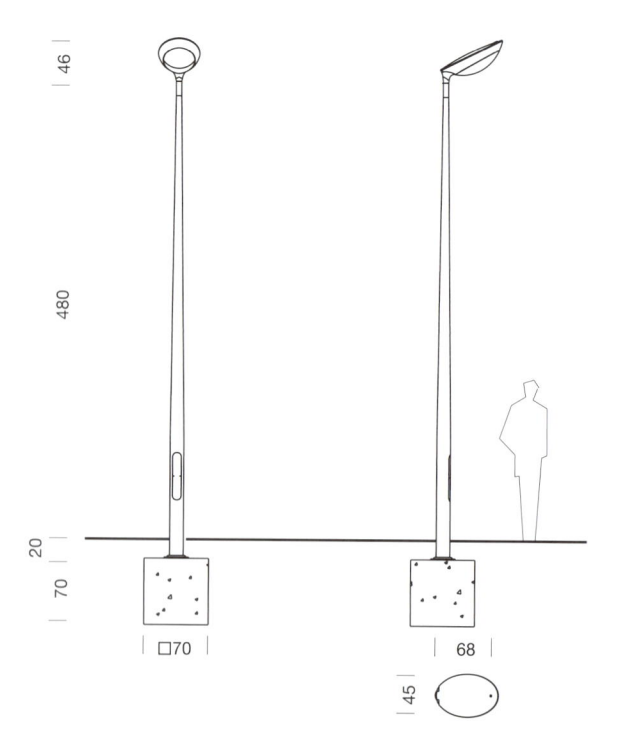

268   LIGHTING

DL 10

Development: **Siteco**

With this pioneering performance the DL 10 demonstrates how outdoor lighting in the future will look, an organically flowing form that ascends from the mast spigot to the luminaire head. The aim of the DL 10 was to implement LED technology to satisfy the demands for the illumination of prestigious squares, roads and city centres in accordance with current standards. The result is impressive. The first Siteco road luminaire incorporating LED technology represents a new luminaire generation, combining state-of-the-art LED technology within an innovative and functional design. The DL 10 provides lighting according to standards for roads and squares with a pleasant white light or coloured accent lighting for the first time with one luminaire. The construction of the luminaire body gives the impression of coming from one casting and is attractively graceful. This light impression is based on the creative potential of the technology used: LED lighting technology allows completely new housing forms and low construction heights – DL 10 has taken good advantage of this bonus. The materials, diecast aluminium with Siteco metallic grey coating as well as an optical enclosure of brilliant, part-matt PMMA that flushly fits into the graceful form rounds off its harmonious appearance.

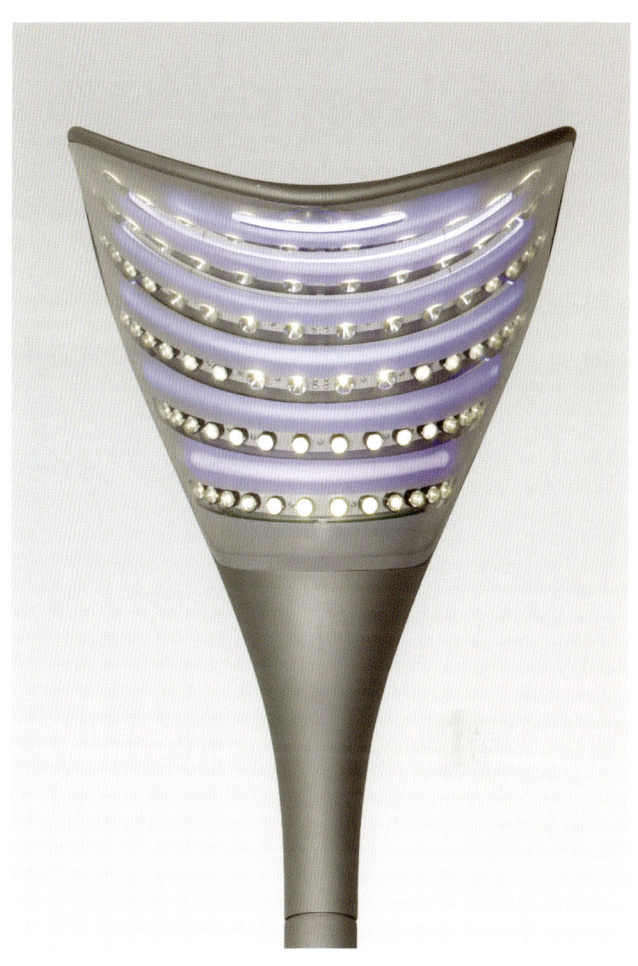

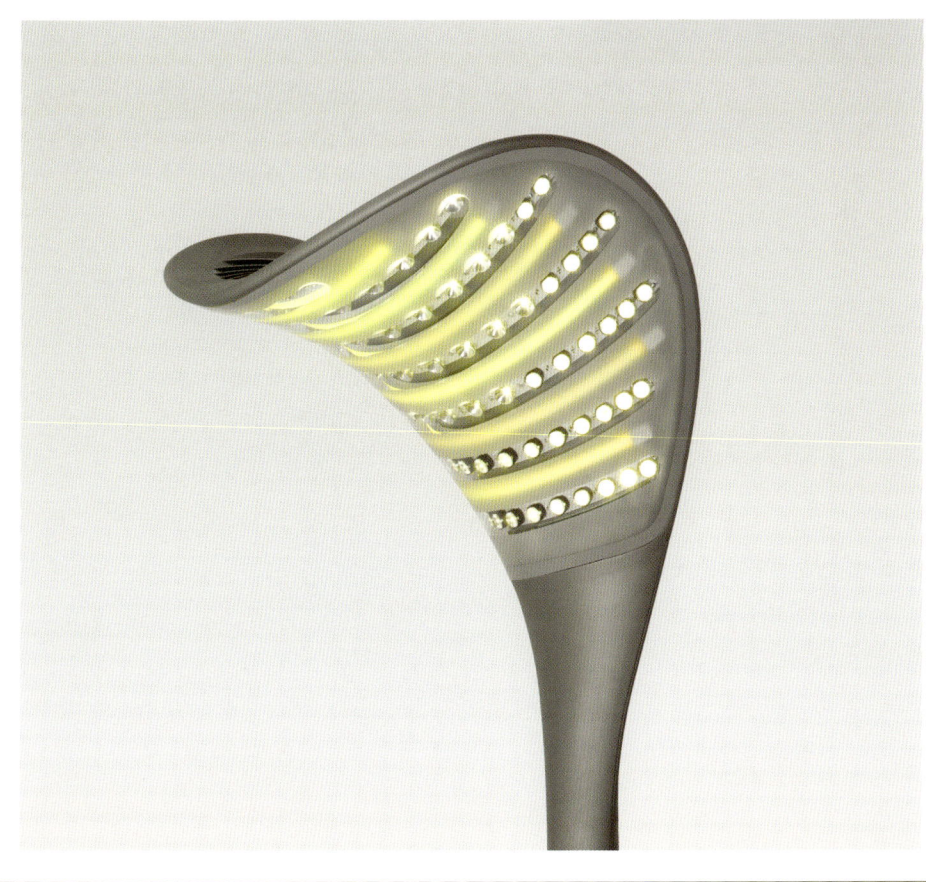

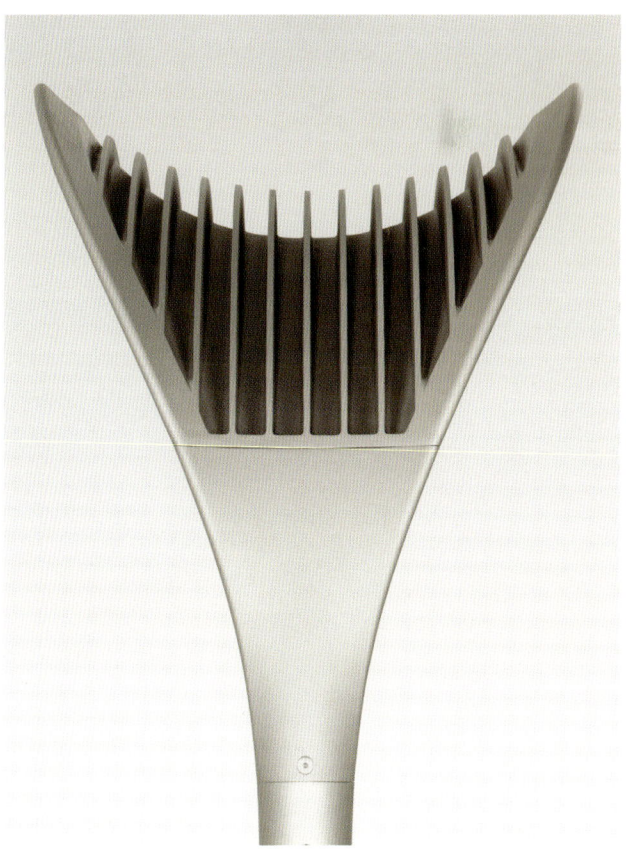

LIGHTING

Donday

Design: **DA2** • Production: **Ghisamestieri**

Donday is a lighting system designed for the illumination of pedestrian areas, parks and gardens. The appearance of these lamps is that of a contemporary and ironic reinterpretation of the traditional globe lights. Its shape is an invitation to implement a series of different curves and inclinations of the supporting post and of the top cover, making a number of different stage settings possible by redirecting the light in unusual and attractive ways. The special calendering of the support pillar instills a fluid, dynamic energy upon the area where the item has been installed, producing the sensation that the lamps are being bent by the wind.

The post has a diameter of 89 mm; it is made of curved steel (Fe 510), with another column of extruded aluminum inside it. The globe is made of white methacrylate and the hat is made of aluminum sheet. The height of the item ranges between 2.350 mm and 3.350 mm. The exterior side of the hat is anthracite grey and the interior side is finished with metalized silver paint. The bolts that secure the lamb to the ground are of stainless steel.

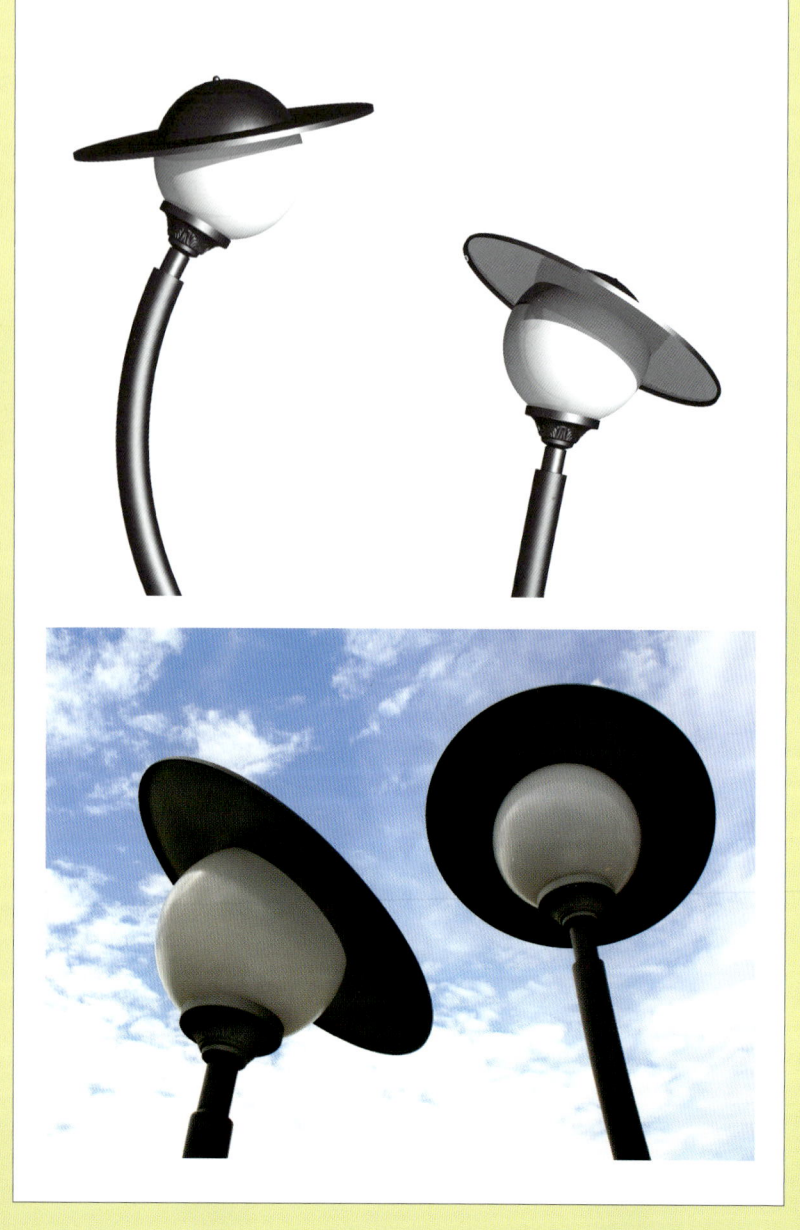

Ecclesia

Design: **Ergo** • Production: **Ghisamestieri**

This street lamp forms part of the Ecclesia street furniture series which incorporates traditional Christian symbols and iconography. The objective of the design is to reflect sacred values in exterior elements.

The shape of the lamp, in the form of a shepherd's crook, is rigidized by the cross inserted within it, and conforms an image which is clearly recognizable at a distance, as if it were a signal announcing the presence of God.

270   LIGHTING

Faf

Design: **Joan Forgas** • Production: **Alis**

The Faf streetlight series is a set of urban lighting elements. The series includes a light for the road, available in two different heights and at different angles and a path light, available in three heights and at different angles. The alternation of the two produces an undulating visual effect. The lights are formed by a 180 cm steel lower post, which incorporates a covered slot for electrical connections and security lock. This allows access to the connections box. Likewise the front section of the post has a plate soldered onto it that serves to attach the light to the pavement. The post is hot galvanized steel and powder paint finished in epoxy RAL 8008, to which a layer of anti-rust and anti-grafitti paint is added. The upper section of the post is a steel tube. The two posts are joined by way of six nuts and bolts. The light fixture is attached via a 5 mm thick fork-shaped steel piece, which is screwed to the upper post.

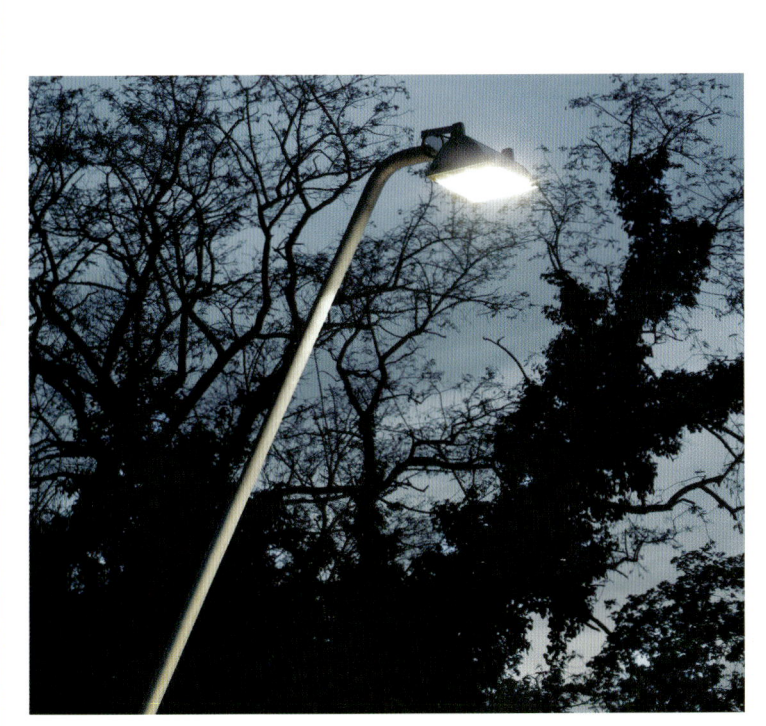

LIGHTING

Faro

Design: Lichtlabor Bartenbach / Klaus Begasse • Production: Hess Form + Licht

The innovative technical concept of the Faro collection is made clearly evident by the characteristics of its design that is based on a secondary, faceted, square reflector, which is made of a special plastic that also reflects the sunlight to great effect during the hours of daylight. The body of the luminaire itself, with a primary source of light and reflection, displays a formal unity with the lamp post, adopting a separate, conical configuration by means of a simple line of shadow. This creates a counterpoint to the secondary reflector located further up, thereby transmitting an overall effect of simplicity that is easy to integrate harmoniously into any environment. The illumination generated in this way is non-blinding, symmetrical and indirect. To achieve a desirable adaptation to different lighting requirements, the posts are supplied in a variety of lengths, with correspondingly adapted secondary reflectors.

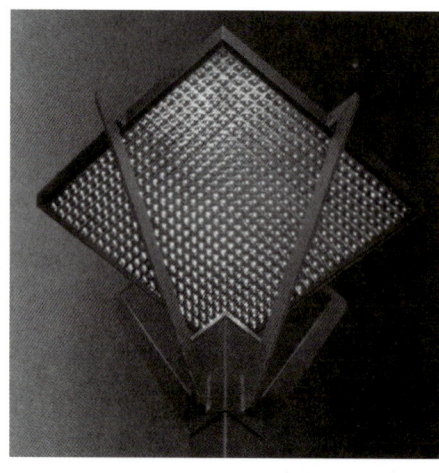

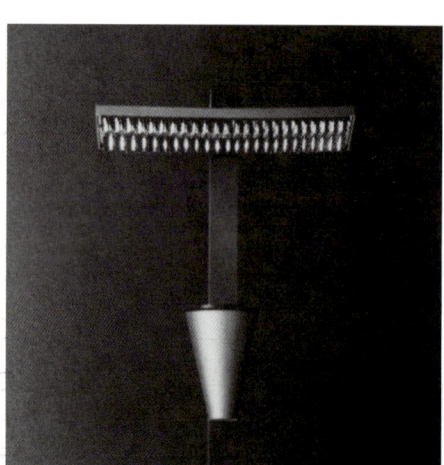

Faro

LIGHTING

Ful

Diseño: Jaume Artigues / Pere Cabrera • Producción: Escofet

The "FUL" range covers 5 models of truncated-cone-shaped columns between 7 and 12 meters in height, made out of galvanized Corten steel, leaning in a variety of angles and following various curved configurations. These arborescent shapes permit a perfect integration into any tree-grown environment; the wide choice of lamps and diffusers ensures an optimally and uniformly distributed flow of light. Designed both for the illumination of traffic lanes as well as for the lighting of pedestrian areas, the light projectors used are small in size, low in power and high in performance, making this a good choice from an environmental standpoint. Choice of a particular projector and its installation ensure the lights vertical fall, reducing luminant contamination of the sky at night. Two 7 meter tall models have been added to the range, which are adequate for the conventional lighting of streets in urban contexts; these can be successfully combined with the other taller members of the family.

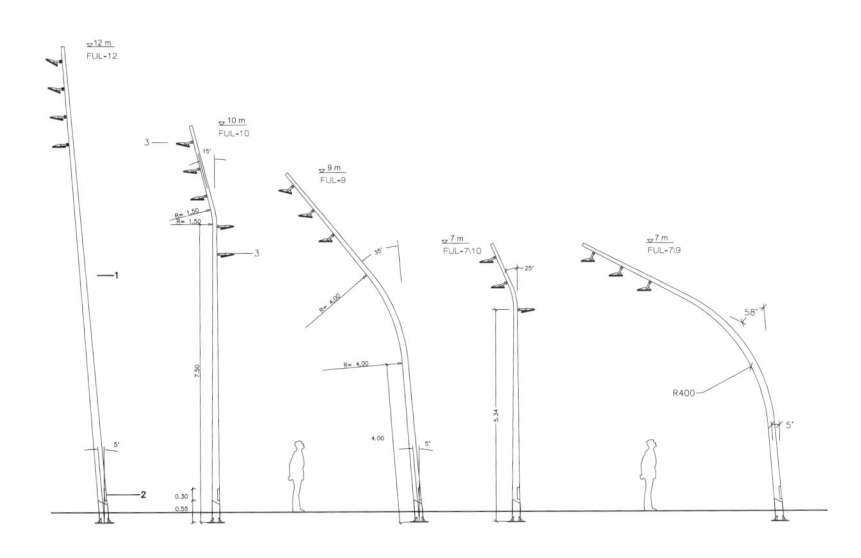

LIGHTING 273

Gabianno

Design and production: **Geohide**

The Gabianno street lamp produces direct down-lighting. The luminaire accessory can be adapted onto new or existing poles of variable diameters (max. 0,24 m). The auto-stable fastening system consists of two transoms. As the article is made entirely of stainless steel, it is resistant and unalterable. The item is supplied normally with a sandblasted finish texture, but other finishes can be made available on request. It has been designed to make assembly simple and quick. The article's dimensions are: length, 3.67 m (12 feet); width 0.50 m (1.64 feet). The luminaire weighs 99 kg (218.196 lb).

Optional accessories are: The c. 501 pole, with a diameter of ø 0.20 meters and a height of 10 meters (32.8 ft) above grade, made of hot-galvanized painted steel (other finishes available on request). The C. 502 extension, with a diameter of ø 0,15 meters and a height of 2.80 meters (9.18 ft) (visible) made of hot-galvanized painted steel (other dimensions and finishes on request).

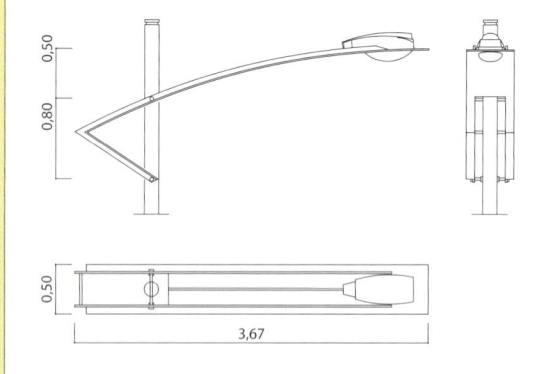

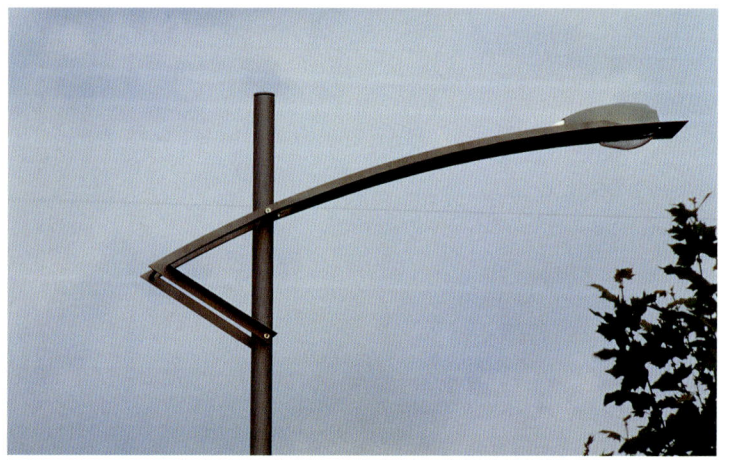

Glowing Places

Design and production: **Philips**

Glowing Places is a concept from an investigation into innovative ways for people to interact with light in public spaces. The plastic seating, embedded with LED (light-emitting diode) strips and sensors, measure the presence of people over time. Both the number of people sitting and the length of time they stay create a 'social interactive pattern' that is translated by patented software into lighting effects in the furniture. Many people sitting for brief periods of time result in lighting activity expressing a busy period, whereas one or two people sitting for a longer period trigger mellow lighting.

274 LIGHTING

Golf

Design: Oriol Guimerà • **Production:** Santa & Cole

This dynamic street lamp, formed by three separate lamps at different heights, combines elements of 1970s classic street lamps with modern materials. The column is made of hot galvanized steel and consists of a base tube that is 160 mm in diameter and 90 cm in height and three upper tubes 50 mm in diameter and of varying lengths. The lamps are made of cast aluminium, sandblasted and powder painted in silver grey. The bottom cover, which supports a flat glaze-finished polycarbonate diffuser, is in sandblasted stainless steel. It uses compact fluorescence lights of 32 or 42 W. The column is fastened using a concrete cube, made on site, and anchoring bolts.

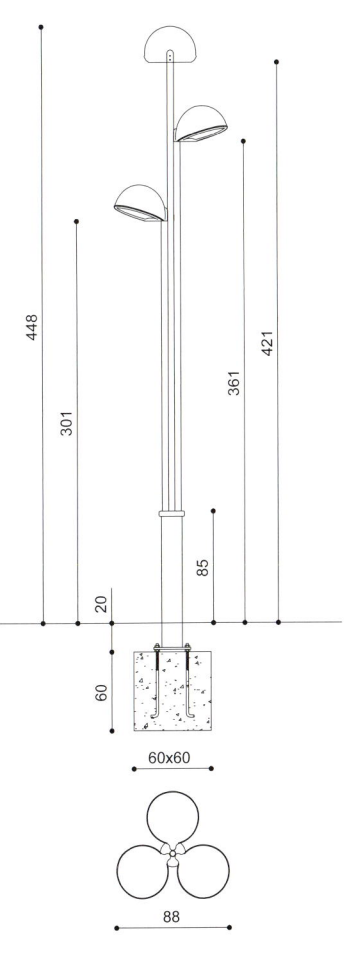

Gropius

Design: Eduardo Albors • **Production:** T&D Cabanes

Gropius consists of a conical post, a head or screen and a terminal (optional), also conical and finished with an item made of injected plastic that houses a small pilot light. The platform of the lamp is fixed to the post and houses a glass diffusing screen and a watertight join. The piece that houses the pilot-light can be red, green, blue or yellow. This little light is a differential accessory added to create a linear play of light when a number of the lamps are installed in a row. These fixtures can be finished in silver gray, graphite, a combination of both, or matt white. The post can be of stainless steel. Also available is an unfinished model without the pilot light, which is then substituted with a watertight lid.

LIGHTING

Heinola Reading Lamps

Design: Vesa Honkonen

Heinola is a town some 130 km north of Helsinki, Finland. Late summer 2004 the Heinola authorities contacted the designer to see if they could use the lighting solution he had created for Raisio, another small town in Finland. Raisio light net, completed 2002, got good response from international press, which raised the image and status of the town. However, Vesa Honkonen had promised Raisio he wouldn't use the same solution in Finland for 7 years, so Heinola was told they would have to be content with something created just for them. They wanted it for a small library plaza; a relatively small urban space, which the designer felt, required some movement. Vesa Honkonen started to dream about the reading lamps stepping out of the library to dance in the street, growing bigger, taking over the street. Having landed in new territory, they started to look over their shoulders, look around, bend down. After a while they calmed down. They started to freeze as they slowly accepted their form and positions. The time for movement was over. They were satisfied and at peace. Their frozen movements took shape as three individual forms. The lower part of the pole is similar in each variation. Three different curved parts permit the fixture to bend in different directions. The lamp head is similar for each variation so three unique fixtures resulted and a total of fifteen units were installed. It was clear form the start that the light source would be metal halide in order to project strong dots of light onto the street and avoid even lighting. It was planned to be a good lighting designer's nightmare, uneven lighting with strong contrasts. Each lamp casts sharp beams onto the street, revealing the shape of the light roaming out of its body. The manufacturer's first model provided extra information about the shape of light, so it was decided to push the lamp deep inside in the body of the fixture to avoid glare. Thus, light bursts out of a black hole in different directions.

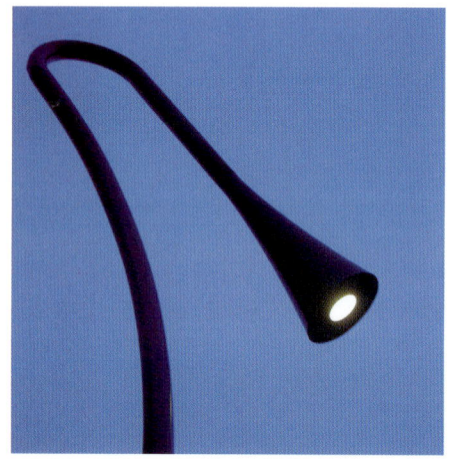

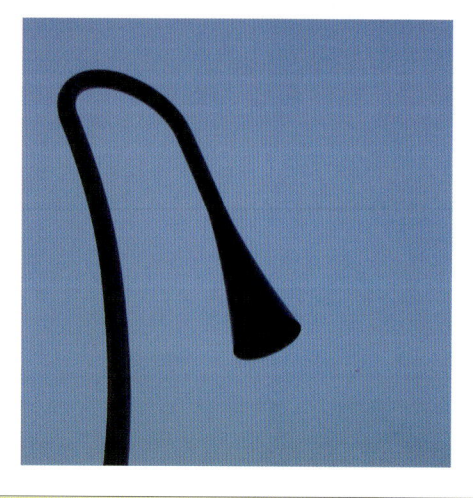

Hom

Design: **Alessandro Caviasca** • Production: **SIARQ**

Hom is photovoltaic lamp of tremendous output. The panels transform solar intake radiation and store electrical power, obtaining a highly efficient illumination system. Each Hom lamp uses 30 led bulbs of the most recent design. The lamp generates no heat, requires no maintenance and provides illumination throughout the entire night, even in the wintertime. No trenches have to be dug to install them; they can be placed in any out-of-the-way location, far from the electrical mains. The lamp has a useful life of 50 000 hours. The design of the lamp represents a human figure that embraces the light of the sun and defines its profile. Hom is ideal for spaces of large dimensions and it saves 255.5 kW/h per year. This translates into a reduction of 153.3 kg of emitted CO_2 with no loss of light power.

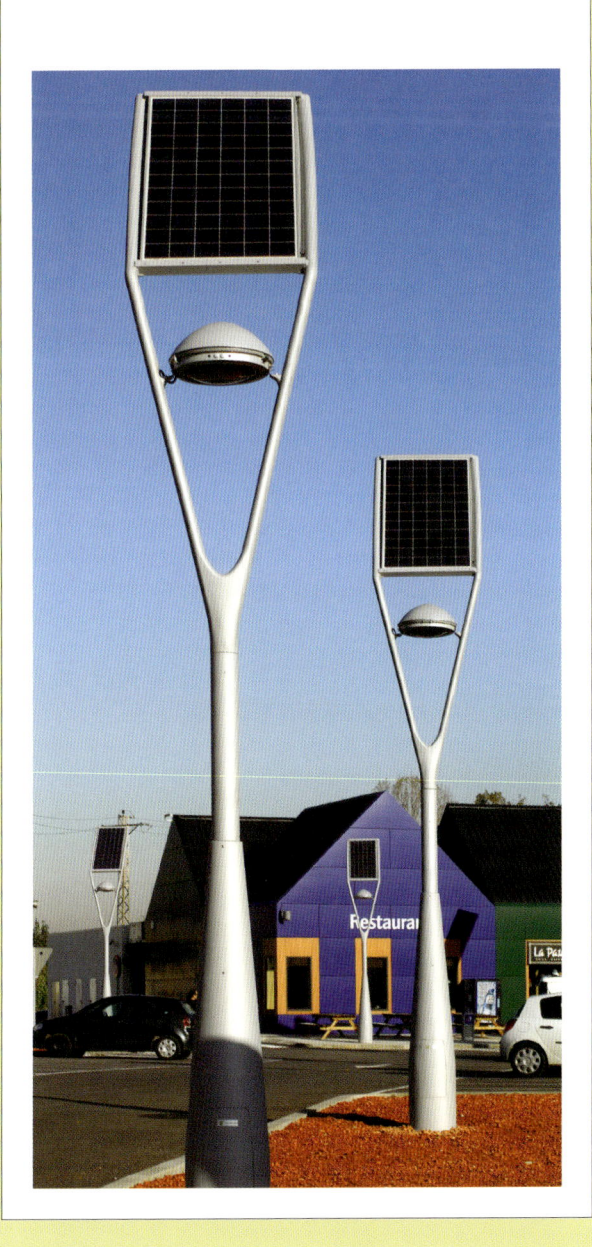

Icon Mini Opal

Design: **Mads Odgård** • Production: **Louis Poulsen**

Icon Mini Opal effectively provides cut-off street lighting with less than 2.5% light distribution above horizontal level. The clear, simplistic design is intentional, since Icon is designed for use in numbers. It combines two geometric forms: a cylinder and a hemisphere. Because of the faintly lit hemisphere, the shape is uniform both night and day. Numerous light source positions in the reflector can make both symmetrical and asymmetrical light distribution possible. Different mounting solutions are available to facilitate optimum positioning and meet individual requirements.

LIGHTING

Ipsilon

Design: **Seste** • Production: **Ghisamestieri**

The Ipsilon lamppost is characterized by the originality of its outline and the materials implemented, wisely used and put together in a harmonious union of shapes and proportions. The system consists of a U-shaped component in drawn aluminium and another in circular section, both having a 170º bend in the upper portion, to house the luminaire. The Ipsilon lamppost, available in two models, consists of a drawn aluminium element in U-section, with maximum dimensions 130 × 150 mm. The channel is 6800 mm high and has a 70º bend. In the double version a second element is joined, circular in section, 6800 mm high, in drawn aluminium, with the same curvature as the first. The connecting elements are realized in aluminium tubes Ø20 mm inside which there is a stainless steel tie M10. The luminaire is in die cast aluminium with a tempered flat glass screen. Ipsilon mounts asymmetric reflectors and metal halide, sodium vapour and mastercolour lamps from 70 to 250 watts. The Ipsilon system can be utilized for lighting medium and large sized avenues and squares, historical centres and residential areas. The light flux Ipsilon emits to its upper hemisphere is nil, in conformity with the strict regulations concerning light pollution.

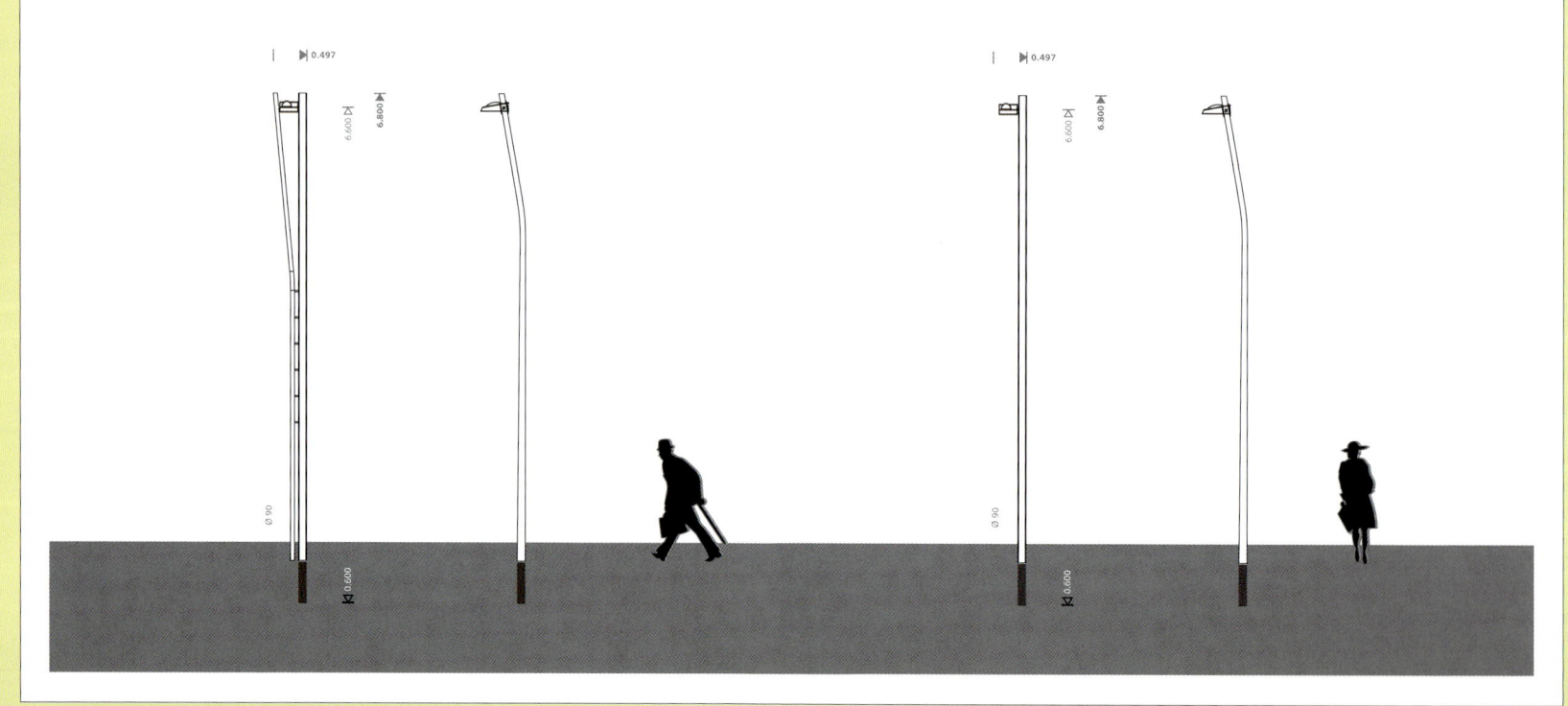

LIGHTING

Java

Design: **Javier Valverde** • Production: **T&D Cabanes**

The minimalistic outline of this lighting item permits an unobtrusive yet interesting integration into all sorts of environments, whether urban or rural, as is illustrated clearly enough in the following images. The body of the column is made of Corten steel. Its section in the form of an isosceles triangle and the angle at which it leans, which corresponds to the exact diagonal of a square polygon, are its main defining features. The electrical equipment consists of an IP-65 light projector situated within the upper end of the column. There is a hinged shutter to close the front of the column in order to facilitate maintenance operations.

Java 2

Design: **Javier Valverde** • Production: **T&D Cabanes**

Java 2 is an illumination system composed of three bodies, square in cross-section, installed at a 90º angle to the horizontal surface of the ground. The luminaire is located inside each body of the lamp, where it is protected by a shutter at the top. The columns or posts are designed to illuminate a wide perimeter in an expansive way, creating a pool of light in the shape of a clover-leaf. The lamp can be provided in stainless steel, galvanized steel or even Corten steel.

LIGHTING

Jupiter

Design: **Emilio Ambasz** • Production: **Ghisamestieri**

Jupiter is proposed as a roadway lighting element of great visual impact. The pole consists of a base decorated with red circular ornaments and three oval section aluminium extrusions joined together by means of a connecting system. A drawn aluminium tube characterizes the upper part with slots lit from the inside. This pole is extremely light and so elegant that it enhances the quality of any specific background, urban or suburban. The base, in hot-galvanized steel, is circular in cross-section; fifteen (15) thermo-rubber collars are inserted into the pole base; three elliptical elements in drawn aluminium set at 120° are joined to the central pole by means of stiffening beads; the central element in drawn aluminium is circular in cross section, where three indentations have been made to house decorative strips of coloured LED lights; the upper ferrule is in cast aluminium; the steel bracket is Ø60 mm in diameter; lighting body is in cast aluminium with an IP66 optical compartment. The Jupiter is suitable for lighting medium and large sized avenues and squares, historical centres and residential areas. The light flux emitted by the Ipsilon system to its upper hemisphere is nil, in conformity with the strictest regulations concerning light pollution.

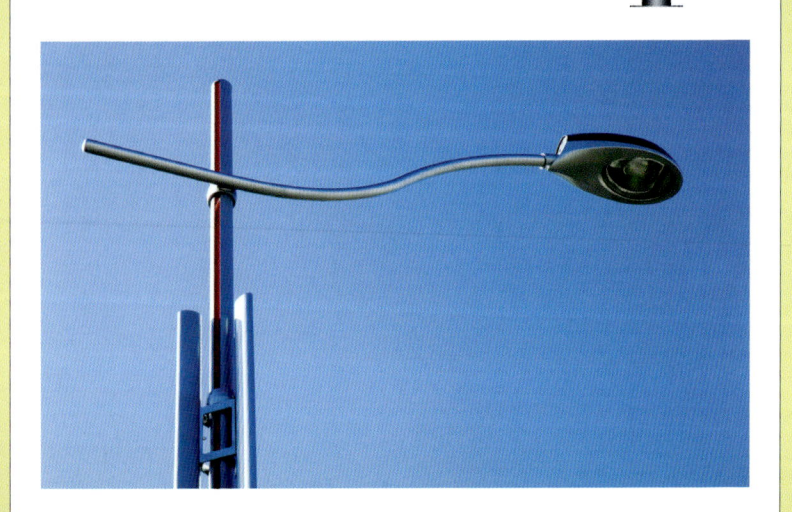

Kanya

Design: **Olga Tarrassó, Jordi Henrich, Jaume Artigues, Miquel Roig**
Production: **Escofet**

The Kanya series of lampposts is intended for lighting large areas, particularly suitable for urban environments and public spaces. They consist of tapered columns in Cor-Ten steel, stainless steel or galvanized steel and stand at an angle of 85°. The heights vary (10, 12 or 15m / 32.20, 39.36 or 49.2 ft). When several are grouped together but facing different ways, attractive lighting effects can be achieved, with endless possibilities thanks to the flexibility of how the pole is positioned and the angle the lights are set at. The column holds circular parabolic floodlights, the number of which varies according to the selected height.

280 LIGHTING

Kipp

Design: Alfred Homann • Production: Louis Poulsen

Kipp Post emits symmetrical downlight. The conical angle of the inner diffuser together with the slightly curved design of the top shade ensures a wide and uniform distribution of the light. The internal diffuser furthermore provides optimal glare-free lighting. Optional finishes are textured and aluminium colored or powder coated grey.
The diffuser is made of high-pressure molded opalescent-white acrylic resin or white spun aluminium. The top shade is black or white pigmented, injection molded ASA. The enclosure is made of injection moulded clear polycarbonate. The frame is die cast aluminum. The various pole options measure (at top): Ø 60mm; Ø 76mm; the QL version Ø 115mm.

Lamparaalta

Design: Beth Galí - Màrius Quintana • Production: Santa & Cole

Lamparaalta, designed as a homage to Alvar Aalto, recovers indirect light for the purpose of lighting public areas, thus transferring a quality of light that is more characteristic of interiors to urban surroundings. The lamp features a curved heat-galvanised steel screen, painted in white. The frame to fasten the screen and the spotlight is in heat-galvanised steel and painted in blue, and the grey cast aluminium spotlight with glass diffuser is sealed with silicone joints, highly resistant to heat. The spotlight itself houses the lamp and the corresponding electrical equipment. It is manufactured in two sizes for metal halide lamps of 150 W or 70 W. The column is fixed using a concrete cube made on site, and anchorage bolts.

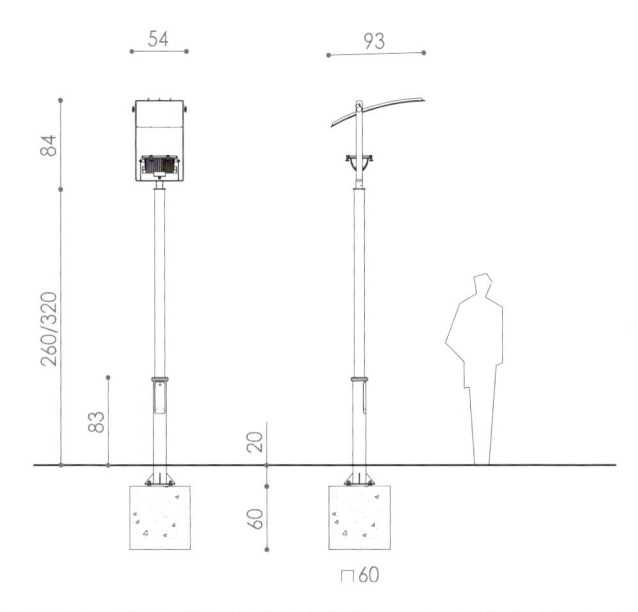

LIGHTING 281

Lampelunas

Design: J.A Martínez Lapeña / Elías Torres • Production: Santa & Cole

This street lamp was conceived with the idea of illuminating public areas with the light of the moon, reproducing the moon's phases using circular reflective screens. These screens gravitate around a 9 or 12 m high tapered cone-shaped column of 5 mm think heat-galvanised steel sheet, reinforced with plates from the base. The circular screens are made from 3 mm thick steel, zinc coated and oven-painted in white polyester, reinforced with plates of the same thickness. There are three or six round spotlights of cast aluminium, oven-painted, which house the lamps and the units. It has a repelled aluminium reflector and a tempered glass diffuser, and uses white light discharge lamps (mercury vapour), with a 250 W recommended maximum. The column is fastened using a reinforced concrete cube, made on site, and anchorage bolts 20 cm below ground level.

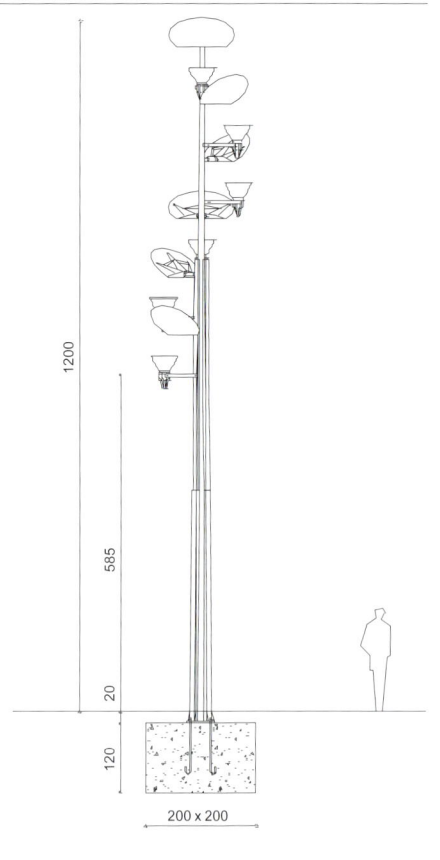

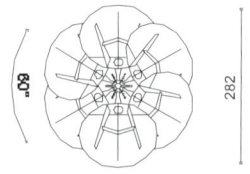

Latina

Design: Beth Galí • Production: Santa & Cole

The Latina public illumination system is an item of extraordinary visual protagonism for large urban spaces, the functional potential of which is befitting to its dimensions: it rises to a height of 15 meters (49.2 ft) and consists of three component elements, the pole, the lamp support and the tension member.

The 7 meter (23 ft) high pole is made of Corten steel and has three parts: a square lower segment and the remaining length which is split in two opposite halves. The support for the luminaires is a tube of hot-galvanized steel, rectangular in cross-section, to carry five PRX-327 type lamps for discharge lamps (max. 250 W).

The tension member that provides the structure with the necessary rigidity is made of a hot-galvanized, round steel tube.

The item's total weight is 895 kg (1972 lb).

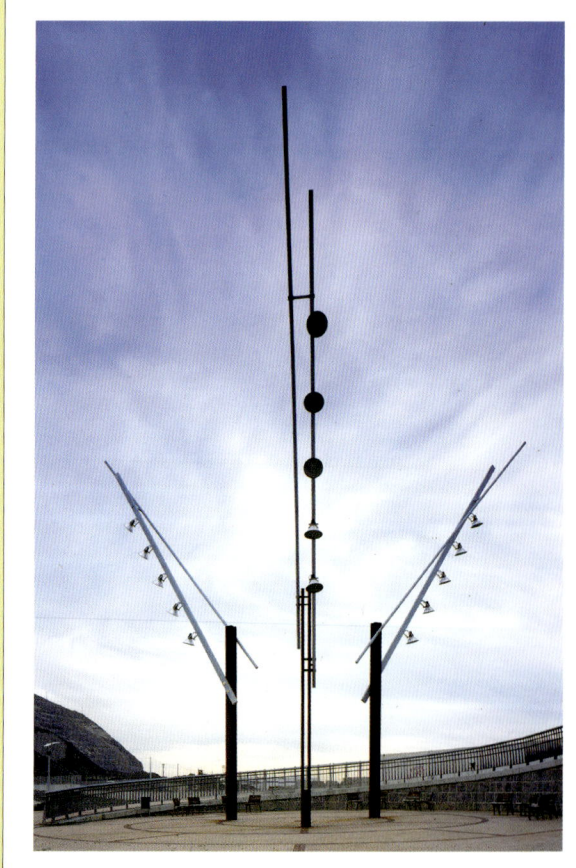

Lausanne

Design: **Carles Valverde** • Production: **Alis**

The work of Carlos Valverde is nourished by the most contemporary trends. One of its characteristics is that it changes according to the space at hand and by the uniqueness of each one of his designs. In this case it is a sober piece of urban sculpture, monumental and elegant, created to resolve a problem of space in a particular location by the recurrent use of Corten steel.

Ledia

Design: **Karsten Winkels** • Production: **Hess Form + Licht**

Two of the items of the Ledia collection are a floor-tile luminaire and a linear luminaire stripe, described as LF and LL respectively. The design and the luminous effect of these products are based on LED technology. The floor tile luminaire consists of a body built of stainless steel V4A, protected by a single-layer sheet of security glass treated with a single coat of anti-slip finish, contained by a built-in frame with a 120 mm deep anchoring system. It is merchandized in four sizes that are adaptable to most of the varieties of paving materials. The linear luminaire consists of a V4A stainless steel coffer to be built into the pavement, and a strip of single-layer security glass with a diffuser side underneath. It is available in different lengths, from 240mm to 910mm. Both luminaires can be supplied in the red, green, blue, amber and white. These fixtures can resist a weight of rubber-wheeled vehicles of up to 1.5 tonnes and require no maintenance.

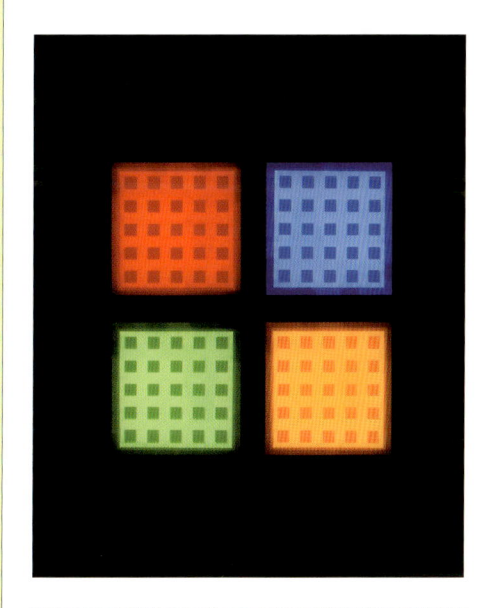

LIGHTING

Lentis

Design: **Alfredo Arribas** • Production: **Santa & Cole**

Alfredo Arribas has designed a modern street lamp with a classic lenticular shape. Thus, he enlarges the projection of light of the classical globe in the bottom half and avoids light pollution with the opaque top half. Alfredo Arribas seeks a classical (lenticular) shape to create a lamp with a modern flavour: the result is the Lentis street lamp. On flattening the dimensions in relation to the classical globe, he increases the area of diffusion and its features. A reflector on the upper half prevents light pollution and increases the performance. The support is a classical cylindrical shaft which leaves full prominence to the lamp. It is a streetlamp adjustable to any kind of urban space. To create the Lentis streetlamp, Arribas found inspiration in the Copa stool, by the same author and very much used within the last twenty years in bars and restaurants. In the late 80's, Arribas was busy designing bars and nightclubs that impressed everyone and established Barcelona's modernity.

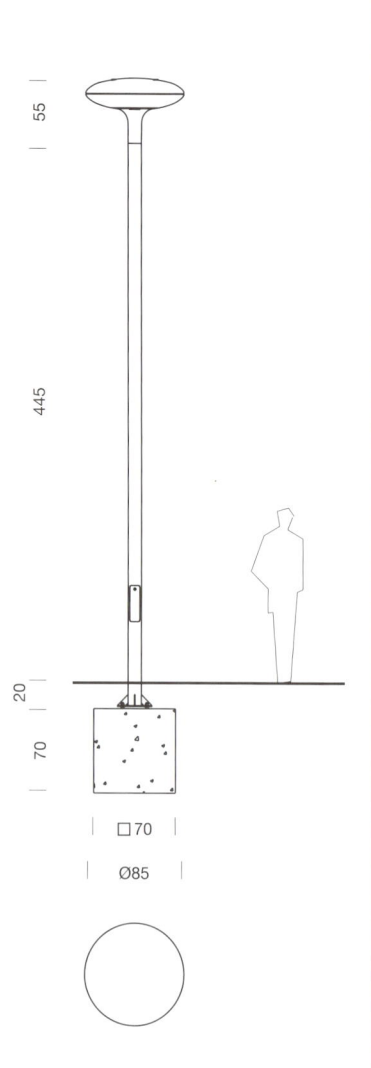

Lightcolumn

Design and production: **Philips**

With its distinctive and contemporary urban design, Lightcolumn is very much the street lamp as 'aesthetic object'. Lightcolumn features Remote Light Source technology, which distributes light from the base to the top, with different perforated masks creating decorative light patterns along the column. These street lamps are ideal for creative applications in relatively large and distinctive areas like business centres, parks and pedestrian zones. The reflective top unit is available in three models: conical, symmetrical and asymmetrical. The column is made from double wall extruded aluminium or die-cast aluminium, and there is an optional enhancing column base cover.

Light Stripe

Design: **SLA** • Production: **GH form**

GH form and SLA have developed a beacon light system in cast iron, the Light Stripe. With the Light Stripe, it is now possible to create modules of up to 30 illuminated meters in length. The Light Stripe is designed to be built into the pavement as a total concept. The starting point of the Light Stripe is located in the kiss and ride space in the city centre of Frederiksberg, where GH form have delivered the cast iron elements. The system consists of a cover plate in cast iron, with LED light spots cast in clear acrylic. For routing of LED light cables and mounting of cast iron elements, a groove in polymeric concrete is used.

Lita

Design: **Gonzalo Milà** • Production: **Macaedis**

Lita is an illumination system for garden areas and paths, which consists of a cylindrical marble element that houses the fixtures and low energy light lamps of great durability. Two versions of the same model are produced, which differ in size, 160 × 500 mm (6.28 × 19.65 inches) and 160 × 800 mm (6.28 × 31.44 inches), allowing for a wider variety of installation possibilities. An innovative and unusual aspect of this product line is that the diffuser screen is made of marble, in the varieties Macael White and Macael Grey to be precise. The medium polish of the object's finish enables it to shed an amiable light with a uniquely charismatic quality. The item is designed to be anchored to the ground by means of built in corrugated rods; its weight varies between 23 and 38 kg (50.7 and 83.75 lb) according to its height.

LIGHTING 285

Llum-i

Design: Albert Viaplana / Helio Piñón • Production: Escofet

Llum-i is a sculpture by day and an atmospheric lamp by night. With its strong geometric lines this piece plays with light and shade and the concrete shapes. It is an ideal lamp for pedestrian areas, with a real sense of human scale, good for marking out routes or alternatively on a larger scale, when several units are grouped together, they turn into a landmark. Made out of reinforced concrete and stainless steel the finish is a granite grey color, stripped and waterproofed. Each piece is anchored down with screws and weighs 340 kg (749 lb).

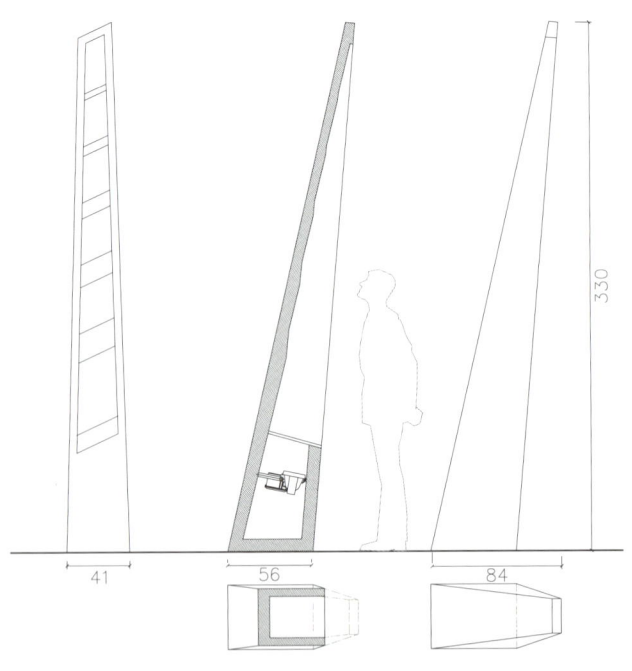

286 LIGHTING

Lux +

Design: **Alessandro Caviasca** • Production: **SIARQ**

Lux+ is a street lamp designed by Siarq with four functions: illumination, solar energy collection, communication and seating. It generates its own solar electricity thus making it an ideal element to respond to the environmental awareness which is required in the design of our public spaces.

It is available in heights from 6 to 7 meters to suit the context. The structure of the lamp is realized in galvanized steel and painted, while the seat is of FSC-certified wood from sustainably managed forests. Thanks to the proportions of the lamp, its additional functions and its strategic design, Lux+ is easily integrated into any context and offers at the same time information and a place to rest.

It is guaranteed to use no more energy than it produces thanks to a system of programmable LEDs which are capable of 14 hours of continuous illumination 365 days of the year. An optional element fixed to the column of the lamp can hold information or advertising.

LIGHTING

Mawson Lakes

Design and production: **Street and Park Furniture**

A major Australian developer, keen to demonstrate his commitment to the sustainable use of resources such as water and electricity, commissioned a design which would do just that in the field of energy. A team from the company Street and Park Furniture were chosen for the job: the resulting solar light is now functioning in the Mawson Lakes area. The striking aspect of this solar-energy light is its unusual curved photovoltaic panel, which was also designed by the same company. As most solar panels are not noted for their interesting design, this curved panel has brought a kind of dynamism to the light while softening the visual impact of the light source. In order to produce a curved solar panel the manufacturers had to perform a lot of trials before finding the best solution. In addition these lights had to be able to light the path so combining design and function was all-important. The mechanism consists of a single curved solar panel of laminated fiberglass, with metallic components of mild steel and aluminum. The solar panel is like a large oval-shaped visor on what seems to be a conventional lamppost. Apart from capturing the sun's energy during the day it acts as a luminous screen at night when the lamp is lit.

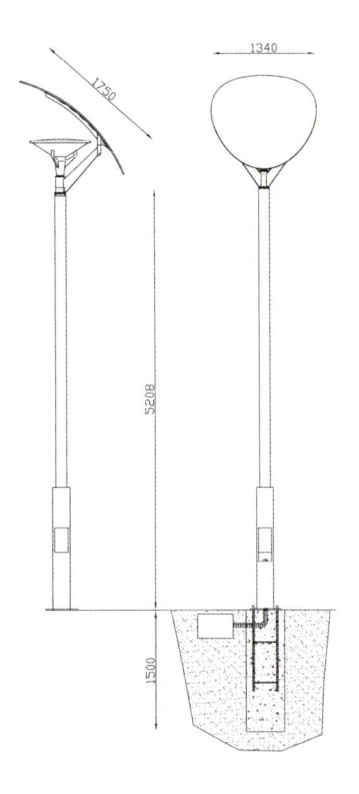

LIGHTING

Mel Dans

Design: DA2 • Production: Ghisamestieri

Mel Dans is a lighting system that has been given an exceptional shape with the intention of making it blend, unnoticed, with the environment in which it is placed. Possessing the utmost versatility, it can be installed suspended on chains or cables, it can be fixed to a wall or any other support, it can be placed facing down or upward, to shed direct or indirect light. It could be defined as a semi-indoor lighting system, which can be installed out of doors if necessary. The basic unit consists of three elements: the luminaire is made of cast aluminum and tempered glass; the polyurethane cover, which conceals the joint; and a curved foot of hot-dip galvanized and painted steel. One of the versions has a steel base with a series of incrustations on the opposite side of the luminaire, which project light by means of LED lamps or tinted methacrylate lenses. The item measures 210 mm in height, 900 mm wide and weighs 12 kg.

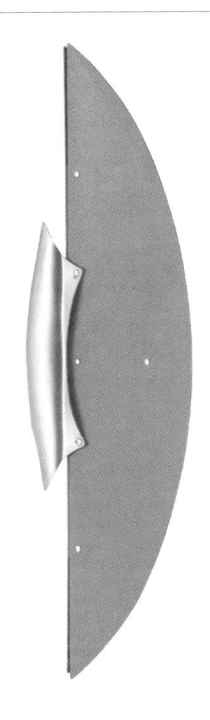

Mota

Design: Iñaki Alday, Margarita Jover, Maurici Giné • Production: Escofet

The design by architects Iñaki Alday/Margarita Jover and the lighting designer Maurici Ginés from ARTEC3 was realised as an initial series of 880 concrete boundary marker/post light units with a built-in light, manufactured by Indalux, to illuminate the walkways of the River Park at Expo Zaragoza 2008. The name Mota was taken from the sixth meaning given in the Dictionary of the Royal Spanish Academy: "A low elevation, natural or artificial, standing alone on a plain." The place where it has been installed certainly fits the definition.

LIGHTING

Nanit

Design: **Ramón Úbeda & Otto Canalda** • Production: **Metalarte**

Nanit has been described by its designers as "a system of exterior illumination and beacon signalling". It consists of a series of fixtures to be installed outdoors, suspended from a fixture or supported on a lamppost. The support pillars of the standard lamps are made of extruded aluminium and the diffuser is made of rotomolded translucent polyethylene, lacquered white or silver. The maintenance locker is located toward the base of the pillar. The system is supplied in heights of 3.34 and 2.26 meters, with an extra-large base shoe, or in heights of 3.00 and 2.26 meters with the normal base shoe. The pillar is finished in white or in silver lacquer. The suspended lamps are also made of rotomolded translucent polyethylene, lacquered white or silver.

Nawa

Design: **Antoni Arola** • Production: **Metalarte**

The Nawa lamp comes in two forms, one is a wall-hanging model and the other is a free-standing element. The structure is made of extruded aluminium, finished in silver lacquer. The light diffuser is made of opalescent methacrylate. The body is 8 cm in diameter and can rise up to 250 cm. It requires an anchoring system.

290   LIGHTING

Olimpia

Design: Frederico Correa, Alfonso Milá • Production: DAE

This lighting column consists of a base composed of three cast iron perlitic steel GG-20 modules, 1980 mm in height, an interior structure of hot-dipped galvanized steel, an exterior structure consisting of a lower rim member, the rings and the hat, all made of steel sheet and protected by an anti-corrosive dip; finally, the light diffuser is made of 4 mm thick molded polycarbonate. The exterior structure is finished with a coat of maximum adherence polyvinyl butyric base paint of zinc phosphate with phenol resins and anti-corrosive pigments, with a polyester-based powder-coating designed to resist harsh outdoor conditions. The standard color is matt black with a wrought iron effect. The base is fixed with four zincified steel M-20 anchoring bolts, 900 mm in length. The approximate weight of the complete item is 557 kg.

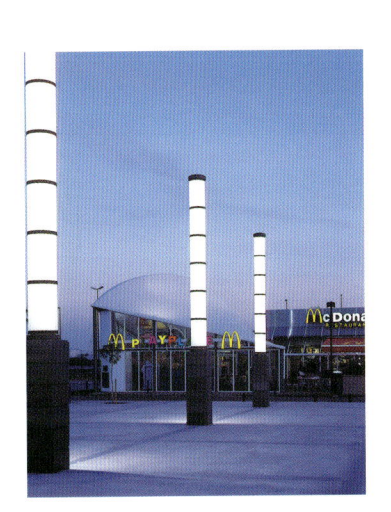

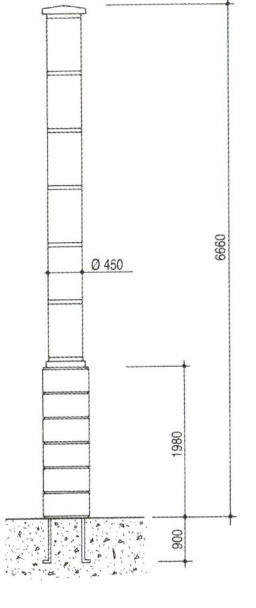

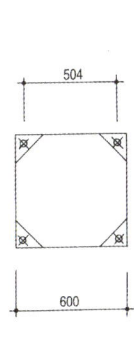

Orbiter Maxi Post

Design: Jens Møller - Jensen • Production: Louis Poulsen

Orbiter Maxi provides symmetrical, glare-free lighting. The design of the top shade directs most of the light downwards, and the anti-glare ring shields the light source from direct view. The top shade and the anti-glare ring are made from form pressed glass fiber, and the enclosure can be injection molded clear or opal white polycarbonate, while the base is die cast aluminum. The lamp can be finished in grey aluminum with a textured surface or graphite with textured surface, powder coated. The pole diameter is 76 mm, and the overall maximum weight is 14.5 kg.

LIGHTING

Palmería

Design: Antonio González Cordón • Production: Santa & Cole

A palm tree trunk, an easy form to recognize, inspired the author in creating this street lamp that emerges from a palm grove like a light totem, symbolizing the union of nature and technology. Its rational and sober silhouette, a one-piece cylinder of hot galvanized "deployé" steel sheet, encloses two fluorescent lamps that create a relaxing and mysterious atmosphere. The idea originated in Almeria, in a large palm grove made into a public garden. Where palm trees formerly stood, these totems, now erect and shining in the dark, blend in and enlarge the area. The result is a forceful, elegant piece. This street lamp is designed as a tall marker that brings personality to the environment, shedding out a soft warm light to accompany us in the night, without imposing its presence.

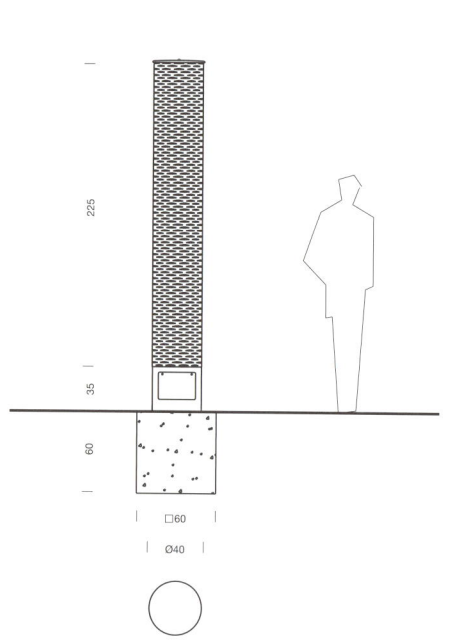

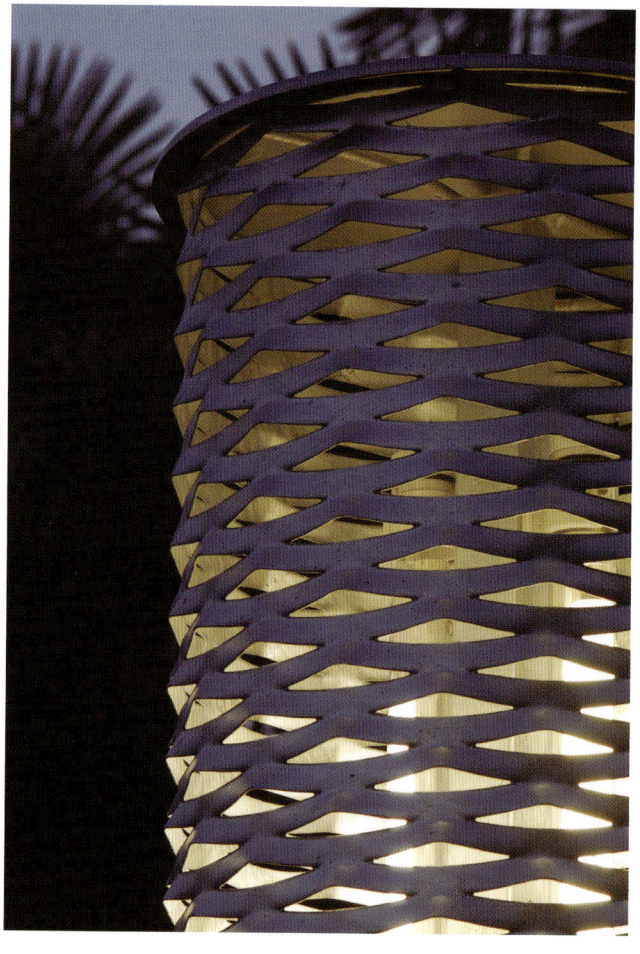

Panamá

Design: Mario Ruiz • Production: Metalarte

This illumination system consists of two simple components, a cylinder and a rectangular prysm with rounded corners. The designer has carried out a dug-out exercise, to eliminate all the unnecessary mass until he had achieved the lightest possible elements to house the sources of light. This series of balanced luminous objects features gentle, rounded profiles, creating an item designed for outdoor areas that intends to avoid the classical tubular beacons. The light source remains hidden, to fulfil a double function: light is projected directly onto the ground while the illuminated edge of the lamp provides the visual signal required.

Piro

Design and production: **Geohide**

This lighting system provides an alternative to the blinding multidirectional street lamps which transform the urban night sky in an opaque black ceiling. The solution is a reflective screen, which bathes the ground in a soft indirect light, free of the hard contrasts of light and shade which are associated with the mystery of night.

The element is constituted of two differentiated parts, the lamppost and the light fixture – composed in turn of the reflector and the light fitting. The post, 5.30 m tall and 0.13 m in diameter is of painted galvanized steel. The dimensions of the reflector are 1.58 by 0.58 meters and it weighs 55 kg. The light fixture can be adapted to posts of different diameters up to a maximum 0.34 m. The fixing is secured by two locking bolts. The element will not degrade as it is fabricated entirely in stainless steel with a matt finish and an underlying reflective layer. The added value of the ensemble is its ease of installation. It is available in a range of finishes.

Poniente

Design: **Silvia López** • Production: **Macaedis**

The design of Poniente has been carried out with the intention of building a light fixture to provide indirect lighting that will not only conceal the light source, but also enhance the natural qualities of the material it is made of. The result is a singularly sculptural piece of urban furniture that illuminates itself and establishes a visual landmark within the area in which it has been installed. It is available in a wide variety of colors, according to the type of natural stone out of which it has been made: Alhambra yellow marble, Eneus marble, white Macael marble, Capri limestone, Iberian cream, black Marquina marble, golden Travertine or green Macael. The item measures 160 × 240 × 650 mm (6.28 × 9.43 × 25.54 inches) and its weight is 28 Kg (61.71 lb). It is designed to be anchored to the ground by means of corrugated steel rods fixed into the pavement.

LIGHTING

Positano

Design: **Karsten Winkels** • Production: **Hess Form + Licht**

Positano is a luminous seat that consists of a single layer box of security glass, the exterior surface of which is characterized by a non-slip finish and a checkerboard pattern of squares, while the interior surface is matt, also displaying a similar pattern of squares to enhance the feeling of three-dimensionality. The shell of the luminaire is of stainless steel V4A, and is fixed into the ground by an anchoring system that is buried some 155 mm under the pavement. The object measures 700 × 400 × 405 mm and is able to withstand a static load of 500 kg. The light that Positano emits is blue.

Rama

Design: **Gonzalo Milà** • Production: **Santa & Cole**

Simple, innovative and versatile, Rama (in Spanish: branch) consists of a cylindrical lamp-post designed to carry one or more lamps, fitted to the post, with clamps. The branches of this "light tree" fulfill a threefold objective: to avoid luminous contamination light is cast downwards to the pavement, the consumtion of electrical power is reduced to a minimum and the system opens the possibility of installing a variable number of luminaires at different heights and positions. The various types of illumination it provides, make the item suitable for any urban area.

The posts are 129 mm(5.07 inches) in diameter and are available in different heights: 4.70m (15.41 ft), 6m (19.68 ft) and 8m (26.24 ft). The material used is hot-galavanized steel or stainless steel AISI 304* with a polished finish texture.

The luminaire and its clamp or made of injected grey polyamide, with an aluminum reflector and a tempered glass diffusor lens. This fixture is designed for compact fluorescent lamps of 57 to 70 W or high pressure discharge sodium vapor lamps or metal halide lamps.

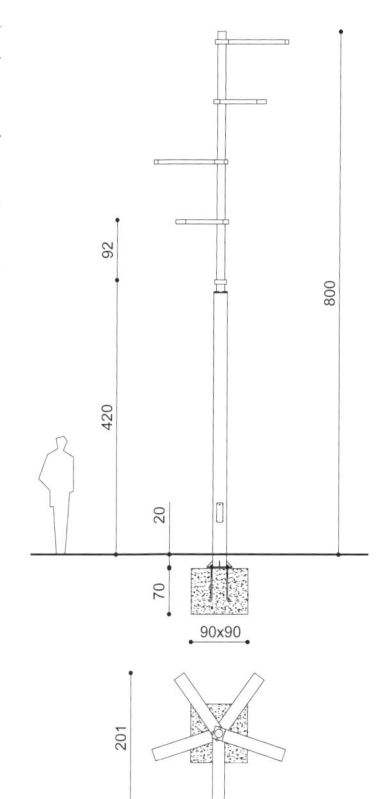

LIGHTING

Romana

Design: Joaquim Carandell • Production: Fundició Dúctil Benito

Romana is a bollard designed with a double function: security and decorative illumination. It is a useful signalling element for pathways, parks and pedestrian areas, with a minimalist design that features essentially purist outlines enhanced by a zincified steel finish.

Rondò

Design: Piero Ravaioli • Production: Ghisamestieri

The suppression of road crossings, gradually transformed into stream roundabouts, has induced Ghisamestieri to design the Rondò system as the answer to the need to find a pleasant way to illuminate and decorate these new urban areas that are now integral parts of any urban landscape. Its harmonic light shape and the chromatic central obelisk allow for the creation of different settings and solutions, in accordance with the background it is placed against.

LIGHTING

Ruta del Quijote

Design: Guillermo Sánchez Gil • Production: T&D Cabanes

Stamped with the mark XQ, "IV Centenario Ruta del Quijote", the creation of this traffic beacon arises from an initially simple flat rectangle that unfolds vertically. It is almost entirely made of 3 mm thick Corten steel plate; the light diffuser is made of stainless steel sheet; the base is a 5 mm thick rectangle of steel plate, anchored to the ground or the pavement. The electrical equipment consists of an IP-67 luminaire with an energy saving 18 W lamp. Access to the electrical system is through an opening at the top of the object, closed by a personalized lid. The result of directing the light from the source towards the pavement is an agreeable indirect illumination that makes everything seem to glow, enhancing the environment of the immediate surroundings.

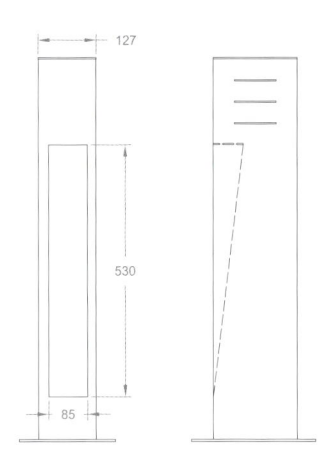

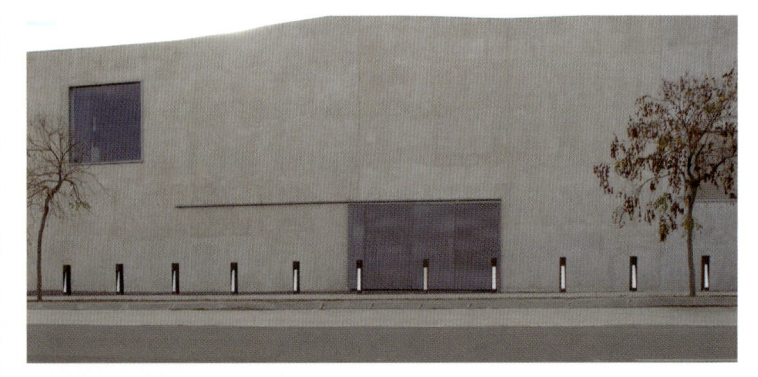

Sara

Design: Beth Galí • Production: Santa & Cole

The Sara street lamp arose from Beth Galí's project in the Irish city of Cork, between Saint Patrick's Street and Grand Parade. The designer wanted to create a unit that would reflect the asymmetrical nature of this crossroads, so she designed a street lamp with two different arms and two lighting systems; one is diffuse, the other is direct. The unit consists of two separate poles leaning at opposite angles and hinged together in the middle; this structure supports the two autonomous illumination systems, one for the street and the other for the pavement.

The tallest of the two poles tapers upward to the height of 10 meters (32.8 ft) and functions as the support for four PRX-327 discharge lamps projectors (maximum 250 W). The other pole, which is 6 meters long (19,68 ft), supports two completely watertight HF-265 type luminaires with 58 W fluorescent lamps.

LIGHTING

Sidney

Design: **Joaquim Carandell** • Production: **Fundició Dúctil Benito**

This urban illumination system features a design that stands out for its solidity and sturdiness. It is adequate for the illumination of highways, industrial estates and public areas. The body is made of hot-dipped galvanized steel with a wrought-iron finish combined with gray.

Skot

Design: **Lauritz Knudsen** • Production: **Louis Poulsen**

Skot is a traditional maritime design, a simplification of the bulkhead lamps on ships. The name is a Danish word for bulkhead. The lamps are used both outside and inside ships. They were protected by a cross or a metal net, which in fact hardly affected the light distribution. This type of light fixture is still used on ships, but due to the influence the maritime context has on fashion, these fixtures have been used in a lot of situations requiring a robust lighting fixture or wanting to suggest a maritime environment. The original design is more than 100 years old. Skot Bollard provides both direct and diffuse lighting with a choice of either clear or white opalescent diffusers. The half-masked cross-guard accentuates the downlight.

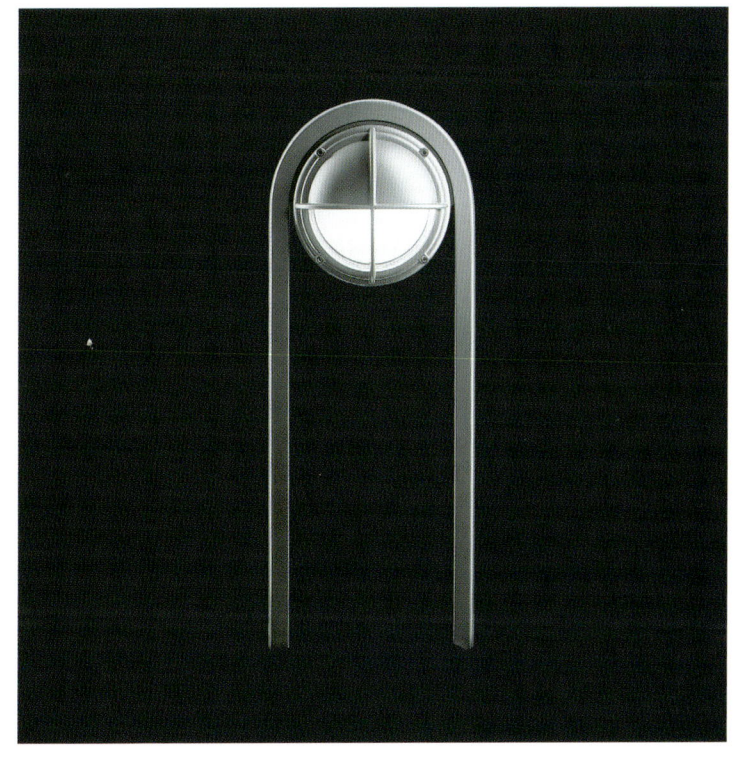

LIGHTING 297

Sloper

Design: **Luis Tabuenca** • Production: **ONN Outside**

The Sloper street lamp range comprises six different models of lighting columns to cover the lighting requirements of any project. The lamp IP66 is designed to generate no light pollution (FHS = 0 %). The versatility of the street lamp is complemented with the possibility of using sodium, metallic halogen or fluorescent lamps.

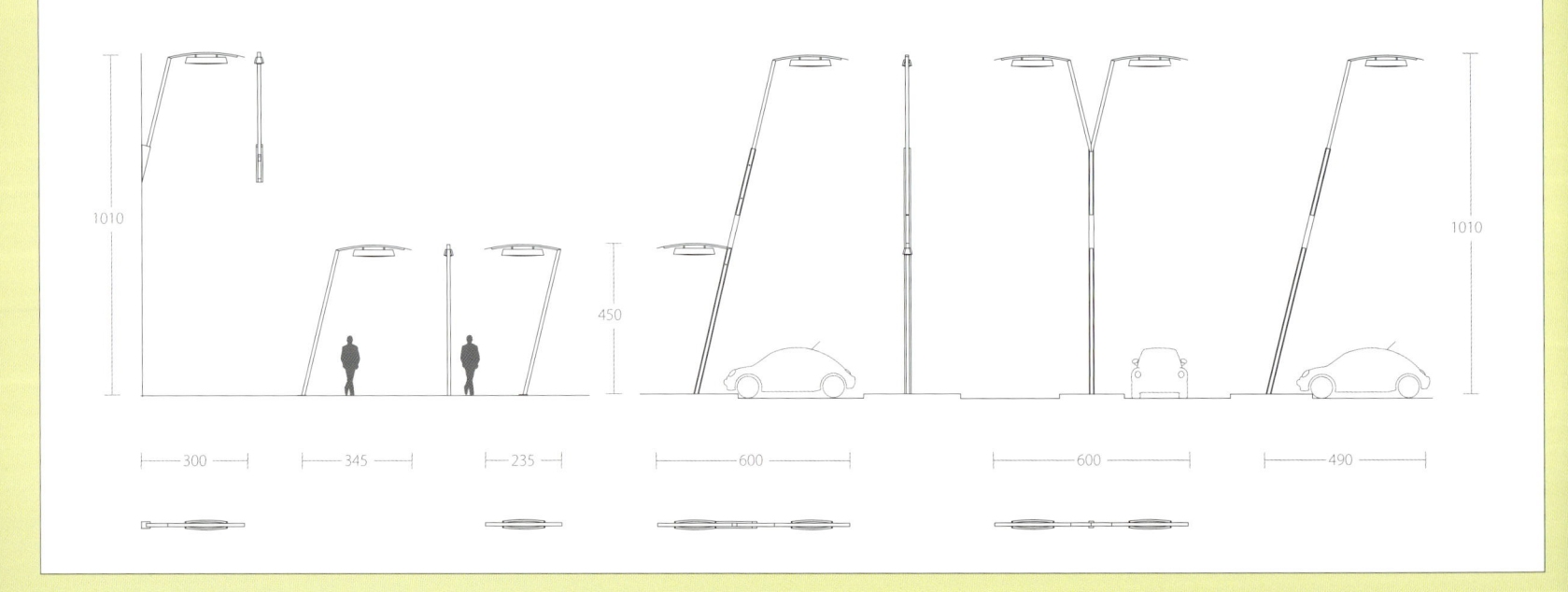

298 LIGHTING

Solar Mallee Trees

Design and production: Street and Park Furniture

The design of these solar trees arose as part of an environmental impact research carried out by the government of Australia to demonstrate its serious involvement in the search for alternative sources of energy. The shape that inspired the project is that of the Mallee, a type of dwarf Eucalyptus tree with various ramifications, native to the environment of southern Australia. The trees were constructed in collaboration with the Street and Park Furniture Studio, who proceeded with the production and installation of the items at the Adelaide Festival Centre. The design displays a new form of dome shaped solar panels, an innovation introduced by the design studio. The dome-shaped oval panels form the treetops and provide the energy to feed the system of programmable LEDs that illuminate the Festival grounds at night. The Solar Mallee Trees include a sound system that is activated by infrared sensors and emits the soundtracks recorded in Adelaide's first "Solar Schools". The materials used to build the metallic parts of the "Mallees" are iron and aluminium; the dome-shaped photovoltaic solar panels are made of laminated fibreglass; the LEDs are controlled electronically, and emit light in the frequencies green, blue and red.

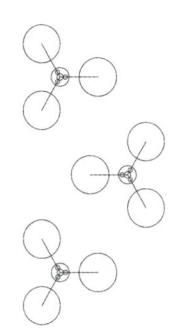

Spiral Light

Design and production: Street and Park Furniture

Street and Park Furniture were provided with details on the type of light fitting required for the project and the designers had to devise a way of fixing the lights to the pole. To create an aesthetically pleasing detail that would give some flair to an otherwise uninteresting pole, they successfully managed to create a spiral out of a flat bar which was attached to the pole and also allowed access for the wiring. Street and Park Furniture are committed to the view that better streets and civic spaces are a vital part of community well being and endeavour to be perceived as a supplier of street furniture for these applications. They aim to provide specifiers and customers with the convenience of a single supply source for most urban projects incorporating street furniture and the support of specialised experience.

LIGHTING

Totem

Design: Studio Itinerante Arquitectura • Production: Siarq

The Totem has a double role as both a streetlight and a photovoltaic plant for generating energy. Its 16 m (52.48 ft) high vertical structure is made of laminated wood. Incorporated into the very top of the structure are two 250 W floodlights which light the surrounding area sufficiently but at the same time guard against light pollution. The plant can generate up to 3,400 kWh of energy which is transferred to the public power supply network, while the energy needed for the floodlights, less than half of what it generates, comes directly from the conventional electric system. In addition to these two functions this structure also creates a recreational area at ground level, which makes it particularly appealing for public spaces. The design of the structure has taken into account more than just aesthetic criteria; the technical and mechanical aspects necessary for generating energy, providing adequate lighting and easy maintenance were given equal importance.

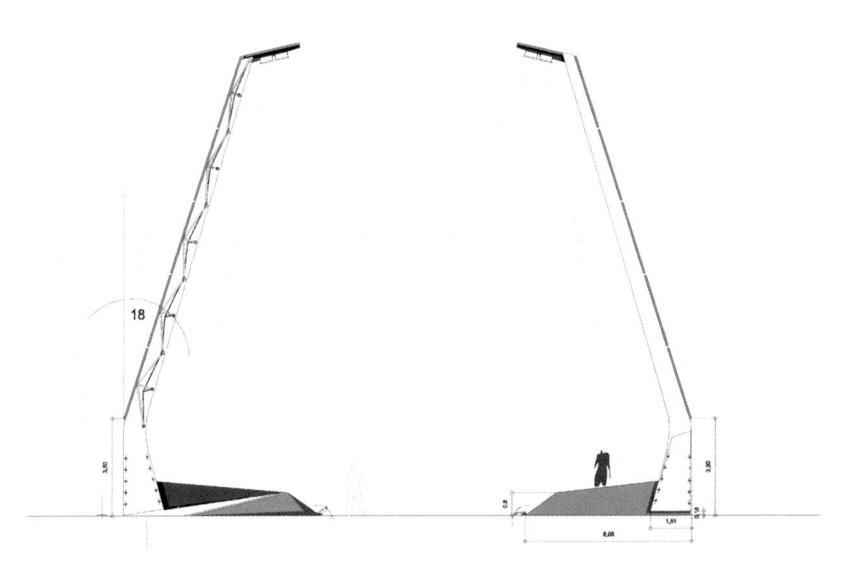

Tournesol

Design: Philippe Starck • Production: JCDecaux

The Tournesol (Sunflower) streetlight has the unmistakable stamp of a Philippe Starck design. Its originality lies in the lamp's movement: during the day it stands in a vertical position but at night it bends over to light the way for pedestrians in the street. It is therefore an enigmatic urban sculpture by day and at night reveals its main function thanks to the rotating lamp head. The shape and texture of the post have a distinctly biological feel and the fact that it moves reinforces the idea of it being almost "alive", which makes it even more attractive.

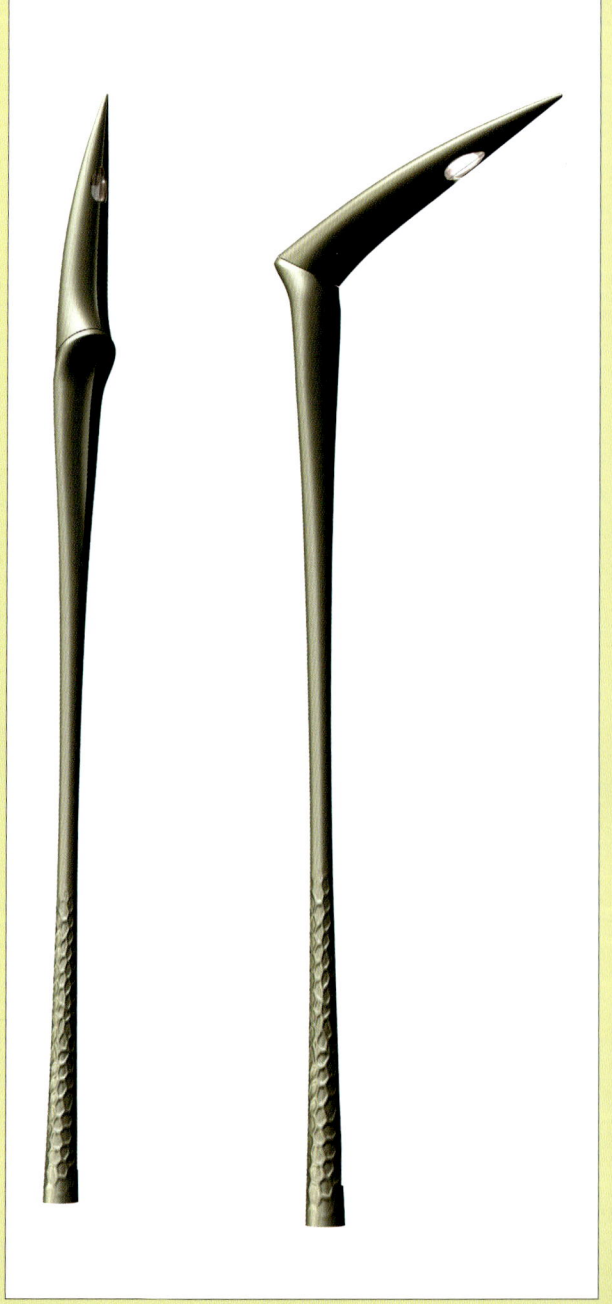

LIGHTING

Treo

Design: Salvador Fraga, Fco. Javier García-Quijada, Manuel Portolés
Production: DAE

The post of the Treo lamp consists of a tube and a base made of hot dip galvanized steel, and a fixture made of cast aluminum L-2520 that holds the projector and the screen, made of polyester reinforced with a metal structure. The aluminum parts of the light source fixture are protected and finished with an undercoat of maximum adherence butyric polyvinyl paint with anti-corrosive pigments and phenol resin with a high zinc chromate content; finally the item is powder coated with a finish especially designed for outdoor performance, based on polyester resins. The standard available color is a silvery metal tone.

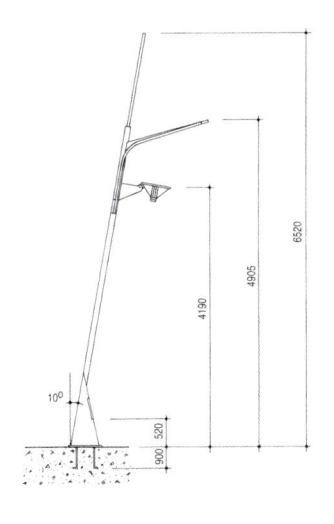

Tres

Design: Marta Ferraz & Paula Cabrera • Production: T&D Cabanes

The triangular geometry of Tres is capable of illuminating the whole perimeter expansively. The illumination is produced by an ice-coloured strip of polycarbonate 20 mm thick, in each side of the object. This, added to its formal subtlety, gives the lamp a sober profile, but produces a special rhythm that is ideal for defining an area or marking out a direction or path.
The shaft is made of galvanized steel painted in a range of colours, available on request. It houses a low energy electronic bulb for the beacon and the lamp uses three 1500mm long 35W fluorescent tubes. The lamp is anchored to the ground by bolts and special security plugs embedded in the pavement.

LIGHTING 301

Triangel

Design and Production: **Philips**

Triangel combines a strong, easily remembered design with a robust and durable construction. Its characteristic lit triangle at the top creates an optical guidance and secondary lighting. It is designed for use in residential areas, shopping areas, car parks, footpaths/pedestrian areas and other urban spaces where its high efficiency reflectors will provide economic lighting. Tempered safety glass makes Triangel vandal-resistant. The housing is made of robust, die-cast aluminium, painted in black or grey (RAL 7021). The cover is made of tempered safety glass - frosted (GF) or clear (GC) - mounted in an aluminium frame, painted in the colour of the housing. The article weighs approximately 12 kg (26,5 lb). It is suitable for a wide variety of lamp types. Mounting brackets are available to permit single, double or quadruple post top mounting.

Upupa

Design and Production: **Geohide**

This indirect lighting system is designed to shed ambient light onto a limited perimetral area, namely onto the banners or flags hanging from the upper part of the poles, giving them a preponderant visual and symbolic role after dark, while providing a subtle light over the area around the flagpole. Installed in groups, a dynamic installation can be choreographed. The luminaire can be adapted to the tops of existing flagpoles or the flagpole accessory can be used.

The pole accessory is a conical cylinder, tapering upward from Ø 0.15m at the base, to Ø 0.07 m at the top, 9 meters (29.52 ft) above the ground.

302 LIGHTING

Vía Láctea

Design: **Enric Batlle - Joan Roig** • Production: **Santa & Cole**

Conceived as a way of drawing lines of light in the sky, Vía Láctea was the first and most remarkable project to use fluorescent lighting in an urban environment. The column is made from 150 x 100 mm base hot-dip galvanized structural steel sections, with a 100 x 50 mm lamppost and inspection door. The screen, which can be single for one lamp or double for two, is rectangular in section and made from the same material. It uses totally weatherproof standard HF-265 lamps for 58W fluorescent tubes, readily available on the market. The column is fixed to the ground through a reinforced concrete cube, made on site 22 cm below the level of the paving, and anchoring bolts.

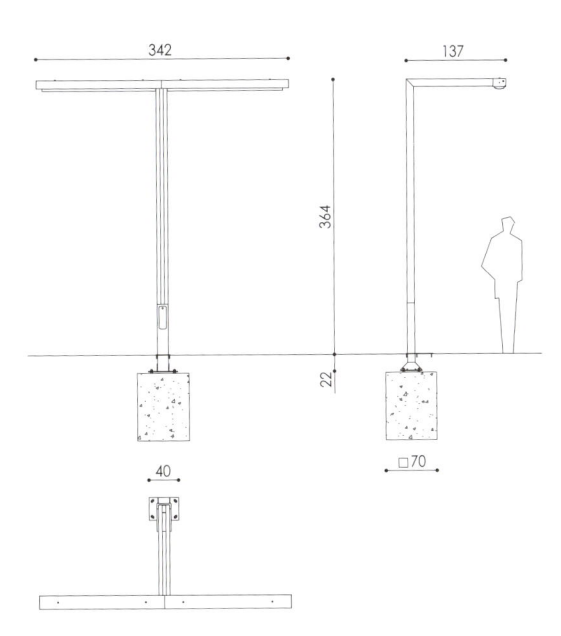

Volcano

Design: **PLH Design** • Production: **Louis Poulsen**

Volcano is designed as an on-ground fixture. The product is mainly suited for image and representative areas due to the fragility of the material. The idea behind the product is a cone, which reflects the light from a reflector placed in the top. When lit the shape of the cone appears as a light profile and makes the light seem weightless. It gives the impression that it has emerged from the landscape, hence its name. The light is directed from the top reflector on to the surface around the Volcano. This causes the Volcano to emit symmetrical light and makes the fixture suitable for indication and landscape lighting.

LIGHTING

Vrellen

Design: UTGM & DA2 • Production: Ghisamestieri

The Vrellen lighting bracket combines function and elegance by using an innovative material for outdoor lighting: the arm connecting the luminaire to the pole is made of structural glass, supported by an almost imperceptible aluminum section. Vrellen is a product range comprising poles of various heights, luminaires in two different sizes, and wall brackets, for different areas of a city to be illuminated by a coherently designed range of articles.

The luminaire is of pressure die-cast aluminum in conformity with CEI regulations. The protection degree is IP 66; made of extra-pure anodized aluminum with a flat, tempered glass lens, the reflector casts a non-symmetrical, mainly transversal light. It has an extractable bayonet plastic shutter, for lamp replacements; heat-resistant rubber gaskets protect the optical compartment. No light is cast upward, following the strictest regulations regarding luminus contamination. The item is 263 mm (10.33 inches) high, Ø600 mm (23.58 inches) wide, and weighs 15 kg (6,80 lb plus wiring).

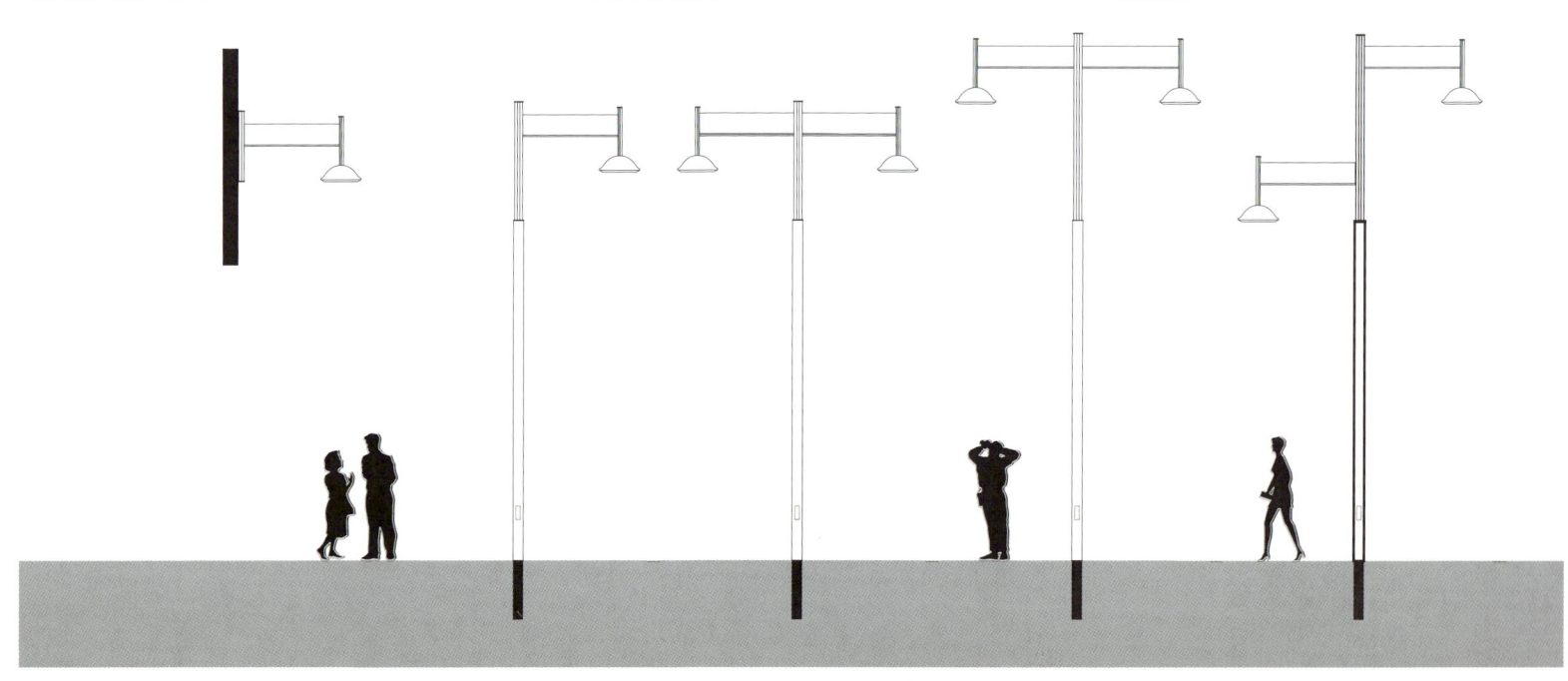

304 LIGHTING

Yumi

Design: **DA2** • Production: **Ghisamestieri**

The wish to tidy up and make room for one piece in the place of the great deal of elements filling our pavements originated the lighting system Yumi. This name echoes oriental essentiality and the shape a Japanese Samurai's long ancient bow called Yumi. This new system integrates street lighting and decoration. Three long curved tubes support the luminaire starting from the base where an integrated planter, or a litter bin on request, is incorporated. The light flux emitted by the Yumi system in its upper hemisphere is null, in conformity with the strictest regulations concerning luminus contamination.
The Yumi system consists of of three circular section steel tubes, 4 mm thick, 60 mm in diameter. One of the three poles is provided with a screw and with a slot where the electric wiring goes in to feed the luminaire.

LIGHTING

Product Index

Seats

10	108
11	2197
11	5050
12	Accesible
12	Agi
13	Agrada
14	AJC
15	Alea
15	Alehop
16	Alfil
17	Ambiente
17	Ameba
18	Ara
19	Arco
20	Armonia
20	Arona
21	Baf
22	Bagdad Café
23	Banca
24	Bancal
25	Banda
25	Banda Doblada
26	BdLove Bench
27	Bench Seat I - Curved
27	Big Bux
28	Bilateral
29	Bilbao
30	Bloop
30	Blue Moon
31	Boa
31	Board
32	Boomerang
33	Botanic
34	Brunea
34	BS9
35	Buque
35	Cado
36	Calma
36	Canapino
37	Catalano
38	Celesta
38	Chill
39	Coma
39	Come Back
40	Comunitario
41	Cornamusa
41	Crusöe
42	Cube
43	Cuc
44	Daciano Da Costa
44	Deca
45	Degrau
45	Divano
46	Dom
47	Elemental
47	Elios
48	Encuentros
48	Equal
49	Essen
49	Fenicia
50	Feris BK
50	Finferlo
51	Flor
52	Fun Bank
52	Godot
53	Grindle
53	Harmony
54	Hebi
54	Hoja
55	Hop hop
56	Horse Shoe
56	Hungaro
57	Iola
57	IP6
58	Isi
59	Islero
60	Katia
60	[K-BENCH]
61	Killy
62	Kimba
62	Lancer
63	Laurede
63	Leichtgewicht
64	Linea
64	Link
65	Literas Urbanas
65	Longlife
66	Longo
67	Loop
67	Lotus
68	Lungo Mare
69	Mateo
69	Metropol
70	Mingle - Shade
70	Miriápodo
71	Mitrum
72	Mix
72	Mobilia
73	Moiré
73	Moon
74	Naguisa
75	Nastra
76	NeoRomántico
77	Nigra
78	Niu
79	Nu
79	Onda
80	Pacú
80	Pagoda
81	Palazzo
81	Pancarè
82	Patrimonial
82	Pausa
83	Perforano
84	Picapiedras
85	Pillet
85	Pinxo
86	Pleamar
86	Pliegue
87	Prat
87	Pure
88	Racional 2
89	Radium
90	Rambla
91	Recte
91	Rehué
92	Riddle Chair
92	Rondine
93	Rough & Ready
94	RS
95	Rua
95	Shape
96	Shoreline
96	Sillarga
97	Sit
97	Sitting-Around
98	Sit
99	Ska
99	Slope
100	So-ffa
100	Sol y Luna
101	Sombra
101	Spring Seat
102	Stay
102	Sumo
103	STO
104-5	The Swiss Benches
106	Szekely
107	Tauranga
107	Tea Tree Gully
108	Tens
108	Terra
109	Tetris
110	Topográfico
111	Trapecio
111	Trasluz
112	Tubbo
113	Tube
114	Twig
115	Vera
116	Vesta
116	Via Augusta
117	Vivanti
118	Walden
118	Wing Pedestal
119	Xurret System
120	Yin-Yang
121	Zen

Planters

124	AJC
124	Arcadia
125	Barcina
125	BdLove Planter
126	Bilbao
127	Botánica
127	Canasto
128	Casicilíndrica
128	Cestae
129	Conical Tree Tubs
129	Cub
130	Dara
130	Diogene
131	Dish
131	Fémina
132	Gardel
132	Highlife Tree Tubs
133	Iona
133	Las Tres Damas
134	Lineafiorne
134	Lolium
135	Marc
135	Morella
136	Plaza
136	Shrubtub
137	Sputnik
138	Tanit L
138	Tram
139	Urbe

Tree Grids

142	Arboré
142	Beiramar
143	Campus
144	Cap i Cua
144	CorTen Tree Grids
145	Helix
145	Iris
146	Pictorial
147	Quadris
147	Rámla
148	Taulat
148	Tree Isles
149	TV
149	Yarg

Bicycle Racks

152	127
152	Arca
153	Ba
153	BCPark
154	Bicilínea
154	Bicipoda
155	Contínuo - Triângulo
156	Ezzo
156	Flo
157	Key

158	Maia 360	189	Cinderello	219	City 90	250	Rondo	283	Lausanne
158	Meandre	190	Cordillo	219	Eco	250	Sagrera	283	Ledia
159	Montana	190	Cornet	220	Edge	251	SD	284	Lentis
159	On	191	Crystal	220	Erandio	251	SE	284	Lightcolumn
160	Quad bike	192	Cube	221	Foster	252	SH	285	Light Stripe
160	Rough & Ready	192	Cylindre	221	Gull Wing	252	Ska	285	Lita
161	Sammy	193	Diagonal	222	Habana	253	SL	286	Llum-i
161	Tatanka	194	Ecclesia	223	Heritage	254	Sloper	287	Lux +
162	Táctil	194	Ecology	223	Kaleidoscope	254	Solid	288	Mawson Lakes
163	Trian	195	Fontana	224	Nimbus	255	SR	289	Mel Dans
163	Velo	195	Grace	225	Pausanias	255	Tente	289	Mota
		196	Imawa	226	Pórtico	256	Tona	290	Nanit
		196	Lakeside	226	Refugio Verde	256	Topino	290	Nawa
	Fountains	197	Laurel & Hardy	227	Regio	257	Tube	291	Olimpia
		197	Lena	228	Rural	257	Vento	291	Orbiter Maxi Post
166	Agua	198	Linea	228	Skandum			292	Palmería
166	Atlántida	198	Litos	229	T Bus		**Lights**	292	Panamá
167	Branca	199	Mantel de Encaje	230	Terminal			293	Piro
167	Chafariz	199	Marte	230	Tokay	260	108	293	Poniente
168	Caudal	200	Maya	231	Tramvia	261	17°	294	Positano
169	Estena	200	Mobilia	232	UMD	262	AJC	294	Rama
170	Fontfosa	201	Nastra	233	UMP	262	Andrea	295	Romana
170	Georgina	201	Net			263	Arken	295	Rondò
171	Lama	202	Pandora		**Limits**	263	Ballerina	296	Ruta del Quijote
171	Lavapiés	202	Paralela			264	Balta	296	Sara
172	Lilla	203	Pitch	236	2994	264	Bd Love lamp	297	Sidney
172	Naia	203	Quattro	236	Bamboo	265	Calaf	297	Skot
173	Periscopio	204	Racional	237	Barriers	265	Camelot	298	Sloper
173	Tana	204	Radium	237	Campus	266	Dinosaurio	299	Solar Mallee Trees
		205	Rambla	238	Cilíndrico	267	Diogene	299	Spiral Light
		205	Rio	238	Consentido	268	Diorama	300	Totem
	Pavements	206	Rodes	239	Haiku	269	DL 10	300	Tournesol
		206	Sacharoff	239	Imawa	270	Donday	301	Treo
176	Ada	207	Saturno	240	Limitot	270	Ecclesia	301	Tres
177	Checkerblock	207	Siriio	240	Linea	271	Faf	302	Triangel
178	Palma	208	Ska	241	Lineapalo - Linealuce	272	Faro	302	Upupa
179	Pass	208	Sloper	241	Luco Mojón	273	Ful	303	Vía Láctea
180	Pictóricos	209	Sócrates	242	Mariosca	274	Gabianno	303	Volcano
181	Redes	209	Starck	242	Morella	274	Glowing Places	304	Vrellen
		210	Trash	243	Murllum	275	Golf	305	Yumi
		210	Urbana	243	Nastra	275	Gropius		
	Wastebaskets	211	Valet	244	Neobarcino	276	Heinola Reading Lamps		
		211	Vega	244	On	277	Hom		
184	2278			245	Onda	277	Icon Mini Opal		
184	377		**Shelters**	245	Paracelso	278	Ipsilon		
185	7kale			246	Pausita	279	Java		
186	Argo	214	Andromeda	246	Petrelli	279	Java 2		
186	Arona	214	APCD	247	Pisolo	280	Jupiter		
187	Balia	215	Apoios de Praia	247	Propeller	280	Kanya		
187	Banquina	215	Arqui	248	Rampante	281	Kipp		
188	Bina	216	Aureo	248	Robert	281	Lamparaalta		
188	Canasto	217	BMG	249	Rodas	282	Lampelunas		
189	Caos	218	Buenos Aires	249	Rough & Ready	282	Latina		

307

Designer Index

Ábalos & Herreros 119
Aguado, Maria Luisa 206
Albero, Roger 41, 109, 113, 145, 257
Albors, Eduardo 275
Alday, Iñaki 289
Alves, Jorge 226
Ambasz, Emilio 280
APCD 214
Arola, Antoni 195, 290
Arribas, Alfredo 181, 284
Arriola, Andreu 32, 133
Arroyo, Eduardo 59
Artigues, Jaume 138, 147, 273, 280
Atelier Mendini 17, 245

Bach, Jaume 125
Barbato e Garzotto 236
Bartenbach, Lichtlabor 272
Basañez, Paúl 112
Batlle, Enric 10, 73, 166, 260, 303
BCQ Arquitectos 100
Begasse, Klaus 272
Benedito, Ramón 268
Bertólez, Guillermo 205
Bijleveld, Eveline 39
Bolaños, Juan Carlos 144
Bollani, Mitzi 50
Bonet, Pep 170
Bosch, Josep 265
Brandt Dam, Erik 200
Brunetti Filipponi Associati 153, 161, 207, 219, 221

Cabeza, Diana 12, 16, 25, 35, 40, 41, 48, 54, 65, 80, 82, 84, 90, 91, 110, 127, 132, 167, 173, 188, 199, 210, 218, 226
Cabrera, Paula 18
Cabrera, Pere 147, 273
Cáceres Zurita, Rafael 231
Camarasa, José Luis 171
Canalda, Otto 290
Cane, Brian 156
Carandell, Joaquim 244, 295, 297
Carvalho de Araújo, J.M. 95
Casamor, Carles 206
Castellnou, Manel 116
Caviasca, Alessandro 277
Chantilly design 134, 238, 242, 246
Churtichaga, Jose María 86

Cierniak, Susanne 25
Cinca, Joan 39
Cipollone, Eugenio 81
Cirici, Cristian 210
Clotet, Lluís 37, 83
Coleman-Davis Pagan Architects 85
Correa, Frederico 291
Cortella, Jean-Luc 116
Cuenca Montilla, Juan 202, 205

Da Costa, Daciano 44
DA2 265, 270, 289, 304, 305
design-people 80
díez+díez diseño 52, 70, 86, 118, 121, 124, 239
Doll, Oscar 167
Duthilleul, Jean-Marie 94

EBDNBA 72
Ergo 194, 270
Espinàs, Julià 24, 28
Estudio Hampton / Rivoira y asociados 187

Farnè, Alfredo 130, 184
Feduchi, Javier 38
Fernández Castro, Roberto 67
Fernández, Franc 88, 204
Fernández, Sergio 46, 108, 195
Ferrándiz, Javier 205
Ferrario, Luigi 49, 158
Ferraz, Marta 301
Figueras, Bet 248
Fiol, Carme 32, 133
Foreign Office Architects - Farshid Moussavi & Alejandro Zaera Polo 43
Forgas, Joan 21, 271
Fortunato, Diego 98, 201
Foster, Norman 221
Fraga, Salvador 301
Franc Dey 49
Frog Design 38, 70, 72, 97, 102, 203
FromAtoB Public Design 229

G&C Arquitectura y Urbanismo 95
Gabás, Maria 206
Galán Lubascher, Lucas 206
Galán Peña, José Luis 206
Galí, Beth 154, 281, 282, 296

García-Quijada, Fco. Javier 301
Gascón, Joseph 48
Gaspar, Joan 139
Giné, Maurici 289
Gómez-Pimienta, Bernardo 23
González Cordón, Antonio 292
Guimerà, Oriol 82, 161, 246, 275

Häberli, Alfredo 104-105
Hastings Pavement Company 177
Healey, Greg 53, 101, 145, 190, 247
Hegmon, Radek 34, 60, 79, 89, 115, 163, 191, 192, 193, 197, 204, 211, 216, 217, 220, 224, 227, 228, 230, 251, 252, 253, 255
Heine, Leandro 218
Henrich, Jordi 79, 280
Herbut, Michelle 33
Homann, Alfred 281
Honkonen, Vesa 276
Hruša & Pelcák Architects 190

ImaginarQ 67
Inés, J.Carlos 96
Irisarri - Piñeda, Jesús 57
Ito, Toyo 74

Jover, Margarita 289

Kaisin, Charles 60
Karásek, David 34, 60, 79, 89, 115, 163, 191, 192, 193, 197, 204, 211, 216, 217, 220, 224, 227, 228, 230, 251, 252, 253, 255
Knudsen, Lauritz 297

Lagranja 157
Larrea, Quim 13, 142
Lauritzen, Vilhelm 69
Llopis Freixa, Mercè 87
Llorian Fueyo, Alberto 31
Lobo, Inês 45
López, Silvia 128, 293
Lotersztain, Alexander 114
Lovegrove, Ross 26, 125, 264
Lozano, Alfredo 38

Machimbarrena, Javier 99, 112, 208, 252
Mangado, Francisco J. 111, 173
Mangado, Patxi 264

Mansilla+Tuñón 51
de Marco, Antonio 162
Marforio, Enrico 20, 186
Marsille, Guido 131
Martínez Lapeña, José Antonio 54, 136, 171, 178, 206, 243, 282
Mateo, Josep Lluís 69
Matorell Pena, Bernat 148
MBM Arquitectes 262
McCurry, Margaret 196
Milá, Alfonso 291
Milà, Gonzalo 96, 128, 188, 197, 285, 294
Milà, Leopoldo 255
Milá, Miguel 76, 197, 248
Minh Nguyen, Tran Thanh 25
Miralles Tintoré, Jordi 179
Miralles, Enric 68, 176
Miró Surroca, Jordi 179
Møller - Jensen, Jens 291
Montes, Antonio 111
Mora, Gabriel 125
Morandi & Citterio 207
Moreno, Pablo 38
Muxart, Josep 29, 102, 126, 250

Nahtrang Design 64
Nebot, Daniel 103, 256
Nouvel, Jean 92
Núñez, Nuria 172

Odgård, Mads 277
Outsign 75, 201, 243

Pereira, Martins 147
Pereira, Pedro 155
Perera, Ernest 149, 160
Pericas, Enric 102, 149, 206
Periel, Montse 77, 111, 240
Piaser, Alessandro 73
Pich-Aguilera Arquitectos 99
Pillet, Christophe 85
Piñón, Helio 22, 135, 238, 241, 242, 286
Pinós, Carme 58
PLH Design 303
Portolés, Manuel 301
Providência, Francisco 155, 261
Pujol, Esther 78

Quintana, Màrius 77, 222, 281
de la Quadra-Salcedo, Cayetana 86

R + B Arquitectos 14
Ramos / Bassols 159, 244
Ravaioli, Piero 295
RCR Arquitectes 57
Rehwaldt Landschaftsarchitekten 50, 71
Repossi, Tobia 44, 47, 133, 152, 153, 172, 189, 247
Riberti, Alessandro 202, 211
Riera Ubia, Ton 30, 61, 62, 91, 138, 240, 249
Rodríquez, Francisco Javier 120
Roig, Joan 10, 73, 166, 260, 303
Roig, Miquel 138, 280
Roqueta, Héctor 159
Roselló Til, Antoni 146, 180, 200, 225, 231, 232, 233
Roviras, Pau 168
Rubio, Germán 19
Ruisanchez, Manuel 66
Ruiz de Castañeda, Adolfo 245
Ruiz, Mario 292
Ruzicka, Tomas 156, 254

Sádaba, Juan 47
Sánchez Gil, Guillermo 296
Sans, Pete 154
Segatori, Lisa 11, 12, 230, 237
Sesplugues, Ferran 159
Seste 278
SLA 143, 285
Smyth, Ted 107
Soto, Vicente 30, 101
Soutinho, Alcino 215
Starck, Philippe 209, 300
Stella, Fausta 100
Studio Ambrozus 53, 192
Studio Itinerante Arquitectura 266, 300
Studio MAO - Emmeazero 97
Studio Rota & Partners 214
Studioata 267
Suriñach, Josep 15, 130, 186
Szekely, Martin 106

Tabuenca, Luis 208, 254, 298
Tagliabue, Benedetta 68, 176
Tarrasó, Olga 24, 28, 79, 280
Teixidó, Gabriel 127

Thesevenhints 63
Thygesen, Rud 118
Torrente, Carlos 168
Torres, Elías 54, 136, 171, 178, 206, 243, 282
Trindade, Jorge 215, 228
Tusquets Blanca, Òscar 37, 83, 131, 248

Úbeda, Ramón 290
Urbanica 196, 239
UTGM 304

Valverde, Carles 283
Valverde, Javier 279
van Eggelen, Ruud 63
Vázquez Consuegra, Guillermo 142
Viaplana, Albert 238, 286
Vila, Daniel 78

Wehberg, Max 35, 117
Winkels, Karsten 283, 294
Winkler, Bernhard 17, 20, 52, 81, 134, 194, 198, 203, 241, 250
Winkler, Thomas 64
Wolfson, Martín 218, 226

Zink, Martina 128, 188

Company Index

Alis
www.alis.es
Tel: +34 93-727-61-72
Fax: +34 93-726-55-26
E-mail: alis@alis.es
21, 23, 81, 92, 159, 244, 271, 283

bd
www.bdbarcelona.com
Tel: +34 93-457-00-52
Fax: +34 93-207-36-97
E-mail: export@bdbarcelona.com
26, 37, 83, 104-105, 125, 210, 264

Botton & Gardiner
www.bottonandgardiner.com.au
Tel: +61 2 9667 8100
Fax: +61 2 9667 2269
E-mail: info@bottonandgardiner.com.au
27, 34

Colomer
www.colomer-es.com
Tel: +34 93-719-08-52
Fax: +34 93-718-78-88
E-mail: info@colomer-es.com
137, 170

Concept Urbain
www.concepturbain.fr
Tel: +33 02-47-29-07-08
Fax: +33 02-47-29-07-09
E-mail: export@colomer-es.com
75, 116, 196, 201, 239, 243

DAE
www.dae.es
Tel: +34 93-814-94-00
Fax: +34 93-893-33-58
E-mail: export@dae.es
67, 86, 102, 111, 139, 142, 145, 154, 167, 170, 172, 173, 255, 257, 262, 291, 301

Durban Studio
www.durbanstudio.com
Tel: +34 659-217-608
Fax: +34 972-574-942
E-mail: info@durbanstudio.com
19, 56, 62

Ecoralia
www.ecoralia.com
Tel: +34 91 5655714
E-mail: ecoralia@ecoralia.com
118

Escofet
www.escofet.com
E-mail: informacion@escofet.com
22, 25, 29, 32, 48, 51, 52, 54, 58, 59, 64, 66, 68, 74, 77, 78, 85, 87, 96, 98, 99,100, 114, 119, 120, 126, 133, 135, 147, 149, 171, 176, 177, 178, 181, 197,201, 209, 238, 241, 242, 243, 248, 250, 273, 280, 286, 289

Esteva
www.esteva.com
Tel: +34 93 772 01 98
Fax: +93 772 10 49
232, 233

Estudio Cabeza
www.estudiocabeza.com
Tel: +54 11-4772-6183
Fax: +54 11-4777-0811
E-mail: info@estudiocabeza.com
12, 16, 25, 35, 40, 41, 48, 54, 65, 80, 82, 84, 90, 91, 110, 127, 132, 167, 173, 187, 188, 199, 210, 226

Euroform
www.euroform-w.it
Tel: +39 0474-678131
Fax: +39 0474-678648
17, 20, 52, 64, 81, 134, 194, 198, 203, 241, 250

Fundició Dúctil Benito
www.benito.com
Tel: +34 93-852-1000
Fax: +34 93-852-1001
E-mail: info@benito.com
15, 49, 125, 130, 148, 186, 206, 244, 295, 297

Geohide
www.geohide.ch
Tel: +41 21-351-50-61
Fax: +41 21-351-50-25
36, 92, 166, 187, 256, 263, 274, 293, 302

GH form
www.ghform.dk
Tel: +45 59-44-0990
Fax: +45 59-44-0440
E-mail: mail@ghform.dk
69, 72, 118, 143, 200, 237, 285

Ghisamestieri
www.ghisamestieri.com
Tel: +39 0543-462-611
Fax: +39 0543-449-111
17, 20, 186, 194, 245, 265, 270, 278, 280, 289, 295, 304, 305

Gitma
www.gitma.es
Tel: +34 94-471-06-13
Fax: +34 94-453-61-21
E-mail: info@gitma.es
86, 134, 198, 238, 242, 246

Hess
www.hess.eu
Tel: +49 7721-920-0
Fax: +49 7721-920-250
E-mail: hess@hess.eu
272, 283, 294

JCDecaux
www.jcdecaux.fr
Tel: +33 130-79-79-79
E-mail: info_ventes@jcdecaux.fr
85, 106, 209, 221, 223, 300

Kühn und Kirste
www.kuehn-und-kirste.de
71

Landscape Forms
www.landscapeforms.com
Tel: +1 800-430-6209
Fax: +1 269-381-3455
E-mail: specify@landscapeforms.com
38, 70, 72, 97, 102, 156, 196, 203, 223

Larus
www.larus.pt
Tel: +351 234-520-600
Fax: +351 234-520-609
E-mail: malmeida@larus.pt
44, 45, 57,67, 69, 95, 147, 155, 214, 215, 226, 228, 261

Louis Poulsen
www.louispoulsen.com
Tel: +49 0211-73279-0
Fax: +49 0211-73279-100
80, 277, 281, 291, 297, 303

Macaedis
www.macaedis.com
Tel: +34 950 12 63 70
Fax: +34 950 12 60 78
E-mail: info@macaedis.com
103, 127, 128, 131, 142, 256, 285, 293

mago:urban
www.magogroup.com
Tel: +34 902 111 893
E-mail: info@magogroup.com
30, 39, 41, 43, 61, 62, 82, 91, 108, 109, 113, 121, 131, 138, 144, 149, 152, 160, 179, 184, 240, 246, 249, 257

Metalarte
www.metalarte.com
Tel: +34 93-477-00-69
Fax: +34 93-477-00-86
E-mail: metalarte@metalarte.com
290, 292

Microarquitectura
www.microarquitectura.com
Tel: +34 93-411-11-91
Fax: +34 93-491-20-97
E-mail: comercial@microarquitectura.com
14, 124, 219, 222, 262

Miramondo
www.miramondo.com
Tel: +43 1 96-90-404
Fax: +43 1 71-41-491
E-mail: office@miramondo.com
27, 55, 63

mmcité
www.mmcite.com
Tel: +420 572 434 298
Fax: +420 572 434 283
E-mail: sales@mmcite.cz
34, 60, 63, 19, 89, 115, 156, 158, 163, 190, 191, 192, 193, 197, 204, 211, 216, 217, 220, 224, 227, 228, 230, 251, 252, 253, 254, 255

Modo
www.modoarredo.com
Tel: +39 049-906-5385
Fax: +39 049-906-5911
44, 47, 49, 50, 73, 97, 100, 133, 152, 153, 158, 172, 189, 202, 207, 211, 214, 236, 247

Neri
www.neri.biz
Tel: + 39 0547-65-21-11
Fax: + 39 0547-54-074
E-mail: neri@neri.biz
11, 130, 184, 236, 267

ONN Outside
www.onnoutside.com
Tel: +34 94-417-10-30
Fax: +34 94-417-03-77
E-mail: info@onnoutside.com
13, 15, 47, 95, 99, 135, 185, 208, 220, 252, 254, 298

ORA Centurelli
www.ora.it
Tel/Fax +39.0731.616010
E-mail: info@ora.it
11, 12, 153, 161, 199, 207, 219, 221, 230, 237

Philips
www.lighting.philips.com
263, 274, 284, 302

Proiek Habita & Equipment
www.proiek.com
Tel: +34 902-541-212
Fax: +34 902-331-902
E-mail: info@proiek.com
112

Runge
www.runge-bank.de
Tel: +49 (0)541 50552-0
Fax: +49 (0)541 505522-2
E-mail: info@mail.runge.de
31, 36, 42, 53, 87, 163, 192

Santa & Cole
www.santacole.com
Tel: +34 938-619-100
Fax: +34 938-711-767
E-mail: info@santacole.com
10, 24, 28, 57, 73, 76, 79, 111, 116, 128, 136, 138, 146, 154, 157, 159, 161, 162, 166, 168, 171, 180, 188, 195, 200, 205, 206, 225, 240, 248, 260, 264, 268, 275, 281, 282, 284, 292, 294, 296, 303

Siarq
www.siarq.net
Tel: +34 93-55-33-913
Fax: +34 93-55-33-765
E-mail: infobcn@siarq.net
266, 277, 287, 300

Siteco
www.siteco.com
Tel: +49 8669-33-0
Fax: +49 8669-33-397
269

Street and Park Furniture
www.streetandpark.com.au
Tel: +61 8 8329 6750
Fax: +61 8 8329 6799
E-mail: sales@streetandpark.com.au
33, 53, 96, 101, 107, 145, 190, 247, 288, 299

Streetlife
www.streetlife.nl
Tel: +31 (0)71-524-6846
Fax: +31 (0)71-524-6849
E-mail: streetlife@streetlife.nl
56, 65, 93, 129, 132, 136, 144, 148, 160, 249

T&D Cabanes
www.tdcabanes.com
Tel: +34-926-25-13-54
Fax: +34 926-22-16-54
E-mail: info@tdcabanes.com
18, 30, 31, 38, 70, 101, 169, 202, 239, 275, 279, 296, 301

Tecam BCN
www.tecambcn.com
46, 88, 108, 129, 195, 204, 205 245, 265

Tecno
www.tecnospa.com
94

Vange
www.vange.be
www.abv.be
Tel: +32(0)4 337 83 23
Fax: +32(0)4 337 78 83
E-mail: sales@abv.be
60

VelopA
www.velopa.com
Tel: +49 (0)20-371-299-716
Fax: +49 (0)20-371-354-81
E-mail: info@velopa.com
39, 45

Westeifel Werke
www.westeifel-werke.de
Tel: +49 0 6591-16-0
Fax: +49 0 6591-16-111
35, 117

Woodform
www.woodbenders.co.nz
Tel: +64 9-835-4107
Fax: +64 9-835-4180
E-mail: dave@woodbenders.co.nz
107